Dual arguments have, in recent years, become standard tools for analysis of problems involving optimization by consumers and producers. The principal aim of this book is to provide a fairly systematic yet simple exposition of the basic structure of such arguments. The emphasis is not on providing mathematically general proofs; instead, a geometric approach is used to provide, in an informal way, an intuitive understanding of duality theory. This book introduces the most common alternative ways of representing preferences and technologies, such as indirect utility and distance functions, expenditure and cost functions, and profit and revenue functions, and it discusses the assumptions under which alternative formulations contain precisely the same information. Results such as Roy's identity, the Hotelling–Wold identity, and Shephard's lemma are fully explained, as are their roles in facilitating analysis of behavior.

In addition to his exposition of duality, Professor Cornes discusses the several applications in which dual arguments have proved particularly helpful. These include the modeling of quantity-constrained choice, productive efficiency and welfare measurement, index numbers, aggregation theory, externalities, and public goods theory. At various points, the usefulness of dual representations in providing a richer menu of econometric specifications is stressed.

Duality and
modern economics

Duality and modern economics

RICHARD CORNES
The Australian National University

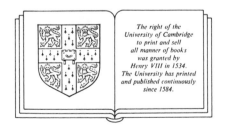

The right of the
University of Cambridge
to print and sell
all manner of books
was granted by
Henry VIII in 1534.
The University has printed
and published continuously
since 1584.

CAMBRIDGE UNIVERSITY PRESS
Cambridge
New York   Port Chester   Melbourne   Sydney

Published by the Press Syndicate of the University of Cambridge
The Pitt Building, Trumpington Street, Cambridge CB2 1RP
40 West 20th Street, New York, NY 10011, USA
10 Stamford Road, Oakleigh, Melbourne 3166, Australia

© Cambridge University Press 1992

First published 1992

Printed in the United States of America

Library of Congress Cataloging-in-Publication Data
Cornes, Richard, 1946–
Duality and modern economics / Richard Cornes.
p. cm.
Includes bibliographical references and index.
ISBN 0-521-33291-5. – ISBN 0-521-33601-5 (pbk.)
1. Demand functions (Economic theory)   2. Duality theory
(Mathematics)   3. Econometric models.   4. Consumer behavior.
5. Microeconomics.   I. Title.
HB801.C635   1992
338.5 – dc20   91–18054
                                                          CIP

A catalog record for this book is available from the British Library

ISBN 0-521-33291-5 hardback
ISBN 0-521-33601-5 paperback

To
STEPHANIE *and* THOMAS

Contents

vii

Preface

Since the early 1970s, the use of dual techniques has become widespread among economists. Familiarity with basic duality theory is now beginning to be taken for granted among graduate students, whether their interest is in economic theory or in empirical applications of that theory. In view of this, the paucity of simple introductory expositions of these techniques is both surprising and disappointing. The existing microeconomic textbooks understandably mix duality in with a lot of other material, which is fine for the current generation of graduate students, but inconvenient for those who have a strong orthodox microeconomic background and who wish to catch up with recent developments in the techniques of modeling. In addition, the textbook treatment typically is limited to presenting a few basic definitions and standard results, together with a demonstration of how the new techniques can facilitate the derivation of well-known standard results. There is little indication of the potential attraction of duality as part of a graduate student's research kit, and therefore little motivation to acquire more than a rudimentary familiarity with dual formulations.

My aim in this book is to provide a brief and informal introduction to the fundamental ideas lying behind duality theory and to show not only the principal results but also how they can be applied to a variety of economic problems. The emphasis is on geometric and economic intuition rather than on rigorous development of general results. Part III, in particular, shows that dual formulations have further uses in addition to the establishment of downward-sloping compensated demand curves, upward-sloping supply curves, and symmetric compensated substitution responses. I hope that readers of this book will subsequently be able to read theoretical and empirical research without being fazed by the presence of dual methods of analysis and will also have the interest, competence, and confidence to exploit dual formulations in their own work.

During the long gestation period of this book, I have incurred a number of debts that I am happy to acknowledge.

xi

In 1977, my colleague Robert Albon introduced me to some of the problems of modeling quantity-constrained choice in the context of work that he was doing on rent control. It was in the course of thinking about these problems that I became interested in the power of dual techniques for handling quantity constraints and in their application to externalities and public goods. Since then I have learned much from collaborative work with Avinash Dixit, Masaaki Homma, Ted Bergstrom, Frank Milne, and, over a prolonged period, Todd Sandler. Both Frank Milne and Todd Sandler have read parts of this manuscript and have made many helpful and encouraging comments, as have Edward Greenberg and Norman Ireland, who were long ago asked by the publishers to read an early version of the manuscript. My colleague Ngo Van Long has also helped to eliminate some sloppy and inaccurate statements from earlier drafts. Patricia Apps made some valuable comments on my treatment of econometric applications and drew my attention to a number of significant references. I want to express special thanks to Ray Rees, who, during a brief visit to the Australian National University, made many helpful and constructive suggestions. I appreciate having a reader who is both sufficiently interested to spend as much time as he did reading another author's manuscript and also sufficiently bold to advise me, gently but firmly, to tear up the initial draft of a whole chapter. Rolf Färe also gave both time and comments generously during his visit to the Australian National University. His contributions significantly improved my treatment of the logical foundations of duality.

The chore of translating handwritten manuscript into typescript was undertaken cheerfully and competently by a number of word-processing experts. I should like to thank Jan Anthony, Marni MacDonald, and Joan O'Neill for their work on parts of the manuscript. It is a pleasure to acknowledge a special debt to Dianne Hodges, who undertook the lion's share of the word processing. Dianne cut her teeth as a mathematical typist on this book. Although she cannot claim to have coped with illegible writing, she has been confronted with seemingly endless revisions and changes of mind, which she has borne with patience and good humor at all times. In the process, she has become a pretty good mathematical typist. It is also a pleasure to thank Val Lyon for drawing the figures so expertly and promptly.

Finally, it is a pleasure to thank Colin Day for the second time. From the first occasion when he listened to the proposal for this book he has been an unfailing source of enthusiastic encouragement and helpful advice. His supportive response has made the difficult task of completing a book-length manuscript a good deal easier than it might otherwise have been.

PART I

Some background

CHAPTER 1

Some formal preliminaries: An informal treatment

The theme of this book is both simple and attractive. It is that the optimizing models that are the daily bread and butter of both theoretical and applied economists can be formulated in a number of different ways and that the investment of a little time and effort in becoming familiar with alternative formulations, together with a little ingenuity in exploiting some simple implications of optimality, can tremendously simplify their formal analysis. The simplicity, and indeed elegance, that can thereby be achieved allows us much more direct insight into the economic intuition that lies behind comparative static and other properties than is afforded by the old-fashioned and rather mechanical procedures that have dominated textbooks in the past. For example, the standard approach to consumer theory once was simply to maximize utility, defined over quantities consumed, subject to the budget constraint. The analysis then proceeded through the tedious and unenlightening manipulation of first- and second-order optimality conditions, through a dense thicket of bordered Hessians, and on to statements about demand behavior whose intuitive explanation, though often simple, was in no way reflected in the tortuous mathematics. We now know that there are at least three alternative ways of stating the consumer's problem and that it pays to think about which one to use before commencing a piece of analysis. One's choice of starting point will be influenced by the nature of the questions to be asked, and some careful thought at this preliminary stage can be tremendously helpful and timesaving. Surprisingly, the exploitation of these ideas requires little more in the way of mathematics than is presumed by the old-fashioned approach. It merely requires a somewhat less mechanical and more creative use of the existing tools of constrained optimization.

I assume that the reader of this book is already familiar with the simple models of consumer behavior and producer behavior set out by, for example, Hirshleifer (1988) and McCloskey (1982), together with their geometric representations using such standard devices as indifference and isoquant maps, production frontiers, and so on.

3

The mathematical prerequisites involve no more than familiarity with the differential calculus and its application to classical optimization problems in which it is assumed that any constraint explicitly listed does in fact hold with equality at the optimum, and quantities consumed or produced are positive. The reader should be able to use the Lagrangian approach to derive the first-order necessary conditions that characterize an optimum and should have some appreciation of the need for, and nature of, the second-order curvature conditions that must also be satisfied in order that a point of tangency between, for example, an indifference curve and a budget constraint will truly chracterize an optimum rather than a pessimum. The algebraic expression of these mathematical ideas was expounded 50 years ago by Allen (1938) in a treatment that, though it is somewhat dated and inelegant, still has a lot to recommend it. More recent treatments have been presented by Intriligator (1971), Chiang (1984), Glaister (1984), and Weintraub (1982). In addition, I use simple matrix and vector notation in order to save space. However, I make little use of any but the most elementary operations, such as the inner product of two vectors and matrix multiplication.

Although the emphasis in this book is on the exploitation of a number of mathematical techniques to facilitate the analysis of optimizing models, the mathematics itself is not developed much beyond the prerequisites stated earlier. This is not a book on mathematics for economists. The tricks that I shall exploit arise from observing a few simple properties of optimizing problems, properties that are easy to grasp both geometrically and intuitively, obvious once understood, but that have been strangely overlooked and underexploited until recent years.

The rest of this chapter is devoted to highlighting those features of optimizing models that provide the basis for the dual tricks to be introduced in subsequent chapters. I have not attempted to be at all exhaustive, but have tried rather to concentrate on presenting a few useful ideas and the relationships between them, while continually referring to the familiar economic examples provided by the utility-maximizing consumer and profit-maximizing production plant.

In consumer theory, if the equality between marginal rates of substitution and relative prices is to characterize a utility maximum, the indifference map must curve "the right way." This leads us to the notions of quasi-concavity and quasi-convexity of a function, which are discussed in Section 1.1. Turning to the model of a profit-maximizing plant, we require the production function to curve "the right way" in order that the equality between value-marginal product and factor price will characterize a profit maximum. In this case, we require slightly stronger curvature restrictions, which lead naturally in Section 1.2 to a discussion of the notions of concavity and convexity of a function. Any function that is concave (convex) is certainly quasi-concave (quasi-convex), but the converse is not true. The relationships between these concepts are discussed in Section 1.3.

If an indifference map in commodity space, or a production frontier, has the appropriate curvature property to ensure that tangency implies optimality, this is because the modeler has made it so by assumption. Many of the functions encountered in this book, by contrast, have inherent curvature properties by virtue of their very definition. For example, the least cost that must be incurred by a consumer in order to attain a given utility level can be expressed as a concave function of the prices faced, as is shown in Chapter 3. In Chapter 5, I show that the maximum profit attained by a competitive production plant can be expressed as a convex function of the input and output prices faced. In these and other examples, such curvature properties, which turn out to have simple and useful implications for behavior, are direct results of the fact that we are dealing with maximum or minimum value functions – that is, functions that express the maximum or minimum value of an objective function in terms of the parameters of the optimizing problem. Section 1.4 discusses such functions and explores their curvature properties in the context of two particularly common classes of optimization problems.

Were it not for the clumsiness of the word, I would be tempted to call this book "Envelopeness and Modern Economics." Among the useful properties of maximum value functions is one known as the envelope property. It is this, as summarized by the envelope theorem in Section 1.5, that provides a close link between maximum value functions on the one hand and the supply and demand functions of maximizing agents on the other. This link enables us to use what we know about the former in order to draw inferences about behavioral functions. The observations that compensated consumer demand curves cannot slope upward and that profit-maximizing output supply curves cannot slope downward are among the many that can be derived in a simple and straightforward manner from the recognition of this link.

Section 1.6 takes the analysis further by considering a second-order, or generalized, envelope property. As its label suggests, this considers further properties of the second derivatives of maximum value functions with respect to the parameters of optimizing problems.

1.1   Quasi-concave and quasi-convex functions

Consider the familiar model of a utility-maximizing consumer. If the equilibrium involves strictly positive consumption of every commodity, then it is characterized by a set of first-order conditions requiring relative prices to equal marginal rates of substitution, represented geometrically as a point of tangency between the budget plane and an indifference surface, *ii*. The tangency requirement is the starting point for the standard analysis of consumer behavior that I present in later chapters. By itself, however, tangency is not sufficient to guarantee even a local, let alone a global, maximum. Only in panel (*a*) of Figure 1.1 does the tangency at *E* pick out a global utility maximum. In all the other cases there are other allocations, shown in the hatched areas, that are feasible and also yield higher utility than the allocation at *E*. In panels (*b*) and (*c*), *E* is not even a local maximum, whereas in (*d*), although *E* looks attractive by comparison with all feasible allocations in its neighborhood, it is not a global maximum. The bundle at *G*, however, is. Because of the linearity of the budget constraint, it is a relatively simple matter to find a set of restrictions on the curvature of indifference surfaces that are sufficient to rule out the situations depicted in panels (*b*), (*c*), and (*d*). We require the indifference curve that touches at *E* to lie otherwise wholly outside the feasible consumption set. If the allocation at *E* not only yields the maximum value of the objective function but also is the only allocation that yields that value, then it is called a strong global maximum. This certainly implies that in the neighborhood of *E* it should curve away from the budget set, so that panels (*b*) and (*c*) are ruled out. Farther away from *E*, we can allow it to curve back, but not by too much. Suppose there is a tangency at *E*, so that it is a local maximum. Then a sufficient condition for it to be also a strong global maximum is that the function $U(\cdot)$ be "strictly quasi-concave at *E*."

Before presenting this and other definitions, I should say something about the functions that appear throughout this book, and also about my conventions concerning notation. A function of *n* variables is simply a rule that associates with every point in some subset *S* of Euclidean *n*-dimensional space, R^n, a point on the real line, or a scalar. Points in R^n are represented by vectors, which are denoted by boldface letters. For example, the utility function $U(\mathbf{q})$ associates with each bundle of *n* commodities, $\mathbf{q} \equiv (q_1, q_2, ..., q_n)$, a real number that represents an individual's utility level. The production function $F(\boldsymbol{\ell})$ associates with each bundle of input quantities, $\boldsymbol{\ell} \equiv (\ell_1, \ell_2, ..., \ell_n)$, a real number that is the maximum attainable output from that bundle in the light of the prevailing

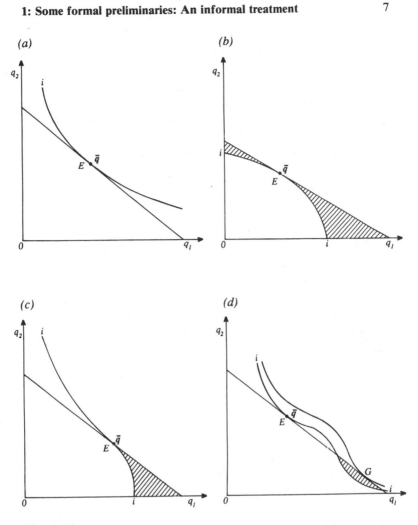

(a)

(b)

(c)

(d)

Figure 1.1

technology. The subset S of R^n over which a function is defined is called the domain of that function. I shall always assume that the domain S of any defined function $f(\cdot)$ is a convex set. The domain can often be taken as R^n itself. However, the economic interpretation of vectors as representing quantities or prices makes it natural often to confine attention to the nonnegative orthant of R^n, which is denoted by R^n_+. In so doing, we are confining attention to vectors whose elements are all either positive or zero. At many points, the argument can be simplified and certain technical problems avoided by further restricting attention to the strictly positive orthant of R^n, denoted by R^n_{++}. The statement "$\mathbf{x} \in S \subset R^n_{++}$" means that the vector $\mathbf{x}$ is an element of a set S that is itself a subset of the strictly positive orthant of Euclidean n-dimensional space, so that every element of $\mathbf{x}$ is strictly positive. For example, if $\mathbf{x}$ were a price vector, such a restriction would have the consequence of ruling out free goods. Let us now turn to the definition of strict quasi-concavity at a point:

Definition 1: Strict quasi-concavity at a point. *The function $f(\mathbf{x})$, defined on the convex set $S \subset R^n$, is strictly quasi-concave at the point $\bar{\mathbf{x}} \in S$ if for any other $\mathbf{x} \in S$ such that $f(\mathbf{x}) \geq f(\bar{\mathbf{x}})$,*

$$f(\bar{\mathbf{x}}) < f(\theta\bar{\mathbf{x}} + [1-\theta]\mathbf{x}) \quad \text{for all } \theta \text{ such that } 0 < \theta < 1.$$

In the context of consumer theory, this means that if an allocation $\mathbf{q}$ is at least as attractive as $\bar{\mathbf{q}}$, then any allocation on the chord joining $\mathbf{q}$ and $\bar{\mathbf{q}}$ is strictly preferred to $\bar{\mathbf{q}}$. This is sufficient to ensure that the tangency at $\bar{\mathbf{q}}$ characterizes a utility maximum.

Figure 1.2 emphasizes that strict quasi-concavity at $\bar{\mathbf{q}}$ is consistent with there being "dents" elsewhere in the indifference surface. The dent along the segment AB is not sufficiently great to mask $\bar{\mathbf{q}}$ from any other point on the surface – wherever $\mathbf{q}$ is chosen on ii, the chord lies wholly above the indifference curve. However, the presence of the dent does mean that had the budget constraint been chosen to touch ii between A and B, that tangency would not have characterized a utility maximum. Because we want a condition that guarantees a maximum at the tangency with any arbitrary budget constraint, our restriction has to be strengthened so as to rule out any dents in indifference surfaces. This leads to the global property of "strict quasi-concavity":

Definition 2: Strict quasi-concavity. *The function $f(\mathbf{x})$, defined on the convex set $S \subset R^n$, is strictly quasi-concave if for any pair of distinct points $\mathbf{x}' \in S$ and $\mathbf{x}'' \in S$ such that $f(\mathbf{x}') \geq f(\mathbf{x}'') = k$, $f(\theta\mathbf{x}' + [1-\theta]\mathbf{x}'') > k$ for all θ such that $0 < \theta < 1$.*

This is certainly true in Figure 1.1(a), but not in the remaining panels. Observe that the definition, unlike the geometry, can handle as many dimensions as desired.

In the context of consumer theory, an immediate and very convenient consequence of strict quasi-concavity is that for any budget constraint consistent with there being a point of tangency, that point is unique and is guaranteed to achieve the maximum attainable utility.

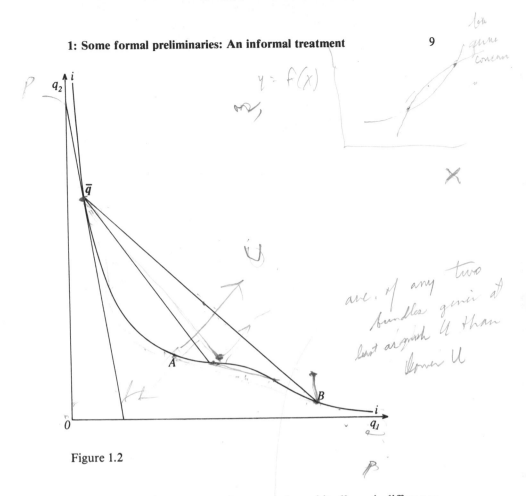

Figure 1.2

Often a slightly weaker property is assumed, and it allows indifference surfaces to have linear portions in them. This is the property of quasi-concavity:

Definition 3: Quasi-concavity. *The function $f(\mathbf{x})$, defined on the convex set $S \subset R^n$, is quasi-concave if for any pair of distinct points $\mathbf{x}' \in S$ and $\mathbf{x}'' \in S$ such that $f(\mathbf{x}') \geq f(\mathbf{x}'') = k$, $f(\theta \mathbf{x}' + [1-\theta]\mathbf{x}'') \geq k$ for all θ such that $0 < \theta < 1$.*

There is another extremely elegant definition in terms of sets. Given any arbitrary point $\hat{\mathbf{x}}$, consider the set of all points $\mathbf{x}$ such that $f(\mathbf{x}) \geq f(\hat{\mathbf{x}})$. Koopmans (1957) calls this the "no-worse-than-$\hat{\mathbf{x}}$" set. Alternatively, it is the upper contour set associated with $\hat{\mathbf{x}}$. For example, if $\hat{\mathbf{x}}$ is identified with $\bar{\mathbf{q}}$ in Figure 1.1(*a*), the no-worse-than-$\hat{\mathbf{x}}$ set is the set of points above and to the right of *ii*. Then we have the following:

Definition 3′: Quasi-concavity. *The function $f(\mathbf{x})$ is quasi-concave if the upper contour set associated with every point $\mathbf{x}$ is convex.*

The statement that preferences are assumed to be convex refers precisely to this assumption on the utility function. A quasi-concave utility function permits an infinite number of allocations consistent with utility maximization. For example, if the linear portion of an indifference curve coincides with a segment of the budget constraint, all points along the common stretch give rise to the same maximized value of utility. This in no way threatens the structure of dual arguments. However, it is convenient to assume that there is a unique maximizing allocation – that is, a strong global maximum – and strict quasi-concavity represents a convenient way to ensure that this is so. Henceforth, I shall generally assume that the maximizing vector $\hat{\mathbf{x}}$ is unique.

Quasi-convex and strictly quasi-convex functions, which are in a natural sense the opposites of quasi-concave and strictly quasi-concave functions, are less commonly encountered in economics. However, an important example is introduced in Chapter 2. Intuition suggests that the maximum attainable utility can be expressed as a function of the prices and income faced by a consumer. Such an indirect utility function turns out to be an inherently quasi-convex function of prices. Quasi-convexity can be defined in a manner similar to that used earlier. This, for example, is done by Intriligator (1971, p. 464). An alternative definition is as follows:

Definition 4: [Strict] Quasi-convexity. *A function $f(\mathbf{x})$ is [strictly] quasi-convex if its negative, $-f(\mathbf{x})$, is [strictly] quasi-concave.*

I leave it to the reader to check, for example, that this definition implies that f is quasi-convex if for any value of $\hat{\mathbf{x}}$, the set of $\mathbf{x}$ such that $f(\mathbf{x}) \leq f(\hat{\mathbf{x}})$ is convex. This, if you like, is the no-better-than-$\hat{\mathbf{x}}$ set, or the lower contour set associated with $\hat{\mathbf{x}}$.

To summarize, quasi-concavity is a property relating to the curvature of the level sets, such as indifference surfaces or isoquants, associated with particular values of a given function, such as a utility or production function. Its particular significance for economists arises from the fact that the quasi-concavity of the utility function $U(\mathbf{q})$, combined with the linearity of the individual's budget constraint, guarantees that the first-order conditions associated with a point of tangency are sufficient as well as necessary for a utility maximum. Strict quasi-concavity ensures that there is only one bundle that yields the maximum utility. Quasi-convexity is simply a mirror image of quasi-concavity.

1.2   Concave and convex functions

Now consider a simple problem drawn from producer theory, that of a competitive profit-maximizing plant. For the moment, let there be one input, ℓ, and one output, y. Their market prices are, respectively, W and P. The problem involves choosing ℓ and y to maximize profit $Py - W\ell$, which is a simple linear function of the quantities ℓ and y, subject to the technology constraint as expressed by the production function, $y = F(\ell)$. The level sets of the profit identity, or iso-profit curves, are parallel straight lines in (y, ℓ) space. The question to be asked is, When can we be certain that fulfillment of the first-order conditions, represented geometrically by a tangency between an iso-profit line and the production function, does indeed represent a true global profit maximum? Before answering this, I should make explicit an assumption concerning the production function. I shall assume that the marginal product of labor is everywhere positive, so that $F(\ell)$ is monotonic increasing. A quick check reveals that in the special case of a function of a single variable, this is sufficient to ensure that it is both strictly quasi-concave and strictly quasi-convex. Figure 1.3 shows that such properties in no way ensure that tangency implies optimality. In panel (a), the allocation T is indeed optimal, but in panels (b) and (c) the curvature of $F(\ell)$ implies feasible allocations that are more profitable than the allocation at the tangent T. In panel (d), T emerges well from local comparisons, but there remain feasible allocations in the hatched area that are more profitable. The most common restriction imposed on the curvature of $F(\cdot)$ to remove such possibilities and to ensure a unique point of tangency is the assumption that $F(\cdot)$ is strictly concave. The definition of a strictly concave function is as follows:

Definition 5: Strict concavity.   *The function $f(\mathbf{x})$, defined on the convex set $S \subset R^n$, is strictly concave if for any pair of distinct points $\mathbf{x}' \in S$ and $\mathbf{x}'' \in S$, $f(\theta\mathbf{x}' + [1-\theta]\mathbf{x}'') > \theta f(\mathbf{x}') + [1-\theta]f(\mathbf{x}'')$ for all θ such that $0 < \theta < 1$.*

A strictly concave function may alternatively be characterized by noting that the tangent at any point consistently lies above the function at every other point. Often it can be helpful to exploit this characterization.

The slightly weaker concept of a concave function allows for linear surfaces:

Definition 6: Concavity.   *The function $f(\mathbf{x})$, defined on the convex set $S \subset R^n$, is concave if for any pair of distinct points $\mathbf{x}' \in S$ and $\mathbf{x}'' \in S$, $f(\theta\mathbf{x}' + [1-\theta]\mathbf{x}'') \geq \theta f(\mathbf{x}') + [1-\theta]f(\mathbf{x}'')$ for all θ such that $0 \leq \theta \leq 1$.*

$f.(\ell) =$

$F(\ell)$

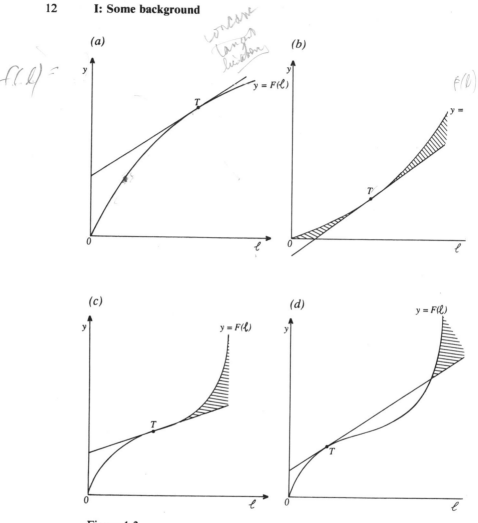

Figure 1.3

As in the preceding section, a definition in terms of sets is available. The function $f(\mathbf{x})$ is concave if and only if the set of points lying on or below $f(\cdot)$ – sometimes called the hypograph of the function – is convex. The statement that a technology is convex refers precisely to this assumption on the production function. In Figure 1.3(a), $F(\ell)$ is clearly concave – indeed, strictly concave.

Had our objective been to minimize, rather than maximize, profit, subject to a single constraint, we would have required the curvature of the constraint function to go the other way. Although profit minimization is a strange thing to wish to do, it is easy to pose reasonable problems for which the required curvature is as shown in Figure 1.3(b) if T is to be an optimum. This leads us to define a convex function as follows:

Definition 7: Convexity.   *The function $f(\mathbf{x})$ is [strictly] convex if its negative, $-f(\mathbf{x})$, is [strictly] concave.*

Thus a convex function is one for which

$$f(\theta\mathbf{x}'+[1-\theta]\mathbf{x}'') \le \theta f(\mathbf{x}')+[1-\theta]f(\mathbf{x}'')$$

for all θ such that $0 \le \theta \le 1$. Further, $f(\mathbf{x})$ is convex if the set of all points on or above the function – sometimes called the epigraph of the function – is a convex set. Again, often it is helpful to use the fact that the tangent to a convex function at any point lies elsewhere on or below the function and therefore provides, if anything, an underestimate of the function for other values of $\mathbf{x}$. Either way, it is clear that $F(\ell)$ in Figure 1.3(b) is strictly convex.

1.3   Quasi-concavity and concavity

The distinction between quasi-concavity and concavity is a fertile source of confusion. To clarify this distinction, consider a function of two variables, $y = f(x_1, x_2)$. Figure 1.4, in which the dependent variable y is measured along the vertical axis, depicts a bell-shaped hillock. To a statistician this might represent a bivariate normal distribution, and to a geographer a hummock. Imagine that all points on or below the surface form a solid mass. To test for quasi-concavity, take a horizontal slice through the hummock. The boundary of the cross section is simply the level set associated with the chosen value of y, that is, the set of points for which $f(x_1, x_2) = \bar{y}$, say. Geographers would simply call this a contour. It is the dashed loop in the figure. Confining attention to this cross section, consider now the hatched area, which is the set of values (x_1, x_2) for which $f(x_1, x_2) \ge \bar{y}$. Consider a particular point $\mathbf{x}^*$ for which $f(\mathbf{x}^*) = \bar{y}$. The hatched area is simply the no-worse-than-$\mathbf{x}^*$ set. If this set is convex for all chosen values of $\bar{y}$, then $f(\cdot)$ is quasi-concave.

The test for quasi-concavity, then, confines attention to the properties of the cross sections, or no-worse-than-$\mathbf{x}^*$ sets, associated with a function. By contrast, the test for concavity involves a more comprehensive examination of the shape of the entire function, in this case the hummock. Because of the flaring toward the base of the figure, the solid mass consisting of all points on or below the surface in Figure 1.4 is not a convex set. For

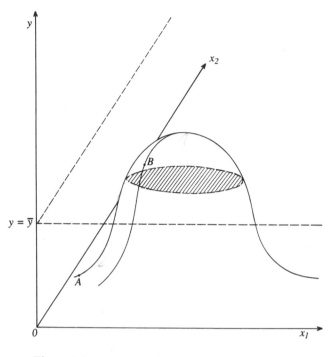

Figure 1.4

example, the straight line passing between *A* and *B* lies at least partially above the surface. By contrast, the surface drawn in Figure 1.5, which depicts a parabolic function of the form $y = K - (x_1 - \gamma_1)^2 - (x_2 - \gamma_2)^2$, where K, γ_1, and γ_2 are constants, has no flaring near its base. It is not only quasi-concave but also concave. Indeed, it is strictly both, because the chord joining any two distinct points on or under the surface itself lies wholly beneath the surface. All functions that are concave must be quasi-concave, but the converse is certainly not true, as Figure 1.4 has demonstrated.

As I have shown, the budget-constrained consumer's problem involves a tangency between a linear surface and a level set – an indifference curve – of the utility function. Consequently, it is simply the curvature properties of level sets that concern us there. Because the budget constraint pins down the scale of operations, those curvature properties that emerge as we move up or down the utility hill are simply not relevant. By contrast, the standard model of the competitive profit-maximizing plant allows the scale of activity to be freely chosen without the restrictions imposed by a

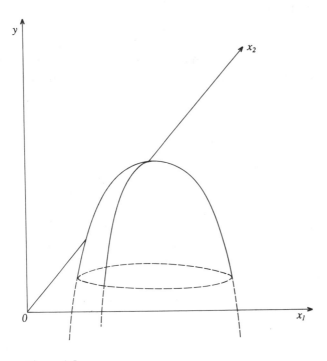

Figure 1.5

budget constraint, and this requires us to check the curvature properties, this time of the production function, in an extra dimension as the dependent variable output is increased or decreased. This extra, more stringent, examination of its curvature properties leads us to impose concavity on the production function if we wish to ensure that any point of tangency corresponds to a global profit maximum.

1.4   Maximum value functions

Optimizing models, of which those of the utility-maximizing consumer and profit-maximizing plant are two particularly important examples, are a basic ingredient of microeconomic theory. In such problems, the optimal attainable value of the objective function clearly depends on the precise set of feasible allocations. If the latter can be described by a set of equalities or inequalities involving the choice variables and a vector of parameters, then the optimal value of the objective function can itself be expressed as a function of those parameters. The consumer's problem is a case in point, the maximum attainable utility being dependent upon the nominal prices and income that describe the budget constraint. More generally, the parameters can also appear in the original objective function. Suppose this can be written as $f(\mathbf{x}, \boldsymbol{\alpha})$, where $\mathbf{x}$ is the vector of choice variables and $\boldsymbol{\alpha}$ the vector of parameters, and let there be a vector of constraints, written $\mathbf{g}(\mathbf{x}, \boldsymbol{\alpha}) \leq 0$. Then the maximum value of $f(\cdot)$ can be expressed as

$$\Omega(\boldsymbol{\alpha}) \equiv \max_{\mathbf{x}}\{f(\mathbf{x}, \boldsymbol{\alpha}) \mid \mathbf{g}(\mathbf{x}, \boldsymbol{\alpha}) \leq 0\}. \tag{1}$$

In the standard consumer's problem the parameters appear only in the single constraint, but other cases are common. The profit-maximizing example involves the input and output price parameters only in the maximand. There are many examples of economic models in which both $f(\cdot)$ and $\mathbf{g}(\cdot)$ contain parameters. For example, if a consumer has some reason for caring directly about prices, perhaps because they are considered to embody information about product quality, then the direct utility function will have prices among its arguments. If the profit-maximizing plant is subjected to rate-of-return regulation, then prices will appear in its constraints. Alternatively, we may be interested in situations involving technical change. If this is conveniently described by a parameter in the production function, the plant's maximum attainable profit can be expressed as

$$\Pi(P, W, \beta) \equiv \max_{y, \ell}\{Py - W\ell \mid y - F(\ell, \beta) \leq 0\},$$

where $F(\cdot)$ is the production function, and P, W, and β are parameters. For example, changes in β may represent simple Harrod- or Hicks-neutral shifts in the production function – see Stoneman (1983). In all these cases, it remains possible to define the maximum value function $\Omega(\boldsymbol{\alpha})$. Much of the rest of this book is devoted to showing why it is also extremely worthwhile to focus attention on maximum value functions. I should stress at this point that minimum value functions – the objective functions of minimization problems – have similarly useful properties. It is from their nature as solutions to optimizing problems that their special characteristics derive.

Under certain special circumstances, the maximum value function has simple curvature characteristics, and it is worth looking at two special cases, both to relate maximum value functions to our earlier discussion of quasi-concavity and concavity and to serve as a useful rehearsal of reasoning that is commonly employed elsewhere in this book.

For simplicity, suppose there is a single constraint. Consider the special case in which the parameters α are absent from the objective function $f(\cdot)$. Then the following proposition can be shown:

Proposition 1.   *Consider this problem:* $\max_x f(\mathbf{x})$ *subject to* $g(\mathbf{x}, \alpha) \le 0$. *If* $g(\mathbf{x}, \alpha)$ *is concave in the parameters* α, *then the maximum value function* $\Omega(\alpha)$ *is quasi-convex in* α.

To demonstrate this, consider two values of the vector of parameters, α' and α'', that give rise to the same value of the maximum value function – say $\Omega(\cdot) = k$. Denote the associated optimal values of the choice variables by $\mathbf{x}'$ and $\mathbf{x}''$. We wish to show that if α^* is a convex combination of α' and α'', then $\Omega(\alpha^*) \le k$. Let $\mathbf{x}^*$ be the optimal value of $\mathbf{x}$, given α^*. Because $\mathbf{x}^*$ is chosen at $\alpha = \alpha^*$, it clearly must be feasible, so that

$$g(\mathbf{x}^*, \alpha^*) \equiv g(\mathbf{x}^*, \theta\alpha' + [1-\theta]\alpha'') \le 0.$$

But because $g(\cdot)$ is concave in α, we know that

$$g(\mathbf{x}^*, \theta\alpha' + [1-\theta]\alpha'') \ge \theta g(\mathbf{x}^*, \alpha') + [1-\theta]g(\mathbf{x}^*, \alpha'').$$

Consequently, the convex combination of $g(\mathbf{x}^*, \alpha')$ and $g(\mathbf{x}^*, \alpha'')$ must itself be nonpositive. Because both θ and $[1-\theta]$ are nonnegative, this must imply that at least one of $g(\mathbf{x}^*, \alpha')$ and $g(\mathbf{x}^*, \alpha'')$ is nonpositive. We can suppose, without any loss of generality, that $g(\mathbf{x}^*, \alpha') \le 0$. But this means that $\mathbf{x}^*$ is feasible given α'. If $\mathbf{x}^*$ is feasible, yet $\mathbf{x}'$ is optimal, it necessarily follows that $\mathbf{x}'$ yields a higher value of $f(\cdot)$ than does $\mathbf{x}^*$. In short,

$$\Omega(\alpha^*) \equiv f(\mathbf{x}^*) \le \Omega(\alpha') = f(\mathbf{x}') = k.$$

This reasoning involves nothing more than the definitions of concavity and quasi-convexity, together with very straightforward manipulations of inequalities. The strategy is simply to note that the optimal choice in any situation must yield as high a value of the objective function as any alternative feasible choice. Once we have determined that $\mathbf{x}^*$ is feasible in a situation in which $\mathbf{x}'$ is actually optimal, the main work is done. Not only is the line of reasoning simple, but also the assumptions are few. I made no assumptions concerning the curvature properties of the objective function, nor did I need any assumption of convexity of $g(\mathbf{x}, \alpha)$ over $\mathbf{x}$, only over α. The only other assumption, which is implicitly lying behind all the analysis of this section, is that a maximum value of $f(\mathbf{x})$ does indeed exist for all values of the parameters under consideration. Finally, an important special case covered by Proposition 1 deserves explicit mention. The standard consumer's problem involves a budget constraint that is linear in prices for given income. Because linearity in α implies concavity (and also, for that matter, convexity) in α, it follows that the maximum value function, which in this case is the indirect utility function, is quasi-convex in prices.

Consider now a problem in which the parameters appear only in the objective function, $f(\mathbf{x}, \alpha)$, not in the constraint, which consequently is written $g(\mathbf{x}) \leq 0$. The following proposition holds:

Proposition 2.   *Consider this problem:* $\max_{\mathbf{x}} f(\mathbf{x}, \alpha)$ *subject to* $g(\mathbf{x}) \leq 0$. *If* $f(\mathbf{x}, \alpha)$ *is convex in the parameters* α, *then the maximum value function* $\Omega(\alpha)$ *is convex in* α.

In this case, we need to show that for any two vectors α' and α'',

$$\Omega(\theta\alpha' + [1-\theta]\alpha'') \leq \theta\Omega(\alpha') + [1-\theta]\Omega(\alpha'').$$

Because $f(\mathbf{x}, \alpha)$ is convex in α', it follows that

$$f(\mathbf{x}^*, \theta\alpha' + [1-\theta]\alpha'') \leq \theta f(\mathbf{x}^*, \alpha') + [1-\theta] f(\mathbf{x}^*, \alpha'').$$

The fact that α does not appear in the constraint means that the feasible set is unaffected by changes in α. Consequently, $\mathbf{x}^*$ must be available both when $\alpha = \alpha'$ and when $\alpha = \alpha''$. Because $\mathbf{x}'$ is optimal given α', whereas $\mathbf{x}^*$ is feasible but not optimal, it follows that $f(\mathbf{x}', \alpha') \geq f(\mathbf{x}^*, \alpha')$. Similarly, $f(\mathbf{x}'', \alpha'') \geq f(\mathbf{x}^*, \alpha'')$. Consequently,

$$f(\mathbf{x}^*, \theta\alpha' + [1-\theta]\alpha'') \leq \theta f(\mathbf{x}', \alpha') + [1-\theta] f(\mathbf{x}'', \alpha'')$$

or

$$\Omega(\alpha^*) \equiv \Omega(\theta\alpha' + [1-\theta]\alpha'') \leq \theta\Omega(\alpha') + [1-\theta]\Omega(\alpha''),$$

which is what I set out to demonstrate. Again, little is assumed beyond the existence of a maximum value of $f(\cdot)$ and the convexity of $f(\mathbf{x}, \alpha)$ in α alone. Consider the profit-maximizing plant's problem. Its objective function $f(\cdot) \equiv Py - W\ell$ is linear and therefore convex in the parameters P and W. These parameters are absent from the constraint function. If the production function is written $y = F(\ell)$, then the constraint function is, in this example, $g(\cdot) \equiv y - F(\ell) \leq 0$. The problem is clearly covered by Proposition 2, and the maximum attainable profit is therefore a convex function of P and W. We shall see in Chapter 5 just how useful this property is.

A further example will be encountered in Chapters 3 and 5. Both utility-maximizing consumers and profit-maximizing plants can be modeled as minimizing the cost of achieving their utility or output level. Minimizing cost is the same as maximizing the negative of cost. Using the same type of reasoning as before, we can show that the minimum cost is a concave function of commodity, or input, prices. Again, it should be emphasized that this property does not depend in any way on the shape of the utility or production function.

1.5   The envelope theorem

It would be legitimate at this stage for the reader to wonder why we should take such an interest in exploring curvature and other properties of maximum value functions. After all, usually we are concerned with the supply and demand behaviors of individuals, rather than with the objective function that lies behind them. The justification is simply that there is a very close connection between the properties of the maximum value function and the behavior of the optimal values of the choice variables expressed as functions of the parameters, $\hat{x}(\alpha)$. In positive models of consumer and producer behavior, these are simply the demand and supply functions. Indeed, there happen to be several formulations of models in both consumer and producer theory, which are special cases covered by Proposition 2, in which individual supply and demand functions can be obtained simply as partial derivatives of the maximum or minimum value function. This close connection is a consequence of what is often called the envelope property of maximum value functions.

I shall maintain the notation already introduced, but now allow explicitly for the possibility of more than one constraint. Each takes the form $g_k(\mathbf{x}, \boldsymbol{\alpha}) = 0$, and there are K constraints, so that $k = 1, 2, \ldots, K$. I assume that the constraints are equalities, or at least that they happen to hold with equality at an optimum. I shall also suppose, purely for convenience, that for any value of the parameters $\boldsymbol{\alpha}$ there is in fact a unique optimal vector of choice variables, and I shall denote this by the vector of functions $\hat{x}(\alpha)$.

Finally, I shall assume that both the objective and the constraints are everywhere differentiable. This last assumption is particularly useful, because the envelope theorem is essentially about the effect on the maximum value function of small – strictly speaking, infinitesimal – perturbations in the parameters.

Let us start by reminding ourselves of the definition of $\Omega(\alpha)$:

$$\Omega(\alpha) \equiv f(\hat{\mathbf{x}}(\alpha), \alpha) = \max_{\mathbf{x}}\{ f(\mathbf{x}, \alpha) \,|\, g_k(\mathbf{x}, \alpha) = 0, k = 1, \ldots, K \}. \qquad (2)$$

Consider the effect of an infinitesimal change in one of the parameters, $d\alpha_j$, on the function $\Omega(\alpha)$. At first, this appears to be potentially complicated, because not only is there the direct effect, $(\partial f(\cdot)/\partial \alpha_j)d\alpha_j$, but also the optimum vector $\hat{\mathbf{x}}$ will itself generally change. A change in relative factor prices, for example, not only affects the cost of the initial mix of inputs employed by a cost-minimizing plant but also generally provokes a change in the optimal mix. Indeed, an increase in the price of commodity purchased by a consumer may make the initial bundle not only suboptimal but also no longer attainable. It would therefore appear that we have to evaluate each endogenous response $d\hat{x}_i$ in order to calculate

$$d\Omega(\alpha) = \sum_i (\partial f(\hat{\mathbf{x}}, \alpha)/\partial x_i)d\hat{x}_i + (\partial f(\hat{\mathbf{x}}, \alpha)/\partial \alpha_j)d\alpha_j. \qquad (3)$$

I have left "hats" over the differentials, $d\hat{x}_i$, to emphasize that these are not arbitrary responses, but are the responses of the optimal values of the choice variables. The envelope theorem tells us that we can, in fact, avoid having to calculate all, and indeed any, of the $d\hat{x}_i$'s. To see how this can be, consider the Lagrangian associated with this problem:

$$L(\mathbf{x}, \alpha, \lambda) = f(\mathbf{x}, \alpha) - \sum_k \lambda_k g_k(\mathbf{x}, \alpha),$$

where λ is the vector of Lagrange multipliers, λ_k being associated with the constraint $g_k(\mathbf{x}, \alpha) = 0$. First-order necessary conditions associated with an optimum are

$$\partial L(\cdot)/\partial x_i = \partial f(\cdot)/\partial x_i - \sum_k \lambda_k \partial g_k(\cdot)/\partial x_i = 0.$$

Therefore,

$$\partial f(\cdot)/\partial x_i = \sum_k \lambda_k \partial g_k(\cdot)/\partial x_i$$

so that, summing over the x_i's,

$$\sum_i (\partial f(\cdot)/\partial x_i)d\hat{x}_i = \sum_i \sum_k \lambda_k (\partial g_k(\cdot)/\partial x_i)d\hat{x}_i. \qquad (4)$$

Now consider a typical constraint. We are assuming that both before and after the exogenous change in α_j each constraint holds. Therefore, because $g_k(\mathbf{x}, \alpha) = 0$ is satisfied throughout, it follows that the changes in the $\hat{x}_i$'s must satisfy the condition that

$$\sum_i (\partial g_k(\cdot)/\partial x_i) d\hat{x}_i + (\partial g_k(\cdot)/\partial \alpha_j) d\alpha_j = 0.$$

Multiplying by λ_k, for reasons that shortly will become apparent,

$$\sum_i \lambda_k (\partial g_k(\cdot)/\partial x_i) d\hat{x}_i = -\lambda_k (\partial g_k(\cdot)/\partial \alpha_j) d\alpha_j. \tag{5}$$

Summing over the constraints, therefore,

$$\sum_k \sum_i \lambda_k (\partial g_k(\cdot)/\partial x_i) d\hat{x}_i = -\sum_k \lambda_k (\partial g_k(\cdot)/\partial \alpha_j) d\alpha_j.$$

Notice what we have done. In equation (4), first-order conditions have been exploited to replace the $\partial f(\cdot)/\partial x_i$ terms by terms involving $\partial g_k(\cdot)/\partial x_i$. Equation (5), in turn, exploits the fact that the constraints hold at all times in order to replace the $\partial g_k(\cdot)/\partial x_i$ terms by terms involving $\partial g_k(\cdot)/\partial \alpha_j$. Substituting (4) into (3), and then (5) into the resulting equation, we obtain

$$d\Omega(\alpha) = -\sum_k \lambda_k (\partial g_k(\cdot)/\partial \alpha_j) d\alpha_j + (\partial f(\cdot)/\partial \alpha_j) d\alpha_j.$$

Inspection of this equation reveals that the right-hand side is simply the partial derivative of the Lagrangian function with respect to α_j:

$$\partial \Omega(\cdot)/\partial \alpha_j = \partial L(\cdot)/\partial \alpha_j = \partial f(\cdot)/\partial \alpha_j - \sum_k \lambda_k \partial g_k(\cdot)/\partial \alpha_j. \tag{6}$$

Therefore, by differentiating the Lagrangian partially with respect to α_j, we can avoid the need to calculate any changes in the $\hat{x}_i$ variables. Their effect on $\Omega(\cdot)$ is of second order and can be ignored in infinitesimal analysis. This is the substance of the envelope theorem.

Although equation (6) has been derived for a maximization problem, it should be clear that the reasoning depends only on properties of first-order necessary conditions and that it therefore applies equally well to minimization problems. All that is assumed is that an optimum, be it a maximum or minimum, exists and that the constraints hold with equality. These, together with the assumption that the objective and constraint functions are differentiable, are all the assumptions needed to derive the envelope theorem, which can be succinctly stated as follows:

The envelope theorem

Consider this problem: $\max_x \{ f(\mathbf{x}, \boldsymbol{\alpha}) \mid g_k(\mathbf{x}, \boldsymbol{\alpha}) = 0, \ k = 1, \dots, K \}$. The partial derivative of the maximum value function $\Omega(\boldsymbol{\alpha})$ with respect to α_j is equal to the partial derivative of the associated Lagrangian:

$$\partial \Omega(\boldsymbol{\alpha})/\partial \alpha_j = \partial L(\hat{\mathbf{x}}, \boldsymbol{\alpha}, \hat{\lambda})/\partial \alpha_j,$$

where $\hat{x}$ and $\hat{\lambda}$ are the values of the choice variables and Lagrange multipliers at the initial optimum.

There is a rather neat alternative way of deriving the envelope theorem. Consider the function $\Phi(\mathbf{x}, \alpha) \equiv \Omega(\alpha) - f(\mathbf{x}, \alpha)$. Because $\Omega(\alpha)$ is the maximum value attained by $f(\cdot)$ when $\mathbf{x} = \hat{\mathbf{x}}$, the function $\Phi(\cdot)$ must be nonnegative, reaching its minimum value of zero at $\mathbf{x} = \hat{\mathbf{x}}$. Now consider what is called the "primal-dual" problem:

$$\min_{\mathbf{x}, \alpha} \{\Omega(\alpha) - f(\mathbf{x}, \alpha) \mid g_k(\mathbf{x}, \alpha) = 0, \ k = 1, \ldots, K\}. \tag{7}$$

Subject to the constraints holding, the objective function $\Phi(\mathbf{x}, \alpha)$ must have a minimum with respect to $\mathbf{x}$ and α when and only when $f(\mathbf{x}, \alpha)$ has a maximum with respect to $\mathbf{x}$. Thus the solution to the original problem must have the same set of first-order conditions as the solution to problem (7). Let us look at them. The Lagrangian function associated with (7) is

$$L^{\dagger}(\mathbf{x}, \alpha, \lambda) = \Omega(\alpha) - f(\mathbf{x}, \alpha) - \sum_k \lambda_k g_k(\mathbf{x}, \alpha).$$

The first-order conditions therefore take the following forms:

$$\partial L^{\dagger}(\cdot)/\partial x_i = \partial f(\cdot)/\partial x_i - \sum_k \lambda_k \partial g_k(\cdot)/\partial x_i = 0,$$

$$\partial L^{\dagger}(\cdot)/\partial \alpha_j = \partial \Omega(\cdot)/\partial \alpha_j - \partial f(\cdot)/\partial \alpha_j - \sum_k \lambda_k \partial g_k(\cdot)/\partial \alpha_j = 0,$$

$$\partial L^{\dagger}(\cdot)/\partial \lambda_k = g_k(\cdot) = 0.$$

The conditions obtained from putting $\partial L^{\dagger}(\cdot)/\partial \alpha_j$ equal to zero are familiar. They are nothing more than the envelope theorem, because they can be written

$$\partial \Omega(\cdot)/\partial \alpha_j = \partial f(\cdot)/\partial \alpha_j + \sum_k \lambda_k \partial g_k(\cdot)/\partial \alpha_j.$$

Two examples may help to justify problem (7). Suppose the original problem is to maximize the direct utility function $U(\mathbf{q})$ subject to the budget constraint $\mathbf{P} \cdot \mathbf{q} = M$. The choice variables, $\mathbf{x}$, are the quantities $\mathbf{q}$, and the parameters α are the prices and income $(\mathbf{P}, M)$. The maximum value function is the indirect utility function $V(\mathbf{P}, M)$. Now write out the problem suggested by (7):

$$\min_{\mathbf{q}, \mathbf{P}, M} \{V(\mathbf{P}, M) - U(\mathbf{q}) \mid \mathbf{P} \cdot \mathbf{q} = M\}.$$

The claim is that $\Phi(\mathbf{P}, M, \mathbf{q})$ $[\equiv V(\mathbf{P}, M) - U(\mathbf{q})]$ is minimized, subject to the budget constraint, when and only when $U(\mathbf{q})$ is maximized. In this example it is particularly easy to see that this is so, because the parameters do not appear in the direct utility function. If $(\mathbf{P}, M)$ are regarded as parameters, so that $V(\cdot)$ is determined, minimizing $F(\cdot)$ with respect to $\mathbf{q}$ is equivalent to minimizing the negative of $U(\mathbf{q})$, or maximizing $U(\mathbf{q})$. With $\mathbf{q}$ regarded as parameters, so that $U(\mathbf{q})$ is given, minimization of $F(\cdot)$ with respect to $(\mathbf{P}, M)$ is equivalent to minimization of $V(\cdot)$. This reasoning appears, not quite as explicitly as I am presenting it now, in Chapter 2. At the consumer's equilibrium, the supporting price vector is the utility-minimizing vector among all those consistent with the chosen point, just as the chosen quantity is the utility-maximizing bundle among all those consistent with the ruling price vector.

The Lagrangian function associated with the primal–dual problem (7) is

$$L^\dagger(\mathbf{q}, \mathbf{P}, M, \lambda) = V(\mathbf{P}, M) - U(\mathbf{q}) + \lambda(\mathbf{P} \cdot \mathbf{q} - M).$$

First-order conditions therefore lead immediately to a number of results that are discussed at greater length in Chapter 2. For example,

$$\partial L^\dagger(\cdot)/\partial M = V_M - \hat{\lambda} = 0,$$

$$\partial L^\dagger(\cdot)/\partial P_j = V_j + \hat{\lambda}\hat{q}_j = 0.$$

The interpretation of λ as the marginal utility of income is among the immediate implications, as is Roy's identity, which links uncompensated demand functions to partial derivatives of $V(\cdot)$. Roy's identity is formally stated and discussed at length in Chapter 2.

The second example is that of profit maximization. If we allow for many outputs and inputs, the vector $\mathbf{x}$ is the vector of output and input levels, $(\mathbf{y}, \boldsymbol{\ell})$, and $\boldsymbol{\alpha}$ is the vector of output and input prices, $(\mathbf{P}, \mathbf{W})$. Denote the technology constraint by the condition $T(\mathbf{y}, \boldsymbol{\ell}) = 0$. Then the Lagrangian is

$$L^\dagger = \Pi(\mathbf{P}, \mathbf{W}) - (\mathbf{P} \cdot \mathbf{y} - \mathbf{W} \cdot \boldsymbol{\ell}) - \lambda[T(\mathbf{y}, \boldsymbol{\ell})],$$

where $\Pi(\cdot)$ is maximum possible profit expressed as a function of input and output prices. I assume that $\Pi(\cdot)$ is a well-defined function; more on this matter in Chapter 5.

First-order conditions yield

$$\partial L^\dagger(\cdot)/\partial P_j = \partial \Pi(\cdot)/\partial P_j - \hat{y}_j = 0, \quad \text{or} \quad \hat{y}_j = \partial \Pi(\cdot)/\partial P_j,$$

and

$$\partial L^\dagger(\cdot)/\partial W_i = \partial \Pi(\cdot)/\partial W_i + \hat{\ell}_i, \quad \text{or} \quad \hat{\ell}_i = \partial \Pi(\cdot)/\partial W_i.$$

The absence of parameters from the constraint, together with the linear form of the objective function, implies that the optimal supplies of outputs and demands for inputs can be generated simply from the partial derivatives of the maximum value function, $\Pi(\cdot)$, with respect to the associated price. Clearly, then, information about partial derivatives of $\Pi(\cdot)$ is information about the plant's supply and demand functions. This point is developed in much greater detail in Chapter 5.

1.6   The second-order envelope theorem

The envelope theorem of the preceding section involves the first derivatives of the maximum value function. We have seen that these can, under certain assumptions, be identified with the supply or demand functions of an individual. In these circumstances, the second derivatives of $\Omega(\alpha)$ are also of particular interest, because they can be identified with supply or demand responses to parameter changes. We already know from Propositions 1 and 2 that under certain circumstances the value function has certain curvature properties. Happily, it is possible to derive some further useful properties of its second derivatives. The substance of these properties is contained in the "second-order" envelope theorem. Return to the problem stated in equation (2). Suppose we are initially at an optimum, where $f(\cdot) = f(\hat{x}(\alpha^*), \alpha^*)$. We already know that the response of $\Omega(\alpha)$ to an infinitesimal change in the parameters is independent of the adjustment in $\hat{x}(\alpha)$. Now consider the consequences of a finite change, which I shall denote by $\Delta\alpha$. I want to compare the effects of this on $\Omega(\cdot)$ under two circumstances. In one, $\hat{x}(\cdot)$ is adjusted, subject to the existing constraints, to ensure continued maximization of $f(\cdot)$. In the other, there is some additional constraint or set of constraints that impede full adjustment. The easiest example to consider is one in which x is partitioned into (x_a, x_f), where x_a is the vector of adjustable quantities, and x_f is the vector of quantities that, for some reason or other, are constrained to remain fixed at their initial levels. A natural economic interpretation is that we are considering a short-run response, in which some subset of input quantities, x_f, cannot be freely varied within the relevant time horizon. I shall write $\Omega(x_f, \alpha)$ to denote the maximum value of the objective function given α, and subject also to the additional constraint that the vector x_f is fixed at its initial level. By assumption, at the initial situation,

$$\Omega(x_f, \alpha^*) = \Omega(\alpha^*). \tag{8}$$

Furthermore when α changes, the imposition of further restrictions on x cannot enhance the value of $\Omega(\cdot)$, and if these restrictions have any bite at all, they can only reduce its value. In short,

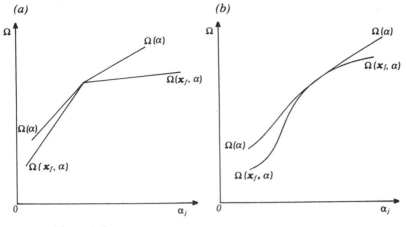

Figure 1.6

$$\Omega(\mathbf{x}_f, \alpha^* + \Delta\alpha) \le \Omega(\alpha^* + \Delta\alpha) \tag{9}$$

for any given value of $\Delta\alpha$. Figure 1.6 summarizes this result. At the initial situation, $\Omega(\cdot)$ takes on the same value under both sets of circumstances, because $\mathbf{x}_f$ is set at its initially optimal level. For other values of α, the presence of additional restrictions cannot raise $\Omega(\cdot)$ and in general will reduce it below the level attained in their absence. The intuition is straightforward: Additional constraints reduce one's feasible set and therefore can only harm, not help, one. Panel (a) of Figure 1.6 reminds us that $\Omega(\alpha)$ is not necessarily everywhere differentiable. Let us assume that it is twice differentiable, at least in the neighborhood of the initial situation. Then panel (b) suggests a simple relationship between the second derivatives $\partial\Omega(\alpha^*)/\partial\alpha_j^2$ and $\partial\Omega(\mathbf{x}_f, \alpha^*)/\partial\alpha_j^2$. I have drawn $\Omega(\alpha)$ with a positive slope at α^*. To the left of α^*, the slope of $\Omega(\mathbf{x}_f, \alpha)$ exceeds that of $\Omega(\alpha)$. At $\alpha = \alpha^*$, their slopes are equal, and as α rises above α^*, the slope of $\Omega(\mathbf{x}_f, \alpha)$ falls short of that of $\Omega(\alpha)$. This suggests that in the neighborhood of α^* the slope of $\Omega(\mathbf{x}_f, \alpha)$ declines more rapidly than that of $\Omega(\alpha)$. In short,

$$\partial^2\Omega(\mathbf{x}_f, \alpha^*)/\partial\alpha_j^2 \le \partial^2\Omega(\alpha^*)/\partial\alpha_j^2. \tag{10}$$

Had $\Omega(\alpha)$ been downward-sloping, the same informal argument would have held, with slight rewording to allow for negative slopes.

The use of the Taylor expansion provides a somewhat more formal and precise justification of (10). To maintain a succinct and simple notation, I shall maintain the assumption that $\Delta\alpha = (0, ..., 0, \Delta\alpha_j, 0, ..., 0)$. Then the Taylor expansion states that

$$\Omega(\alpha^* + \Delta\alpha) = \Omega(\alpha^*) + (\partial\Omega(\alpha^*)/\partial\alpha_j)\Delta\alpha_j + \tfrac{1}{2}(\partial^2\Omega(\alpha^*)/\partial\alpha_j^2)(\Delta\alpha_j)^2 + \cdots$$
(11)

and

$$\Omega(x_f, \alpha^* + \Delta\alpha) = \Omega(x_f, \alpha^*) + (\partial\Omega(x_f, \alpha^*)/\partial\alpha_j)\Delta\alpha_j$$
$$+ \tfrac{1}{2}(\partial^2\Omega(x_f, \alpha^*)/\partial\alpha_j^2)(\Delta\alpha_j)^2 + \cdots .$$
(12)

We already know that by virtue of $\Omega(\cdot)$ being a maximum value function,

$$\Omega(\alpha^* + \Delta\alpha) \geq \Omega(x_f, \alpha^* + \Delta\alpha).$$

In applying this inequality to the right-hand sides of (11) and (12), two further observations should be recalled. First, because x_f is assumed to be optimal given α^*, we know that $\Omega(\alpha^*) = \Omega(x_f, \alpha^*)$. Second, we know that the slopes of $\Omega(\alpha)$ and $\Omega(x_f, \alpha)$ coincide at α^*, so that $\partial\Omega(\alpha^*)/\partial\alpha_j = \partial\Omega(x_f, \alpha^*)/\partial\alpha_j$. Consequently, we know that the quadratic and higher-order terms in (11) and (12) obey the following inequality:

$$\tfrac{1}{2}(\partial^2\Omega(\alpha^*)/\partial\alpha_j^2)(\Delta\alpha_j)^2 + \cdots \geq \tfrac{1}{2}(\partial^2\Omega(x_f, \alpha^*)/\partial\alpha_j^2)(\Delta\alpha_j)^2 + \cdots .$$

For this inequality to be guaranteed for any value of $\Delta\alpha_j$ it is necessary that the quadratic term stated explicitly on the left-hand side be at least as great as its counterpart on the right-hand side. This implies that

$$\partial^2\Omega(\alpha^*)/\partial\alpha_j^2 \geq \partial^2\Omega(x_f, \alpha^*)/\partial\alpha_j^2.$$

This is the second-order envelope property. I have already indicated that it holds in the presence of a more general class of additional constraints than the straight rationing assumed earlier, and I shall now state it in a more general setting:

The generalized envelope theorem

Consider the following two maximum value functions:

$$\Omega(\alpha) \equiv \max_{x}\{f(x, \alpha) \mid g_k(x, \alpha) = 0, k = 1, \ldots, K\}$$
(I)

$$\Omega^c(\alpha) \equiv \max_{x}\{f(x, \alpha) \mid g_k(x, \alpha) = 0,$$

$$k = 1, \ldots, K, h_m(x, \alpha) = 0, m = 1, \ldots, M\}$$
(II)

(Problem II is simply Problem I with additional constraints imposed.) Suppose that for a particular vector of parameters α^*, the additional constraints are only just binding, so that $\Omega(\alpha^*) = f(\hat{x}(\alpha^*), \alpha^*) = \Omega^c(\alpha^*)$. Then in the neighborhood of the optimum,

$$\partial\Omega(\alpha^*)/\partial\alpha_j = \partial\Omega^c(\alpha^*)/\partial\alpha_j,$$

and

$$\partial^2\Omega(\alpha^*)/\partial\alpha_j^2 \geq \partial^2\Omega^c(\alpha^*)/\partial\alpha_j^2, \quad \text{for all } j. \tag{13}$$

The inequality (13) is particularly interesting in any context in which the partial derivatives of $\Omega(\cdot)$ generate the optimal vector $\hat{x}(\alpha^*)$, because the second-order envelope theorem then has direct implications for comparative static responses under varying degrees of constraint. The collection of results from this analysis goes under the heading of Le Chatelier's principle.

1.7 Concluding comments and suggestions for further study

Convex and concave functions, together with their various generalizations, have been studied by mathematicians and engineers as well as by economists. In preparing Sections 1.1 to 1.3, I have found the following discussions of nonlinear programming useful: Mangasarian (1969), Avriel (1976), and Bazaraa and Shetty (1979). The generalization to quasi-concavity is of particular interest to economists, and its implications for optimization have been thoroughly explored by Arrow and Enthoven (1961). Chapters 2–4 of Avriel et al. (1988) provide a good discussion of the present state of understanding of quasi-concavity and quasi-convexity.

The properties of maximum value functions have been largely the concern of economists, because of their implications for the kind of comparative static analysis with which economics abounds. A characteristically elegant treatment is given by Dixit (1976, esp. ch. 3), who also discusses first- and second-order envelope properties. As an introduction to such matters, his treatment may be a little terse and cryptic for some. If so, I recommend that the reader return to it after gaining more of a feel for the dual approach.

For cryptic allusions to the subject matter of this book, none compares with Samuelson: The first-order envelope property of a constrained maximization problem is disposed of in a single sentence (Samuelson 1947, p. 34), and Le Chatelier's principle is worked out two pages later. Samuelson's work is peppered with arguments that exploit the envelope property and the dual techniques that it permits, as a quick perusal of his collected works will verify.

Since Samuelson's contribution, envelope theorems have been further studied by Silberberg (1974, 1978, pp. 168–72, 284–99) and by Pauwels

(1979). Silberberg (1971) also discusses Le Chatelier's principle. More recently, Gorman (1984) has provided an informal but sophisticated discussion of the principle; this is, perhaps, more informative to the experienced microeconomist than to the beginner.

PART II

Modeling individual consumer and producer behavior

CHAPTER 2

Individual consumer behavior: Direct and indirect utility functions

It is known that utility functions are themselves the consequences of assumptions, or axioms, imposed on individuals' rankings over commodity bundles. The literature usually begins by demonstrating the existence of a direct utility function $U(\mathbf{q})$ and proceeds from there. It transpires that this is not a convenient strategy for analyzing demand functions of the form $q_i = x_i(\mathbf{P}, M)$, but is admirably suited for analysis of inverse demand functions of the form $P_i/M = \phi_i(\mathbf{q})$. The key result here is known as the Hotelling–Wold identity. If one develops the observation that the maximum attainable utility in a competitive situation is determined by the prices faced and income received, one arrives naturally at the idea of an indirect utility function, $V(\mathbf{P}, M)$. Just as the Hotelling–Wold identity generates inverse demand functions from $U(\mathbf{q})$, so a similar result, Roy's identity, generates demand functions from $V(\mathbf{P}, M)$. Under certain assumptions, of which convexity of preferences is a crucial one, $U(\mathbf{q})$ and $V(\mathbf{P}, M)$ are dual functions – that is, they offer alternative ways of representing a given set of preferences. We are then free to choose whichever is more convenient for the purpose at hand, because both contain precisely the same information, the one in terms of quantities, the other in terms of prices. From an informational point of view the situation is analogous to that confronting an econometrician or statistician who can choose between a number of alternative ways of representing a probability distribution, either by writing out the density function or by listing its moments. Duality involves a fair bit more than the existence of alternative, informationally equivalent formulations. As suggested by the similarities between the Hotelling–Wold identity and Roy's identity, there are important symmetries linking the quantity space inhabited by $U(\mathbf{q})$ and the price space of $V(\mathbf{P}, M)$. These symmetries lie at the heart of the duality between these two representations of utility, representations that form the subject of this chapter.

2.1   Preferences and utility

A rational consumer is one whose ranking of various alternative outcomes, which in the present context are synonymous with bundles or vectors of commodities, exhibits a certain coherence. More precisely, I suppose that the individual's choices between alternative bundles are consistent with a set of axioms, or basic assumptions, from which the remaining implications of the model can be logically deduced. I shall adopt six axioms similar to those stated and discussed by Deaton and Muellbauer (1980*a*, pp. 26–30). These are the axioms of reflexivity, completeness, transitivity, continuity, nonsatiation, and convexity. To these I add an axiom of differentiability. This addition, together with a slight tightening of the convexity axiom, though by no means necessary for the development of duality theory, considerably simplifies the subsequent exposition. The first four axioms are in some sense the more fundamental, because they enable us to define a utility function such that the statement "the consumer chooses the most preferred bundle from his constraint set" can be translated into the statement "the consumer acts so as to maximize utility subject to remaining in his constraint set." The significance of this translation is that by formulating the problem as one of constrained maximization of a function, we immediately have at our disposal the whole armory of mathematical optimization theory. Even that elementary part of the theory that we exploit is remarkably powerful. The remaining three axioms put extra structure into preferences and therefore into the utility function that represents them.

Let $\mathbf{q}^0$ and $\mathbf{q}^1$ denote two different commodity bundles. The statement $\mathbf{q}^0 \succsim \mathbf{q}^1$ means that the consumer either finds $\mathbf{q}^0$ preferable or is indifferent between the two bundles. More succinctly, $\mathbf{q}^0$ is said to be weakly preferred to $\mathbf{q}^1$. We now run through the axioms.

Axiom 1: Reflexivity. $\mathbf{q}^0 \succsim \mathbf{q}^0$ *for any given bundle.*

Axiom 2: Completeness.   *For any two bundles* $\mathbf{q}^0$ *and* $\mathbf{q}^1$, *either* $\mathbf{q}^0 \succsim \mathbf{q}^1$ *or* $\mathbf{q}^1 \succsim \mathbf{q}^0$.

Axiom 3: Transitivity.   *For any three bundles* $\mathbf{q}^0$, $\mathbf{q}^1$, *and* $\mathbf{q}^2$, *if* $\mathbf{q}^0 \succsim \mathbf{q}^1$ *and* $\mathbf{q}^1 \succsim \mathbf{q}^2$, *then* $\mathbf{q}^0 \succsim \mathbf{q}^2$.

Axiom 4: Continuity.   *For every bundle* $\mathbf{q}^0$, *the no-worse-than-*$\mathbf{q}^0$ *set* $A \equiv \{\mathbf{q} \mid \mathbf{q} \succsim \mathbf{q}^0\}$ *and the no-better-than-*$\mathbf{q}^0$ *set* $B \equiv \{\mathbf{q} \mid \mathbf{q} \precsim \mathbf{q}^0\}$ *are closed sets.*

Less formally, Axiom 4 implies that if, for example, $\mathbf{q}^1$ is strictly preferred to $\mathbf{q}^0$, then bundles that are sufficiently similar to $\mathbf{q}^1$ will also be strictly preferred to $\mathbf{q}^0$. Conversely, if $\mathbf{q}^1$ is less attractive to an individual than is $\mathbf{q}^0$, so will be other bundles that are sufficiently similar to $\mathbf{q}^1$. (The vagueness of the phrase "sufficiently similar to" points to the value of a more precise formal characterization.)

The central result of this section is the following. If Axioms 1–4 hold, then there exists a function $U(\mathbf{q})$ that associates with each bundle of commodities a real number such that the statement "$\mathbf{q}^0$ is weakly preferred to $\mathbf{q}^1$" both implies and is implied by the statement that "the number associated with $\mathbf{q}^0$ is at least as great as the number associated with $\mathbf{q}^1$." More succinctly,

$$\mathbf{q}^0 \succsim \mathbf{q}^1 \Leftrightarrow U(\mathbf{q}^0) \geq U(\mathbf{q}^1).$$

An ideal name for the function $U(\mathbf{q})$ would be a preference indicator function. Unfortunately, the habit of calling it a utility function, with the misleading cardinal overtones that this suggests, is too deeply ingrained to be changed. I shall follow custom and refer to it henceforth as a utility function.

The remaining axioms are as follows:

Axiom 5: Nonsatiation.   *Suppose the bundle $\mathbf{q}^1$ has at least as much of every commodity as does $\mathbf{q}^0$, and strictly more of at least one commodity. That is, $\mathbf{q}^1 \geq \mathbf{q}^0$ and $\mathbf{q}^1 \neq \mathbf{q}^0$. Then $\mathbf{q}^1 > \mathbf{q}^0$.*

This form of nonsatiation axiom is stated by Varian (1984*b*), who calls it "strong monotonicity" to distinguish it from other, weaker notions of nonsatiation. It implies that each commodity is, indeed, regarded as a good.

Axiom 6: Convexity.   *If $\mathbf{q}^0 \succsim \mathbf{q}_1$, then for any scalar λ such that $0 \leq \lambda \leq 1$, $\lambda \mathbf{q}^0 + (1-\lambda)\mathbf{q}^1 \succsim \mathbf{q}^1$.*

Axioms 1–6 are sufficient to develop duality theory. However, the exposition can be greatly simplified by adopting a slightly stronger version of Axiom 6 and by introducing an additional assumption. The extra assumptions both relate to the curvature properties of the indifference map. First is the strengthened version of the convexity axiom, which I shall label 6S:

Axiom 6S: Strict convexity.   *If $\mathbf{q}^0 \succsim \mathbf{q}^1$, then for any scalar λ such that $0 < \lambda < 1$, $\lambda \mathbf{q}^0 + (1-\lambda)\mathbf{q}^1 > \mathbf{q}^1$.*

This rules out linear segments of indifference surfaces. It implies that any plane in quantity space has only a single point of tangency with an indifference surface, so that to every budget line there corresponds just one optimal bundle. The last axiom, applied directly to the utility function, allows us to make straightforward use of the differential calculus in characterizing a consumer optimum and conducting comparative static analysis:

Axiom 7: Differentiability. $U(\mathbf{q})$ *is everywhere twice continuously differentiable.*

Geometrically, the adoption of this axiom means that each indifference curve in quantity space has a unique tangent at each point. The assumption that the first derivatives, $\partial U(\mathbf{q})/\partial q_i$, are continuous also ensures that the values of the second derivatives at any point will not depend on the order in which the differentiation is done, so that $\partial^2 U(\mathbf{q})/\partial q_i \partial q_j = \partial^2 U(\mathbf{q})/\partial q_j \partial q_i$. At a more intuitive level, the axiom imposes a certain smoothness on indifference surfaces, by ruling out kinks or corners.

The motivation of Axioms 6S and 7 is clearly demonstrated in Figure 2.1. In each panel, the enclosed area marked B represents the set of all budget constraints, and Q represents the set of all quantity bundles. In panel (a) there are many bundles that represent an optimum for the consumer facing the given budget constraint. Axiom 6S rules out this possibility. In panel (b) there are many budget lines consistent with $\mathbf{q}^*$ being the chosen bundle. Axiom 7 rules out this possibility. Together the two axioms leave us with panel (c), in which there is a one-to-one mapping between budget constraints and optimal bundles. Let me emphasize again that duality relationships in no way require these last two assumptions. They are adopted purely to simplify the exposition, by allowing us to define optimal quantities as functions of prices, and demand prices as functions of chosen quantities, instead of having to deal with correspondences.

2.2   The price-taking consumer's problem

Recall the traditional formulation of the consumer's problem as set out, for example, by Hirshleifer (1988). Faced with a given money price vector $\mathbf{P}$ for the n marketed commodities on which he may spend a given sum of money M, his problem is to choose that feasible vector of quantities $\mathbf{q}$ that will maximize the value of his utility function. Formally, the problem is

$$\max_{\mathbf{q}} U(\mathbf{q}) \quad \text{subject to } \mathbf{P} \cdot \mathbf{q} \le M, \, \mathbf{q} \ge 0.$$

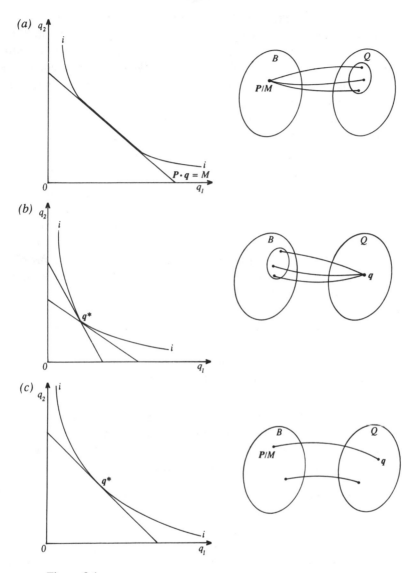

Figure 2.1

To keep things simple, we assume that the solution involves purchasing a strictly positive quantity of each commodity, so that the nonnegativity constraints are not binding. In addition, we avoid certain complications of a technical nature by restricting attention to a strictly positive price vector.

Axioms 1–5, 6S, and 7 ensure that the traditional formulation can be tackled with differential calculus and that it has convenient properties –

for example, that the equilibrium **q** is indeed unique and varies continuously with prices and incomes. For the moment, however, just recall the conventional route to the standard comparative static results of demand theory. This proceeds by writing out the first-order necessary conditions for the problem stated earlier and by differentiating them totally with respect to the exogenous parameters **P** and M. The result is a set of $(n+1)$ equations. Apart from the one derived from the budget constraint, they each contain *all* of the unknown quantity changes, $d\mathbf{q}$, and just *one* of the exogenous price changes. At this point, the manipulations become tedious and not very enlightening, because the usual objective is to explore the properties of so-called uncompensated demand functions by generating a set of equations each of which expresses the endogenous change in just *one* quantity – say dq_1 – as a function of *all* the exogenous parameter changes, $d\mathbf{P}$ and dM. Furthermore, having inverted the system of equations to achieve this end, the results come as something of an anticlimax. For example, much to the glee of critics of this tradition, the income effects associated with a price change prevent us from concluding even that demand curves are downward-sloping.

The difficulties of the procedure that we have outlined stem from two sources. First, the desired uncompensated demand functions express quantities as functions of prices and money income, whereas the utility function from which the analysis started has as its arguments not prices and income but the quantities consumed. In addition, the most interesting and powerful results, from both theoretical and practical viewpoints, come from breaking down the price responses associated with the uncompensated functions and separating out the "real income" and "compensated" components. This suggests the following three observations:

1. When we are primarily interested in generating, and deriving properties of, uncompensated demand functions, this may best be done by casting the consumer's problem in such a form that **P** and M appear as arguments from the outset.

2. Analysis of compensated price responses may best be done not with uncompensated demand functions but with "compensated" demand functions that express quantities demanded as functions of **P** and u. The convenience of this approach, if it can be done, is apparent, because the compensated price responses are simply the partial derivatives of quantity with respect to price.

3. The formulation of the consumer's problem that uses the function $U(\mathbf{q})$ is most appropriate in situations in which the independent variables are the quantities consumed.

2.3   The Hotelling–Wold identity

Let us do the traditional optimizing problem stated in the preceding section. The Lagrangian expression from which the first-order conditions are generated is

$$L = U(\mathbf{q}) - \lambda[\mathbf{P} \cdot \mathbf{q} - M].$$

Recall that the optimal bundle is assumed to contain a positive quantity of each commodity, so that the first-order conditions are

$$\partial L/\partial q_i = \partial U(\mathbf{q})/\partial q_i - \lambda P_i = 0, \quad i = 1, \dots, n,$$

$$\partial L/\partial \lambda = \mathbf{P} \cdot \mathbf{q} - M = 0.$$

Eliminating λ, the first n conditions may be expressed as

$$P_i/P_j = U_i(\mathbf{q})/U_j(\mathbf{q}) = F_{ij}(\mathbf{q}). \tag{1}$$

This is all elementary and familiar. Notice, however, the precise form of equation (1). It expresses a single relative price, P_i/P_j, as a function of the quantities of all the commodities. It may be called an inverse demand function, because ordinary demand functions express a single quantity as a function of all prices. It is useful to call equation (1) an uncompensated inverse demand function, in order to distinguish it from its compensated variant, to be discussed later. If we were analyzing a situation in which quantities were given, and we wished to determine the prices at which the consumer would be prepared to consume those quantities, equation (1) would be a useful starting point. An alternative statement expresses each nominal price relative to money income, P_i/M, as a function of the quantity bundle. Combining the budget constraint with (1) yields

$$(U_1/U_i)P_i q_1 + \cdots + P_i q_i + \cdots + (U_n/U_i)P_i q_n = M;$$

$$\therefore \ P_i/M = U_i \bigg/ \sum_{j=1}^{n} q_j U_j = \phi_i(\mathbf{q}), \quad i = 1, \dots, n. \tag{2}$$

This relationship between the market price and the partial derivatives of $U(\mathbf{q})$ is often referred to as the Hotelling–Wold identity, in acknowledgment of two economists who were among the first to derive it.

There are, indeed, occasions when we are interested in expressing price as a function of quantities. Ironically, the Hotelling–Wold identity has, in the past, more often been used en route to expressing quantities as functions of prices and income. For this purpose it is not particularly convenient. Equation (2) provides n equations, each relating a single price to the vector of quantities $\mathbf{q}$. This system has to be inverted if we are to generate and explore the properties of uncompensated demand functions, each expressing a single quantity q_i as a function of the vector of prices and money income. In our later discussion of the indirect utility function we shall show a less cumbersome, more economically transparent way of approaching such demand functions. In keeping with the spirit of the dual approach, we shall find that such an approach has strong parallels with the method just shown of deriving uncompensated inverse demand functions from the direct utility function.

2.4   The indirect utility function

We have observed that the solution to the consumer's budget-constrained utility maximization problem yields a set of behavioral equations – the ordinary or uncompensated demand functions – of the form $\mathbf{x}(\mathbf{P}, M)$, where $\mathbf{x}$ denotes the optimal bundle of quantities. This suggests writing utility itself as a function of $\mathbf{P}$ and M. Indeed, it is perfectly natural to think of one's utility as depending on the set of prices that confront one, together with one's exogenous money income. Because the particular bundle that the consumer chooses depends upon the prices he faces and his money income, so does the associated level of utility, which by definition is the maximum attainable by him. When the level of utility is expressed in this way, in terms of $\mathbf{P}$ and M, the resulting function is called the indirect utility function, which I shall write as $V(\mathbf{P}, M)$. We now explore further the various useful properties of $V(\mathbf{P}, M)$. Formally, we can write

$$\max_{\mathbf{q}} \{U(\mathbf{q}) \mid \mathbf{P} \cdot \mathbf{q} \le M\} = F[\mathbf{x}(\mathbf{P}, M)] \equiv V(\mathbf{P}, M), \tag{3}$$

where $\mathbf{x}(\cdot)$ is the vector of utility-maximizing values of $\mathbf{q}$, expressed as a function of $\mathbf{P}$ and M. The function $V(\mathbf{P}, M)$ embodies an optimizing process that the function $U(\mathbf{q})$ does not; it presupposes that the consumer chooses the best bundle from those that his budget constraint makes available. Nevertheless, there are close analogies. To begin with, it can be represented geometrically by an indifference map in the commodity price space. First, though, we perform the trick of "normalizing" prices. Clearly, if all prices and money income are changed by exactly the same proportion, the consumer's constraint set is unchanged. If he is interested only in the quantities consumed, and has no preferences concerning nominal prices as such, his behavior is, in turn, unaffected. The objects that matter to him are the nominal prices relative to income, P_i/M. We are therefore at liberty to pin down nominal magnitudes by normalizing prices.

In situations where exogenous income M is assumed positive, we can define normalized prices, $p_j \equiv P_j/M$, and a normalized price vector, $\mathbf{p} \equiv (p_1, p_2, \ldots, p_n) \equiv (P_1/M, P_2/M, \ldots, P_n/M)$. A moment's further reflection should persuade the reader that we can analyze the consumer's problem with the normalized prices $\mathbf{p}$ instead of the absolute, or money, prices $\mathbf{P}$, because the latter appear only in the budget constraint,

$$\mathbf{P} \cdot \mathbf{q} \leq M,$$

which can simply be rewritten,

$$(\mathbf{P}/M) \cdot \mathbf{q} \leq 1 \quad \text{or} \quad \mathbf{p} \cdot \mathbf{q} \leq 1.$$

The advantage of conducting the analysis with prices normalized in this way is that it reveals with great clarity the symmetries that lie at the heart of duality relationships. Using normalized prices, equation (3) becomes

$$\max_{\mathbf{q}} \{U(\mathbf{q}) \mid \mathbf{p} \cdot \mathbf{q} \leq 1\} = F[\mathbf{x}(\mathbf{p})] = V(\mathbf{p}). \tag{4}$$

We can now generate indifference curves in the commodity price space. In Figure 2.2, normalized prices are measured along the axes for the two-commodity example. Suppose that initially the consumer faces prices p_1^0 and p_2^0 and that he chooses the bundle containing the quantities q_1^0 and q_2^0 of commodities 1 and 2, respectively. Associated with this bundle is the utility level u^0. We wish to locate other pairs of prices, (p_1, p_2), which just enable the consumer to attain u^0, and to generate the locus of all such pairs. To begin with, such pairs of values cannot lie either above and to the right or below and to the left of (p_1^0, p_2^0). If both prices rise, the consumer must become worse off, whereas if they both fall he will become better off. In Figure 2.2, such pairs must lie in the unhatched areas. Now consider the line DD. This passes through (p_1^0, p_2^0) and is the locus of values of $\mathbf{p}$ that would just enable the consumer to purchase the bundle (q_1^0, q_2^0). Its equation is therefore

$$p_1 q_1^0 + p_2 q_2^0 = 1.$$

The slope of DD is clearly $(-q_1^0/q_2^0)$. The reader will already have noticed the parallels and contrasts with the traditional quantity diagram – in Figure 2.2 price vectors are points, whereas the slope of DD represents a ratio of quantities. Now suppose prices happen to change in such a way that we stay on the line DD. By definition, this cannot make the consumer worse off, because he can still afford his previous optimal bundle. Indeed, it will generally make him better off, because if his preferences exhibit any degree of substitutability he will be able to move to a strictly

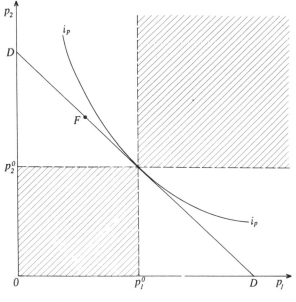

Figure 2.2

preferred bundle. Consequently, any price vector within the triangle $0DD$ must yield a strictly higher utility level than is possible at (p_1^0, p_2^0). The locus of normalized prices that just enable the consumer to attain the utility level u^0 therefore lies everywhere on or above the line DD. Applying this argument to every point of the locus, we conclude that the indifference curve must lie everywhere on or above the tangent to any point and must look convex from the origin. It cannot have dents in it. The locus $i_p i_p$ is just such a curve.

The indifference map in price space looks much like its familiar counterpart in quantity space. Two important differences, however, should be noted. First, higher normalized prices clearly imply lower levels of the maximum attainable utility. The farther out is an indifference curve from the origin, the lower is its associated utility level. Our discussion of the shapes of indifference curves in price space may be summed up by the statement that for any two price vectors $\mathbf{p}^0$ and $\mathbf{p}^1$,

$$\max[V(\mathbf{p}^0), V(\mathbf{p}^1)] \geq V[\lambda \mathbf{p}^0 + (1-\lambda)\mathbf{p}^1] \quad \text{for all } 0 \leq \lambda \leq 1.$$

In other words, if we consider any straight line segment in price space, the maximum utility is attained at one of the endpoints of the segment. More formally, $V(\mathbf{p})$ is quasi-convex.

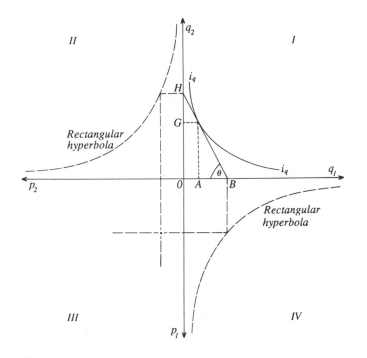

Figure 2.3

The second important difference between $U(\cdot)$ and $V(\cdot)$ is that the quasi-convexity of the latter is not the consequence of any special assumptions imposed upon preferences. In this respect, it is quite different from the quasi-concavity assumption often imposed on the direct utility function. Even if preferences defined over quantities are not convex – that is, the indifference curves in quantity space have dents in them – $V(\mathbf{p})$ will be quasi-convex. This robust property follows simply as a consequence of the definition of $V(\mathbf{p})$ as the solution of a maximization problem.

2.5   The duality between $U(\mathbf{q})$ and $V(\mathbf{p})$.

We now provide an informal geometric treatment of the link between indifference curves in quantity space and their counterparts defined over prices, before undertaking a more formal analysis of the so-called duality between $U(\mathbf{q})$ and $V(\mathbf{p})$.

In quadrant I of Figure 2.3, a conventional indifference curve, i_q, is drawn in quantity space. It has smooth curvature everywhere, with no kinks or dents in it. In short, it reflects extremely well behaved convex preferences. Our aim is to use the information contained in i_q to generate an indifference curve in price space. Pick an arbitrary point on i_q – say $\mathbf{q}^0$. Under our assumptions there is just one price line that touches i_q at $\mathbf{q}^0$ and that therefore will lead the price-taking consumer to choose $\mathbf{q}^0$ as his most preferred bundle. Denote by B the intersection of this price line with the horizontal axis. Then the distance $0B$ is equal to $1/p_1^0$. This is so because $0B$ is the value of (q_1^0, q_2^0) expressed in terms of units of good 1, $(p_1^0 q_1^0 + p_2^0 q_2^0)/p_1^0$. Recall our normalization, which puts $p_1^0 q_1^0 + p_2^0 q_2^0$ equal to unity. Then the distance $0B$ is equal to $1/p_1^0$. Similar reasoning shows that $0H$ equals $1/p_2^0$. Now draw rectangular hyperbolae in quadrants II and IV. Recall that the equation of a rectangular hyperbola is $xy = k$, or $x = k/y$. If k is set equal to unity, the hyperbola transforms the variable x into its reciprocal. In the present context, the hyperbola in quadrant IV transforms the variable $1/p_1$, measured along the horizontal axis, into its reciprocal p_1, measured along the vertical axis that projects downward from 0. In quadrant II, $1/p_2$ undergoes the same transformation. Quadrant III contains the desired price vector, which it represents as the point $\mathbf{p}^0$. By starting from other points on i_q, an entire indifference curve may be generated in price space. It would be a useful exercise for the reader to generate additional points on the "price indifference curve" and to confirm the earlier claim that it looks convex from the origin. The best way to do this is to start with an extreme example in which the "quantity indifference curve" is L-shaped, and then consider what happens when the possibility of some substitution is allowed.

Further reflection on Figure 2.3 reveals an important fact: Not only can i_p be generated from i_q, but also we can start with i_p and generate i_q. This means that $U(\mathbf{q})$ and $V(\mathbf{p})$ offer alternative but precisely equivalent representations of the individual's preferences. Because they both contain precisely the same information, it does not matter which we use, and our choice may be made according to which is more convenient, or offers clearer insights, for the particular problem at hand. The present discussion stops far short of the most general and rigorous examination of the assumptions that must be made for the equivalence between U and V to hold, but it is easy to see that convexity of preferences is vital. If there are nonconvexities, or dents, in i_q, it is still possible to generate i_p, but we cannot regenerate i_q from i_p. In Figure 2.4, that part of i_q lying between R and S simply gets overlooked in the process by which i_p is generated. In this case, although $V(\mathbf{p})$ certainly can be defined, it does not contain all the information contained in $U(\mathbf{q})$. Convexity of preferences, then, is

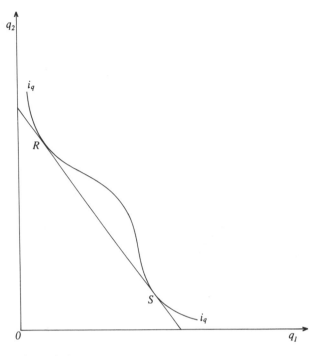

Figure 2.4

necessary for $U(\mathbf{q})$ and $V(\mathbf{p})$ to be logically equivalent representations of preferences.

The equivalence, or duality, of U and V is useful because it allows one, for example, to use $V(\mathbf{p})$ in the confident knowledge that one's assumptions imply a coherent preference ordering over quantities that can in turn be represented by a well-behaved direct utility function. The choice between the two representations will depend upon which is more convenient and offers greater economic insights. I have already suggested, and shortly will try to demonstrate, that the less common indirect utility function may have advantages in certain contexts.

This duality, already evident in our geometry, comes through equally clearly in the algebra. We can write

$$\min_{\mathbf{p}} \{ V(\mathbf{p}) \mid \mathbf{p} \cdot \mathbf{q} \leq 1 \} = G[\mathbf{p}(\mathbf{q})] = U(\mathbf{q}). \qquad (5)$$

Consider a given vector $\mathbf{q}^0$. The formulation given by (5) invites us to consider all those price lines passing through $\mathbf{q}^0$ in Figure 2.5 and to pick out that one for which $\mathbf{q}^0$ is the optimal attainable bundle. This line is the

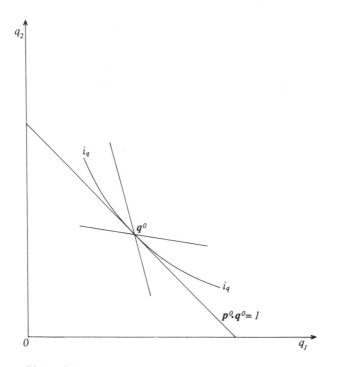

Figure 2.5

tangent to the quantity indifference curve at $\mathbf{q}^0$, and we denote its associated price vector by $\mathbf{p}^0$. The price line $\mathbf{p}^0 \cdot \mathbf{q}^0 = 1$ attains maximum utility at $\mathbf{q}^0$, whereas the remaining price lines under consideration would enable higher utility levels to be attained. It is in this sense that $\mathbf{p}^0$ minimizes the maximum attainable utility level, the value of which itself depends on the choice of consumption bundle, $\mathbf{q}^0$. The symmetries between equations (4) and (5) are obvious.

More rigorous discussions of the duality between $U(\cdot)$ and $V(\cdot)$ dispense with certain assumptions, such as differentiability, and also have to worry about extending the functions so that they will be defined when one or more of the quantities, or prices, are zero. It is worth mentioning the special case in which the commodities – say left shoes and right shoes – are demanded in fixed proportions. Such Leontief preferences imply L-shaped indifference curves in quantity space and are not very convenient to handle using calculus, because the derivatives of $U(\cdot)$, and therefore of the indifference curves, are not well defined at precisely those points of particular economic interest. In price space, the indifference curves are parallel straight lines, and $V(\mathbf{p})$ is everywhere differentiable. We shall see in Chapter 5 that a fixed-coefficients production technology is more conveniently handled by moving from quantity space into price space. The reader may also confirm that parallel linear indifference curves in quantity space imply and are implied by L-shaped indifference curves in price space. Recall that earlier in this chapter we explicitly confined attention to strictly positive price and optimal quantity vectors. The extension of $U(\cdot)$ and $V(\cdot)$ to cover the nonnegative orthants and still remain continuous functions involves technicalities of little interest to the general reader. Having taken care of these matters, the duality relationship asserts that the existence of a continuous, positive monotonic and quasi-concave direct utility function both implies and is implied by the existence of a continuous, negative monotonic and quasi-convex indirect utility function. Thus we can use either formulation, being guided by convenience for the task at hand, because both contain precisely the same information regarding preferences.

2.6   Roy's identity

I have derived equation (5) not simply because of the aesthetic appeal of its duality with (4), which is remarkable, but also because it is a natural starting point for some important comparative statics. We assume that $V(\mathbf{p})$ is everywhere differentiable. Set up the Lagrangian expression associated with the minimizing problem stated in (5):

$$L = V(\mathbf{p}) - \mu[\mathbf{p} \cdot \mathbf{q} - 1].$$

The first-order conditions are

$$V_i/V_j = q_i/q_j \text{ for all } i, j, \quad \text{and} \quad \mathbf{p} \cdot \mathbf{q} = 1,$$

where $V_i \equiv \partial V(\mathbf{p})/\partial p_i$. Now suppose we want to solve for q_k in terms of all prices. The first-order conditions enable us to write $q_i = V_i q_k / V_k$ for all $i \neq k$. Substituting for all the q_i's in the budget constraint and rearranging,

$$q_k = x_k(\mathbf{p}) = V_k(\mathbf{p}) \bigg/ \sum_{i=1}^{n} p_i V_i(\mathbf{p}). \tag{6}$$

Equation (6) is called Roy's identity. It shows that we can generate demand functions of the form $x_k(\mathbf{p})$ from expressions involving simple partial derivatives of the indirect utility function.

These demand functions look more familiar when expressed in terms of money prices. Roy's identity becomes

$$q_k = V_k(\mathbf{P}, M) \bigg/ \sum_i (P_i/M) V_i(\mathbf{P}, M). \tag{7}$$

Now if all prices and income change by the same proportion, nothing real changes. $V(\mathbf{P}, M)$ is, in other words, homogeneous of degree zero in $\mathbf{P}$ and M. Thus,

$$\sum_i P_i V_i(\mathbf{P}, M) + M V_M(\mathbf{P}, M) = 0,$$

so that (7) may be written

$$q_k = x_k(\mathbf{P}, M) = -V_k(\mathbf{P}, M)/V_M(\mathbf{P}, M). \tag{8}$$

Equation (8), as well as providing a neat statement of Roy's identity, clarifies its economic content. The reader may find it instructive to try the following exercise. First, on the assumption that the direct utility function is of the form $U(q_1, q_2) = q_1^\alpha q_2^{(1-\alpha)}$, derive the Marshallian demand functions. Then perform the same exercise starting from the indirect utility function

$$V(P_1, P_2, M) = M(\alpha/P_1)^\alpha([1-\alpha]/P_2)^{1-\alpha},$$

and exploiting Roy's identity.

It is instructive to remind ourselves of the consequences of choosing a vector $\mathbf{p}^*$ at which $V(\mathbf{p})$ is not differentiable. In quantity space, this corresponds to a linear segment of an indifference curve, as shown in panel (a) of Figure 2.1. There is, in this case, a set of many quantity vectors consistent with optimization. In price space, the relevant indifference curve has a kink in it, so that there is not a unique tangent at $\mathbf{p}^*$. Because the tangent, or supporting hyperplane, is associated with a particular quantity vector, it again follows that there is not a unique solution for quantities. In short, demand functions cannot be defined, though correspondences can. We shall henceforth assume $V(\mathbf{p})$ to be everywhere differentiable, so that the tangent to any point of an indifference curve in price space is unique. Roy's identity then generates the implied set of demands as functions of normalized prices.

What restrictions can be imposed on the functions $x_i(\mathbf{P}, M)$ as a consequence of their being individual demand functions? It turns out that relatively little can be said about them using the analysis of this chapter without a lot of hard effort, and what can easily be said follows in a straightforward way from the budget constraint. There are four properties of use to us:

1. The adding-up restriction: This states that $\mathbf{P} \cdot \mathbf{x}(\mathbf{P}, M) = M$. The demand functions must collectively be consistent with the budget constraint.
2. Homogeneity: Let θ be a nonnegative scalar. Then $\mathbf{x}(\theta\mathbf{P}, \theta M) = \mathbf{x}(\mathbf{P}, M)$. Equal proportional changes in all P values and M leave the budget set unchanged, and hence demands are unchanged. I exploited this property when I introduced the idea of normalized prices.
3. Engel aggregation: $\sum_j P_j(\partial x_j / \partial M) = 1$. Because the budget constraint must at all times be obeyed, differentiation with respect to income gives the result that the sum of marginal propensities to consume must be unity.
4. Cournot aggregation: $\sum_j P_j(\partial x_j / \partial P_k) + x_k = 0$. Again, this follows from the budget constraint in a straightforward way, this time by differentiation with respect to P_k.

Nothing in these results tells us much about individual responses. We cannot infer, for example, that $\partial x_i / \partial M$ is positive for any i, although we know that there is at least one value of i for which it is true. More disappointing is our inability to conclude that $\partial x_i / \partial P_i$ is negative – that is, that orthodox uncompensated demand curves are downward-sloping. To shed more light on the structure of individual demand systems, we must use the compensated demand functions that are introduced in Chapter 3.

2.7 Some convenient functional forms for economists and econometricians

Most of the qualitative and quantitative applications of demand theory require that we impose other restrictions on preferences in addition to those implied by the axioms. For example, when trade theorists analyze the implications of factor endowments for comparative advantage and trade patterns, they try to abstract from demand complications by assuming that preferences are homothetic. This implies that the direct utility function can be written in the form

$$U(\mathbf{q}) = f(g(\mathbf{q})),$$

where the function $g(\cdot)$ is homogeneous of degree 1, and $f(\cdot)$ is monotonic increasing. This in turn implies that marginal rates of substitution are unaffected by equal proportional changes in all quantities, so that income expansion paths are straight lines through the origin, as in Figure

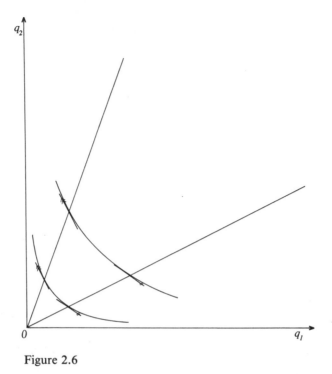

Figure 2.6

2.6, and income elasticities are unity. The attraction for trade theorists is that if preferences are of this form, and are identical in each of two countries, any difference in their autarkic prices must be due to supply side differences. Such assumptions are the economist's (poor) substitute for the physical scientist's controlled experiment. Let us look at some further preference structures, beginning with the direct utility function and then moving on to the indirect utility function.

Functional forms of direct utility functions

There is a class of preferences that often is assumed in introductory and intermediate economics without an explicit statement of the utility function. Such preferences are called quasi-linear, and the associated quasi-linear direct utility function takes the form

$$U(\mathbf{q}) = q_1 + F(q_2, ..., q_n). \tag{9}$$

This implies that inverse demand functions of the kind defined in equation (1) are independent of q_1. Income expansion paths are therefore parallel to the q_1 axis. Clearly, then, the preferences represented by (9) are not homothetic. Given a single indifference curve, all others can be obtained as horizontal displacements. If a consumer with such a preference map initially consumes all commodities, then any extra income received will be entirely spent on commodity 1: $P_1 \partial x_1(\cdot)/\partial M = 1$, and $P_j \partial x_j(\cdot)/\partial M = 0$ for $j = 2, \ldots, n$. It is this assumption that provides a rigorous justification of partial equilibrium demand functions of the form $q_j = D_j(P_j)$, for $j \neq 1$, and of their use as the basis for calculations of consumer's surplus – see Varian (1984b, pp. 278–83).

We shall encounter a generalization of (9) in Chapter 10, when we discuss public goods. Let

$$U(\mathbf{q}) = F(q_2, \ldots, q_n)q_1 + G(q_2, \ldots, q_n), \tag{10}$$

where the functions $F(\cdot)$ and $G(\cdot)$ are consistent with $U(\cdot)$ being strictly quasi-concave and increasing in $\mathbf{q}$. Now the inverse demand functions are

$$P_i/P_1 = \frac{(\partial F(\cdot)/\partial q_i)q_1 + \partial G(\cdot)/\partial q_i}{F(\cdot)}$$

$$= f(q_2, \ldots, q_n)q_1 + g(q_2, \ldots, q_n).$$

The relative demand price is no longer independent of q_1, but is a simple linear function of it. Such a property can substantially simplify the analysis of certain aspects of public good and rationing theory.

The standard workhorse of classroom and textbook is the Cobb–Douglas direct utility function:

$$U(\mathbf{q}) = A q_1^{\alpha_1} q_2^{\alpha_2} \cdots q_n^{\alpha_n}, \tag{11}$$

where A and $\alpha_1, \ldots, \alpha_n$ are positive parameters. It is certainly homothetic, because it can be expressed as

$$U(\mathbf{q}) = A[(q_1^{\alpha_1} \cdots q_n^{\alpha_n})^{1/(\alpha_1 + \alpha_2 + \cdots + \alpha_n)}]^{(\alpha_1 + \alpha_2 + \cdots + \alpha_n)}$$

$$= A[g(\mathbf{q})]^{(\alpha_1 + \alpha_2 + \cdots + \alpha_n)},$$

where $g(\mathbf{q})$ is homogeneous of degree 1. Homotheticity is confirmed by looking at the first-order conditions, which imply

$$P_i/P_j = \alpha_i q_j/\alpha_j q_i, \quad i, j = 1, \ldots, n.$$

Alternatively, applying the Hotelling–Wold identity presented in (2), we obtain the inverse uncompensated demand functions:

$$P_i/M = \alpha_i \bigg/ \left(q_i \sum_{j=1}^{n} \alpha_j\right), \quad i = 1, \ldots, n. \tag{12}$$

In terms of budget shares,

$$P_i q_i / M = \alpha_i \Big/ \sum_j \alpha_j = k_i \text{ (a constant).}$$

The special structure of the Cobb–Douglas function is such that it is easy in this case to write out ordinary uncompensated demand functions, because

$$q_i = \left(\alpha_i \Big/ \sum_j \alpha_j\right) M/P_i = k_i M/P_i. \tag{13}$$

Notice that the demand and inverse demand functions have very special forms. The demand for each commodity depends only on its own price and total income, so that the uncompensated cross-price responses $\partial x_i(\cdot)/\partial P_j$ are zero, as are their inverse analogues $\partial \phi_i(\cdot)/\partial q_j$.

Its extreme simplicity is both a strength and a weakness of the Cobb–Douglas form. Empirically, it is not sensible to impose unit income elasticities and zero uncompensated cross-price responses, because both generally conflict with empirical findings. A widely used modification, which at least allows income expansion paths to avoid the origin, is the "linear expenditure system." Consider the following direct utility function:

$$U(\mathbf{q}) = A(q_1 - \gamma_1)^{\alpha_1}(q_2 - \gamma_2)^{\alpha_2} \cdots (q_n - \gamma_n)^{\alpha_n}, \tag{14}$$

where the γ_i's are parameters. This is often called the Stone–Geary utility function. For it to be economically meaningful, we must restrict attention to situations in which $q_i \geq \gamma_i$ for all i.

A moment's reflection reveals that this is a Cobb–Douglas function defined over the variables $(q_i - \gamma_i)$. Suppose the consumer's budget constraint allows him to consume a basic subsistence bundle $(\gamma_1, \ldots, \gamma_n)$. Equation (14) implies that any expenditure over and above this level is allocated according to Cobb–Douglas preferences. Figure 2.7 should make clear what is implied. All income expansion paths are straight lines passing through the point (γ_1, γ_2). From the point $0'$, the indifference map is the Cobb–Douglas variety.

Although it allows greater freedom in the determination of income elasticities, this system continues to impose stringent restrictions on price responses. Taking logarithms reveals that the utility function in (14) can be transformed into one that has the following additive structure:

$$U(\mathbf{q}) = f_1(q_1) + f_2(q_2) + \cdots + f_n(q_n). \tag{15}$$

Rather than impose such an assumption at the outset, econometricians have sought forms that allow us to suspend judgment on such matters as

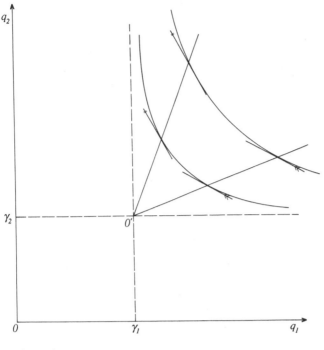

Figure 2.7

additive separability. The use of "flexible functional forms" allows us to do just that.

Suppose that instead of using a functional form such as Cobb–Douglas, which imposes substantial a priori structure on demand functions in addition to that required by theoretical consistency – for example, it immediately forces $\partial x_i(\mathbf{P}, M)/\partial P_j$ to be zero for $i \neq j$ – we want to let the data, as it were, do more of the talking. In short, we want a more flexible specification of preferences. An algebraic function representing, say, a utility function is said to be "second-order" flexible at a given set of prices if by suitable choice of parameters the implied demand functions and their own and cross-price responses, together with income responses, can take on any arbitrary values at the given set of prices subject only to the restriction implied by optimization. Because it has been known for a long time that Taylor's series provides a way of approximating a large class of functions, it is not surprising that this has provided a popular way of generating the sort of flexible form that is sought.

A linear approximation of $U(\mathbf{q})$ is hardly satisfactory, but a quadratic approximation using the Taylor series gives us curvature in the implied indifference map. At any point $\mathbf{q}$ in the neighborhood of the point $\mathbf{q}^0$, $U(\mathbf{q})$ is approximated by $U^A(\mathbf{q})$, which is defined as

$$U^A(\mathbf{q}) \equiv U(\mathbf{q}^0) + \sum_i (q_i - q_i^0) U_i(\mathbf{q}^0) + \frac{1}{2} \sum_i \sum_j (q_i - q_i^0)(q_j - q_j^0) U_{ij}(\mathbf{q}^0).$$

Regroup the right-hand side into a constant term involving just the elements of the given vector $\mathbf{q}^0$, terms involving the variables q_i, and quadratic terms involving $q_i q_j$:

$$U^A(\mathbf{q}) = \left[U(\mathbf{q}^0) - \sum_i q_i^0 U_i(\mathbf{q}^0) + \frac{1}{2} \sum_i \sum_j q_i^0 q_j^0 U_{ij}(\mathbf{q}^0) \right]$$

$$+ \sum_i \left[U_i(\mathbf{q}^0) - \sum_j q_j^0 U_{ij}(\mathbf{q}^0) \right] q_i$$

$$+ \frac{1}{2} \sum_i \sum_j [U_{ij}(\mathbf{q}^0)] q_i q_j. \tag{16}$$

The terms in square brackets are constants, which we might as well denote more briefly. Accordingly, we can write

$$U^A(\mathbf{q}) = \alpha_0 + \sum_i \alpha_i q_i + \frac{1}{2} \sum_i \sum_j \beta_{ij} q_i q_j, \tag{17}$$

where α_0, α_i, and β_{ij} are constant coefficients, each defined as the corresponding term in square brackets in (16). Notice particularly that, because the β_{ij} terms are second derivatives, they are symmetric: $\beta_{ij} = \beta_{ji}$ for all i and j. Applying the Hotelling–Wold identity to (17),

$$P_k / M = \frac{\alpha_k + \sum_j \beta_{kj} q_j}{\sum_i (\alpha_i + \sum_j \beta_{ij} q_j)}, \quad k = 1, \ldots, n. \tag{18}$$

This represents a system of inverse demand functions that can be estimated. One problem with (18) should be noted. Because it is the ratio of two expressions, each of which is linear in the parameters, the inverse demand function itself cannot be linear in those parameters. This generates econometric complications, but these are no longer as serious a problem as they once were.

A slight variant of (17) is obtained by observing that because differentiation of $U(\cdot)$ with respect to the logarithms of quantities yields budget-share equations, we might base Taylor's approximation on the logarithms. Then (17) is replaced by

$$U^A(\mathbf{q}) = \alpha^0 + \sum_i \alpha_i \ln q_i + \frac{1}{2} \sum_i \sum_j \beta_{ij} \ln q_i \ln q_j \tag{19}$$

where α_0, α_i, and β_{ij} are, as before, coefficients. Budget shares are given by

$$\omega_k \equiv \frac{P_k q_k}{M} = \frac{\partial U(\cdot)/\partial \ln q_k}{\Sigma_i \, \partial U(\cdot)/\partial \ln q_i} = \frac{\alpha_k + \Sigma_j \beta_{kj} q_j}{\Sigma_i (\alpha_i + \Sigma_j \beta_{ij} q_j)}$$

This particular approximation is generally called the direct "transcendental logarithmic," or translog, utility function.

Functional forms of indirect utility functions

The assumption of homothetic preferences is easily represented by the indirect utility function, which factorizes into the following simple form:

$$V(\mathbf{P}, M) = f(M)g(\mathbf{P}). \tag{20}$$

Roy's identity quickly confirms that this form does indeed imply that $x_i(\cdot)/x_j(\cdot)$ is independent of income for all i, j. The quasi-linear preferences shown in (9) also have a straightforward representation in terms of the indirect utility function. By solving $x_i(\cdot)$ and substituting into (9), it can be seen that quasi-linear preferences are representable by

$$V(\mathbf{P}, M) = M/P_1 + g(P_2/P_1, \dots, P_n/P_1). \tag{21}$$

However, the generalization of quasi-linear preferences captured by (10) does not, in general, have a convenient representation in terms of $V(\cdot)$. This is possible only if restrictions are placed on the functions $F(\cdot)$ and $G(\cdot)$. Indeed the quasi-linear form is obtained by putting $F(\cdot)$ identically equal to unity. There is a class of preferences, however, for which the indirect utility function has a form similar to that possessed by $U(\cdot)$ in (10). The Gorman polar-form indirect utility function can be written as

$$V(\mathbf{P}, M) = A(\mathbf{P})M + B(\mathbf{P}). \tag{22}$$

This implies, through Roy's identity, demand functions of the form

$$x_i(\mathbf{P}, M) = a_i(\mathbf{P})M + b_i(\mathbf{P}),$$

where $a_i(\cdot) \equiv (\partial A(\cdot)/\partial P_i)/A(\cdot)$ and $b_i(\cdot) \equiv (\partial B(\cdot)/\partial P_i)/A(\cdot)$. Uncompensated demands are linear functions of income, so that income expansion paths are linear, but do not pass through the origin. This class of preference is important in aggregation theory and is further discussed in Chapter 8. Without restrictions on $A(\mathbf{P})$ and $B(\mathbf{P})$, the preferences represented by (22) have no simple representation in terms of $U(\mathbf{q})$.

The preferences represented by the Cobb–Douglas direct utility function, on the other hand, do have a simple indirect representation. That this should be the case is strongly suggested by the symmetric way in which P_i and q_i appear in the budget-share equation, $P_i q_i / M = k_i$. It can be confirmed that the indirect function corresponding to the preferences represented by (11) is

$$V(\mathbf{P}, M) = BM^{\alpha_1 + \cdots + \alpha_n} / P_1^{\alpha_1} P_2^{\alpha_2} \cdots P_n^{\alpha_n}. \tag{23}$$

The linear expenditure system represented by (15) also is readily characterized by an indirect utility function. We know that the quantities $(q_i - \gamma_i)$ are related to supernumerary income $M - \Sigma_i P_i \gamma_i$ in a Cobb–Douglas fashion:

$$(q_i - \gamma_i) = \alpha_i \left(M - \sum_j P_j \gamma_i \right) \Big/ P_i.$$

Consequently, substitution into the direct utility function yields

$$V(\mathbf{P}, M) = B \cdot \left(M - \sum_j P_j \gamma_j \right)^{\alpha_1 + \alpha_2 + \cdots + \alpha_n} \Big/ P_i^{\alpha_1} P_2^{\alpha_2} \cdots P_n^{\alpha_n}.$$

An earlier example of the use of a particular form of $V(\cdot)$ is that by Houthakker (1960) of the additive indirect utility function. The specific form he used was

$$V(\mathbf{p}) = \sum_{i=1}^{n} \alpha_i p_i^{\beta_i}. \tag{24}$$

Roy's identity generates the demand functions

$$x_i(:\,) = (\alpha_i \beta_i p_i^{\beta_i - 1}) \Big/ \left(\sum_j \alpha_j \beta_j p_j^{\beta_j} \right), \quad i = 1, \ldots, n.$$

Alternatively, the budget-share equations are

$$\omega_i \equiv p_i x_i \Big/ \sum_j p_j x_j = p_i x_i = (\alpha_i \beta_i p_i^{\beta_i}) \Big/ \left(\sum_j \alpha_j \beta_j p_j^{\beta_j} \right), \quad i = 1, \ldots, n.$$

Again, there appears to be the slight inconvenience of requiring estimation of an equation that is nonlinear in parameters. However, this can be avoided in the present case by considering the ratio $x_i(\cdot)/x_j(\cdot)$ and taking logarithms:

$$\ln(x_i(\cdot)/x_j(\cdot)) = \ln(\alpha_i \beta_i / \alpha_j \beta_j) + (\beta_i - 1) \ln(p_i/p_j).$$

This provides a linear form in parameters.

The ease with which Roy's identity enables us to generate demand functions makes the indirect utility function a more attractive candidate for approximation by flexible functional forms than is its direct counterpart. An obvious procedure is to use Taylor's series to provide a quadratic approximation:

$$V^A(\mathbf{p}) = \alpha_0 + \sum_i \alpha_i p_i + \frac{1}{2} \sum_i \sum_j \beta_{ij} p_i p_j. \tag{25}$$

Roy's identity yields the system of uncompensated demand functions in the usual way:

$$x_k(\mathbf{p}) = \frac{\partial V(\cdot)/\partial p_k}{\sum_i p_i \partial V(\cdot)/\partial p_i} = \frac{\alpha_k + \sum_j \beta_{kj} p_j}{\sum_i (\alpha_i + \sum_j \beta_{ij} p_j)}.$$

The derivation of (25) proceeds precisely in the same way as that of the quadratic approximation of the direct utility function (17). This means, for example, that the β coefficients are symmetric, because they are the cross partial derivatives of $V(\mathbf{p})$.

Applying the Taylor series to obtain a quadratic approximation in the logarithms of normalized prices yields the translog indirect utility function:

$$V^A(\mathbf{p}) = \alpha_0 + \sum_i \alpha_i \ln p_i + \frac{1}{2} \sum_i \sum_j \beta_{ij} \ln p_i \ln p_j. \tag{26}$$

Budget-share equations are obtained using the logarithmic version of Roy's identity, because

$$\omega_k \equiv P_k x_k(\cdot)/M = p_k x_k = \frac{\partial V^A(\cdot)/\partial p_k}{\sum_i \partial V^A(\cdot)/\partial p_i}$$

$$= \frac{\alpha_k + \sum_j \beta_{kj} \ln p_j}{\sum_i (\alpha_i + \sum_j \beta_{ij} \ln p_j)}.$$

Because of the ease with which budget shares can be expressed as functions of $\mathbf{p}$, the translog form has become quite widely used. An early example is provided by Wales and Woodland (1976) in a study of household labor supply. They consider the reciprocal of the indirect utility function, $H(\mathbf{p}) \equiv 1/V(\mathbf{p})$, rather than $V(\mathbf{p})$ itself, but this is no more than a cosmetic modification. They then assume the translog form for $H(\cdot)$. The same authors also use an alternative flexible functional form, the "generalized Cobb–Douglas." The latter is also briefly discussed by Wales and Woodland (1977).

One last form should be mentioned. This is the "generalized Leontief indirect utility function," suggested by Diewert (1971, 1974b), and again usually stated in terms of the inverse indirect utility function $H(\mathbf{p}) \equiv 1/V(\mathbf{p})$. The Taylor series expansion of $H(\cdot)$ is applied not to the p_i variables but to their square roots:

$$H^A(\mathbf{p}) = \alpha_0 + 2 \sum_i \alpha_i \sqrt{p_i} + \sum_i \sum_j \beta_{ij} \sqrt{p_i p_j}. \tag{27}$$

Demand functions are

$$x_k(\mathbf{p}) = \frac{\partial H^A(\cdot)/\partial p_k}{\sum_i p_i \partial H^A(\cdot)/\partial p_i}$$

$$= \frac{(\alpha_k/\sqrt{p_k}) + \sum_j \beta_{kj} \sqrt{p_j/p_k}}{\sum_i [\alpha_i \sqrt{p_i} + \sum_j \beta_{ij} \sqrt{p_i p_j}]}.$$

In writing (27), the linear and quadratic terms of the Taylor series have been multiplied by 2 in order to keep the resulting demand function clean of fractions.

Given that the reciprocal indirect utility function is of the generalized Leontief form, preferences are homothetic if and only if $\alpha_0 = \alpha_1 = \cdots = \alpha_n = 0$. The reason for the label applied to this class of preferences becomes apparent when the further restriction is imposed that $\beta_{ij} = 0$ for all $i \neq j$.

2.8   Some pioneers of indirect utility functions

Giovanni Antonelli (1858–1944)

Just over a century ago, in 1886, Giovanni Battista Antonelli published a pamphlet entitled "Sulla Teoria Matematica della Economia Politica." Antonelli went on to enjoy a prominent career as a civil engineer, and this pamphlet was his sole published contribution to economic theory. This makes all the more remarkable the number of important ideas to be found there that remained overlooked and unexploited for nearly half a century until independently rediscovered by (and, in at least one prominent case, named after) others. In particular, his development of the functional relationship between utility, on the one hand, and the budget constraint as described by the set of nominal prices and nominal income, on the other, is a key element in the modern dual approach to consumer theory.

Antonelli observed that the maximum utility attained by a price-taking consumer can be expressed as a function of the parameters describing the budget constraint – in short, as an indirect utility function, $V(P_1, \ldots, P_n, M)$. Antonelli used this function, at least implicitly, to derive commodity demand functions. His notation and the details of his analysis make his argument a little obscure for modern readers. However, the spirit of his approach is fairly captured by the following reasoning.

Given the direct utility function, we know that the change in utility arising from arbitrary infinitesimal changes in $\mathbf{q}$ may be written as

$$dU(\cdot) = \sum_{i=1}^{n} (\partial U/\partial q_i)dq_i. \tag{28}$$

If a utility maximizer chooses an interior bundle, then it is well known that marginal rates of substitution are equated to relative prices for every pair of commodities. In other words, marginal utilities are proportional to money prices: $\partial U/\partial q_i = \lambda P_i$ for all i, where λ is a positive scalar. Substituting for the marginal utilities in (28),

$$dU(\cdot) = \lambda \sum_{i=1}^{n} P_i d\hat{q}_i. \tag{29}$$

The "hats" are to remind us that the quantities appearing in (29) are the optimal, or utility-maximizing, quantities. Any response in quantities provoked by price or money income changes must be consistent with the budget constraint, $\sum_{i=1}^{n} P_i q_i = M$. Consequently, we require that the $d\hat{q}_i$'s satisfy the condition

$$\sum_{i=1}^{n} P_i d\hat{q}_i + \sum_{i=1}^{n} \hat{q}_i dP_i = dM. \tag{30}$$

This can now be used to substitute into (29), so that the response of utility to a set of infinitesimal changes in prices and income may be expressed as

$$dU(\cdot) = \lambda \left[dM - \sum_{i=1}^{n} \hat{q}_i dP_i \right]. \tag{31}$$

Notice that the change in utility has, in (31), been expressed as a function of changes in prices and income. This suggests that we could regard utility explicitly as a function of prices and income, the indirect utility function $V(P_1, \ldots, P_n, M)$, with $dU = dV$. The total differential of V can be written

$$dV(\mathbf{P}, M) = (\partial V/\partial M)dM + \sum_{i=1}^{n} (\partial V/\partial P_i)dP_i. \tag{31'}$$

Because (31) and (31') are simply alternative statements of the same relationship and hold for any arbitrary infinitesimal changes in $\mathbf{P}$ and M, we can identify the coefficients in (4) with the corresponding coefficients in (31'), so that

$$\partial V(\cdot)/\partial M = \lambda, \tag{32}$$

and

$$\partial V(\cdot)/\partial P_i = -\lambda \hat{q}_i,$$
(33)

from which the quantity demanded, $\hat{q}_i$, can be expressed as the ratio of the partial derivatives of $V(\mathbf{P}, M)$, and therefore as a function of prices and income:

$$\hat{q}_i = -\frac{\partial V(\cdot)/\partial P_i}{\partial V(\cdot)/\partial M} = x_i(P_i, \ldots, P_n, M),$$
(34)

which is, of course, Roy's identity.

René Roy (1894–1977)

Antonelli's derivation of demand functions as simple ratios of derivatives of $V(\mathbf{P}, M)$ made no immediate impact. This is particularly surprising in view of the fact that writers such as Pareto were certainly aware of his pamphlet. Relationships (32) and (33) were independently rediscovered much later, for example by Allen (1933). However, Allen did not go on to write the demand function explicitly, his main interest being in the interpretation of the scalar λ, the marginal utility of income. Hotelling (1932) also alluded to the idea of defining utility as a function of prices, but did not develop the idea in a way that later writers found congenial. I shall have more to say about Hotelling in Chapter 3. Konüs (1939) and Ville (1951–2) both expressed utility as a function of prices, but it was Roy (1942, 1947) who not only rediscovered equation (34) but also drew the attention of economists and econometricians to its potential importance. This relationship has since become known – and, as Chipman and Moore (1980) ruefully remark, mispronounced – as Roy's identity. The term indirect utility function seems to have been suggested by Houthakker (1951–2).

Whereas Antonelli's analysis started from the direct utility function and exploited the indirect function only in the differential form provided by (31), Roy began with the indirect utility function itself, expressed in terms of normalized prices

$$U = V(P_1, \ldots, P_n, M) = V(\mathbf{P}, M),$$
$$= V(P_1/M, \ldots, P_n/M) = V(\mathbf{p}).$$

This formulation invites one from the outset to think in terms of preferences over budget constraints. Roy himself had no doubts about the potential importance of the indirect utility function both in economic theory and in econometrics. Experience has justified his belief that in many contexts $V(\mathbf{P}, M)$ provides a more convenient representation of preferences than does $U(\mathbf{q})$.

2.9   Concluding comments and suggestions for further study

In addition to Deaton and Muellbauer (1980a), others have provided useful general discussions of the axioms: Green (1971, pp. 21–45), Simmons (1974, pp. 4–13), and Pearce (1964, pp. 16–38). Beware of Pearce's terminology – the property that I and the rest of the economics profession refer to as "quasi-concavity" is called by Pearce "quasi-convexity." The existence of a utility function is a mathematical problem that is addressed by Debreu (1954b). The derivation of demand functions and their properties from the direct utility function, an activity that I do not recommend to the fainthearted, has been undertaken by Hicks (1946, pp. 305–11), Samuelson (1947, pp. 96–116), Pearce (1964, pp. 43–57), and Intriligator (1971, pp. 148–63). A glance at any of these will reveal the tedious and unenlightening nature of the mathematical manipulations involved.

Inverse demand functions are less commonly encountered, though Pearce (1964, pp. 57–64) discusses them in a section that develops an "antidemand theory." Hicks (1956, pp. 83–94) calls them marginal valuation functions. They are used, with earlier references cited, by Bronsard, Salvas-Bronsard, and Delisle (1978). More recently, Barten and Bettendorf (1989) have used them to analyze the determination of fish prices. Like ordinary demand functions, the uncompensated variant discussed in this chapter is less interesting, from the point of view of generating a priori restrictions on behavioral parameters, than the compensated functions defined later in Chapter 3. Further references can be found there. Inverse demand, or marginal valuation, or willingness-to-pay functions come into their own in analysis of situations involving exogenously imposed quantity constraints. They therefore feature prominently in models of rationed choice (see Chapter 7) and externalities (see Chapter 10).

The duality between $U(\cdot)$ and $V(\cdot)$ is treated by Shephard (1970, pp. 301–5) and Diewert (1974b, pp. 120–4), as well as in a useful expository summary by Weymark (1980). A brief discussion and further references have been provided by Diewert (1982, pp. 556–9).

Roy's identity is also treated by Weymark (1980) and, in a useful geometric exposition that uses the four-quadrant diagram, by Darrough and Southey (1977). I particularly recommend these last two sources for an initial foray into the literature.

The literature on flexible functional forms is growing rapidly. Lau (1977) discusses the use of indirect utility functions for the purpose of generating econometrically tractable demand systems and also discusses the several flexible functional forms mentioned earlier, together with the generalized Cobb–Douglas form suggested by Diewert (1973*b*) and applied by Berndt, Darrough, and Diewert (1977). Deaton and Muellbauer (1980*a*, ch. 3) discuss some of the issues involved and criticize the Christensen, Jorgenson, and Lau (1975) interpretation of the results of statistical tests of symmetry in the context of the translog model. Simmons and Weiserbs (1979) offer a similar criticism and spell out very clearly what is involved in the Taylor series approximation. Most recently, researchers have started to explore alternatives to the Taylor series, such as the Fourier series, as a way of generating an approximation – see, for example, Gallant (1981). The motive for exploring alternatives derives from two considerations. First, statistical tests applied to the estimated systems often reject the hypothesis of optimizing behavior. For example, if the symmetry restriction on the β_{ij} coefficients is not initially imposed, symmetry is often rejected. This might, as Christensen et al. (1975) suggest, imply that the optimization assumption is a bad one. Alternatively, it might imply that the particular class of approximation used cannot accommodate the data thrown up by optimizing behavior without itself having to violate the symmetry condition. Exploration of alternatives can shed light on this problem. Second, even though an estimated flexible functional form may possess the "correct" curvature in the neighborhood of the point in quantity or price space about which the approximation is taken, it is often the case that for points farther away such convenient properties break down. The problems to which this gives rise, and ways of dealing with them, are discussed by Diewert and Wales (1987), albeit mainly in the context of expenditure functions.

Lau (1986) has recently addressed the principal issues raised in the choice of functional form. He identifies a number of properties that one might want such a form to possess. These may be classified into five categories: theoretical consistency, domain of applicability, flexibility, computational facility, and factual conformity. After explaining the meaning of each of these, and expressing the various desiderata with proper precision, Lau demonstrates an impossibility theorem. As a matter of logic, it seems, there do not exist functional forms that satisfy all the properties that we would ideally desire. We are inevitably confronted with trade-offs.

Inspired by the earlier work of Afriat (1967), a number of writers have recently explored a "nonparametric" approach both to the construction of utility functions and to testing for various restrictions, such as homotheticity. The idea here is simple. The assumption of a particular functional form typically injects a lot more a priori structure into an individual's preferences than is implied by the maximizing nature of the problem. Even "flexible functional forms" inject a good deal of gratuitous structure as one moves away from the given set of prices at which they are "second-order" flexible. A given set of data, estimated using different flexible functional forms, will produce different indifference maps.

The nonparametric approach tries to make use of no more than the implications of the axioms stated in Section 2.1. In this context, the key axiom is that of transitivity. If we were confident that our data contained no measurement errors, then it would be easy to see how confrontation with data would enable, indeed compel, us to reject the model. If an individual were to choose $(q_1^0, q_2^0) = (2, 5)$ when faced with $(P_1^0, P_2^0, M^0) = (1, 2, 12)$ and also to choose $(q_1^1, q_2^1) = (5, 2)$ when faced with $(P_1^1, P_2^1, M^1) = (2, 1, 12)$, we would be forced to conclude that this behavior was inconsistent with our model. The first choice suggests that because $\mathbf{q}^0$ was chosen when $\mathbf{q}^1$ was available, it is revealed preferred to the latter. The second choice suggests precisely the opposite. Such "revealed preference" arguments can be extended and used not only to detect violations of transitivity but also in some sense to place bounds on the positions of indifference curves generated by data that are consistent with the axioms. Varian (1982, 1983) provides a useful discussion of the economic content of this approach and suggests ways of incorporating measurement errors into the analysis (Varian 1985).

My discussion of Antonelli's contribution relies on the English translation in Chipman et al. (1971). It is accompanied by helpful annotations and a brief biographical sketch of this remarkable man. As I have already indicated, his derivation of Roy's identity is far from being the sole contribution of his pamphlet. He was particularly interested, like many mathematical economists since, in the so-called integrability problem. Suppose someone presents us with a set of equations that purport to be a system of demand functions pertaining to a utility-maximizing consumer. If we have suspicious minds, or simply an abundance of intellectual curiosity, we may want to determine if, indeed, they can be what they are claimed to be. An obvious first point to check is whether or not for any admissible set of prices and income the implied demands are consistent with the budget constraint. There are also some less obvious properties that must be satisfied if the individual's behavior, as described by the functions, is to be consistent with maximization of a utility function. We know that if we start from a utility function, the individual's behavioral functions can be generated by differentiation. The integrability problem requires us to go in the opposite direction. Starting with a system of behavioral functions, we wish to know under what conditions they can, in principle, be

integrated so as to recover a utility function. Antonelli's approach starts
with inverse demand functions. These characterize the individual's behavior by expressing the marginal rates of substitution, or demand prices,
as functions of the bundle of quantities, taking the form $P_i/P_1 = \phi_i(\mathbf{q})$,
$i = 2, \ldots, n$. He then shows that if they are the products of optimizing
behavior, it must be true that

$$\phi_{ij} - \phi_j\phi_{i1} = \phi_{ji} - \phi_i\phi_{j1} \quad \text{for all } i,j,$$

where $\phi_{ij} \equiv \partial\phi_i(\cdot)/\partial q_j$. The symmetric matrix composed of such terms is
called the Antonelli matrix. We shall encounter it in Chapter 3. Anton-
elli's integrability conditions are not complete, his assumptions are more
stringent than necessary, and he did not explore the integrability conditions associated with demand functions of the form $q_i(\mathbf{P}, M)$. Subsequent literature has taken up all these points. The interested reader is
referred to the useful survey by Hurwicz (1971) for further discussion and
references. Another idea that can be found in Antonelli's pamphlet concerns aggregation over consumers. He observes that if the aggregate demand for a commodity is to behave just like that of an individual, then
each consumer's demand must be a linear function of income, and the
coefficient attached to income must be the same for all consumers. This
idea and its implications for the structure of the utility function are discussed further in Chapter 8.

The paper by Roy (1947) has not, to my knowledge, been translated
from the original French. The algebra is laid out so clearly, however, that
it repays study even by a reader whose command of that language is rudimentary.

Finally, in addition to the material contained in the surveys by Diewert
(1974b, 1982), I should mention the more recent surveys by Deaton (1986)
and Blundell (1988). The former covers, somewhat tersely, many of the
topics of this and the following chapter and also discusses econometric
aspects and the extension of demand analysis to deal with demographic
aspects, intertemporal choices, and quality choice. The latter surveys recent applied work that uses and extends the models encountered in this
book.

CHAPTER 3

Individual consumer behavior: Expenditure and distance functions

Chapter 2 introduced a number of axioms concerning consumer preferences. Of these, the first three – reflexivity, completeness, and transitivity – comprise the essence of what we there called rationality on the part of the individual consumer. The fourth – continuity – gives access to the help of some simple optimization theory. A large part of economic theory uses no more than these axioms, together with the last two – nonsatiation and (strict) convexity – in its handling of consumers. Yet, apart from some fairly obvious and not very startling properties obtained directly from the budget constraint, our subsequent discussion of demand behavior in Chapter 2 turned up disappointingly little concerning the properties of demand systems. To have any hope of uncovering further a priori restrictions on demand behavior, we must try a slightly different tack. This is the task of the present chapter.

We begin, in Section 3.1, by identifying a "law of demand" and by suggesting an associated type of function – a compensated demand function – in which money income is replaced by the utility level as an argument. Investigation of such functions reveals further powerful and far from intuitively obvious properties of demand behavior that are direct consequences of the axioms of rational behavior. Section 3.2 introduces the idea that at any equilibrium the consumer is minimizing the cost of attaining his realized utility level at the prevailing prices, and it defines the resulting minimum expenditure function, whose properties are discussed in Section 3.3. Of particular importance is the ease with which it can be used to generate compensated demand functions and to derive their properties. This topic, accordingly, receives a separate discussion in Section 3.4.

For certain purposes, inverse compensated demand functions are useful. To derive and explain these, Section 3.5 first introduces the distance function. Its properties, in particular its relationship with inverse compensated demand functions, are briefly discussed in Section 3.6. Section 3.7 mentions some specific functional forms of expenditure and distance functions that have been found useful. Finally, suggestions for further reading are given in Section 3.8.

3.1   Compensated demand functions

Consider the following thought experiment: Suppose that initial prices and income are $\mathbf{P}^0$ and M^0, respectively, and a consumer responds by choosing $\mathbf{q}^0$. Now suppose P_j falls, perhaps by a finite amount. At the same time, the omniscient experimenter changes M so that in the new situation $(\mathbf{P}^1, M^1)$ the most preferred bundle, $\mathbf{q}^1$, is viewed by the consumer as no better, and no worse, than $\mathbf{q}^0$. He is, in short, indifferent between $\mathbf{q}^0$ and $\mathbf{q}^1$. A natural question is, What happens to q_j? To answer this, note first that the change in income precisely compensates the consumer for the price change, in that it leaves the maximum attainable utility level unchanged. We are, in effect, asking a question about the "compensated" demand function for the jth good, $c_j(\mathbf{P}, u)$. The question can be answered using very straightforward reasoning. We are told that the individual is indifferent between $\mathbf{q}^0$ and $\mathbf{q}^1$ and that when confronted with $\mathbf{P}^0$ he chooses $\mathbf{q}^0$, not $\mathbf{q}^1$. Therefore, valued at $\mathbf{P}^0$, $\mathbf{q}^1$ cannot be cheaper than $\mathbf{q}^0$. If it were, the consumer would not have chosen the more costly of the two alternatives. In short, we can conclude that

$$\mathbf{P}^0 \cdot \mathbf{q}^0 \le \mathbf{P}^0 \cdot \mathbf{q}^1.$$

By similar reasoning, we can infer that

$$\mathbf{P}^1 \cdot \mathbf{q}^1 \le \mathbf{P}^1 \cdot \mathbf{q}^0.$$

Therefore, adding these together,

$$\mathbf{P}^0 \cdot \mathbf{q}^0 + \mathbf{P}^1 \cdot \mathbf{q}^1 \le \mathbf{P}^0 \cdot \mathbf{q}^1 + \mathbf{P}^1 \cdot \mathbf{q}^0,$$

or

$$(\mathbf{P}^0 - \mathbf{P}^1) \cdot (\mathbf{q}^0 - \mathbf{q}^1) \le 0.$$

If P_j changes by the amount ΔP_j while all others are held constant, and if the change in the quantity q_j is denoted by Δq_j, this inequality becomes

$$\Delta P_j \Delta q_j \le 0.$$

This, at last, is a law of demand. If P_j is increased while utility is held constant, then q_j must either fall or remain constant. Compensated demand curves cannot slope upward.

If the change in P_j is infinitesimal, the inequality becomes $dP_j dq_j \leq 0$. Assuming the function $c_j(\mathbf{P}, u)$ to be differentiable, the law of demand can be stated as

$$dq_j = (\partial c_j / \partial P_j) dP_j, \quad \text{so that} \quad dq_j dP_j = (\partial c_j / \partial P_j)(dP_j)^2 \leq 0,$$

or

$$\partial c_j(\mathbf{P}, u) / \partial P_j \leq 0. \tag{1}$$

This is the most simple of the properties of compensated demand functions. There are, however, many more properties waiting to be uncovered by systematic analysis of such functions. To help us in this task, we must first examine more closely their derivation and their relationship with the expenditure function. This we do in the next two sections.

3.2   The expenditure function defined

The formulation of the consumer's problem in terms of the indirect utility function is a very natural one. After all, from the consumer's point of view the set of feasible consumption bundles is defined by the exogenous price and income parameters on which, therefore, his optimal choice and utility level depend. However, there are alternative and, for some purposes, more convenient formulations.

Let us ask the following question: How much would it cost to enable a consumer, who faces a given set of commodity prices, to attain a particular standard of living? As always, I shall assume that all prices are strictly positive. In Figure 3.1, the individual is required to consume a bundle in, or on the boundary of, the hatched area for which $U(\mathbf{q}) \geq u$. The given prices determine the slope of the iso-cost, or iso-expenditure, lines. Of those drawn in the figure, that corresponding to $\mathbf{P} \cdot \mathbf{q} = M'$ fails to make the target u attainable, whereas an expenditure of M'' is more than enough to make u attainable. An expenditure of M^0 represents the lowest level consistent with achievement of the utility target. Formally, given that by assumption $\mathbf{P} \in R^n_{++}$, $\mathbf{q}^0$ solves the problem

$$\min_{\mathbf{q}} \{ \mathbf{P} \cdot \mathbf{q} \mid U(\mathbf{q}) \geq u \}. \tag{2}$$

The solution to this problem defines a function, the expenditure function, that expresses the minimum required expenditure as a function of the utility target to be achieved and the money prices faced by the consumer. We shall henceforth write this as $E(\mathbf{P}, u)$.

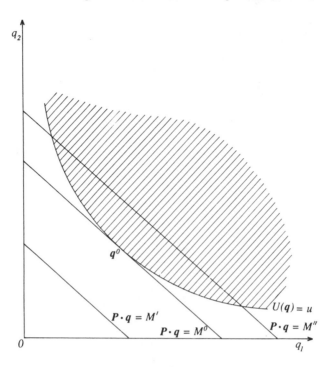

Figure 3.1

At the consumer's optimum, the value of $E(\cdot)$ will in fact equal the individual's money income, M. Because utility is monotonically increasing with income, the equation $E(\mathbf{P}, u) = M$ can be inverted so as to express utility as a function of prices and money income – indeed, this yields precisely the indirect utility function that was introduced in Chapter 2. Bearing in mind that u can always be solved out if desired, it is still useful to explore the properties of $E(\mathbf{P}, u)$ on the basis of an exogenous value for u. As we shall see, the expenditure function greatly simplifies the evaluation and measurement of welfare changes; it provides a natural building block in the theory of index numbers; last, but by no means least, it enables us to obtain the central propositions of demand theory in a way that greatly reduces the mathematical complications and clarifies their economic content. It does this by generating, in a very direct manner, a set of compensated demand functions that express the quantities demanded as functions of prices and of the utility level. We now consider the properties of $E(\mathbf{P}, u)$.

3.3 Properties of the expenditure function

Consider the properties of the expenditure function

$$E(\mathbf{P}, u) \equiv \min_{\mathbf{q}}\{\mathbf{P} \cdot \mathbf{q} \mid U(\mathbf{q}) \geq u\}. \tag{3}$$

First, it is an increasing function of prices. So long as the optimal consumption point involves strictly positive quantities of all goods, an increase in any individual price will, by itself, reduce the maximum attainable utility. To maintain his original utility level, the consumer must be allowed an increase in expenditure.

Second, if all prices change by the same proportion, say from $\mathbf{P}$ to $\theta\mathbf{P}$, the level of expenditure required to attain a fixed utility target must also change by the same proportion. In short, $E(\mathbf{P}, u)$ is homogeneous of degree 1 in all prices:

$$E(\theta\mathbf{P}, u) = \theta E(\mathbf{P}, u).$$

Third, $E(\mathbf{P}, u)$ is concave in prices. Let $\mathbf{q}^1$ denote the least-cost way of attaining u given $\mathbf{P}^1$, and let $\mathbf{q}^0$ be any other bundle that precisely attains u. Then, by definition,

$$E(\mathbf{P}^1, u) = \mathbf{P}^1 \cdot \mathbf{q}^1 \leq \mathbf{P}^1 \cdot \mathbf{q}^0. \tag{4}$$

Now denote by $\mathbf{P}^0$ the vector of prices at which $\mathbf{q}^0$ represents the least-cost way of attaining u. Then by simply adding $\mathbf{P}^0 \cdot \mathbf{q}^0$ to the right-hand side of (4) and simultaneously subtracting it, we have

$$E(\mathbf{P}^1, u) \leq \mathbf{P}^0 \cdot \mathbf{q}^0 + \mathbf{P}^1 \cdot \mathbf{q}^0 - \mathbf{P}^0 \cdot \mathbf{q}^0$$

$$\leq E(\mathbf{P}^0, u) + (\mathbf{P}^1 - \mathbf{P}^0) \cdot \mathbf{q}^0. \tag{5}$$

The meaning of this is clarified by panel (*a*) of Figure 3.2, which graphs $E(\mathbf{P}, u)$ against the price of, say, commodity j when all other money prices and utility are held constant.

Suppose that the individual initially faces the price vector $\mathbf{P}^0$ and chooses the bundle $\mathbf{q}^0$. Now let P_j increase from P_j^0 to P_j^1, while other prices remain unchanged. If the consumer were constrained to consume an unchanged bundle – that is, to remain consuming precisely $\mathbf{q}^0$ – then the level of required expenditure would vary linearly with P_j, along the line through the point A with slope q_j^0. This must be so because the required expenditure must equal $\sum_i P_i q_i^0$, and the only term that has varied is P_j. If constrained to consume $\mathbf{q}^0$ when the price of commodity j is P_j^1, the consumer

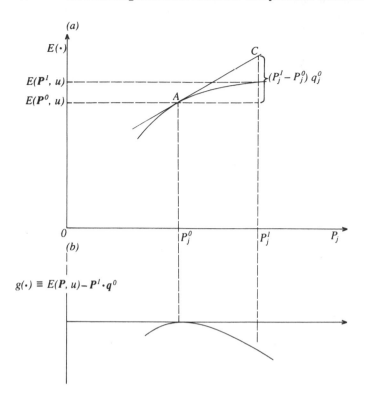

Figure 3.2

will be at the point C, where expenditure equals the initial value, $E(\mathbf{P}^0, u)$, plus the change in the cost of commodity 1, $(P_j^1 - P_j^0)q_j^0$. However, if the consumer is able to adjust his consumption pattern in response to the relative price change, he will generally choose to do so, thereby attaining a bundle preferred to $\mathbf{q}^0$. Thus, for him to remain no better off than he was initially, he requires less expenditure than at C. This line of reasoning implies that the minimum expenditure required to reach the target utility at the set of prices $\mathbf{P}^1$, $E(\mathbf{P}^1, u)$, is less than that represented by C. More generally, the tangent at any point of the individual's expenditure curve in Figure 3.2 will, if anything, overestimate the expenditure required at other values of P_j. The algebra leading to (5) is rather more powerful than Figure 3.2 suggests, because it allows more than one price to vary in the comparison between $\mathbf{P}^0$ and $\mathbf{P}^1$. It also establishes the concavity of $E(\mathbf{P}, u)$ in prices.

The property of concavity is inherent in the definition of $E(\mathbf{P}, u)$, for it is because the problem is one of minimization that the inequality appears in the expression (5). Further properties that are not inherent often are assumed for convenience. For example, we assume from now on that it is twice differentiable with respect to all arguments. This means, for example, that the function drawn in Figure 3.2 has no kinks in it, but has smooth curvature everywhere. It also means rather more than this, because if we graph the derivative $\partial E/\partial P_j$ against P_j, the resulting function must also be smoothly curved everywhere. The homogeneity and concavity of $E(\mathbf{P}, u)$ in prices imply a number of properties for its various partial derivatives, but before stating these we should draw attention to a particularly important proposition. Indeed, it is sufficiently important to have a section of this chapter to itself. It also has a name – Shephard's lemma.

3.4   Shephard's lemma

We have shown that the graph of $E(\cdot)$ against P_j lies everywhere on or below the tangent at any point. This concavity property is quite consistent with the graph having kinks in it. However, let us assume that the derivative $\partial E/\partial P_j$ exists at all positive values of P_j, so that the curvature is smooth. Then the slope at any point yields the optimal demand at that point. Consider the price vector $\mathbf{P}^0$, and denote the associated cost-minimizing bundle by $\mathbf{q}^0$. Then, by definition,

$$E(\mathbf{P}^0, u) = \sum_i P_i^0 q_i^0.$$

Let P_j change while all other prices and utility level remain constant. In response to such a compensated change, the individual will generally adjust the quantities of all goods in his consumption bundle. Differentiation yields

$$dE(\cdot) = q_j^0 dP_j + \sum_i P_i^0 dq_i. \tag{6}$$

Because utility is assumed constant, the changes dq_i must satisfy the condition that

$$dU = \sum_i U_i dq_i = 0.$$

But the first-order conditions associated with expenditure minimization tell us that $P_i^0 = \lambda U_i$, where λ is reciprocal of the marginal utility of income. Hence

$$\sum_i U_i dq_i = \lambda \sum_i P_i^0 dq_i = 0;$$

$$\therefore \ \sum_i P_i^0 dq_i = 0.$$

Consequently, even though the consumer will generally rearrange his consumption in response to a small price change, such an adjustment will have a negligible effect on the minimum expenditure required to achieve the given utility target, so that with all other prices and utility constant, (6) becomes

$$dE(\mathbf{P}^0, u) = q_j^0 dP_j. \tag{7}$$

The reasoning leading to (7) is no more than the envelope property discussed in Chapter 1. Hence, the quantity q_j^0 is equal to the partial derivative of $E(\cdot)$ with respect to P_j, evaluated at the initial point. Because the partial derivative is a function of $\mathbf{P}^0$ and u, so is q_j^0.

An alternative, and quicker, derivation uses the primal-dual formulation of the envelope result. Define the function

$$g(\mathbf{P}, u) \equiv E(\mathbf{P}, u) - \mathbf{P} \cdot \mathbf{q}^0,$$

where $\mathbf{q}^0$ is fixed, and is the bundle chosen when $\mathbf{P} = \mathbf{P}^0$. Panel (b) of Figure 3.2 graphs this function, which is simply the vertical distance between $E(\cdot)$ and its tangent at A, against P_j. By definition, $g(\cdot)$ is everywhere nonpositive. As P_j varies, $g(\cdot)$ attains its maximum of zero when $P_j = P_j^0$. Remembering that $\mathbf{q}^0$ is fixed in this thought experiment, the first-order condition yields

$$\partial g(\mathbf{P}^0, u)/\partial P_j = \partial E(\mathbf{P}^0, u)/\partial P_j - q_j^0 = 0,$$

so that $q_j^0 = \partial E(\mathbf{P}^0, u)/\partial P_j$. Put briefly, we have the following:

Shephard's lemma. *If $E(\mathbf{P}, u)$ is differentiable with respect to all prices at the point $\mathbf{P}^0$, then*

$$\partial E(\mathbf{P}^0, u)/\partial P_j = c_j(\mathbf{P}^0, u) \quad \text{for all } j.$$

This relationship between the expenditure function and compensated demand functions is exciting, especially to those of us originally trained in the more traditional and circuitous route to demand functions via the direct utility function.

Properly speaking, the lemma due to Shephard is somewhat more profound than that stated earlier. We set out with a utility function, showed that an expenditure function could be defined, and then showed that its derivative with respect to P_j was a compensated demand curve. Shephard did not start with $U(\cdot)$, but was concerned to show that if we start off with information on costs and prices, this can, under certain assumptions, be used to generate demand functions and primal representations of preferences. In this context, Shephard's lemma takes on added significance as an important bridge from dual representations using prices to primal representations in terms of quantities. The analysis presented earlier, though its conclusion is algebraically identical with Shephard's result, is really no more than the first-order envelope theorem. It allows us to derive those properties of the compensated demand functions that result from optimizing behavior as simple consequences of the properties of $E(\cdot)$, particularly its homogeneity and concavity.

First, note that $c_j(\mathbf{P}, u)$ is homogeneous of degree 0 in all prices – that is, $c_j(\theta\mathbf{P}, u) = c_j(\mathbf{P}, u)$ for any positive scalar θ. This can be seen either by recalling that $E(\cdot)$ is homogeneous of degree 1, so that its partial derivatives are homogeneous of degree 0, or alternatively by applying common sense. Relative prices are unchanged and so, too, by assumption, is the utility level. Therefore the consumer's real situation is unchanged. We assume that $c_i(\mathbf{P}, u)$ is itself differentiable with respect to all arguments. The homogeneity property implies that

$$\sum_j (\partial c_i / \partial P_j) P_j = \sum_j c_{ij} P_j = 0 \quad \text{for all } i. \tag{8}$$

Thus the price-weighted sum of the compensated price responses of c_i is zero. This means that if $(n-1)$ of these responses are known, so is the nth.

We have already noted that the own-price response cannot be positive. Another simple, but remarkable, property is the symmetry of compensated cross-price responses. This has no intuitive explanation, but is a simple consequence of Shephard's lemma and of the continuity properties of $E(\cdot)$. There is a useful result in the differential calculus, known as Young's theorem, stating that if a function $F(\mathbf{y})$ has continuous second derivatives, then the cross partial derivatives are equal. That is,

$$\partial^2 F(\cdot)/\partial y_i \partial y_j = \partial^2 F(\cdot)/\partial y_j \partial y_i.$$

If we assume that the second derivatives of $E(\mathbf{P}, u)$ with respect to prices are continuous, application of Young's theorem tells us that because $c_i(\mathbf{P}, u) = \partial E(\mathbf{P}, u)/\partial P_i$,

$$c_{ij} = \partial^2 E/\partial P_i \partial P_j = \partial^2 E/\partial P_j \partial P_i = c_{ji}. \tag{9}$$

With utility held constant, the response of demand for bread to a change in the price of wine is equal to the response of demand for wine to a change in the price of bread. This provides a further powerful set of a priori restrictions, because it means that once c_{ij} is known, so is c_{ji}. The symmetry result may be combined with (8) to yield the further restriction

$$\sum_i (\partial c_i / \partial P_j) P_i = \sum_i c_{ij} P_i = 0. \tag{10}$$

The fact that the own-price response is nonpositive is a reflection of the concavity of $E(\cdot)$. Concavity, however, has additional implications. If one can picture the graph of $E(\cdot)$ in the space of all prices, and further imagine the hyperplane that is a tangent at some point, then this is on or above the graph for any move in any direction from that point, not just for moves parallel to one axis. Algebraically, concavity of $E(\mathbf{P}, u)$ in prices implies that the matrix of second derivatives $\partial^2 E / \partial P_i \partial P_j$, or c_{ij}, is negative semidefinite. This, in turn, implies the following set of inequalities:

$$c_{ii} \le 0,$$

$$\begin{vmatrix} c_{ii} & c_{ij} \\ c_{ji} & c_{jj} \end{vmatrix} \ge 0,$$

$$\begin{vmatrix} c_{ii} & c_{ij} & c_{ik} \\ c_{ji} & c_{jj} & c_{jk} \\ c_{ki} & c_{kj} & c_{kk} \end{vmatrix} \le 0, \tag{11}$$

$$|\{c_{ij}\}| = 0.$$

The last of these conditions refers to the $(n \times n)$ determinant formed by all the price responses. It is zero because of the homogeneity of the demand system. The various other subdeterminants typically are assumed to be nonzero. Equations (8), (9), (10), and (11) together summarize the a priori restrictions implied for demand by the assumption of utility-maximizing, or rational, behavior.

3.5   The distance function

The last, and least familiar, of our quartet of functions is the distance function. Although it appears, like the expenditure function, a rather artificial formulation, the basic idea behind it is essentially quite simple. However, because experience shows that students have more difficulty in getting to grips with the distance function than with the other three approaches, I want to start by providing some preliminary motivation.

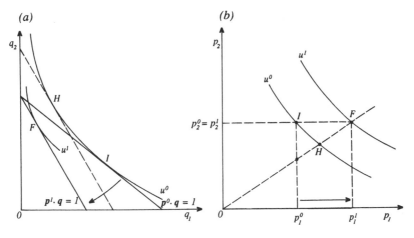

Figure 3.3

Recall the Slutsky (or, more properly, the Hicksian) decomposition of an uncompensated price response into compensated and real income components. This decomposition is depicted in panels (a) and (b) of Figure 3.3. Panel (a) is the more usual representation. The compensated substitution response to an increase in p_1 takes the consumer from the initial equilibrium I to the "Hicks" point H. The real income response takes him from H to the final equilibrium F. Panel (b) shows these responses in normalized price space. The postulated change in p_1 again takes the individual from I to F. The compensated response, from I to H, can be thought of as coming about as a result of a proportional scaling down of all normalized prices so that the initial utility level is maintained. At H, the increase in p_1 has been accompanied by an appropriate scaling down of all normalized prices. Now consider inverse demand functions. In Chapter 2, I defined uncompensated inverse demand functions, $p_i = \phi_i(\mathbf{q})$. I want now to show that the response $\partial \phi_i / \partial q_j$ can be decomposed into compensated and real income components, just like the parameters of the ordinary uncompensated demand functions, $\partial x_i / \partial p_j$, and that the compensated responses have properties qualitatively similar to those of the Slutsky price responses. Figure 3.4, panels (a) and (b), represents the decomposition that is here envisaged. In panel (b), the initial quantities are given as the point I. At I, the relative prices are represented by the normal to the tangent. Their absolute value is pinned down by imposing the normalization that $\mathbf{p} \cdot \mathbf{q}^0 = 1$. The move from I to the final allocation F is decomposed into two components. First, we imagine that the increase in q_1 is accompanied by proportional reductions in all quantities.

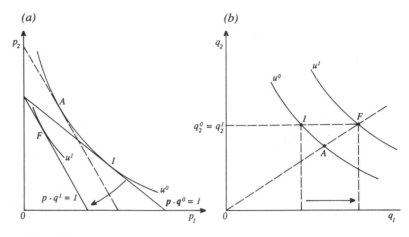

Figure 3.4

This reduction keeps all ratios of quantities at the values implied at F and is of such a magnitude as to maintain the initial utility level. This takes us to the point A, the "Antonelli" point. I use this label because it was Antonelli who first alluded to compensated responses implied by the move from I to A. Panel (a) of Figure 3.4 shows the same thought experiment in price space, and it has the great advantage over panel (b) of allowing us to read off the response of demand prices to the shift from I to A explicitly. It shows clearly that an increase in q_1, accompanied by the compensating proportional reductions in all quantities, must reduce p_1 and increase p_2 – or at least leave them unchanged. The move from A to F captures the effect on $\mathbf{p}$ of the real income consequences of the change in q_1. The two panels of Figure 3.4 should, I hope, make clear what is meant when we write a compensated inverse demand function, $\psi_i(\mathbf{q}, u)$. Such a function picks out a reference bundle $\mathbf{q}$, scales it up or down to that bundle $\hat{\mathbf{q}}$ that just attains the utility target u, and generates the normalized price of commodity i associated with the budget constraint that supports consumption of $\hat{\mathbf{q}}$. The striking parallels between Figures 3.3 and 3.4 suggest strongly that the functions $\psi_i(\mathbf{q}, u)$ have properties similar to those of the compensated demand functions $c_i(\mathbf{p}, u)$. The distance function, which I shall now introduce, leads us to these properties in the same way that the expenditure function led us to the properties of the compensated demand system.

The decomposition of an uncompensated price response that is provided by Figure 3.4 requires us at one point to consider a reference quantity

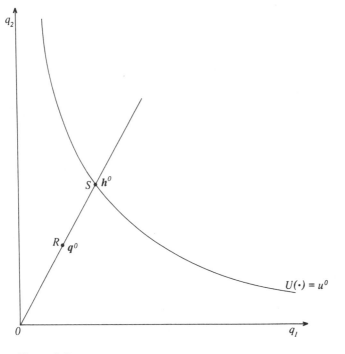

Figure 3.5

bundle (q_1^1, q_2^1) and a level of utility associated not with (q_1^1, q_2^1) but with a scalar multiple of this bundle – the point A in panel (b). There is a straightforward way of defining the allocation A, and this is provided by the distance function.

Let $\mathbf{q}^0$ be an arbitrary reference bundle of commodities. In Figure 3.5 it is the point R. Now consider an arbitrary indifference curve in quantity space, which we associate with the utility level u^0. In general, $\mathbf{q}^0$ does not lie on u^0. As drawn, the bundle $\mathbf{q}^0$ does not enable the consumer to attain u^0. However, if the quantities of all the commodities in the bundle are increased by the same proportion so as to take him to S, then u^0 is just attainable. Denote the hypothetical bundle of commodities associated with S by $\mathbf{h}^0$. By construction, $\mathbf{q}^0$ and $\mathbf{h}^0$ are scalar multiples of one another, so that we can define a scalar, δ^0, such that $\mathbf{q}^0 = \delta^0 \mathbf{h}^0$, or $\mathbf{q}^0/\delta^0 = \mathbf{h}^0$. In the diagram, $\delta^0 = 0R/0S$, and it simply expresses the reference bundle $\mathbf{q}^0$ as a fraction of the scalar multiple $\mathbf{h}^0$ that attains the utility target u^0. If we chose $\delta < \delta^0$, then its division into $\mathbf{q}^0$ would produce a bundle that would be more than sufficient to attain u^0. On the other hand, if $\delta > \delta^0$, the resulting bundle would fall short of that required to attain u^0. δ^0 can therefore be defined as the maximum value of δ such that $U(\mathbf{q}^0/\delta) \geq u^0$. Its value will depend on the selected reference bundle and utility target, and this functional dependence defines the so-called distance function, $D(\mathbf{q}, u)$. Formally, the distance function is defined as

$$D(\mathbf{q}, u) \equiv \max_{\delta}\{\delta \mid U(\mathbf{q}/\delta) \geq u\}. \tag{12}$$

Had $\mathbf{q}^0$ and u^0 been chosen such that $U(\mathbf{q}^0) = u^0$, then $D(\mathbf{q}^0, u^0) = 1$, because $\mathbf{q}^0$ and $\mathbf{h}^0$ would have coincided.

This definition of the distance function makes no mention of, and is in no way reliant upon, a price system. It is, however, useful to provide an alternative characterization in which competitive prices play a role. This displays the duality between the distance function $D(\mathbf{q}, u)$ and the expenditure function $E(\mathbf{P}, u)$ particularly clearly and provides a convenient point of departure for deriving the properties of distance functions.

Suppose the consumer has a fixed money income, $\bar{M}$. I shall put $\bar{M}$ equal to unity throughout the following thought experiment, which is equivalent to working with the normalized prices $p_i \equiv P_i/\bar{M}$. I shall also assume that preferences are convex. To every hypothetical bundle $\mathbf{h}$ that generates the target utility level there corresponds a price vector $\mathbf{p}$ such that the implied budget constraint touches the indifference curve at $\mathbf{h}$, so that $V(\mathbf{p}) = u^0$ and $E(\mathbf{p}, u^0) = \mathbf{p} \cdot \mathbf{h} = 1$. In Figure 3.6, the intersection between such a budget line and the ray $0R$ is denoted by the point C. Let γ be the ratio $0R/0C$. Then γ can be expressed as

$$\gamma = 0R/0C = \mathbf{p} \cdot \mathbf{q}^0/\mathbf{p} \cdot \mathbf{h} = \mathbf{p} \cdot \mathbf{q}^0.$$

The value of γ is minimized when the normalized price vector touches the target indifference curve at the point S, at which $\mathbf{h} = \mathbf{h}^0$. Moreover, at that point, γ is precisely equal to the distance function. Now that the intuitive argument is complete, we can drop subscripts and write

$$D(\mathbf{q}, u) \equiv \min_{\mathbf{p}}\{\mathbf{p} \cdot \mathbf{q} \mid E(\mathbf{p}, u) = 1\}. \tag{13}$$

In short, from among all the normalized price vectors that just make the target utility level u attainable, (13) picks out the one that minimizes the value of the reference bundle $\mathbf{q}$.

Now recall the definition of $E(\mathbf{p}, u)$. We know that if a vector $\mathbf{q}$ attains the utility level u, then $D(\mathbf{q}, u) = 1$. Hence the expenditure function originally defined in (3) can be expressed alternatively as

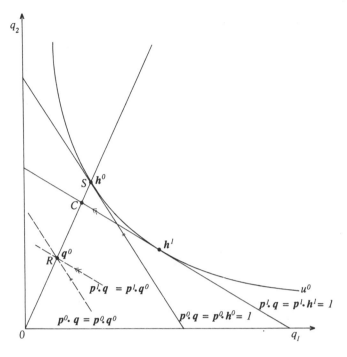

Figure 3.6

$$E(\mathbf{p}, u) \equiv \min_{\mathbf{q}}\{\mathbf{p} \cdot \mathbf{q} \mid D(\mathbf{q}, u) = 1\}. \tag{14}$$

The pleasing symmetry of equations (13) and (14) is striking. However, they form a significant pair of relationships for deeper reasons. Together, they express what may be termed Shephard duality. Equation (13) tells us that given the information summarized by the expenditure function in price space, a simple optimizing problem will generate a representation of preferences in terms of quantities, using the distance function. Equation (14) tells us that given the information summarized by the distance function concerning quantities, an equally simple optimizing problem will generate a representation of preferences in terms of prices using the expenditure function. $D(\cdot)$ and $E(\cdot)$ are, in short, dual functions that contain equivalent information. It should again be emphasized that for this to be so, the assumption that preferences are convex is necessary. Shephard duality was introduced in the context of producer theory (Shephard 1953, pp. 17–22) and later was discussed further (Shephard 1970, pp. 159–67).

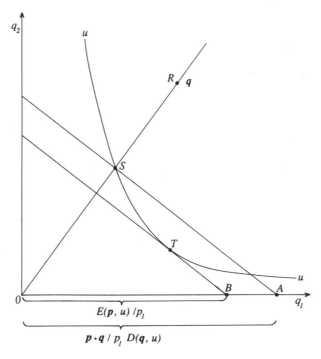

Figure 3.7

The duality between $D(\mathbf{q}, u)$ and $E(\mathbf{p}, u)$ is also reflected in a further relationship between them. Suppose we choose arbitrary quantity and price vectors, $\mathbf{q}$ and $\mathbf{p}$, together with an arbitrary utility target, u, These are shown in Figure 3.7. By the definition of $D(\cdot)$, the allocation S is simply $\mathbf{q}/D(\mathbf{q}, u)$. At the price vector $\mathbf{p}$ the value of this allocation is $\mathbf{p}\cdot\mathbf{q}/D(\mathbf{q}, u)$. For completeness, I have shown the distance $0A$, which is simply this value deflated by p_1 so as to express it in units of commodity 1. Because we started with arbitrary values for $\mathbf{p}$, $\mathbf{q}$, and u, the allocation S generally will not represent the minimum-cost way of achieving u when faced with $\mathbf{p}$. The cost-minimizing allocation is the point T, and the associated value of expenditure is simply $E(\mathbf{p}, u)$. In terms of commodity 1, it is the distance $0B$. Because this is cost-minimizing, we know that $0B \leq 0A$, or

$$E(\mathbf{p}, u) \leq (\mathbf{p}\cdot\mathbf{q})/D(\mathbf{q}, u),$$

which implies

$$E(\mathbf{p}, u)D(\mathbf{q}, u) \leq \mathbf{p}\cdot\mathbf{q}.$$

This inequality must hold for any arbitrary values of **q**, **p**, and u, and the diagram clearly suggests that it is an equality if **p** is the price vector that happens to support consumption, or touch the indifference curve, at S. If, furthermore, **q** is chosen as a point on the indifference curve corresponding to u, we can go further, because we know that in this case, $D(\mathbf{q}, u) = 1$. The points R, S, and T all coincide. In short, if **q** is the optimal bundle given **p**, and if it generates the utility level u, the relationship holds as an equality. Blackorby, Primont, and Russell (1978b, pp. 26–33) derived this relationship more formally, and Färe (1988) used it to show how measures of scale elasticity could be expressed using either cost measures or measures involving input quantities. There are doubtless other contexts in which it provides a useful gateway between price and quantity treatments of problems.

3.6 Properties of the distance function

To begin with, $D(\mathbf{q}, u)$ is a decreasing function of u. As u increases, the unchanged bundle **q** becomes smaller by comparison with the scalar multiple bundle that just attains u. Similarly, elementary reasoning indicates that $D(\mathbf{q}, u)$ is an increasing function of **q**. Indeed, it is homogeneous of degree 1 in **q**, as is revealed by inspection of (12).

In addition, $D(\mathbf{q}, u)$ is a concave function of **q**. As in the case of the expenditure function, this follows directly from the fact that $D(\cdot)$ is defined as a minimum function. Equation (13) implies that there is a $\mathbf{p}^0$ such that

$$D(\mathbf{q}^0, u) = \mathbf{p}^0 \cdot \mathbf{q}^0 \le \mathbf{p} \cdot \mathbf{q}^0$$

for any **p** consistent with $E(\mathbf{p}, u) = 1$. Now consider some other arbitrary $\mathbf{q}^1$ and a price vector $\mathbf{p}^1$ that solves (13). Then we have

$$D(\mathbf{q}^0, u) \le \mathbf{p}^1 \cdot \mathbf{q}^1 - \mathbf{p}^1 \cdot \mathbf{q}^1 + \mathbf{p}^1 \cdot \mathbf{q}^0$$
$$\le D(\mathbf{q}^1, u) + (\mathbf{q}^0 - \mathbf{q}^1) \cdot \mathbf{p}^1,$$

where $\mathbf{p}^1$ is the price vector that supports consumption at $\mathbf{q}^1$. The parallel with the argument establishing concavity of $E(\cdot)$ is apparent. The vectors **p** and **q** are simply interchanged. The reader is invited to develop the analogous diagrammatic treatment if desired.

The argument hinges on the general proposition that the consumption bundle supported by a given budget line – for example, $\mathbf{p}^1 \cdot \mathbf{q} = 1$ – is preferred to other bundles, such as C, that are attainable with that budget line. Applying this reasoning at all points on the function $D(\cdot)$, we conclude that it must everywhere lie on or below the tangent to any point on it. Its concavity, at least with respect to changes in a single quantity, is thereby established. As in the case of the minimum expenditure function, the algebra establishes concavity in a more general sense, allowing as it does for any arbitrary change in the vector of quantities.

If $D(\mathbf{q}, u)$ is twice differentiable, a further set of results, analogous to our treatment of compensated demand functions, can be obtained. Their derivation proceeds along lines that by now should be familiar. By virtue of (14), we know that for any given $\mathbf{p}^1$ satisfying $E(\mathbf{p}, u) = 1$,

$$D(\mathbf{q}, u) = \mathbf{p} \cdot \mathbf{q} \le \mathbf{p}^1 \cdot \mathbf{q} \quad \text{or} \quad f(\mathbf{q}, u) \equiv D(\mathbf{q}, u) - \mathbf{p}^1 \cdot \mathbf{q} \le 0.$$

The function $f(\cdot)$ equals zero, and hence attains its maximum value, when $\mathbf{q} = \mathbf{q}^1$. At this value of $\mathbf{q}$, $\partial f(\cdot)/\partial q_k = 0$ for each K:

$$\partial f(\cdot)/\partial q_k = \partial D(\mathbf{q}^1, u)/\partial q_k - p_k^1 = 0;$$
$$\therefore \; \partial D(\mathbf{q}^1, u)/\partial q_k = p_k^1. \tag{15}$$

The associated price p_k^1 depends on the values of $\mathbf{q}^1$ and u, so that (15) defines a function, which we shall write as

$$p_k = \psi_k(\mathbf{q}, u), \quad k = 1, \dots, n. \tag{16}$$

The function $\psi_k(\cdot)$ is a compensated valuation, or inverse demand, function, and it expresses the value to the individual of an extra unit of the commodity k as a function of the reference bundle and of the target utility level.

Because $D(\mathbf{q}, u)$ is concave, and because $\partial D/\partial q_i = \psi_i(\mathbf{q}, u)$, the inverse compensated demand function for the ith commodity, it should come as no surprise that $\psi_i(\cdot)$ enjoys properties similar to those of the ordinary compensated demand functions, $c_i(\mathbf{P}, u)$. Specifically,

$$\psi_{ij} = \psi_{ji},$$

$$\psi_{ii} \le 0,$$

$$\begin{vmatrix} \psi_{ii} & \psi_{ij} \\ \psi_{ji} & \psi_{jj} \end{vmatrix} \ge 0 \quad \text{and so on,}$$

$$|\{\psi_{ij}\}| = 0.$$

The world of inverse compensated demand functions is very much the mirror image of that of ordinary compensated demand functions.

Although the $\psi_i(\cdot)$ functions are not as well known as their quantity counterparts, they have a respectable history. The matrix $\{\psi_{ij}\}$ is known as the Antonelli matrix – Antonelli discussed its properties as long ago as 1886. More recently, the ψ_{ij} terms have been used by Hicks (1956) to provide a criterion by which to classify goods as complements or substitutes. He calls i and j q-substitutes if $\psi_{ij} < 0$. Given relatively more bread, but kept on the same indifference curve, the individual's valuation of cake may be expected to fall. However, bread and butter are likely to be q-complements, corresponding to $\psi_{ij} > 0$. Given relatively more bread, at constant utility, the valuation of butter is likely to rise.

3.7   Some convenient functional forms for economists and econometricians

The most commonly encountered classes of preferences were originally represented by utility functions. However, if a class of preferences has a simple representation using the indirect utility function, then it usually has an equally simple expenditure function. Similarly, the direct utility function often can be manipulated to yield the distance function. Going from $U(\mathbf{q})$ to $E(\mathbf{P}, u)$ or from $V(\mathbf{P}, M)$ to $D(\mathbf{q}, u)$ can, however, be more problematic. The difficulty here was noted in Section 2.4 in Chapter 2.

Although it is useful to know that the common classes of preferences often have simple representations in terms of $E(\mathbf{P}, u)$ or $D(\mathbf{q}, u)$, it is also important to realize that now that we know their general properties, we can use expenditure or distance functions as the starting point for generating further classes of preferences. Let us now consider some functional forms, starting with the expenditure function.

The expenditure function

Consider first expenditure functions implied by the more common forms of utility functions. Usually it is easy to write down the expenditure function that represents the same preferences as a given indirect utility function. For example, by solving for M as a function of $\mathbf{P}$ and u, it is easy to see that homothetic preferences for which $V(\cdot) = f(\mathbf{P})g(M)$ can be represented by an expenditure function of the form

$$E(\mathbf{P}, u) = F(\mathbf{P})G(u),$$

where $F(\mathbf{P})$ is homogeneous of degree 1 and concave in $\mathbf{P}$, and $G(u)$ is an increasing function. Shephard's lemma readily confirms that the ratios $c_i(\cdot)/c_j(\cdot)$ are independent of u for all i and j.

Because the Gorman polar form of indirect utility function implies a linear relationship between utility and expenditure level, the expenditure function has a particularly convenient form. Because $V(\cdot) = A(\mathbf{P})M + B(\mathbf{P})$, solving for M yields

$$M = E(\mathbf{P}, u) = (u - B(\mathbf{P}))/A(\mathbf{P})$$
$$= \alpha(\mathbf{P})u + \beta(\mathbf{P}).$$

The function $\beta(\mathbf{P})$ is sometimes interpreted as a base level of expenditure for a poor individual, for whom $u = 0$; $\alpha(\mathbf{P})$ is the marginal cost of utility. Compensated demand functions, too, are linear in utility. Shephard's lemma yields functions of the form

$$c_i(\mathbf{P}, u) = \alpha_i(\mathbf{P})u + \beta_i(\mathbf{P}),$$

where $\alpha_i(\cdot) \equiv \partial\alpha(\cdot)/\partial P_i$ and $\beta_i(\cdot) = \partial\beta(\cdot)/\partial P_i$. Quasi-linear preferences clearly are special cases of Gorman polar form for which $\alpha(\mathbf{P}) = 1/A(\mathbf{P}) = P_1$. Compensated demands for commodities $2, \ldots, n$ are then independent of the utility level.

Cobb-Douglas preferences, too, have a straightforward representation in terms of $E(\cdot)$. Because the indirect utility function for such preferences can be written as $V(\cdot) = BM/(P_1^{\alpha_1} \cdots P_n^{\alpha_n})$, where $\Sigma \alpha_i = 1$, the expenditure function is $E(\cdot) = P_1^{\alpha_1} P_2^{\alpha_2} \cdots P_n^{\alpha_n} u/B$. The expenditure function corresponding to the linear expenditure system is easy to write down if one exploits the observation that this system is simply a Cobb-Douglas structure defined with respect to the supernumerary quantities, $(q_i - \gamma_i)$.

The expenditure function also has been used as the starting point for generating flexible functional forms along the lines indicated in Chapter 2. Diewert (1971) has suggested the following "generalized Leontief" expenditure function:

$$E(\mathbf{P}, u) = \left(\sum_{i=1}^{n} \sum_{j=1}^{n} b_{ij} \sqrt{P_i P_j} \right) u,$$

where $b_{ij} = b_{ji}$. Shephard's lemma readily generates compensated demand functions:

$$c_i(\mathbf{P}, u) = \left(\sum_{j=1}^{n} b_{ij} \sqrt{P_j/P_i} \right) u, \quad i = 1, \ldots, n.$$

Inspection of the demand system shows that the symmetry restriction on the b_{ij}'s is required in order to yield the appropriate symmetric compensated price responses. It also reveals the reason for the label. If $b_{ij} = 0$ for

all $i \neq j$, preferences exhibit no substitutability between commodities. Indifference curves are L-shaped.

Another flexible functional form is the translog expenditure function:

$$E(\mathbf{P}, u) = \left(\alpha_0 + \sum_{i=1}^{n} \alpha_i \ln P_i + \frac{1}{2} \sum_{i=1}^{n} \sum_{j=1}^{n} \alpha_{ij} \ln P_i \ln P_j \right) u,$$

where $\sum_{i=1}^{n} \alpha_i = 1$, $\alpha_{ij} = \alpha_{ji}$, and $\sum_{j=1}^{n} \alpha_{ij} = 0$ for all i. These conditions
on the parameters ensure the necessary homogeneity. The use of $E(\cdot)$ as
a starting point for estimation of demand systems has one notable advantage and one disadvantage. Observe that because the demand functions
are simple derivatives of $E(\cdot)$, they are conveniently linear in the parameters to be estimated. This contrasts with the use of Roy's identity to produce uncompensated demand functions as ratios of linear functions of
parameters. The disadvantage is that one of the independent variables in
$E(\mathbf{P}, u)$ is the unobservable quantity, u. For econometric work this has
to be replaced by something observable. Fortunately it can be shown that
even if the expenditure function is unknown, but is approximated by a
flexible functional form, index numbers can be defined and estimated that
allow us to estimate "real income," a proxy for utility. See the last section
of this chapter for sources.

The distance function

Given a direct utility function, the implied distance function can, in principle, be generated in a straightforward way by considering the requirement that $U((1/\delta)\mathbf{q}) = u$. Sometimes this is easy. If preferences are homothetic, so that $U(\cdot) = f(g(\mathbf{q}))$, where $g(\cdot)$ is homogeneous of degree 1 in
$\mathbf{q}$, then the distance function factorizes:

$$f(g(\mathbf{q}/\delta)) = u,$$

$$f((1/\delta)g(\mathbf{q})) = u,$$

$$(1/\delta)g(\mathbf{q}) = f^{-1}(u),$$

$$\delta = g(\mathbf{q})/f^{-1}(u);$$

$$\therefore \ \delta = D(\mathbf{q}, u) = F(\mathbf{q})G(u).$$

Sometimes, however, derivation of $D(\mathbf{q}, u)$ is a little more difficult. Suppose the direct utility function represents quasi-linear preferences, taking
the form $U(\cdot) = q_1 + \sqrt{q_2}$. The distance function is generated by solving
the following equality for δ:

$$q_1/\delta + \sqrt{q_2/\delta} = u.$$

The solution involves a quadratic, of which the larger root is taken, because δ is defined as the solution of a maximizing problem. The result is

$$\delta = D(q_1, q_2, u) = \frac{q_2 + 2q_1u + \sqrt{q_2^2 + 4q_1q_2u}}{2u^2}.$$

One can be forgiven for thinking that $U(\cdot)$ may be the easier form to work with.

Cobb–Douglas preferences, however, have a simple representation in terms of $D(\mathbf{q}, u)$. Because $U(\cdot) = Aq_1^{\alpha_1} \cdots q_n^{\alpha_n}$, the distance function can be obtained by writing

$$A(q_1/\delta)^{\alpha_1} \cdots (q_j/\delta)^{\alpha_n} = u.$$

There is no harm in scaling the α's so that $\sum \alpha_i = 1$. If this is done, the solution for δ is

$$\delta = D(\mathbf{q}, u) = Aq_1^{\alpha_1} \cdots q_n^{\alpha_n}/u.$$

I am not aware of any work done in consumer theory in which a flexible functional form is introduced for $D(\mathbf{q}, u)$. As an approach to estimating a demand system, it shares an advantage with the expenditure function in that it leads to inverse compensated demand functions that are linear in parameters. It also shares the disadvantage of generating a system in which utility is an independent variable.

3.8   Concluding comments and suggestions for further study

The pioneers in the development of the expenditure function approach the matter from rather different perspectives. Hicks (1946, p. 331) briefly refers to the idea of regarding expenditure as the dependent variable in the course of a discussion of welfare change. The direct utility function is assumed to exist. Shephard (1953) is concerned to show that if an expenditure function with certain regularity conditions can be defined, this implies the existence of a direct utility function capable of representing the same preferences. Finally, McKenzie (1957) shows that the expenditure function provides a way of representing preferences that obviates the need even to mention utility. After all, the requirement that the individual be on or above a given indifference curve can be expressed by requiring that the bundle chosen be weakly preferred to some specified reference bundle, $\mathbf{q}^r$, so that (2) may be written

$$\min_{\mathbf{q}}\{\mathbf{P}\cdot\mathbf{q}\,|\,\mathbf{q}\gtrsim\mathbf{q}^r\}.$$

Although it is now widely appreciated that reference to utility does not unduly contaminate the analysis with cardinal overtones, it is worth reading McKenzie's paper.

I mentioned in Chapter 1 that Shephard's lemma can be found in Hicks (1946) and is indeed based on the same idea as the result stated by Hotelling (1932) in the context of profit functions. The profit function is a maximum value function, to be explored in Chapter 5, whereas the expenditure function is a minimum value function. In both cases the endogenous responses to small exogenous price changes have only a second-order effect on the value of the objective function. Diamond and McFadden (1974) provide a simple treatment and cite Gorman as the source of a simple demonstration of Shephard's lemma. Gorman eventually committed himself to print (Gorman 1976). See also Karlin (1959, pp. 271–2). The convenient properties of maximum and minimum value functions are lucidly expounded by Dixit (1976).

The distance function is used by Shephard (1953, 1970) in the context of producer theory as an alternative way of representing preferences in quantity space. There is a classic paper on index numbers by Malmquist (1953) that, in effect, uses the distance function to define a quantity index. Its various applications to consumer theory are developed in an expository paper by Deaton (1979), who refers to earlier literature. The properties of inverse compensated demand functions are treated later in Chapter 4, and the use of the distance function in defining certain common index numbers is mentioned in Chapter 9. Further references can be found there.

Diewert (1974b, pp. 108–16) gives a useful discussion of expenditure functions and provides examples of flexible functional forms. The more recent discussion of flexible functional forms by Lau (1986), to which I referred in Chapter 2, is again relevant, together with the survey by Deaton (1986, pp. 1788–93). An example of estimating demand functions derived from flexible functional forms of the expenditure function is provided by Swamy and Binswanger (1983). They briefly discuss the problem of providing an index of real income, to which Diewert (1976, 1978b) provides a solution. Explorations of alternative flexible forms, and interpretation of the empirical results obtained from them, are topics that clearly will continue to attract a good deal of attention.

CHAPTER 4

Individual consumer behavior: Further useful relationships and formulations

Having assembled the basic ingredients of the demand theory, we can now set to work relating them to one another and demonstrating their various uses. We already know that the direct and indirect utility functions are related, each being the dual of the other. Similarly, the minimum expenditure and distance functions are duals. Sections 4.1 and 4.2 point out the simple relationships between the two pairs of functions. Section 4.3 is perhaps the most important. On the one hand, uncompensated demand functions are the most natural and most commonly used form, especially in the estimation of demand systems, whereas it is the system of compensated demand functions that directly reflects the a priori restrictions on behavior implied by rationality. Clearly, it is important to relate the two types of functions, so that analysis that uses the uncompensated formulation can still exploit those restrictions. This is done in Section 4.3; as with demand functions, so too with inverse demand functions, as Section 4.4 demonstrates. Section 4.5 explores the local duality relationships between demand and inverse demand systems as reflected in the relationship between the Slutsky and Antonelli matrices.

I asserted in Chapter 3 that the concept of a utility function is a direct implication of the first four axioms. Even so, the use of the word "utility" continues to worry students into thinking that economic theory has injected some unsatisfactorily metaphysical concept into the works. Section 4.6 emphasizes that it is the notion of an indifference relationship, not utility, that is important. If desired, the word "utility" can easily be removed and replaced by a phrase concerning indifference. The price to be paid for this consists of occasionally tiresome circumlocutions, but no more. Section 4.7 draws attention to two further "laws of demand" that are of interest in their own right, in addition to providing alternative ways of decomposing total price responses into substitution and real income effects. Suggestions for further reading will be found in the concluding section.

4.1 The indirect utility function and the expenditure function

As we saw in Chapter 2, the direct and indirect utility functions are dual functions. One represents preferences in quantity space, and the other does so in price space. Similarly, we found in Chapter 3 that the expenditure and distance functions are dual to one another. It is also straightforward to relate the former pair of functions to the latter. Consider the indirect utility function $V(\mathbf{P}, M)$. Because goods are everywhere goods – there is no satiation – an increase in M will always increase the utility level. Therefore, because V is a strictly increasing and continuous function of M, the function may be "inverted" to express income, or expenditure, as a function of nominal prices and the utility target. For example, suppose the indirect utility function is

$$u = V(P_1, P_2, M) = kM/(P_1^\alpha P_2^\beta),$$

where k, α, and β are parameters and $\alpha + \beta = 1$. Then the minimum expenditure function is obtained by solving for M:

$$M = E(P_1, P_2, u) = P_1^\alpha P_2^\beta u/k.$$

The ease with which either function can be obtained from the other is useful because it means that if we are given, say, the indirect utility function, we can derive both uncompensated demand functions, through Roy's identity, and compensated demand functions, by first generating $E(\mathbf{P}, u)$ and then by applying Shephard's lemma.

4.2 The direct utility function and the distance function

Like the indirect utility and minimum expenditure functions, the direct utility and distance functions are easily related. The distance function, it may be recalled, generates a scalar δ such that $u = U(\mathbf{q}/\delta)$. Again, so long as goods are goods, this may be inverted to give $\delta = D(\mathbf{q}, u)$, the distance function itself. Given either $U(\cdot)$ or $D(\cdot)$, the other can, in principle, be obtained by simple inversion. For example, suppose we are given the distance function

$$\delta = D(q_1, q_2, u) = A q_1^\alpha q_2^\beta/u,$$

where $\alpha + \beta = 1$. Then the direct utility function is obtained by solving for u:

$$u = A q_1^\alpha q_2^\beta/\delta = A(q_1/\delta)^\alpha (q_2/\delta)^\beta.$$

This tells us what the implied utility level is if a reference bundle (q_1, q_2) is taken and then scaled up or down by dividing each quantity by the scalar δ. If, as is natural when characterizing preferences, we choose the reference vector to lie on the indifference curve associated with the target utility level, then $\delta = 1$, and preferences are clearly representable by a Cobb–Douglas direct utility function.

4.3   Compensated and uncompensated demand functions

We succeeded in Chapter 3 in generating substantial restrictions on parameters associated with the compensated demand functions, $c_i(\mathbf{P}, u)$. Because typically these are not directly observed or estimated, the reader may legitimately wonder how useful this is. In fact, the parameters of uncompensated demand functions are related to those of compensated functions, so that our results imply substantial and useful restrictions on the observable values of uncompensated responses of demand to price changes. The links between the two types of functions are easily established, as we now show. The decomposition of the uncompensated price response, $\partial x_i(\mathbf{P}, M)/\partial P_j$, into pure compensated substitution and real income effects is a standard exercise. By making use of our analysis of demand functions, we can also make it a straightforward exercise. The consumer's behavior may be described equally well by either compensated or uncompensated demand functions, and at an optimum we can write

$$x_i(\mathbf{P}, M) = c_i(\mathbf{P}, u). \tag{1}$$

M itself is a function of prices and utility and may be replaced by the expenditure function:

$$x_i(\mathbf{P}, E(\mathbf{P}, u)) = c_i(\mathbf{P}, u). \tag{2}$$

It is important to understand that equation (2) is an identity that holds for any set of values of $\mathbf{P}$ and u. The difference between the two sides is that $c_i(\cdot)$ expresses the demand for commodity directly as a function of $\mathbf{P}$ and u, whereas $x_i(\cdot)$ expresses exactly the same quantity as a function of $\mathbf{P}$ and M, where M itself is treated as a function of $\mathbf{P}$ and u. Because it holds true as an identity, and not just at a single point, the adjustments dx_i and dc_i provoked by changes in $\mathbf{P}$ or u can also be equated. Now change P_j while holding constant all other prices and utility. P_j appears twice on the left-hand side of (2), and differentiation yields

$$\partial x_i/\partial P_j + (\partial x_i/\partial M)(\partial E/\partial P_j) = \partial c_i/\partial P_j. \tag{3}$$

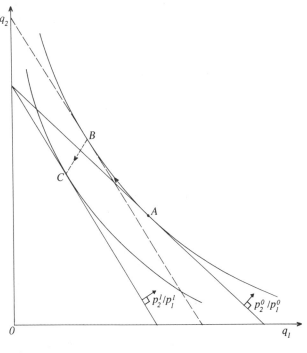

Figure 4.1

Shephard's lemma allows us to replace $\partial E/\partial P_j$ by the quantity demanded, c_j $(= x_j)$. Slutsky's well-known decomposition of an uncompensated response into compensated and real income components follows immediately, without a bordered Hessian in sight:

$$\partial x_i/\partial P_j = \partial c_i/\partial P_j - x_j \, \partial x_i/\partial M. \tag{4}$$

Slutsky's decomposition is shown in Figure 4.1. The initial equilibrium at A is disturbed by a rise in P_1. The consumer's response takes him to C and is split up into the compensated response, A to B, and the real income response, B to C. The power of a priori restrictions in reducing the number of independent parameters that need to be estimated in order to estimate a demand system can be appreciated by considering a three-commodity example. The responses of a consumer of three commodities to changes in prices and money income are entirely characterized by 12 parameters – there are the price responses, $\partial x_i/\partial P_j$, and the income responses, $\partial x_i/\partial M$, $i, j = 1, 2, 3$. The Engel and Cournot aggregation theorems tell us that these are not independent – for example, once we know

$\partial x_1/\partial M$ and $\partial x_2/\partial M$, we also know $\partial x_3/\partial M$. Further, knowing $\partial x_1/\partial P_j$ and $\partial x_2/\partial P_j$ is sufficient to determine $\partial x_3/\partial P_j$. These observations leave us with 8 parameters that, once determined, imply the rest. If we now exploit Slutsky's equation, the number of independent parameters can be seen to be not 8, but 5. Suppose we have estimates of $\partial x_1/\partial P_1$, $\partial x_2/\partial P_2$, $\partial x_2/\partial P_1$, $\partial x_1/\partial M$, and $\partial x_2/\partial M$. The Engel aggregation result gives us $\partial x_3/\partial M$. Slutsky's equation allows us to determine c_{11}, c_{22}, and c_{12} (and therefore c_{21}). Then $\partial x_1/\partial P_3$ can be determined, either from the Cournot aggregation result or from c_{13}, which is now known, followed by application of Slutsky's equation. From c_{21} and c_{22} we can determine c_{23}, and therefore c_{32}. Knowing c_{13} and c_{23}, we can finally pin down c_{33}. Application of Slutsky's equation reveals the values of the remaining uncompensated price responses. Consequently, although the c_{ij}'s are not directly observed, the relationships between them permeate the system of uncompensated demands and imply substantial and potentially useful a priori restrictions on the observable behavior of a rational, or utility-maximizing, consumer. Alternatively, independent estimates of demand parameters can be used to provide tests of the theory.

4.4   Compensated and uncompensated inverse demand functions

It should come as no surprise that the response of an individual's marginal valuations to a change in one of the quantities consumed can be decomposed into compensated and real income components analogous to the Slutsky decomposition of quantity responses. Indeed, the geometric representation of this decomposition was sketched in Section 3.5. The uncompensated inverse demand function can be written in the following way:

$$p_i = \zeta_i(\mathbf{q}, \delta), \quad i = 1, \ldots, n. \tag{5}$$

The interpretation of this is as follows: Consider the reference vector $\mathbf{q}$ and the scalar δ; p_i is the value placed by the individual on an extra unit of i in the neighborhood of $\mathbf{q}/\delta$ when prices are normalized by requiring $E(\mathbf{p}, u) = 1$, where $u = U(\mathbf{q}/\delta)$. The general strategy follows that adopted for the Slutsky decomposition. The trick is to choose a convenient substitution. Observe that (5) enables us to write

$$p_i = \zeta_i(\mathbf{q}, D(\mathbf{q}, u)) = \psi_i(\mathbf{q}, u). \tag{6}$$

Like equation (2), from which we derived Slutsky's equation, this is an identity. Let q_j change while all other reference quantities and the utility target remain constant. Differentiation of (6) yields

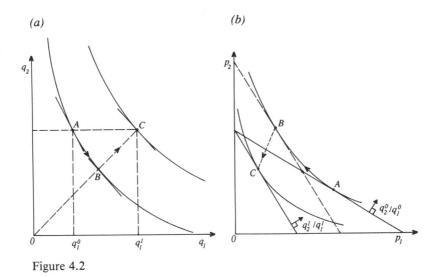

Figure 4.2

$$\partial \zeta_i / \partial q_j + (\partial \zeta_i / \partial \delta)(\partial D / \partial q_j) = \partial \psi_i / \partial q_j. \tag{7}$$

We already know that $\partial D / \partial q_j$ provides the valuation of commodity j, say $\zeta_j(\mathbf{q}, \delta)$. Equation (7) therefore can be written

$$\partial \zeta_i / \partial q_j = \partial \psi_i / \partial q_j - \zeta_j (\partial \zeta_i / \partial \delta). \tag{8}$$

This expression is the inverse demand system's analogue of the Slutsky equation. Panels (a) and (b) of Figure 4.2 show the decomposition in the spaces of quantities and prices, respectively. The initial reference bundle is the point A. In the figure, δ is initially assumed equal to unity, so that the target utility level is represented by an indifference curve through A. Let q_1 rise. The term $\partial \psi_i / \partial q_j$ is the change in the (normalized) valuation of commodity i when the increase in q_j is accompanied by the change in δ required to maintain the initial utility level. In both panels the consumer now moves to point B. We see that δ has fallen below unity – in panel (a) it is represented by $0B/0C$ – to maintain utility unchanged. Panel (b) is perhaps more enlightening, because it shows p_1 and p_2 separately, whereas panel (a) shows the ratio p_1/p_2. Notice, too, the parallels between Figure 4.2(b) and Figure 4.1. They are identical except for the transposition of p's and q's. The move from B to C in both panels captures the response to the real income change that is implied by the change in q_1 given that δ is, in fact, kept constant. This link between compensated and uncompensated parameters is as interesting to students of inverse demand systems as is the Slutsky equation to students of conventional demand systems.

Because the functions $\psi_i(\cdot)$ and $\zeta_i(\cdot)$ are unlikely to be familiar, an illustrative example may help to show what is going on. Suppose preferences are Cobb–Douglas, representable by $U(\mathbf{q}) = q_1 q_2$. The distance function is then $D(q_1, q_2, u) = \sqrt{q_1 q_2/u}$. From this the compensated inverse demand functions can be derived by differentiation:

$$\psi_1(q_1, q_2, u) = \tfrac{1}{2}\sqrt{q_2/q_1 u}, \tag{9}$$

and

$$\psi_2(q_1, q_2 u) = \tfrac{1}{2}\sqrt{q_1/q_2 u}. \tag{10}$$

Now we must derive $\zeta_1(q_1, q_2, \delta)$ and $\zeta_2(q_1, q_2, \delta)$. Given the reference bundle (q_1, q_2) and the value of δ, the ratio $\zeta_1(\cdot)/\zeta_2(\cdot)$ is the marginal rate of substitution, or ratio of demand prices, at $(q_1/\delta, q_2/\delta)$. Given the Cobb–Douglas form, at that point the utility level is

$$u = U(q_1/\delta, q_2/\delta) = (q_1/\delta)(q_2/\delta) = q_1 q_2/\delta^2.$$

Therefore,

$$\begin{aligned}\zeta_1(\cdot)/\zeta_2(\cdot) &= (\partial U(\cdot)/\partial(q_1/\delta))/(\partial U(\cdot)/\partial(q_2/\delta)) \\ &= (\partial U(\cdot)/\partial q_1)/(\partial U(\cdot)/\partial q_2) \\ &= q_2/q_1.\end{aligned}$$

Recall that the prices ζ_1 and ζ_2 are normalized so that

$$(\zeta_1 q_1/\delta) + (\zeta_2 q_2/\delta) = 1.$$

We can therefore solve for ζ_1 and ζ_2:

$$\zeta_1(q_1, q_2, \delta) = \delta/2q_1, \qquad \zeta_2(q_1, q_2, \delta) = \delta/2q_2. \tag{11}$$

Figure 4.3 is intended to reinforce understanding further. Suppose that the initial bundle is $\mathbf{q}$, represented by the point R, and the initial value of δ is given by $0R/0S$. Then ζ_1/ζ_2 is the marginal rate of substitution at the point S, the bundle $(q_1/\delta, q_2/\delta)$; $\zeta_i(\cdot)$ is the normalized price of commodity i. If q_1 alone increases by dq_1, while q_2 is constant, the new reference bundle is at Y. If δ is also held constant at $0R/0S = 0Y/0Z$, the prices ζ_1 and ζ_2 are now evaluated at the point Z, because $\zeta_i(\cdot) = \zeta_i((q_1 + dq_1)/\delta, q_2/\delta)$. The responses $\partial\zeta_1(\cdot)/\partial q_1$ and $\partial\zeta_2(\cdot)/\partial q_1$ are, then, the uncompensated responses of normalized demand prices as the reference bundle changes from R to Y, and the bundle at which evaluation is made changes from S to Z.

Returning from the intuitive discussion to the decomposition shown in equation (8), we can now check that it is certainly satisfied by the Cobb–

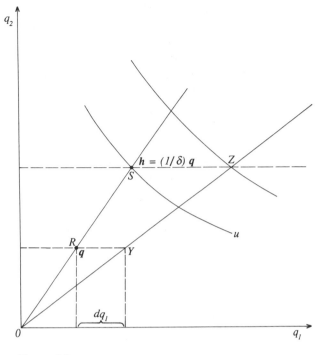

Figure 4.3

Douglas example. Consider the response $\partial \zeta_1 / \partial q_2$. From (11), this is zero. The right-hand side of (8) is easily evaluated using (9) and (11):

$$\partial \psi_1 / \partial q_2 - \zeta_2 \partial \zeta_1 / \partial \delta = \tfrac{1}{4} \sqrt{1/q_1 q_2 u} - (\delta/2q_2)(1/2q_1).$$

But $\delta = \sqrt{q_1 q_2 / u}$. Therefore,

$$\partial \psi_1 / \partial q_2 - \zeta_2 \partial \zeta_1 / \partial \delta = \tfrac{1}{4} \sqrt{1/q_1 q_2 u} - \tfrac{1}{4} (\sqrt{q_1 q_2 / u} / q_1 q_2)$$

Equation (8), then, is satisfied in this case, both sides being zero. The reader may readily check that (8) is satisfied when $i = j$. It is worth noticing a ubiquitous characteristic of Cobb–Douglas preferences. Just as $x_i(\cdot)$ is independent of P_j for $i \neq j$, so $\zeta_i(\cdot)$ is independent of q_j.

4.5   Compensated demand and inverse demand functions

Chapter 3 investigated, among other things, the duality between $D(\mathbf{q}, u)$ and $E(\mathbf{P}, u)$ – that is, the idea that under certain circumstances these two functions contain precisely the same information about an individual's preferences, the one in quantity space, and the other in price space. In many contexts, all we know and, indeed, need to know about preferences is their local behavior. For example, perhaps we know only the values of all the first derivatives of the compensated demand system in the neighborhood of a given bundle. The duality between $D(\cdot)$ and $E(\cdot)$ suggests that this information should enable us, if we so desire, to infer the values of the first derivatives of the inverse compensated demand system in that same neighborhood of commodity space. To put it another way, if we have a linear approximation to the compensated system $\mathbf{c}(\mathbf{P}, u)$ at some set of prices and utility target, we should be able to calculate the corresponding linear approximation to the inverse compensated system $\psi(\mathbf{q}, u)$ in the neighborhood of $(\mathbf{q}, u)$, where $\mathbf{q} = \mathbf{c}(\mathbf{P}, u)$.

This can be done, and it is a useful exercise in the handling of demand systems. It is tempting to argue as follows: Starting with a given $\mathbf{P}$ and u, the linear approximation of the responses of quantities to a small change in the price vector if u is held constant is

$$d\mathbf{q} = \{c_{ij}\}d\mathbf{P} = (1/M)\{c_{ij}\}d\mathbf{p}.$$

If, instead, we think of quantities as being changed exogenously, the linear approximation of the price responses is given by

$$d\mathbf{q} = (q/M)\{\psi_{ij}\}^{-1}d\mathbf{p},$$

where $\{\psi_{ij}\}^{-1}$ is the inverse of the matrix $\{\psi_{ij}\}$, as defined, for example, by Chiang (1984, pp. 84-7) and Glaister (1984, pp. 61-8). Such a temptation should, however, be resisted. The homogeneity of demand systems ensures that both $\{c_{ij}\}$ and $\{\psi_{ij}\}$ are singular, so that such inverses are not defined. There is, however, a sense in which they are "generalized" inverses of one another.

Because the ψ's are normalized prices, it is helpful to begin by expressing expenditure and compensated demand functions in terms of the normalized system $\mathbf{p}$. First, observe that because $E(\mathbf{P}, u)$ is homogeneous of degree 1 in $\mathbf{P}$, $E(\theta\mathbf{P}, u) = \theta E(\mathbf{P}, u)$ for any scalar $\theta > 0$. Putting $\theta = 1/M$, this implies that $E(\mathbf{p}, u) = (1/M)E(\mathbf{P}, u)$. Also, because $c_i(\mathbf{P}, u)$ is homogeneous of degree 0 in $\mathbf{P}$, $c_i(\mathbf{P}, u) = c_i(\mathbf{p}, u)$. Consequently, $\partial c_i(\mathbf{P}, u)/\partial P_j = (\partial c_i(\mathbf{p}, u)/\partial p_j)(dp_j/dP_j) = (1/M)\partial c_i(\mathbf{p}, u)/\partial p_j$. We distinguish the compensated demand function expressed in terms of normalized prices, and its derivatives, by a dagger superscript. Hence, $c_i(\mathbf{p}, u) \equiv c_i^{\dagger}(\cdot)$, and $c_{ij}^{\dagger} \equiv \partial c_i^{\dagger}(\mathbf{p}, u)/\partial p_j$.

Now turn to Figure 4.4. There, the bundle demanded at prices $\mathbf{p}$ and utility target u is denoted by $\mathbf{h}$, the ith element of which is $h_i = c_i^{\dagger}(\mathbf{p}, u)$.

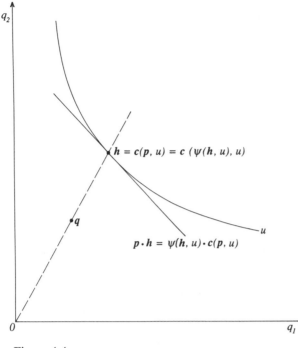

$h = c(p, u) = c \ (\psi(h, u), u)$

$\bullet q$

u

$p \cdot h = \psi(h, u) \cdot c(p, u)$

Figure 4.4

The price vector $\mathbf{p}$ can be replaced, using Cook's trick (1972), by the functions $\psi(\mathbf{h}, u)$. If the trick is applied again to replace $\mathbf{h}$ by the functions $\mathbf{c}^{\dagger}(\mathbf{p}, u)$, the result is a system of equations in which the p_i's, together with u, are the independent variables on both sides:

$$\mathbf{c}^{\dagger}(\mathbf{p}, u) = \mathbf{c}^{\dagger}(\psi(\mathbf{h}, u), u) = \mathbf{c}^{\dagger}(\psi(\mathbf{c}^{\dagger}(\mathbf{p}, u), u), u). \tag{12}$$

Because by definition $\mathbf{h} = \mathbf{c}^{\dagger}(\cdot)$ is the bundle chosen when facing $\mathbf{p}$, and $\mathbf{p} = \psi(\cdot)$ is the price vector supporting consumption at $\mathbf{h}$, equation (12) must be satisfied both before and after any change in $\mathbf{p}$. To illustrate what this implies, consider the two-commodity example, and focus on the response of $c_1^{\dagger}(\cdot)$ to a change in p_2. We have

$$c_1^{\dagger}(\mathbf{p}, u) = c_1^{\dagger}(\psi_1(c_1^{\dagger}(\mathbf{p}, u), c_2^{\dagger}(\mathbf{p}, u), u), \psi_2(c_1^{\dagger}(\mathbf{p}, u), c_2^{\dagger}(\mathbf{p}, u), u), u);$$

$$\therefore \ c_{12}^{\dagger} = c_{11}^{\dagger}\psi_{11}c_{12}^{\dagger} + c_{11}^{\dagger}\psi_{12}c_{22}^{\dagger} + c_{12}^{\dagger}\psi_{21}c_{12}^{\dagger} + c_{12}^{\dagger}\psi_{22}c_{22}^{\dagger}.$$

More generally, for n commodities,

$$c_{ij}^{\dagger} = \sum_{r=1}^{n} \sum_{s=1}^{n} c_{ir}^{\dagger}\psi_{rs}c_{sj}^{\dagger}.$$

This is the representative element of the matrix of compensated responses. The whole system can be written as

$$\{c_{ij}^\dagger\} = \{c_{ij}^\dagger\}\{\psi_{ij}\}\{c_{ij}^\dagger\}.$$

Using the fact that $c_{ij}^\dagger = Mc_{ij}$, this implies that in terms of the usual $c_i(\mathbf{P}, u)$ functions,

$$\{c_{ij}\} = M\{c_{ij}\}\{\psi_{ij}\}\{c_{ij}\}.$$

The singularity of $\{c_{ij}\}$ and $\{\psi_{ij}\}$ prevents us from concluding that their product yields the identity matrix. However, it is possible and sometimes useful to express their product explicitly. Turning to Figure 4.4 again, the reference bundle $\mathbf{q}$ is, by definition, equal to $D(\mathbf{q}, u)\mathbf{h}$. Consequently,

$$q_i = D(\mathbf{q}, u)c_i^\dagger(\mathbf{p}, u);$$

$$\therefore \quad q_i = D(\mathbf{q}, u)c_i^\dagger(\psi(\mathbf{q}, u), u). \tag{13}$$

Notice that the quantity arguments of $\psi(\cdot)$ are the q_j's, not the h_j's. I can write this because the $\psi_i(\cdot)$ functions are homogeneous of degree 0 in quantities, so that $\psi_j(\mathbf{q}, u) = \psi_j(\delta\mathbf{h}, u) = \psi_j(\mathbf{h}, u)$. I wish to write it because now the independent variables are the same on both sides of (13). I can now differentiate (13), first with respect to q_i:

$$1 = c_i^\dagger(\cdot)\partial D(\cdot)/\partial q_i + D(\cdot)\sum_{j=1}^{n}(\partial c_i^\dagger(\cdot)/\partial\psi_j)(\partial\psi_j(\cdot)/\partial q_i).$$

If initially $\mathbf{q} = \mathbf{h}$, or $D(\mathbf{q}, u) = 1$, then $D(\cdot)$ may be omitted. The expression becomes, with a little rearranging,

$$\sum_j c_{ij}^\dagger\psi_{ji} = 1 - h_i p_i. \tag{14}$$

Now return to (13) and differentiate with respect to q_k, $k \neq i$. Because only q_k changes, while q_i remains constant, $dq_i = 0$:

$$0 = c_i^\dagger(\cdot)\partial D(\cdot)/\partial q_k + D(\cdot)\sum_j(\partial c_i^\dagger(\cdot)/\partial\psi_j)(\partial\psi_j(\cdot)/\partial q_k).$$

In the same way as before, this leads to

$$\sum_j c_{ij}^\dagger\psi_{jk} = -h_i p_k. \tag{15}$$

Equations (14) and (15) form a system of equations that in matrix notation are written

$$\{c_{ij}^\dagger\}\{\psi_{ij}\} = \mathbf{I} - \mathbf{h}\cdot\mathbf{p}. \tag{16}$$

Instead of starting with the relationship $\mathbf{q} = D(\mathbf{q}, u)\mathbf{c}(\mathbf{p}, u)$ and arriving at (16), we could have started with the "dual" observation that $P_i = E(\mathbf{P}, u)\psi_i$, so that $\mathbf{P} = E(\mathbf{P}, u)\,\psi(\mathbf{h}, u)$, and arrived at the transpose of (16).

4.6 Demand theory without utility

Utility has been referred to on many occasions in the preceding pages, both as a function $U(\mathbf{q})$ and also as a variable, u. In view of the observation, encountered in almost every textbook on consumer behavior, that the concept of a cardinally measurable entity "utility" is in no way necessary for the model, we should indicate at this point how we can do without it. It happens that the minimum expenditure and distance functions can easily be rewritten so as to make no reference to utility whatsoever, thus providing natural formulations for those purists who wish to purge their language of any hint of measurable utility. The expenditure function $E(\mathbf{P}, u)$, for example, can be replaced by the function $K(\mathbf{P}, \mathbf{q}')$, which denotes the minimum expenditure required, at prices $\mathbf{P}$, to acquire a commodity bundle at least as good as the reference bundle $\mathbf{q}'$:

$$K(\mathbf{P}, \mathbf{q}') \equiv \min_{\mathbf{q}}\{\mathbf{P}\cdot\mathbf{q} \mid \mathbf{q} \gtrsim \mathbf{q}'\}.$$

All that is being done here is that instead of identifying an indifference surface by reference to a utility level, we identify it by picking out one of the bundles that lie on the surface. Indeed, the classic article by McKenzie (1957) discussing the minimum expenditure function was entitled "Demand Theory Without a Utility Index" and developed the comparative statics of consumer behavior without reference to utility, except to mention its superfluity.

The minimum expenditure, considered as a function of $\mathbf{P}$ and $\mathbf{q}'$, is sometimes called the money-metric utility function, sometimes the direct compensation function. If $\mathbf{P}$ is fixed, and $K(\mathbf{P}, \mathbf{q}')$ is regarded as a function of $\mathbf{q}'$, it is in fact a utility function. This is a simple consequence of the fact that if goods are goods, then $K(\mathbf{P}, \mathbf{q}^0) \geq K(\mathbf{P}, \mathbf{q}^1)$ if and only if $\mathbf{q}^0$ is weakly preferred to $\mathbf{q}^1$. It seems, then, that in the very act of ridding ourselves of "utility" we have generated a perfectly acceptable utility function! We develop this theme later in Chapter 9.

A slight variation on this theme is to observe that utility can be replaced not only by $\mathbf{q}'$ but also by $(\mathbf{P}', M')$, using the indirect utility function. This defines an indirect compensation function:

$$\Gamma(\mathbf{P}, \mathbf{P}', M') = E(\mathbf{P}, V(\mathbf{P}', M')).$$

$\Gamma(\cdot)$ is the minimum expenditure required, when facing prices $\mathbf{P}$, to do at least as well as one can when faced with the reference budget constraint $(\mathbf{P}^r, M^r)$. Again, for a fixed $\mathbf{P}$, this is a perfectly acceptable indirect utility function. Both the direct and the indirect compensation functions are convenient formulations that occur quite naturally in welfare economics.

Like the minimum expenditure function, the distance function can be purged of all utilitarian language. Although it is undoubtedly useful to know this, and be reminded that for many purposes utility is a redundant fifth wheel, most economists seem to find it convenient to retain the word in their vocabulary. There are certainly occasions on which its use helps to avoid tedious circumlocutions.

4.7   Two more laws of demand

In Section 3.1 we stated the following law of demand:

Law of compensated demand.   *If P_j falls, while income is adjusted so that the individual is precisely as well off after the price change as he was before it, his demand for commodity j will generally rise, and cannot fall.*

In short, the compensated demand curve cannot slope upward. A pragmatic objection to this "law" is that, even in principle, we cannot directly observe it in action unless we know enough about the individual's preferences to be able to identify the appropriate income compensation. In view of this objection, it is worth noting that there are at least two other "laws of demand" that involve only observable magnitudes. Such laws may be of more interest to the skeptic.

Now suppose, instead, that the change in P_j is accompanied by an adjustment in income that keeps the initially chosen bundle, $\mathbf{q}^0$, just affordable. At the new set of prices, the bundle actually chosen, $\mathbf{q}^1$, has the same value as $\mathbf{q}^0$:

$$\mathbf{P}^1 \cdot \mathbf{q}^0 = \mathbf{P}^1 \cdot \mathbf{q}^1. \tag{17}$$

The type of argument used in Section 3.1 can be used again. The consumer's choice of $\mathbf{q}^1$ in the new situation reveals that $\mathbf{q}^1$ is preferred to $\mathbf{q}^0$, because $\mathbf{q}^0$ is still available but is not chosen. Hence, at the initial prices, $\mathbf{q}^1$ must have been unattainable, because $\mathbf{q}^0$ was chosen. Therefore, we can infer that

$$\mathbf{P}^0 \cdot \mathbf{q}^0 < \mathbf{P}^0 \cdot \mathbf{q}^1. \tag{18}$$

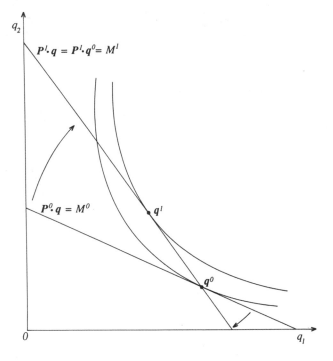

Figure 4.5

All that remains to be done is to subtract $\mathbf{P}^1 \cdot \mathbf{q}^0$ from the left-hand side of (18) and $\mathbf{P}^1 \cdot \mathbf{q}^1$ from the right-hand side, to obtain

$$(\mathbf{P}^0 - \mathbf{P}^1) \cdot (\mathbf{q}^0 - \mathbf{q}^1) \equiv \Delta \mathbf{P} \cdot \Delta \mathbf{q} < 0. \tag{19}$$

If, say, P_2 falls while all other prices remain constant, this becomes the second law of demand. It is shown in Figure 4.5:

Law of overcompensated demand. *If P_j falls, while income is adjusted so that the individual is just able to afford his initially chosen bundle, his demand for commodity j will generally rise, and cannot fall.*

As already mentioned, an important feature of this "law" is that everything is observable. We do not need any information about tastes in order to perform the experiment. I have called it the law of overcompensated demand because the amount of income compensation envisaged is more than enough to maintain the initial utility level.

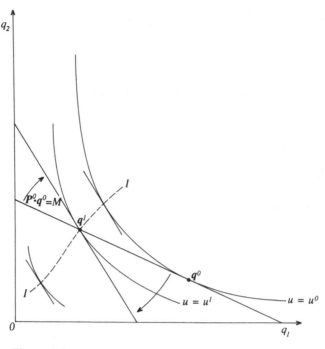

Figure 4.6

Finally, there is a law of undercompensated demand. Suppose now that starting from $(\mathbf{P}^0, M^0)$ and $\mathbf{q}^0$, P_j changes, while income is adjusted in such a way that the individual, choosing the cost-minimizing bundle at the new set of prices, consumes a bundle that lies on his original budget line. In Figure 4.6, when P_2 has fallen, income is adjusted so that $\mathbf{q}^1$ lies at the intersection of the income expansion path, II, with the original budget line along which $\mathbf{P}^0 \cdot \mathbf{q}^0 = M^0$. Algebraically, $\mathbf{q}^1$ is defined in the following way: In the light of the new price vector, it is by definition a cost-minimizing way of attaining the associated utility level, u^1, because $\mathbf{q}^1$ is chosen in the new situation. It can therefore be represented by the vector of compensated demands, $\mathbf{c}(\mathbf{P}^1, u^1)$. To determine u^1, note that $\mathbf{q}^0$ and $\mathbf{q}^1$ have the same value at the initial price vector, $\mathbf{P}^0$, so that $\mathbf{P}^0 \cdot \mathbf{c}(\mathbf{P}^1, u^1) = \mathbf{P}^0 \cdot \mathbf{q}^0$, or $\sum_{i=1}^{n} P_i^0 \partial E(\mathbf{P}^1, u^1)/\partial P_i = \mathbf{P}^0 \cdot \mathbf{q}^0$. This may be used to solve for u^1 as a function of $\mathbf{P}^0$, $\mathbf{P}^1$, and $\mathbf{q}^0$. A simple revealed preference argument leads to the third law of demand. Initially, $\mathbf{q}^0$ and $\mathbf{q}^1$ cost the same, but $\mathbf{q}^0$ was chosen. Therefore, $\mathbf{q}^0 \succsim \mathbf{q}^1$. In the new situation, because $\mathbf{q}^1$ is chosen, $\mathbf{q}^0$ must cost more than $\mathbf{q}^1$. In short, we have

$$\mathbf{P}^0 \cdot \mathbf{q}^1 = \mathbf{P}^0 \cdot \mathbf{q}^0 \quad \text{and} \quad \mathbf{P}^1 \cdot \mathbf{q}^1 < \mathbf{P}^1 \cdot \mathbf{q}^0.$$

Therefore, subtracting and rearranging,

$$\Delta \mathbf{P} \cdot \Delta \mathbf{q} < 0.$$

In particular, if only P_j changes, we have our third law of demand, which may be termed the law of undercompensated demand, because for a finite price change the individual's income is not changed sufficiently to maintain his initial utility level:

Law of undercompensated demand. *If P_j falls, while income is adjusted so that the value of the new chosen bundle, valued at the initial prices, is equal to that of the initial bundle, the individual's demand for commodity j will generally rise, and cannot fall.*

It may be rigorously shown that if prices are perturbed infinitesimally away from an initial equilibrium, the three thought experiments that lie behind the three laws amount to the same thing. For finite changes, however, they represent significantly different experiments and provide three alternative ways of decomposing the response to actual price changes. The second and third laws both use only observable magnitudes, and indeed both arise naturally in certain contexts. For example, imagine a consumer endowed with a given bundle of commodities that he consumes. We can think of him as facing a set of prices at which his endowment bundle is the most preferred. Now he is presented with the opportunity to trade at some arbitrary new set of given prices, giving up part of his endowments of some goods in exchange for others. This opening up of trade corresponds precisely to the second thought experiment. Now consider, instead, a consumer who initially faces a set of producer prices. He is the representative individual in a single-consumer economy with a constant-costs technology. Now a tax is imposed on his consumption of commodity j. Its revenue is paid back in a lump-sum manner. This situation is precisely captured by the third thought experiment. Again, the imposition of a tariff in a single-consumer open economy facing fixed world prices involves precisely the same mechanism.

4.8   Concluding comments and suggestions for further study

The various relationships between the four formulations of the consumer's problem are dealt with in many of the sources cited in Chapters 2 and 3. Indeed, this is true of a number of the matters treated in this chapter. They are conveniently summarized by Blackorby, Primont, and Russell (1978b, pp. 38–40). The Slutsky equation is derived in the more tedious way using bordered Hessians in many places – see Hicks (1946, pp. 29–33, 307–10) and Samuelson (1947, pp. 100–7) for standard treatments.

The trick of substituting $E(\cdot)$ for income in the uncompensated demand function, or alternatively $V(\cdot)$ for utility in the compensated demand function, is suggested by Cook (1972) in his simple derivation of Slutsky's equation. The same procedure has been adopted by McKenzie (1957), but a little more effort is required to find it in his analysis. This trick is used many times in subsequent pages and is worth remembering.

The properties of inverse demand systems, in particular the Antonelli equation that relates compensated and uncompensated responses of demand prices to quantity changes, are discussed by Anderson (1980). Bronsard and Salvas-Bronsard (1984) discuss some of the relevant considerations in deciding whether to estimate a demand system or an inverse demand system, and they argue that the level of commodity aggregation is important. The link between the Slutsky and Antonelli matrices is treated by Deaton (1979) and suggested as an exercise by Deaton and Muellbauer (1980a, p. 58). My experience is that students have some difficulty with this, and therefore I have spelled out the necessary manipulations in some detail. Stern (1986) has taken the analysis further in an investigation of the relationship between $\{c_{ij}\}$, $\{\psi_{ij}\}$, and $\{U_{ij}\}$. He has sensible things to say about the usefulness of, and some limitations of, the distance functions.

It has been noted in the literature that the Slutsky decomposition does not really capture Slutsky's own thought experiment, but rather that of later writers such as Hicks. Slutsky's own analysis corresponds to what I have called the law of overcompensated demand, a result that Samuelson (1953b) develops further. This was pointed out by Mosak (1942). More recently, Hatta and Willke (1982), followed by Diewert and Edlefsen (1984), have pursued the relationships between alternative substitution matrices. Their analyses draw considerably on duality theory. The conclusion from this work is that for infinitesimal changes, Slutsky's and Hicks's decompositions amount to the same thing. For finite changes, they differ.

The work by McKenzie (1957) on demand theory without a utility index has been influential in promoting the use of the expenditure function. Hurwicz and Uzawa (1971) make use of "income compensation" functions, which are identical with what I called indirect compensation functions, in their discussion of the integrability problem. The same function is exploited by Chipman and Moore (1980) in their analysis of welfare measurement. It will be encountered again in Chapter 9.

The papers by Samuelson, by Hatta and Willke, and by Diewert and Edlefsen cited earlier in this section are all relevant to the discussion of alternative laws of demand. Of particular interest is the observation that although the law of compensated demand uses unobservables, the compensated response may be approximated by an appropriate linear combination of overcompensated and undercompensated responses, both of which are more easily observable. In short, the assessment by Blaug (1980, p. 163) of the paucity of general results from demand theory seems overly harsh.

CHAPTER 5

Producer behavior

From the point of view of duality theory, the ideas that we have encountered in consumer theory carry over very naturally into the analysis of production. There are no fundamentally new ideas, simply old ones in a slightly different guise. Whereas the consumer can be thought of as using commodities to generate utility, the production plant uses factor inputs to generate output, and thereby profits. The principal differences are as follows: First, utility is a derived concept, whereas output is a primitive concept. Second, production theory has to be able to deal with situations involving vectors of many outputs, whereas the consumer's output, utility, is a scalar. Finally, the precise forms of the objectives and constraints usually assumed in producer theory imply the absence of any response analogous to the real income component of a consumer's price response. The extension to many outputs does not greatly complicate matters if duality is properly exploited, and the two remaining features of production theory serve, if anything, to simplify it.

5.1 Direct and indirect production functions

Let us begin by considering the production of a single homogeneous output, y, from a vector of input services, ℓ. A common description of the production possibility set specifies the maximum attainable output as a function of the input vector. This is the *direct production function, $F(\ell)$*:

$$F(\ell) \equiv \max_{y} \{ y \mid (y, \ell) \text{ feasible} \}. \tag{1}$$

Shephard (1970) provides an advanced analysis of the assumptions necessary to ensure the existence of such a function. $F(\ell)$ is production theory's analogue of the direct utility function encountered in Chapter 2. The main difference is that output has objective existence and is perfectly measurable, whereas utility, by contrast, is an ordinal concept, being itself the logical consequence of the axioms concerning the consumer's

104

preference ordering. These differences do not reveal themselves in the algebra.

Now assume that inputs are available at a given vector of competitive prices, $\mathbf{W}$. Suppose for the moment that there is a budget constraint that requires the expenditure on factor inputs not to exceed, say, M. Consider the problem of producing the maximum output subject to the cost constraint. This is formally identical with the consumer's utility maximization problem. Consequently, we can define the *indirect production function,* $G(\mathbf{W}, M)$, which expresses that output level as a function of the exogenous economic variables:

$$G(\mathbf{W}, M) \equiv \max_{\ell}\{F(\ell) \mid \mathbf{W} \cdot \ell \le M\}. \tag{2}$$

Like the indirect utility function, $G(\cdot)$ may be expressed as a function of normalized prices, because the budget constraint may be written as $(\mathbf{W}/M) \cdot \ell \le 1$, or $\mathbf{w} \cdot \ell \le 1$.

Because the formal structure of this problem is identical with the consumer's utility maximization problem, there should be no need to devote further space to such matters as the derivation of the properties of $G(\cdot)$, the generation of isoquants in factor price space, and the duality between $F(\ell)$ and $G(\mathbf{w})$. All that is involved is a change of symbols and slightly different terminology. For example, duality between $F(\ell)$ and $G(\mathbf{w})$ requires that the set of input combinations capable of attaining or exceeding any given target output level be convex. This is production theory's analogue of convex preferences. If this condition is satisfied, we say that the production possibility set possesses a convex input structure. This implies that if each of two input bundles, ℓ' and ℓ'', is capable of producing $\bar{y}$ units of output, so is any convex combination of them.

A further reason for not wishing to devote further space to $G(\mathbf{w})$ is simply that it is rarely encountered. The reason is simple: Typically, production theory does not assume a budget constraint. There has been a recent revival of interest in indirect production functions, and this literature is cited in Section 5.11.

By contrast, production theory has extensively exploited the cost function, which is precisely analogous to the consumer's expenditure function analyzed in Chapter 3. Although there is no budget constraint, it is reasonable to suppose, and is universally assumed in production theory, that plant managers have a keen interest in minimizing the cost of whatever they choose to produce. Let us, therefore, take a brief look at the cost function.

5.2   The cost function

Suppose the manager of a production plant has already determined the output target to be y. Factor inputs are available at given prices, $\mathbf{W}$. For simplicity I shall assume, as usual, that all factor prices are strictly positive. The objective is to combine inputs so as to minimize the cost of attaining y. This defines the plant's minimum cost function:

$$C(\mathbf{W}, y) \equiv \min_{\ell} \{\mathbf{W} \cdot \ell \,|\, F(\ell) \geq y\}. \tag{3}$$

Our assumptions concerning the input requirement set allow us to define an isoquant corresponding to the output level y that has precisely the same properties as the indifference curves encountered in consumer theory. Indeed, comparison of equation (3) with equation (3) of Chapter 3 reveals that the game is the same – only the names have changed. The utility target has become an output target, consumable commodities have become factor inputs, and commodity prices have become factor input prices, or factor rentals. The cost function $C(\cdot)$ therefore has precisely the same properties as the consumer's expenditure function $E(\cdot)$, so that this section can be kept short. Let us simply recapitulate the properties of $C(\cdot)$, without repeating their derivation. First, $C(\mathbf{W}, y)$ is an increasing function of input prices. Second, it is homogeneous of degree 1 in all input prices. Third, it is concave in prices. Finally, its derivative with respect to W_i yields the demand for the ith factor input as a function of $\mathbf{W}$ and y. This last result is Shephard's lemma again:

Shephard's lemma.   *If $C(\mathbf{W}, y)$ is differentiable with respect to all input prices at $(\mathbf{W}, y)$, then*

$$\partial C(\mathbf{W}, y)/\partial W_i = v_i^*(\mathbf{W}, y) \quad \text{for all } i. \tag{4}$$

The significance of the asterisk attached to the factor demand function $v_i^*(\cdot)$ will shortly be revealed. The derivative of the cost function with respect to output is, by definition, the marginal cost:

$$\partial C(\mathbf{W}, y)/\partial y = m^*(\mathbf{W}, y).$$

Application of Young's theorem yields a further symmetry result:

$$\partial m^*(\cdot)/\partial W_i = \partial^2 C(\cdot)/\partial W_i \partial y = \partial^2 C(\cdot)/\partial y \partial W_i = \partial v_i^*(\cdot)/\partial y,$$

that is, the response of marginal cost to a change in the price of factor i is equal to the response of demand for factor i to a change in output.

In production theory, additional structure often is imposed on the technology in the form of further assumptions concerning the form of $C(\cdot)$. For example, it is commonly assumed that it can be factorized:

$$C(\mathbf{W}, y) = f(y)g(\mathbf{W}).\tag{5}$$

Shephard's lemma, applied to (5), yields

$$v_i^*(\cdot) = f(y)(\partial g(\cdot)/\partial W_i) = f(y)g_i(\mathbf{W}).$$

Consequently,

$$v_i^*(\cdot)/v_j^*(\cdot) = g_i(\mathbf{W})/g_j(\mathbf{W}) = h(\mathbf{W}).\tag{6}$$

Equation (6) shows that the ratio of factor demands is independent of the level of output. Such a technology, for which expansion paths are rays through the origin, is known as homothetic.

A further common assumption identifies the function $f(y)$ with y itself. If $C(\mathbf{W}, y) = yg(\mathbf{W})$, then the marginal cost is independent of the level of output, as is the average cost, because

$$m^*(\mathbf{W}, y) = \partial C(\cdot)/\partial y = g(\mathbf{W}) = C(\mathbf{W}, y)/y.$$

In this case, the function $g(\mathbf{W})$ may be interpreted as the unit cost of production, which is independent of the scale of production. Application of Shephard's lemma reveals that the demand for the ith factor is then

$$v_i^*(\cdot) = yg_i(\mathbf{W}).\tag{7}$$

Thus, $g_i(\mathbf{W}) \equiv \partial g(\mathbf{W})/\partial W_i$ has a straightforward interpretation as the demand for factor i per unit output. Such unit demand functions are often denoted by $a_i(\mathbf{W})$. Finally, observe that because $C(\cdot)$ is homogeneous of degree 1 in factor prices, Euler's theorem implies that

$$C(\mathbf{W}, y) = \sum_{i=1}^{n} C_i(\cdot)W_i.$$

If $C(\cdot) = yg(\mathbf{W})$, therefore, we can write

$$C(\mathbf{W}, y) = y\sum_{i=1}^{n} a_i(\mathbf{W})W_i,$$

so that the unit cost is

$$g(\mathbf{W}) = C(\mathbf{W}, y)/y = \sum_{i=1}^{n} a_i(\mathbf{W})W_i.\tag{8}$$

Unit cost functions written in this form are familiar to trade theorists, following their use by Jones (1965), and have become increasingly popular

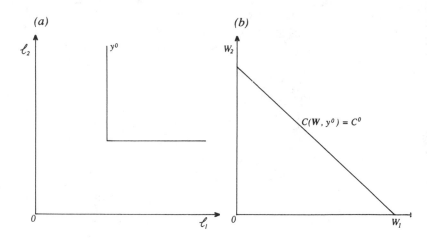

Figure 5.1

in the comparative static analysis of simple general equilibrium systems in such areas as public economics – see, for example, Atkinson and Stiglitz (1980, Lecture 6).

Let us consider a further special case. Suppose the cost function takes the following form:

$$C(\mathbf{W}, y) = \sum_{i=1}^{n} f_i(y)W_i. \tag{9}$$

What does this imply for the isoquant in quantity space, and for the iso-cost locus in factor price space? Shephard's lemma implies that the demand for input i is a function of y alone, $f_i(y)$. It is independent of $\mathbf{W}$. This immediately suggests an L-shaped isoquant, as in panel (a) of Figure 5.1. Furthermore, if we consider changes in the factor price vector that leave the cost unchanged, we find they are related by the condition that

$$dC = 0 = \sum_i f_i(y)dW_i.$$

For the given output target, then, the factor prices are linearly related. Panel (b) of Figure 5.1 shows a representative iso-cost curve, corresponding to an exogenously chosen cost level C^0, in the same way that values of (P_1, P_2) on an indifference curve in price space just enable the consumer to attain the target utility level u at minimum cost equal to money income M^0. The present example corresponds precisely to that of a consumer who consumes goods in fixed proportions.

A final special case involves the following form of cost function:

$$C(\mathbf{W}, y) = y \sum_i a_i W_i,$$

where a_i is a constant and is interpreted as the requirement of the ith factor per unit output. Not only are isoquants L-shaped, but this technology also is homothetic and, indeed, exhibits constant returns to scale. Although the extreme simplicity of such assumptions may offend some theorists, they have proved of great importance in facilitating empirical analysis of the production sector along the lines pioneered by Leontief's input–output analysis. The cost function is particularly convenient in this special case because it is differentiable. The production function, by contrast, is not.

5.3 Profit maximization

We have seen that for a given output target, the cost minimization assumption is sufficient to determine the behavior of the production plant. This is convenient, because there is not unanimous agreement concerning the appropriate model of output determination. Perusal of the literature will uncover a number of hypotheses concerning the objective of production units. Profit maximization, maximization of rate of growth of sales, maintenance of existing market share, and various other managerial utility functions have all been suggested. However, there is much more agreement concerning the proposition that however output may be determined, typically it will be produced at minimum cost. Our analysis suggests that we can, if desired, model the production decision in two stages, grafting the cost minimization exercise on to whatever is the chosen model of output determination.

In fact, we shall confine attention to the simple model of competitive profit maximization. This is the natural model to concentrate on, because we are talking about physical production plants rather than the legal entities called firms. The profit maximization assumption is the standard one in the treatment of production in abstract general equilibrium theory and also its application to such topics as international trade and public economics.

The single-input, single-output profit maximizer

The simplest model avoids the problem of optimal factor mix by assuming that there is a single input. Output and input levels are related by the production function, $y = F(\ell)$. I assume $F(\cdot)$ is strictly increasing and twice differentiable. Further necessary restrictions will be uncovered during the course of the analysis. The properties of $F(\cdot)$ enable us to define its inverse, the input requirement function $\ell = F^{-1}(y)$, which is also strictly increasing and twice differentiable. The immediate objective is to define and derive the properties of the profit function, which expresses the plant's maximum attainable profit as a function of its economic environment, summarized by the exogenous prices faced:

$$\Pi(P, W) \equiv \max_{y, \ell} \{ Py - W\ell \mid y = F(\ell) \}. \tag{10}$$

Alternative expressions, obtained from using the production relationship to substitute for ℓ or y, are

$$\Pi(P, W) \equiv \max_{\ell} \{ PF(\ell) - W\ell \}, \tag{11}$$

and

$$\Pi(P, W) \equiv \max_{y} \{ Py - WF^{-1}(y) \}. \tag{12}$$

It is important to begin by checking that there is a finite positive level of input, therefore of output, associated with a maximum value of $\Pi(\cdot)$. Consider the first- and second-order conditions for an allocation (y^0, ℓ^0) to represent a profit maximum. The profit associated with (y^0, ℓ^0) is

$$\Pi = Py^0 - W\ell^0 = PF(\ell^0) - W\ell^0.$$

The first-order necessary condition therefore requires that

$$d\Pi = PF'(\ell^0)d\ell - Wd\ell = 0,$$

from which

$$F'(\ell^0) = W/P. \tag{13}$$

This is the familiar equality of marginal product with the real wage. But this establishes only a stationary value, not necessarily a maximum value, for Π. For (y^0, ℓ^0) to represent a local maximum, we require

$$d^2\Pi = PF''(\ell^0) < 0.$$

That is, the marginal product of ℓ must be diminishing as ℓ increases in the neighborhood of ℓ^0. Even this is not quite enough, because such a local condition is still consistent with Π being negative at (y^0, ℓ^0). If such were the case, the plant would do better by abstaining from all production, thereby earning zero profit. We therefore require that

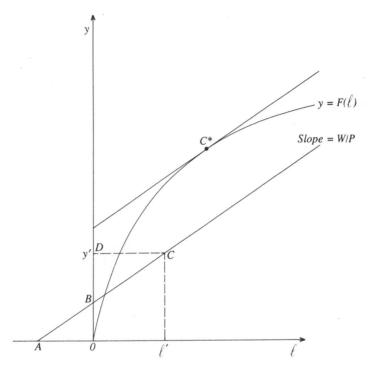

Figure 5.2

$$PF(\ell^0) - W\ell^0 \geq 0,$$

or

$$F(\ell^0)/\ell^0 \geq W/P. \tag{14}$$

Combining this with the first-order condition (13), it is necessary that at (y^0, ℓ^0) the average product of the input should at least equal its marginal product. The most commonly encountered class of production functions that guarantee this are those that are homogeneous of degree r, where $0 < r < 1$. Such a function is characterized by the relationship

$$F(\theta\ell) = \theta^r F(\ell) \quad \text{for all} \ \theta > 0. \tag{15}$$

Figure 5.2 shows how the level of profit can be depicted in the diagram, showing the production relationship $y = F(\ell)$, as well as demonstrating the importance of the assumption of diminishing returns to the input. Taking P and W as exogenously given, pick an arbitrary allocation, say (y', ℓ'). The level of profit associated with this association is

$$\Pi' = Py' - W\ell'.$$

Now trace out all those allocations (y, ℓ), feasible or not, that would, if realized, yield the profit Π'. Along the iso-profit locus thereby defined, $d\Pi = Pdy - Wd\ell = 0$, so that $dy/d\ell = W/P$. The straight line ABC is the required locus. In particular, the distance $0B$ measures profit in terms of output. This follows from the observation that $0D$ measures the output level y', and elementary trigonometry implies that $BD/DC = \tan \alpha = W/P$. But DC measures ℓ'. Therefore, BD represents $W\ell'/P$, the value of the input measured in terms of the output at the prevailing prices. Hence, finally, $0B = 0D - BD = y' - W\ell'/P = (Py' - W\ell')/P = \Pi'/P$, the level of profit expressed in units of output. By similar reasoning, $0A$ measures the same profit, but in units of the input ℓ. Corresponding to a given pair of values (P, W) there is a family of iso-profit loci consisting of a set of parallel straight lines in Figure 5.2. The profit-maximizing allocation is that feasible allocation that corresponds to the highest such locus. Clearly the point C does not maximize profit, but the point C^* does.

The importance of the second-order conditions should be clear from Figure 5.3. In panel (a) there are constant returns to scale. In the single-input model this implies that $F'(\ell)$ is a constant. If $W/P > F'(\ell)$, the profit-maximizing allocation is the origin. If $W/P = F'(\ell)$, then any point on the production function yields the maximum attainable profit of zero. If $W/P < F'(\ell)$, there is no finite quantity of input that maximizes profit, because profits can always be increased by increasing ℓ further. While a point such as C implies positive profits, it can be improved upon by moving up the production function. In panel (b), which reflects universal increasing returns to the input, for all finite values of W/P profits can be increased by further expansion – there is no finite profit-maximizing allocation. In panel (c), the curvature of $F(\ell)$ is consistent with local profit maximization at the allocation C, but the global condition is not met, because profits at C are negative at the indicated prices. The true profit maximum is at the origin. Finally, in panel (d), the curvature of $F(\ell)$ is inconsistent with profit maximization at C, even if the first-order tangency condition is met.

For the moment, let us assume that there are universal decreasing returns to scale, implying that $F''(\ell)$, which I assume is everywhere defined, is also everywhere negative. On this assumption, consider the relationship between the maximum attainable profit and the input price W, given a fixed output price P. It is convenient to think of P as being equal to unity throughout.

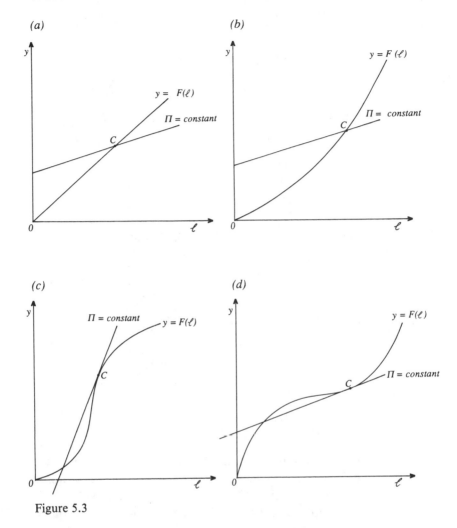

Figure 5.3

Figure 5.4 shows the production function in quadrant I. For a particular value of W the profit-maximizing allocation C^* is as shown. We know that the intersection of the relevant iso-profit locus with the vertical axis provides a measure of the associated profit. This is transferred to the vertical axis in quadrant II and, using the 45° line shown there, is finally measured along the horizontal axis in quadrant III. To represent the variable W, or W/P, return to quadrant I and draw the line parallel to the ℓ-axis representing $y = 1$. Through the origin draw a ray parallel to the price line through C^*. We know that $\tan \alpha = W/P = W = EF/0F$. But by

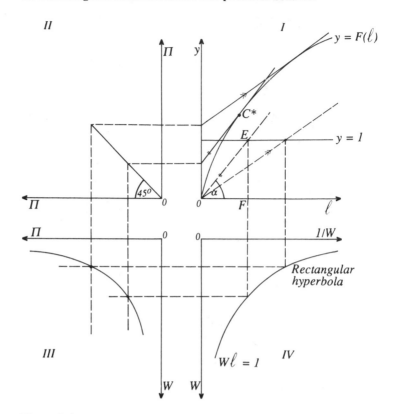

Figure 5.4

construction EF is unity. Therefore $0F$ measures $1/W$. This is transferred to the horizontal axis of quadrant IV. By the simple and familiar expedient of drawing a rectangular hyperbola in quadrant IV, $1/W$ can be transformed into W, measured along the vertical axis of quadrant IV. By this means, we have succeeded in representing Π and W by distances along the axes of Figure 5.4, and in quadrant III Π is graphed against W.

Though the details differ, the general nature of this geometric exercise is similar to the derivation in Chapter 3 of indifference curves in price space corresponding to indifference curves in quantity space. Again, it must be admitted that the geometry is somewhat mechanical. However, it does emphasize some important truths. Careful construction would reveal that the profit function is not only a decreasing but also a convex function of W. More apparent from the geometry is the fact that given the profit function, the procedure can be reversed to generate the production function. Starting from the graph in quadrant III one can generate a family of straight lines in quadrant I that are the tangents to points such as C^*. This family of curves forms the "envelope" of the production function. As in Chapter 3, the strict duality between $\Pi(\cdot)$ and $F(\cdot)$ as representations of the technology depends upon technology being convex. Our assumption that $F''(\cdot) < 0$ guarantees this, but if the production function were as shown in Figure 5.3, panel (c), strict duality would not hold. However, $\Pi(\cdot)$ would still be well defined.

Convexity of $\Pi(P, W)$ in W had better be demonstrated. Let s^i and v^i denote the profit-maximizing output supply and input demand, respectively, when the input price is W^i. By definition, recalling that P is at present being held constant throughout,

$$\Pi(P, W^1) \geq Ps^0 - W^1v^0 \tag{16}$$

$$\geq Ps^0 - W^0v^0 + W^0v^0 - W^1v^0$$

$$\geq \Pi(P, W^0) + (W^0 - W^1)v^0, \tag{17}$$

which establishes convexity. Geometrically, the tangent at any point on the curve in Figure 5.5 yields an underestimate of $\Pi(\cdot)$ for other values of W. The inequality (17) is also a convenient point of departure for Hotelling's lemma, which in the present context states that the negative of the partial derivative of $\Pi(\cdot)$ with respect to W yields the factor demand function $v(P, W)$. To see this, observe from (16) that

$$g(P, W^1) = \Pi(P, W^1) - Ps^0 + W^1v^0 \geq 0,$$

where s^0 and v^0 are constants. By definition, $g(\cdot)$ attains its minimum value of zero when W^1 is put equal to W^0. Therefore,

$$\partial g(P, W^0)/\partial W = \partial \Pi(P, W^0)/\partial W + v^0 = 0,$$

which immediately implies the general result that

$$\partial \Pi(P, W)/\partial W = -v(P, W).$$

It may be a useful exercise to vary the foregoing analysis by fixing W and considering $\Pi(\cdot)$ as a function of the variable P. Similar reasoning establishes that $\Pi(\cdot)$ is an increasing convex function of P, and Hotelling's lemma provides a further useful result. Let us state the lemma:

Hotelling's lemma. *Suppose the profit function is well defined, and its first derivatives exist everywhere. Then*

$$\frac{\partial \Pi(P, W)}{\partial P} = s(P, W) \quad and \quad \frac{\partial \Pi(P, W)}{\partial W} = -v(P, W).$$

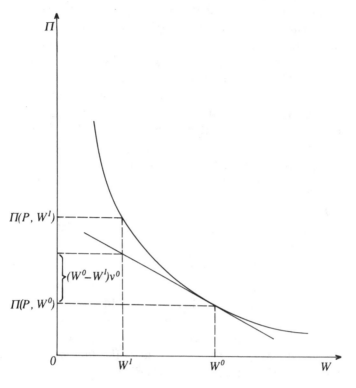

Figure 5.5

The usefulness of this lemma should by now be evident. If we have a function that satisfies those properties that make it admissible as a profit function, and if it is everywhere differentiable, then straightforward differentiation is enough to generate behavioral functions.

5.4   Properties of the profit function

The properties of the profit function extend easily to situations involving many inputs and outputs. Indeed, its ability to cope with larger dimensions without substantial extra complexity is one of its attractions. Because the discussion of the single-input, single-output example has been fairly discursive, it may help to summarize the properties of $\Pi(\cdot)$ in the more general context. Let $\mathbf{y}$ and ℓ be output and input vectors, and let their price vectors be $\mathbf{P}$ and $\mathbf{W}$. Suppose there exists a well-defined profit function, the definition of which is given by

$$\Pi(\mathbf{P},\mathbf{W}) \equiv \max_{\mathbf{y},\ell}\{\mathbf{P}\cdot\mathbf{y} - \mathbf{W}\cdot\boldsymbol{\ell} \mid (\mathbf{y},\boldsymbol{\ell})\ \text{feasible}\}.$$

Then $\Pi(\cdot)$ possesses the following properties:

1. $\Pi(\cdot)$ is nondecreasing in $\mathbf{P}$.
2. $\Pi(\cdot)$ is nonincreasing in $\mathbf{W}$.
3. $\Pi(\cdot)$ is homogeneous of degree 1 in $(\mathbf{P},\mathbf{W})$.
4. $\Pi(\cdot)$ is convex in $(\mathbf{P},\mathbf{W})$.
5. If its derivatives exist at $(\mathbf{P},\mathbf{W})$, then

$$\partial\Pi(\mathbf{P},\mathbf{W})/\partial P_j = s_j(\mathbf{P},\mathbf{W}),$$

$$\partial\Pi(\mathbf{P},\mathbf{W})/\partial W_i = -v_i(\mathbf{P},\mathbf{W}),$$

where $s_j(\cdot)$ is the profit-maximizing supply of the jth output, and $v_i(\cdot)$ is the profit-maximizing demand for the ith input.

Demonstration of these properties is a straightforward matter of adapting the arguments already used in the single-input, single-output example. Indeed, the general approach is the same as that employed in earlier analysis of expenditure and cost functions. An explicit treatment is provided by Diewert (1974*b*).

5.5   Output supply and input demand functions

Consider first the input demand functions we generated in earlier sections. The analysis of the cost-minimizing plant led to demand functions of the form $v_i^*(\mathbf{W},\mathbf{y})$. Factor demands are here expressed as functions of input prices and output levels. The analysis of profit-maximizing behavior then leads to functions of the form $v_i(\mathbf{W},\mathbf{P})$, in which output prices, not quantities, are independent variables. These functions are, of couse, different. Suppose W_k changes. Then the response of demand for the ith factor input will generally depend on whether the output levels are assumed to remain constant or are allowed to adjust to their new profit-maximizing levels. It is to emphasize this difference that the cost minimizer's demand functions have been distinguished by an asterisk.

The factor demand functions $v_i^*(\mathbf{W},\mathbf{y})$ bear the same relationship to the cost function as do the consumer's compensated demand functions to the expenditure function. Their properties are therefore the same. In particular, because $v_i^*(\mathbf{W},\mathbf{y})$ is a derivative of a concave cost function,

$$v_{ij}^* \ (\equiv \partial v_i^*(\cdot)/\partial W_j) = v_{ji}^* \quad \text{for all } i \text{ and } j,\ i \neq j,$$

$$v_{ii}^* \leq 0,$$

$$\begin{vmatrix} v_{ii}^* & v_{ij}^* \\ v_{ji}^* & v_{jj}^* \end{vmatrix} \geq 0 \quad \text{for all } i \text{ and } j, \; i \neq j,$$

$$\begin{vmatrix} v_{ii}^* & v_{ij}^* & v_{ik}^* \\ v_{ji}^* & v_{jj}^* & v_{jk}^* \\ v_{ki}^* & v_{kj}^* & v_{kk}^* \end{vmatrix} \leq 0 \quad \text{for all } i, j, \text{ and } k, \; i \neq j \neq k,$$

$$|\{v_{ij}^*\}| = 0.$$

The last of these conditions refers to the determinant formed by the full array of all input price responses. If there are m inputs, this will be an $(m \times m)$ determinant. It is zero because of the homogeneity of the demand system with respect to input prices when the output quantity is held constant. If all input prices were, say, doubled, the real allocation would remain unchanged. The own response, v_{ii}^*, is everywhere strictly negative if there are no kinks in the isoquant.

The properties of the price-taking demand functions are qualitatively the same. Recall that $v_i(\mathbf{P}, \mathbf{W})$ is minus the partial derivative of the profit function with respect to W_i and that the profit function, being a maximum value function, is convex in $\mathbf{P}$ and $\mathbf{W}$. This leads directly to the following properties:

$$v_{ij} \; (\equiv \partial v_i(\cdot)/\partial W_j) = v_{ji} \quad \text{for all } i \text{ and } j, \; i \neq j,$$

$$v_{ii} \leq 0,$$

$$\begin{vmatrix} v_{ii} & v_{ij} \\ v_{ji} & v_{jj} \end{vmatrix} \geq 0 \quad \text{for all } i \text{ and } j, \; i \neq j,$$

$$\begin{vmatrix} v_{ii} & v_{ij} & v_{ik} \\ v_{ji} & v_{jj} & v_{jk} \\ v_{ki} & v_{kj} & v_{kk} \end{vmatrix} \leq 0 \quad \text{for all } i, j, \text{ and } k, \; i \neq j \neq k,$$

$$|\{v_{ij}\}|(-1)^n \geq 0.$$

The full determinant will generally be nonzero, by contrast with that of the $v_i^*(\cdot)$ system, because equal proportional changes in all input prices, with output price held constant, typically will have a real effect.

Although the qualitative behaviors of $v_i^*(\cdot)$ and $v_i(\cdot)$ are similar, the magnitudes of their various partial derivatives generally differ. Before investigating this matter further, let us turn briefly to the properties of the output supply functions associated with the profit function. Because these are first derivatives with respect to output prices of a function that is convex in those prices, it follows that

$$s_{ij} \ (\equiv \partial s_i(\cdot)/\partial P_j) = s_{ji} \quad \text{for all } i \text{ and } j, \ i \neq j,$$

$$s_{ii} \geq 0,$$

$$\begin{vmatrix} s_{ii} & s_{ij} \\ s_{ji} & s_{jj} \end{vmatrix} \geq 0 \quad \text{for all } i \text{ and } j, \ i \neq j,$$

$$\begin{vmatrix} s_{ii} & s_{ij} & s_{ik} \\ s_{ji} & s_{jj} & s_{jk} \\ s_{ki} & s_{kj} & s_{kk} \end{vmatrix} \geq 0 \quad \text{for all } i, j, \text{ and } k, \ i \neq j \neq k,$$

$$|\{s_{ij}\}| \geq 0.$$

Again, $s_{ii} > 0$ if the relevant portion of the production surface has no kinks in it. If the plant produces n outputs, this last expression is an $(n \times n)$ determinant. The reasoning behind these properties should by now be thoroughly familiar. Notice that output supply functions cannot be downward-sloping. Similarly, input demand functions, whether output quantity or price is held constant, cannot be upward-sloping. There is no analogue of those income effects that pervade consumer theory and that place doubt over the signs of a consumer's uncompensated own-price responses.

This analysis of price-taking behavior has looked at only a subset of parameters. What about the responses of output quantities to changes in input price? To investigate these responses, I shall write down the matrix of second derivatives of the profit function with respect to **P** and **W** in partitioned form. Consider the matrix

$$\begin{bmatrix} \mathbf{\Pi}_{PP} & \mathbf{\Pi}_{WP} \\ \mathbf{\Pi}_{PW} & \mathbf{\Pi}_{WW} \end{bmatrix} \equiv \begin{bmatrix} \{\partial^2 \Pi/\partial P_i \partial P_j\} & \{\partial^2 \Pi/\partial W_i \partial P_j\} \\ \{\partial^2 \Pi/\partial P_i \partial W_j\} & \{\partial^2 \Pi/\partial W_i \partial W_j\} \end{bmatrix}.$$

Our analysis of the properties of behavioral functions has concentrated on the matrices $\mathbf{\Pi}_{PP}$ and $\mathbf{\Pi}_{WW}$. What can be said of $\mathbf{\Pi}_{PW}$ and $\mathbf{\Pi}_{WP}$? To begin with, one is simply the transpose of the other. Because Young's theorem implies, for example, that $\partial^2 \Pi/\partial W_i \partial P_j = \partial^2 \Pi/\partial P_j \partial W_i$, Shephard's lemma may be invoked to generate further symmetry results. These are sometimes called reciprocity relations:

$$\partial s_j(\cdot)/\partial W_i = -\partial v_i(\cdot)/\partial P_j, \quad i = 1, \ldots, m, \ j = 1, \ldots, n.$$

Without specific assumptions concerning the structure of the technology, the profit-maximizing model does not allow us to sign these responses. Intuitively, one may feel that an increase in an input price should, if anything, reduce the optimal output levels. It is worthwhile to consider assumptions that imply such a result. To keep notation under control, suppose there is a single output, the optimal level of which is $s(P, \mathbf{W})$. The reciprocity relation tells us that $\partial s(\cdot)/\partial W_i = -\partial v_i(\cdot)/\partial P$. What can be said about the response of demand for factor i to a change in the price of the output? It can be related to other parameters by a substitution that should now be familiar. By their definitions, it must be true that $v_i^*(\cdot)$ and $v_i(\cdot)$ are identically equal if the output level appearing in the former is the profit-maximizing level:

$$v_i^*(\mathbf{W}, s(P, \mathbf{W})) = v_i(\mathbf{W}, P). \tag{18}$$

Now consider a change in output price, holding $\mathbf{W}$ constant:

$$(\partial v_i^*(\cdot)/\partial y)(\partial s(\cdot)/\partial P) = \partial v_i(\cdot)/\partial P.$$

Combined with the reciprocity relationship, this implies that

$$\partial s(\cdot)/\partial W_i = -(\partial v_i^*(\cdot)/\partial y)(\partial s(\cdot)/\partial P).$$

We already know that $\partial s(\cdot)/\partial P$ is positive. Consequently, we know that $\partial s(\cdot)/\partial W_i$ and $\partial v_i^*(\cdot)/\partial y$ have opposite signs. This is an interesting result, because $\partial v_i^*(\cdot)/\partial y$ has a very natural interpretation. Consider the standard isoquant diagram. Given input prices, trace out the locus of cost-minimizing input vectors as the output target is varied. This generates an expansion path similar to the income expansion path encountered in consumer theory. If the path is upward-sloping, so that $\partial v_i^*(\cdot)/\partial y$ is positive for all $i = 1, \ldots, m$, then all factors are said to be normal. However, it is possible for the path to bend backward toward one of the axes, as in Figure 5.6. In this case, input 1 is, over a certain range, said to be an inferior input.

There is a further result associated with factor input inferiority. Consider the marginal cost function

$$m^*(\mathbf{W}, y) = \partial C(\mathbf{W}, y)/\partial y.$$

Again, Young's theorem and Shephard's lemma enable us to infer that

$$\partial m^*(\cdot)/\partial W_i = \partial^2 C(\cdot)/\partial W_i \partial y = \partial^2 C(\cdot)/\partial y \partial W_i = \partial v_i^*(\cdot)/\partial y.$$

Consequently, an increase in W_i lowers marginal cost if and only if factor i is inferior.

The common assumption that isoquants are homothetic with respect to the origin is more than enough to rule out the occurrence of inferior inputs.

Equation (18) is the starting point for a further celebrated property of input demand functions. It is known that both $v_{ii}(\cdot)$ and $v_{ii}^*(\cdot)$ are

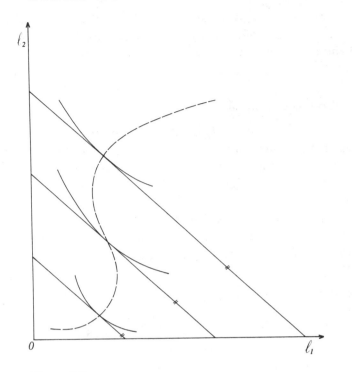

Figure 5.6

negative. We can show that the absolute value of $v_{ii}^*(\cdot)$ is less than that of $v_{ii}(\cdot)$. Consider a change in W_i alone, holding all other input prices and the output price(s) fixed. Differentiation of (18) yields

$$v_{ii}^* + v_{iy}^*(\partial s/\partial W_i) = v_{ii}.$$

We have just shown that v_{iy}^* and $\partial s/\partial W_i$ are of opposite signs. Their product is therefore negative. Consequently,

$$v_{ii}^* > v_{ii}.$$

This means that the response $\partial v_i^*(\mathbf{W}, y)/\partial W_i$ is a smaller negative number than the response $\partial v_i(\mathbf{W}, P)/\partial W_i$, which is the desired result. This is often interpreted as involving a comparison between short-run and long-run responses. Suppose initially a plant is maximizing profits. Suppose further that in the period immediately following a change in the input price the quantity of output that can be sold is fixed. It may be prohibitively costly to break contracts to supply existing customers, or it may take time to generate new orders for one's product. In the long run, output can be adjusted. Then the result states that the short-run own-price response is numerically smaller than the long-run response. This is an example of the Le Chatelier principle, which we shall encounter again in Chapter 7.

5.6   The revenue function

Consider the problem facing a plant that for some reason cannot choose input levels, but instead is already committed to a given endowment vector ℓ. Perhaps contractual arrangements make adjustments through further hiring or firing impossible to achieve. Given its endowment, and a set of given prices for outputs and inputs, the remaining problem is to produce the mix of outputs that will maximize profits, $\mathbf{P} \cdot \mathbf{y} - \mathbf{W} \cdot \ell$. But with ℓ and $\mathbf{W}$ both exogenous, this is equivalent to choosing y to maximize the revenue, $\mathbf{P} \cdot \mathbf{y}$. This problem is summarized by the revenue function, $R(\mathbf{P}, \ell)$:

$$R(\mathbf{P}, \ell) \equiv \max_{y} \{ \mathbf{P} \cdot \mathbf{y} \,|\, (\ell, \mathbf{y}) \text{ feasible} \}. \tag{19}$$

Figure 5.7 shows the revenue-maximizing bundle, $\mathbf{y}^0$, in the two-output example when the output price vector is $\mathbf{P}^0$. The feasible set $0AB$ is determined by the input endowment and available technology. The definition of $R(\cdot)$ does not depend on this set being convex, although an exact duality between $R(\cdot)$ and certain other representations of technology requires such an assumption. Its properties are as follows:

1. $R(\mathbf{P}, \ell)$ is increasing in output prices.
2. $R(\mathbf{P}, \ell)$ is increasing in input quantities.
3. $R(\mathbf{P}, \ell)$ is homogeneous of degree 1 in $\mathbf{P}$.
4. $R(\mathbf{P}, \ell)$ is convex in $\mathbf{P}$.

If $R(\mathbf{P}, \ell)$ is twice differentiable, then its partial derivatives with respect to output prices generate output supply functions:

5. $\partial R(\cdot)/\partial P_j = s_j^*(\mathbf{P}, \ell)$.

In the usual way, the derivative properties of these functions reflect the fact that they themselves are derivatives of a function that is convex in $\mathbf{P}$.

Let us compare the own-price supply response $\partial s_j^*(\mathbf{P}, \ell)/\partial P_j$ with that associated with price-taking behavior, $\partial s_j(\mathbf{P}, \mathbf{W})/\partial P_j$. For notational simplicity, suppose there is a single input. The supply function of a price-taking profit maximizer can be written using $s_j^*(\cdot)$, as long as the "rationed"

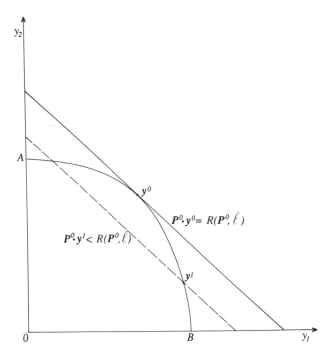

Figure 5.7

input level is put equal to the profit-maximizing level. By definition, then, it must be true that

$$s_j^*(\mathbf{P}, v(\mathbf{P}, W)) = s_j(\mathbf{P}, W). \tag{20}$$

Differentiating with respect to P_j,

$$s_{jj}^* + s_{j\ell}^* v_j = s_{jj}, \tag{21}$$

where $s_{j\ell}^* \equiv \partial s_j^*(\cdot)/\partial \ell$, and $v_j = \partial v(\mathbf{P}, W)/\partial P_j$. To compare s_{jj}^* and s_{jj}, we must say something about $s_{j\ell}^*$ and v_j. Consider the consequences of changing W alone. Differentiating (20) with respect to W,

$$s_{j\ell}^* v_w = s_{jw}.$$

The reciprocity relationship allows us to replace s_{jw} with $-v_j$. Recall that there is a single input, the own-price response of which is negative. Consequently, because $s_{j\ell}^* v_w = -v_j$ and $v_w < 0$, it follows that $s_{j\ell}^*$ and v_j are of the same sign. Their product is therefore positive, so that (21) tells us that $s_{jj} > s_{jj}^*$. This result obviously is similar to the relationship derived in Section 5.5 between short-run and long-run own-price factor demand responses.

5.7   The restricted profit function

The profit function that was discussed in Section 5.4 imagines the plant manager as being able to determine the levels of all outputs and inputs subject only to the technological constraints. Suppose now that some subset of outputs and inputs is fixed in quantity. Partition the output and input vectors and their associated price vectors so that $\mathbf{y} = (\mathbf{y}_m, \mathbf{y}_r)$, $\ell = (\ell_m, \ell_r)$, and so on, where $\mathbf{y}_m$ is the vector of competitively chosen, or marketed, outputs, and $\mathbf{y}_r$ is the vector of exogenously fixed, or rationed, outputs. The manager now chooses $\mathbf{y}_m$ and ℓ_m to maximize profits, given $\mathbf{y}_r$, ℓ_r, and current technology. This defines a restricted profit function:

$$\Pi^*(\mathbf{P}_m, \mathbf{y}_r, \mathbf{W}_m, \ell_r)$$

$$\equiv \max_{\mathbf{y}_m, \ell_m} \{\mathbf{P}_m \cdot \mathbf{y}_m + \mathbf{P}_r \cdot \mathbf{y}_r - \mathbf{W}_m \cdot \ell_m - \mathbf{W}_r \cdot \ell_r \mid (\mathbf{y}, \ell) \text{ feasible}, \mathbf{y}_r, \ell_r \text{ given}\}$$

$$= \mathbf{P}_r \cdot \mathbf{y}_r - \mathbf{W}_r \cdot \ell_r + \max_{\mathbf{y}_m, \ell_m} \{\mathbf{P}_m \cdot \mathbf{y}_m - \mathbf{W}_m \cdot \ell_m \mid (\mathbf{y}, \ell) \text{ feasible}, \mathbf{y}_r, \ell_r \text{ given}\}.$$

Because all prices are exogenous, as are $\mathbf{y}_r$ and ℓ_r, maximization of this expression is equivalent to maximizing $\mathbf{P}_m \cdot \mathbf{y}_m - \mathbf{W}_m \cdot \ell_m$. There should be no need to run through the properties of $\Pi^*(\cdot)$, because they and their derivation should by now be routine. Observe, however, that we have already analyzed special cases. The cost function was obtained by fixing all outputs, thereby focusing attention on the input mix. With all outputs exogenous and all inputs freely chosen, maximizing $\mathbf{P}_r \cdot \mathbf{y}_r - \mathbf{W}_m \cdot \ell_m$ is equivalent to minimizing $\mathbf{W}_m \cdot \ell_m$. The revenue function, by contrast, fixes all input quantities and examines the choice of output mix. I leave it as an exercise for the reader to derive the properties of $\Pi^*(\cdot)$ and, in particular, to generate the supply and demand functions for marketed outputs and inputs, and the inverse supply and demand functions for rationed outputs and inputs.

5.8   The distance function

The technology of a plant that produces a single output may be described, as we did in Section 5.1, by the direct production function. If there are many outputs, however, an alternative representation in quantity space is

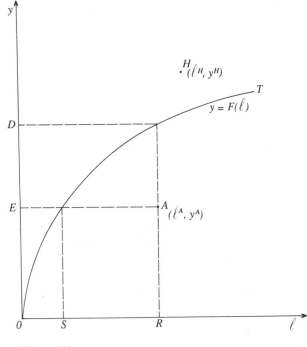

Figure 5.8

provided by the distance function. This turns out to have some advantages. In the first place, the distance function is a dual of the cost function. Second, only under certain special circumstances can a multiple-output technology be described by a set of production functions, one for each output. Although such a description is often employed, I suspect that many who write down a set of production functions are unaware of the assumptions necessary to justify such a procedure. The distance function, by contrast, provides a much more general description of a technology.

Although the distance function comes into its own when the technology involves many inputs and many outputs, the single-input, single-output example provides a useful introduction to its use in production theory. Suppose a technology is represented by $0T$ in Figure 5.8. One can think of many reasons why one might observe a pair of input and output levels that do not lie on the production function defining the maximum output given the prevailing input, but instead lie elsewhere within the feasible set. Suppose we observe the point A. If we believed that the true production function was graphed by $0T$, we would conclude that the same level of output y^A, could be produced using only a fraction, $0S/0R$, of the observed input quantity, ℓ^A. Apart from the fact that we have only one input, this thought experiment is clearly similar to that of Section 3.5, where we introduced the distance function in consumer theory by considering the fraction of the observed bundle that was just sufficient to attain a target utility level. If we take the proportion $0S/0R$ of the input level ℓ^A, this will provide just enough to produce the given output level, y^A. By convention, we consider the reciprocal: $0R/0S$ is the largest scalar by which we can divide ℓ^A and still be able to produce y^A. Formally, consider the scalar δ^*, defined by the maximizing problem:

$$\delta^* \equiv D_I(\ell^A, y^A) \equiv \max_{\delta}\{\delta \mid F(\ell^A/\delta) \geq y^A\}. \tag{22}$$

As I have indicated, the maximum value of δ depends on the choice of ℓ^A and y^A. The function that expresses this dependence is a distance function. Comparison of (22) with equation (12) of Chapter 3 reveals that I have added a subscript. $D_I(\cdot)$ is known as an input distance function, and it concerns a rescaling of the input level consistent with a given target output. Confronted with allocation A in Figure 5.8, one might equally well consider the maximum amount by which output could be expanded in the light of the given technology and the observed input level ℓ^A. As drawn, the quantity ℓ^A permits us, at most, to produce $0D/0E$ times the output level y^A. Again, it is more usual to focus on the reciprocal: $0E/0D$ is the smallest scalar by which we can divide y^A and still be able to produce the implied output level with ℓ^A. Formally, consider the scalar θ^*, defined by the minimizing problem:

$$\theta^* \equiv D_0(\ell^A, y^A) \equiv \min_{\theta}\{\theta \mid y^A/\theta \leq F(\ell^A)\}. \tag{23}$$

The distance function $D_0(\cdot)$ considers rescalings of output consistent with a given technology and a given input quantity ℓ^A. It is called an output distance function.

At the beginning of this section I invited the reader to imagine an actual, or observed, allocation (ℓ^A, y^A). Necessarily, an observed allocation must lie in the feasible set, on or below $0T$ in Figure 5.8. Had (ℓ^A, y^A) happened to lie on $0T$, both the input and the output distance functions would have taken the value 1. At points such as A, which suggest inefficiency of some kind, in that input is not being used to full advantage, it is easy to check that $D_I(\cdot) > 1$ and $D_0(\cdot) < 1$. There is nothing to stop us from imagining hypothetical allocations such as H, outside the feasible set. Both distance functions can be defined at such points. At H, the input

ℓ^H would need to be increased in order to render y^H obtainable. Conversely, y^H would have to be reduced in order to generate an output target that would be feasible given ℓ^H. Thus, at H, $D_I(\cdot) < 1$ and $D_0(\cdot) > 1$.

In Chapter 3, my discussion of the distance function concentrated on the input distance function, because this has been the more widely discussed of the two. For the same reason, the rest of this chapter will also concentrate on the input distance function. I include source citations to the output distance function at the end of the chapter. I now introduce the notion of the input distance function when there are many inputs and many outputs.

Suppose there is a technology that determines what output mixes, denoted by the vector $\mathbf{y}$, can be obtained from various given input endowments ℓ. The production possibilities set is that set of values of ℓ and $\mathbf{y}$ such that $(\mathbf{y}, \ell)$ is feasible. Suppose now we take an arbitrary pair of vectors, $\mathbf{y}^0$ and ℓ^0, and that it so happens that ℓ^0 is more than sufficient to enable production of $\mathbf{y}^0$. Then ℓ^0 can be scaled down – that is, every component of ℓ^0 can be reduced by the same proportion – and still allow $\mathbf{y}^0$ to be produced. There is some proportional reduction in ℓ^0 that just, but only just, permits production of the target $\mathbf{y}^0$. This thought experiment leads to our definition of the distance function. For given vectors ℓ and $\mathbf{y}$, it is defined as

$$D_I(\mathbf{y}, \ell) \equiv \max_{\delta}\{\delta \mid (1/\delta)\ell, \mathbf{y}) \text{ feasible}\}. \qquad (24)$$

If there is only one output, then the definition is formally identical with that given in Chapter 3 in the context of consumer theory. The replacement of a scalar output by a vector introduces no new complications. The properties of $D_I(\mathbf{y}, \ell)$ are unchanged, and their demonstration is along the lines used in Chapter 3. Specifically:

1. $D_I(\mathbf{y}, \ell)$ is decreasing in each output level.
2. $D_I(\mathbf{y}, \ell)$ is increasing in each input level.
3. $D_I(\mathbf{y}, \ell)$ is homogeneous of degree 1 in ℓ.
4. $D_I(\mathbf{y}, \ell)$ is concave in ℓ.

Finally, if $D_I(\mathbf{y}, \ell)$ is everywhere twice differentiable, then we know that

5. $\partial D_I(\mathbf{y}, \ell)/\partial \ell_i = \omega_i(\mathbf{y}, \ell)$, the marginal product, or inverse demand function, of input i.

The properties of the derivatives of $\omega_i(\cdot)$, such as negative own-quantity responses, symmetry, and so on, can be generated by analyzing the second derivatives of the concave distance function.

It remains possible, as we saw in Section 3.6, to define the distance function in a way that makes its duality with the cost function explicit – indeed, this is the natural way to generate $\omega_i(\cdot)$. We normalize input prices so that the minimum cost of producing the target vector of outputs is unity – that is, put $C(\mathbf{W}, \mathbf{y}) = 1$. Then the distance function can be defined as

$$D_I(\boldsymbol{\ell}, \mathbf{y}) \equiv \min_{\mathbf{W}} \{\mathbf{W} \cdot \boldsymbol{\ell} \mid C(\mathbf{W}, \mathbf{y}) = 1\}. \tag{25}$$

The symmetric expression for the cost function is

$$C(\mathbf{W}, \mathbf{y}) \equiv \min_{\boldsymbol{\ell}} \{\mathbf{W} \cdot \boldsymbol{\ell} \mid D_I(\boldsymbol{\ell}, \mathbf{y}) = 1\}. \tag{26}$$

This is Shephard duality again, in the context of producer theory. It may help to recall that putting $D_I(\cdot)$ equal to unity is equivalent to choosing input and output vectors on the boundary of the feasible production set. This duality is useful in establishing one further property concerning the partial derivative $\partial D_I(\cdot)/\partial y_i$. Suppose that initially $D_I(\boldsymbol{\ell}, \mathbf{y})$ is unity. Consider a change in y_i. The envelope theorem tells us that the derivative $\partial D_I(\cdot)/\partial y_i$ is equal to the derivative $\partial L(\cdot)/\partial y_i$, where $L(\cdot)$ is the Lagrangian associated with (25). Consequently,

$$\partial D_I(\cdot)/\partial y_i = \lambda \partial C(\cdot)/\partial y_i,$$

where λ is the Lagrangian multiplier. However, the first-order condition associated with the minimization problem requires that $\partial L(\cdot)/\partial W_k = \ell_k + \lambda \partial C(\cdot)/\partial W_k = 0$. But if $D_I(\cdot)$ is unity, then the reference quantity ℓ_k and the quantity that just attains $\mathbf{y}$ are one and the same, so that $\lambda = -1$. Consequently, we can infer

$$-\partial D_I(\boldsymbol{\ell}, \mathbf{y})/\partial y_i = \partial C(\mathbf{W}, \mathbf{y})/\partial y_i.$$

This is simply the marginal cost of the ith output, $\phi_i(\boldsymbol{\ell}, \mathbf{y})$.

A further interpretation of the multipliers associated with (25) and (26) is possible and may be helpful in some contexts. We define a slightly modified cost function, $C^*(\boldsymbol{\ell}, \mathbf{y}, \alpha)$, as

$$C^*(\boldsymbol{\ell}, \mathbf{y}, \alpha) \equiv \min_{\boldsymbol{\ell}} \{\mathbf{W} \cdot \boldsymbol{\ell} \mid D(\boldsymbol{\ell}, \mathbf{y}) = \alpha\}. \tag{26'}$$

It is easy to see that $C^*(\cdot)$ is homogeneous of degree 1 in α. In Figure 5.9 an isoquant is shown as a continuous curve. Along the isoquant, $D(\boldsymbol{\ell}, \mathbf{y}) = 1$. Values of ℓ_1 and ℓ_2 for which $D(\boldsymbol{\ell}, \mathbf{y}) = 2$ lie on the dashed line that is simply a radial expansion of the original isoquant. It is the locus of points Y such that $0Y = 20X$. Conversely, values of ℓ_1 and ℓ_2 for which $D(\boldsymbol{\ell}, \mathbf{y}) = \frac{1}{2}$ are on a locus of points such as Z, where $0Z = 0X/2$. These

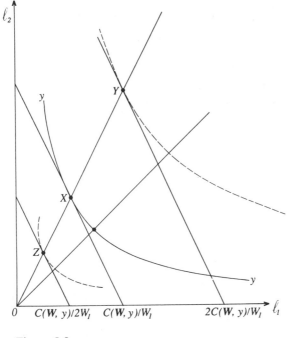

Figure 5.9

dashed curves, which are not, in general, isoquants, but are simply defined, as before, as radial expansions or contractions of the original isoquant, form a homothetic system. The geometry makes very clear the fact
that

$$C^*(\mathbf{W}, \mathbf{y}, 2) = 2C^*(\mathbf{W}, \mathbf{y}, 1) = 2C(\mathbf{W}, \mathbf{y}),$$

and

$$C^*(\mathbf{W}, \mathbf{y}, \tfrac{1}{2}) = \tfrac{1}{2}C^*(\mathbf{W}, \mathbf{y}, 1) = \tfrac{1}{2}C(\mathbf{W}, \mathbf{y}).$$

More generally,

$$C^*(\mathbf{W}, \mathbf{y}, \alpha) = \alpha C(\mathbf{W}, \mathbf{y}).$$

If we now return to (26′), consider the associated Lagrangian, $L(\cdot)$, and
exploit the envelope theorem, we find that

$$\partial C^*(\cdot)/\partial \alpha = \partial L(\cdot)/\partial \alpha = \lambda(\mathbf{W}, \mathbf{y}, \alpha),$$

where $\lambda(\cdot)$ is the multiplier. In the neighborhood of $\alpha = 1$, therefore, using
the observation that $C^*(\cdot) = \alpha C(\cdot)$, we have

$$C(\mathbf{W}, \mathbf{y}) = \lambda(\mathbf{W}, \mathbf{y}).$$

The value of the Lagrange multiplier at the optimum, in short, can be interpreted as the minimum cost of producing $\mathbf{y}$ when facing input prices $\mathbf{W}$. This is derived by Jacobsen (1972) and Färe (1988, pp. 90–1), and as the latter author points out, it can help to provide useful interpretations of certain relationships. This interpretation carries over into consumer theory just as the results discussed in Section 3.5 carry over into production theory.

5.9   Example of a distance function

Consider the following example of an input distance function describing a two-input, two-output homothetic technology:

$$D_I(\ell, \mathbf{y}) = \sqrt{\ell_1 \ell_2} / \sqrt{y_1^2 + y_2^2}. \tag{27}$$

For given values of the inputs, the attainable outputs are calculated by putting $D_I(\cdot) = 1$. The implied production possibilities frontier is then given by $\sqrt{y_1^2 + y_2^2} = \sqrt{\ell_1 \ell_2}$, which is a constant. It is therefore a quarter circle, and the production possibilities set is clearly convex. If, on the other hand, output levels are fixed, then the isoquant in input space is a rectangular hyperbola. Furthermore, if $(\ell_1^0, \ell_2^0, y_1^0, y_2^0)$ is just feasible, so is $(\theta\ell_1^0, \theta\ell_2^0, \theta y_1^0, \theta y_2^0)$. $D(\cdot)$ therefore describes a constant-returns-to-scale technology that is convex.

Let us generate the cost function of this technology. We know that it can be defined as

$$C(\mathbf{W}, \mathbf{y}) \equiv \min_{\ell} \{ \mathbf{W} \cdot \ell \mid \sqrt{\ell_1 \ell_2} / \sqrt{y_1^2 + y_2^2} = 1 \}.$$

The first-order conditions imply that the optimal input levels are

$$v_1^*(\cdot) = \sqrt{W_2(y_1^2 + y_2^2)/W_1} \quad \text{and} \quad v_2^*(\cdot) = \sqrt{W_1(y_1^2 + y_2^2)/W_2}.$$

Substituting these factor input demand functions into the expression for costs yields

$$C(\mathbf{W}, \mathbf{y}) = \mathbf{W} \cdot \mathbf{v}^*(\cdot) = 2\sqrt{W_1 W_2(y_1^2 + y_2^2)}.$$

If we had been given $C(\cdot)$, a similar chain of reasoning would have generated the distance function (25), thereby demonstrating the informational equivalence of the two functions. $C(\cdot)$ and $D_I(\cdot)$ describe the same technology.

Now consider the partial derivative $\partial D_I(\cdot)/\partial \ell_i$. This equals $D_I(\cdot)/2\ell_i$. If $(\ell, \mathbf{y})$ is chosen to be on the production possibilities frontier, so that $D_I(\cdot)$ is initially unity, we therefore have

$$\partial D_I(\cdot)/\partial \ell_i = \omega_i(\ell, \mathbf{y}) = 1/2\ell_i.$$

Recall that $\partial D_I(\cdot)/\partial \ell_i$ is the demand, or virtual, price of factor i. The inverse demand function, $\omega_i(\cdot)$, is independent of all output levels and all factor input levels save ℓ_i. In elasticity form,

$$(\partial D_I(\cdot)/\partial \ell_i)(\ell_i/D_I(\cdot)) = \omega_i(\cdot)\ell_i = \tfrac{1}{2}.$$

This says that when valued at its demand price, the cost of input i is $\tfrac{1}{2}$. Upon reflection, this is not surprising. The present example reflects, on the input side, a Cobb–Douglas technology. This is easily seen by replacing the joint outputs by a single output, so that $D_I(\cdot) = \sqrt{\ell_1 \ell_2}/y$. Differentiating the cost function yields the dual result

$$\partial C(\cdot)/\partial W_i \equiv v_i(\mathbf{W}, y) = C(\cdot)/2W_i,$$

from which

$$(\partial C(\cdot)/\partial W_i)(W_i/C(\cdot)) = W_i v_i(\cdot)/C(\cdot) = \tfrac{1}{2}.$$

This is the familiar Cobb–Douglas property that states that if factors are chosen to minimize costs, then factor i's share in the total cost is constant – in this case, it equals $\tfrac{1}{2}$.

As a further exercise, consider the implied revenue function:

$$R(\ell, \mathbf{P}) = \max\{\mathbf{P} \cdot \mathbf{y} \mid \sqrt{\ell_1 \ell_2}/\sqrt{y_1^2 + y_2^2} = 1\}.$$

The first-order conditions imply output supply functions of the form

$$s_1^*(\cdot) = P_1\sqrt{\ell_1 \ell_2}/(P_1^2 + P_2^2), \qquad s_2^*(\cdot) = P_2\sqrt{\ell_1 \ell_2}/(P_1^2 + P_2^2).$$

The revenue function itself is obtained by substituting for these optimal values of output:

$$R(\cdot) = P_1 s_1^*(\cdot) + P_2 s_2^*(\cdot) = \sqrt{\ell_1 \ell_2 (P_1^2 + P_2^2)}.$$

Notice that the ratio of outputs, $s_1^*(\cdot)/s_2^*(\cdot)$, is independent of both ℓ_1 and ℓ_2. It is easy to check that the responses $\partial s_j^*(\ell, \mathbf{P})/\partial \ell_i$ are all positive. This contrasts with the properties of such responses in a well-known model of production, the Heckscher–Ohlin model, which we shall encounter in Chapter 6.

The derivatives of $R(\cdot)$ with respect to input levels yield inverse demand functions. To distinguish these from the $\omega_i(\cdot)$ functions derived from $D_I(\cdot)$, denote them by $\omega_i^*(\cdot)$:

$$\partial R(\cdot)/\partial \ell_1 = \omega_1^*(\ell, \mathbf{P}) = \sqrt{(\ell_2/\ell_1)(P_1^2 + P_2^2)}/2$$
$$= R(\cdot)/2\ell_1.$$

If input prices are normalized by requiring $R(\cdot) = 1$, this immediately confirms that the virtual price, or marginal productivity, of input i depends on ℓ_1 alone. Because the technology reflects constant returns to scale, this normalization is equivalent to setting the cost function equal to unity.

The constant-returns-to-scale assumption has one further significant implication – namely, the fact that a price-taking profit function $\Pi(\mathbf{P}, \mathbf{W})$ is not well defined. Any attempt to derive it will confirm this and will result in a condition involving $\mathbf{P}$ and $\mathbf{W}$ that requires zero profits. If this condition is met, input and output choices are not uniquely determined. In other circumstances, either the zero level of activity is the unique optimum or else further expansion of activity will always increase profits, thereby implying no finite profit-maximizing allocation.

A slight modification of the example enables us to model variable returns to scale and, in the case of decreasing returns, to define the profit function $\Pi(\mathbf{P}, \mathbf{W})$. Consider the following generalization of (25):

$$D_I(\cdot) = \sqrt{\ell_1 \ell_2}/(y_1^2 + y_2^2)^\rho. \tag{28}$$

If $\rho > \frac{1}{2}$, there are decreasing returns, because a doubling of inputs will be associated with less than a doubling of outputs if $D_I(\cdot) = 1$. Suppose $\rho = 1$. The profit function is defined as

$$\Pi(\mathbf{P}, \mathbf{W}) = \max_{y, \ell} \{\mathbf{P} \cdot \mathbf{y} - \mathbf{W} \cdot \ell \mid \sqrt{\ell_1 \ell_2} = y_1^2 + y_2^2\}.$$

Slightly tedious manipulation of first-order conditions yields the following input demand and output supply functions:

$$v_1(\cdot) = \frac{P_1^2 + P_2^2}{16 W_1 W_2} \sqrt{W_2/W_1}, \qquad v_2(\cdot) = \frac{P_1^2 + P_2^2}{16 W_1 W_2} \sqrt{W_1/W_2},$$
$$s_1(\cdot) = P_1/4\sqrt{W_1 W_2}, \qquad s_2(\cdot) = P_2/4\sqrt{W_1 W_2}.$$

Substitution of these functions into the profit function yields

$$\Pi(\mathbf{P}, \mathbf{W}) = \mathbf{P} \cdot \mathbf{s}(\cdot) - \mathbf{W} \cdot \mathbf{v}(\cdot) = (P_1^2 + P_2^2)/8\sqrt{W_1 W_2}. \tag{29}$$

This, then, is the profit function representation of the technology described by (26) when $\rho = 1$.

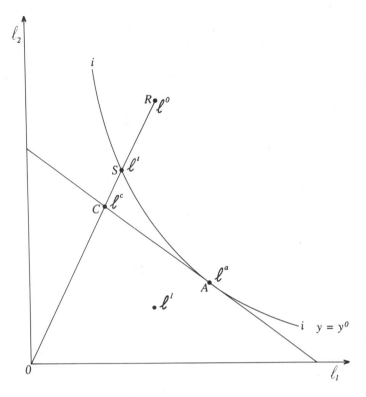

Figure 5.10

This example should be sufficient to substantiate the claim that the distance function contains all economically relevant information about the technology. A further significant aspect of the example will be discussed in Chapter 6.

5.10 The measurement of production efficiency

Consider a production plant with access to a constant-returns-to-scale technology for converting two inputs into a single homogeneous output. Figure 5.10 shows the isoquant ii corresponding to the level of output y^0. By definition, if the input mix ℓ^1 lies below and to the left of ii, we shall not observe the allocation (y^0, ℓ^1). However, it is quite conceivable that we might observe the allocation (y^0, ℓ^0), where ℓ^0 lies above and to the right of ii. The input bundle ℓ^0 is more than enough to produce y^0, but one can imagine the plant failing to use its resources as efficiently as the best available technology allows. This raises the possibility of defining a measure of the extent of such inefficiency. One such measure is suggested by Farrell (1957). The point S represents an efficient way of producing the output y^0 given that factors are employed in the same ratio as at the point R. The output y^0 can therefore just be produced using the fraction $0S/0R$ of the quantities (ℓ_1^0, ℓ_2^0). Conversely, in view of the constant-returns-to-scale assumption, the input vector (ℓ_1^0, ℓ_2^0) can, if used efficiently, produce $0R/0S$ times as much output as the level y^0. Farrell suggests using the ratio $0S/0R$ as a measure of the technical efficiency associated with the allocation (y^0, ℓ^0). A plant that manages to attain the output level implied by its production function, by employing the technically efficient vector ℓ', operates with a technical efficiency of unity, or 100%, whereas if it falls short of this goal its technical efficiency lies between zero and 100%. Notice that Farrell's measure of technical efficiency is simply the inverse of the distance function. It is also identical with Debreu's notion of the coefficient of resource utilization (Debreu 1951, pp. 284–5; 1954a, p. 14).

Suppose that the plant is operating at 100% technical efficiency at, say, S. This is not enough to ensure that it is operating with economic efficiency in the sense that it is minimizing the cost of producing y^0. Suppose it faces given factor prices, and the relative price is reflected in the slope of the tangent at A. Then A represents the least-cost way of producing y^0. Farrell suggests using the ratio $0C/0S$ as a measure of what he calls the price efficiency (and other authors call allocative efficiency) of the allocation S. This is simply the ratio of the minimum cost of producing y^0, attained by using the allocatively efficient vector ℓ^a, to the cost of the technically efficient allocation at S, (y^0, ℓ'). If the observed quantities are (y^0, ℓ^0), the overall efficiency of the plant can be measured by the ratio $0C/0R$, which is simply the product of the measures of technical and allocative efficiency. If the relative factor prices that support production at A are denoted by $\mathbf{W}$, this statement can be summarized as

$$(\mathbf{W} \cdot \ell^a / \mathbf{W} \cdot \ell')(\mathbf{W} \cdot \ell' / \mathbf{W} \cdot \ell^0) = \mathbf{W} \cdot \ell^a / \mathbf{W} \cdot \ell^0 \qquad (30)$$

$$\left(\begin{array}{c}\text{index of}\\\text{allocative efficiency}\end{array}\right)\left(\begin{array}{c}\text{index of}\\\text{technical efficiency}\end{array}\right) = \begin{array}{c}\text{index of}\\\text{overall efficiency.}\end{array}$$

Subsequent literature, cited at the end of this chapter, has addressed a number of questions raised by Farrell's seminal contribution and has generalized his analysis. For example, the assumption that the production function exhibits constant returns to scale has been relaxed, as has that of homotheticity. In addition, the implications of congestion have been explored. Input congestion arises when an increase in some input leads to a reduction in the maximum attainable output, and it is represented by positively sloped sections of isoquants. Output congestion arises when a reduction in some output is not possible with the given inputs. For example, it may not be possible to reduce the output of toxic chemical wastes while maintaining a given steel output.

Of more interest to readers of this book is the observation that our knowledge of the production process may be embodied in a cost function rather than in a production function. It is therefore useful to be able to derive the efficiency measures from the cost function. Suppose $C(\mathbf{W}, y)$ is known. The variables whose values are known are y^0, ℓ^0, and $\mathbf{W}$. The task is to solve for ℓ^a, ℓ^c, and ℓ^t.

Kopp and Diewert (1982) suggest a procedure that uses the information contained in $C(\mathbf{W}, y)$ to solve for these three vectors of input quantities. After suitable manipulation, their algorithm involves solving $(2n-1)$ equations. More recently, Zieschang (1983) has suggested an alternative procedure that involves solving only $(n-1)$ equations. If n is large, this may involve a considerable saving of computing effort. Like all neat ideas, Zieschang's observation is simple once understood. First, let us express the decomposition of overall efficiency into allocative and technical components slightly differently. We have

$$\begin{pmatrix} \text{index of} \\ \text{overall efficiency} \end{pmatrix} = \begin{pmatrix} \text{index of} \\ \text{allocative efficiency} \end{pmatrix} \begin{pmatrix} \text{index of} \\ \text{technical efficiency} \end{pmatrix}$$

$$0C/0R = (0C/0S)(0S/0R) \tag{31}$$

$$C(\mathbf{W}, y)/\mathbf{W} \cdot \ell^0 = (0C/0S)(1/D(\ell^0, y)).$$

Because $\mathbf{W}$, y, and ℓ^0 are observed and $C(\mathbf{W}, y)$ is assumed to be known, all that is required is that we solve for $D(\cdot)$. This can be done without bothering to produce explicit solutions for the unobserved input quantities, by simply exploiting Shephard duality. Recall the duality relationship expressed in equation (23). Writing out the Lagrangian expression associated with the minimizing problem, and equating the appropriate partial derivatives to zero, we obtain

$$\ell_i - \lambda \partial C(\mathbf{W}, y)/\partial W_i = 0, \quad i = 1, \dots, n,$$

$$C(\mathbf{W}, y) = 1.$$

Although there are $(n+1)$ equations here, the fact that we are not interested in solving for λ, together with the homogeneity properties of $C(\cdot)$ with respect to $\mathbf{W}$, allows us to collapse it to a system of $(n-1)$

equations that can be used to solve for the $(n-1)$ relative input prices $W_1/W_n, W_2/W_n, \ldots, W_{n-1}/W_n$ in terms of ℓ and y. Because, at an optimum, $C(\mathbf{W}, y) = \mathbf{W} \cdot \ell = 1$, W_n is readily expressed as

$$W_n = 1/[(W_1/W_n)\ell_1 + (W_2/W_n)\ell_2 + \cdots + (W_{n-1}/W_n)\ell_{n-1} + \ell_n].$$

The hard work, then, is the derivation of solutions for W_i/W_n for $i = 1, \ldots, (n-1)$. Having done this, the solutions can be plugged into the objective function in (25). This yields the desired distance function, because the W_i variables have been replaced by ℓ and y, the true arguments of a distance function. This done, (31) allows us to calculate the overall index, the technical efficiency index, and thereby as a residual the allocative efficiency index, in a straightforward manner. Duality makes the analysis relatively simple. The difficult part is the collection of data and their transformation into an accurate representation of the technology.

5.11   Concluding comments and suggestions for further study

An important reference for anyone wishing to learn more about the use of duality in modern production theory is the two-volume collection of papers edited by Fuss and McFadden (1978). In particular, McFadden (1978) discusses most of the functions referred to in this chapter and the relationships between them. Diewert (1973a, 1974a) discusses some of the flexible functional forms that might be used for profit, revenue, and other functions of interest in producer theory. Chambers (1988) provides a useful book-length exposition. His selection of topics is a little different from mine, which makes his book a useful complement to this one. For example, he does not use the distance function. He does, however, discuss technical change and also the empirical applications of production theory.

Indirect production functions are discussed by Shephard (1970, pp. 105–13), who calls them cost-limited maximal output functions. Diewert (1978a) and Hanoch (1978) also briefly mention them. Shephard (1974) provides a more extended analysis of their properties, and his Preface briefly provides some motivation. Because indirect production functions are concerned with what can be obtained from a given expenditure on inputs, and because public-sector firms, in particular, often operate under explicit restrictions on their budgets, it would seem that indirect production functions do have relevance for the evaluation of their performance. This theme has been taken up recently by Färe, Grosskopf, and Lovell (1988). An indirect production function is estimated by Kim (1988).

Profit functions were used by Hotelling (1932), who exploited the envelope property enshrined in Hotelling's lemma. His model was of a consumer, but contained no explicit budget constraint. This reflects the idea that in any single period, the consumer can lend or borrow at given rates. A suitable reinterpretation of Hotelling's model yields precisely the firm's profit function. His analysis is closely related to the idea of Frisch demand functions, which are discussed in Chapter 6. The Fuss–McFadden volumes include a useful analysis of profit functions by Lau (1978).

The likelihood of inferior inputs and their comparative static implications have attracted some interest – see, for example, Bear (1965) and Silberberg (1974). Among the comparative static results that have been derived, most of which are straightforward if the appropriate dual formulation is used, the most celebrated are those that reflect Le Chatelier's principle. Samuelson (1947) introduced this to economists, and Gorman (1984) has provided a more modern treatment.

Revenue functions arise very naturally in trade theorists' models. Woodland (1977) provided a rigorous justification of modeling the competitive production sector by means of a single revenue, or national product, function, a device earlier exploited by Samuelson (1953a), Pearce (1970), Chipman (1972), and Wegge (1974). Dixit and Norman (1980, pp. 30–43) and Woodland (1982, pp. 53–6, 123–34) have provided simple expositions. The restricted profit function was covered by Lau (1976).

In view of the prominence given to the distance function by Shephard (1953, 1970) in his development of duality theorems, it is surprising that it has received so little attention since then. The output distance function first appeared in the work of Shephard (1970). Färe (1988) discussed both the input and output distance functions and analyzed the relationship between the two. Distance functions are mentioned sporadically in the Fuss and McFadden (1978) volumes, but are rarely exploited systematically in producer theory. Perhaps their time is yet to come.

I thought at one time that the example given in Section 5.9 was novel, but should have known better – see Samuelson (1966). I shall have occasion to refer to this example again in Chapter 6, where the potential usefulness of the distance function as a representation of technology in quantity space is emphasized.

It is still worthwhile to read Farrell's lucid discussion of the measurement of productive efficiency. Much subsequent work has drawn heavily on his suggestions. At the same time, a number of modifications and extensions have been developed. Färe and Lovell (1978) set out a number of desirable characteristics that should be possessed by an efficiency measure, and they argued that Farrell's measure possesses them only under very restrictive assumptions. They then suggested an alternative measure that has desirable properties under more general assumptions regarding technology than those employed by Farrell. Kopp (1981) generalized the analysis to nonhomothetic production technologies and estimated the underlying technology using frontier production functions. The use of frontier functions as the basis for estimating a technology has been surveyed by Schmidt (1985–6). Zieschang's suggested decomposition algorithm involves recovering the reciprocal of $D(\cdot)$ rather than $D(\cdot)$ itself. The optimizing problem is therefore slightly different from the one stated in Section 5.10. However, the present treatment accurately conveys the essence of the approach. A useful and comprehensive discussion of many alternative measures and of their properties can be found in Färe, Grosskopf, and Lovell (1985).

The nonparametric approach to estimation and testing, to which I briefly referred in Chapter 2 in the context of consumer theory, has also been applied to producer theory. Again, Afriat (1972) was a pioneer, and Varian (1984a) has provided a development and exposition of the economic elements of this approach. Other important papers are those by Hanoch and Rothschild (1972) and Diewert and Parkan (1983). Readers will quickly discover much common ground between this body of literature and the analysis of productive efficiency.

CHAPTER 6

Consumer and producer behavior: More useful topics

Many theoretical and empirical applications of the models of consumer and producer behavior make use of substantial modifications, extensions, or simple special cases of the structure set out in Chapters 2 to 5. This chapter deals with a number of these variations on the basic theme in which the insights of duality prove especially helpful.

6.1   Induced preferences

The characteristics model

The basic model of consumer behavior assumes that the individual has preferences over a set of objects, called commodities, and that those same commodities can be exchanged in competitive markets. Consequently, the same quantities appear in both the utility function and the budget constraint. A number of authors, among them Gorman (1956) and Lancaster (1966, 1971), have explored models that distinguish between the commodities bought and sold in markets and the characteristics that consumers care about. For example, suppose we are concerned with foodstuffs simply from a nutritional point of view. The objects bought in the market are the foodstuffs, but the objects of preference are vitamins and calories. The household production model, of which Lancaster's characteristics approach is a special case, imagines a technology whereby marketed goods generate characteristics. The elements of such a model are as follows:

1.   A utility function defined over characteristics:

$$U(\cdot) = U(\mathbf{z}),$$

where $\mathbf{z}$ is a vector of characteristics. For the moment, I shall suppose that $U(\cdot)$ has the usual properties. It is a continuous, twice-differentiable, strictly increasing and strictly quasi-concave function of $\mathbf{z}$.

139

2.   A mapping from marketed goods to characteristics. This reflects, essentially, a production technology of the kind analyzed in Chapter 5. Marketed goods are the inputs, and characteristics are the outputs. In any application, specific structure will be imposed on this mapping. For the moment, denote it by the distance function:

$$D(\mathbf{q}, \mathbf{z}) \geq 1.$$

3.   A budget constraint:

$$\mathbf{P} \cdot \mathbf{q} \leq M.$$

The original purpose for which Lancaster developed this model made it important for him to render explicit the process by which goods are transformed into characteristics and to perform his analysis in terms of characteristics. However, there are situations in which, having started with characteristics, we wish to consider how the utility function is related to goods. To put this another way, we wish to study the properties of the implied, or induced, preferences over marketed goods. Under common assumptions, we can define a utility function $\hat{U}(\mathbf{q})$ and establish simple properties that $\hat{U}(\cdot)$ must possess.

As an example, consider Lancaster's own model. Suppose that each unit of marketed good i generates a fixed amount, β_{ij}, of the characteristic j. This reflects a constant-coefficients technology. We can allow each good to produce jointly a number of characteristics – a unit of milk, for example, generates calories, proteins, vitamins, and so on – and each characteristic has many potential sources. The technological constraint can be written as a set of linear relationships:

$$z_1 = \beta_{11}q_1 + \beta_{21}q_2 + \cdots + \beta_{m1}q_m$$
$$\vdots$$
$$z_n = \beta_{1n}q_1 + \qquad \cdots \qquad + \beta_{mn}q_m.$$

Note that no assumption has been made concerning the relative numbers of goods and characteristics. None, indeed, is necessary for the main result that I wish to show. This is the claim that the individual's preferences may be represented by a utility function defined over marketed goods, $\hat{U}(\mathbf{q})$, that is itself quasi-concave. To establish the existence of a function $\hat{U}(\cdot)$ is beyond the scope of this treatment. If existence is taken for granted, quasi-concavity is easy to show. Suppose that when confronted with the vector $\mathbf{q}'$ the individual can generate the vector of characteristics $\mathbf{z}' = \mathbf{B} \cdot \mathbf{q}'$ and can attain the utility level $u' = \hat{U}(\mathbf{q}') = U(\mathbf{z}')$. Similarly, suppose that the vector $\mathbf{q}''$ implies $\mathbf{z}'' = \mathbf{B} \cdot \mathbf{q}''$ and $u'' = \hat{U}(\mathbf{q}'') =$

$U(\mathbf{z}'')$. Without loss of generality, assume $u' \ge u''$. Then the convex combination $\theta \mathbf{q}' + (1 - \theta)\mathbf{q}''$, where $0 \le \theta \le 1$, permits attainment of the vector of characteristics $\mathbf{B} \cdot (\theta \mathbf{q}' + (1 - \theta)\mathbf{q}'')$, which in turn is a convex combination of the vectors $\mathbf{z}'$ and $\mathbf{z}''$, because

$$\mathbf{B} \cdot (\theta \mathbf{q}' + (1 - \theta)\mathbf{q}'') = \theta(\mathbf{B} \cdot \mathbf{q}') + (1 - \theta)(\mathbf{B} \cdot \mathbf{q}'')$$
$$= \theta \mathbf{z}' + (1 - \theta)\mathbf{z}''.$$

Because $U(\mathbf{z})$ is quasi-concave, the bundle of characteristics $\theta \mathbf{z}' + (1 - \theta)\mathbf{z}''$ generates at least as high a level of utility as u''. But this bundle is itself generated by the linear combination of goods $\theta \mathbf{q}' + (1 - \theta)\mathbf{q}''$. Hence,

$$\hat{U}(\theta \mathbf{q}' + (1 - \theta)\mathbf{q}'') \ge \hat{U}(\mathbf{q}'').$$

This confirms that $\hat{U}(\mathbf{q})$ is quasi-concave. A consumer with Lancaster's problem can therefore be modeled, if we wish, as maximizing an orthodox utility function $\hat{U}(\mathbf{q})$ subject to the single budget constraint $\mathbf{P} \cdot \mathbf{q} = M$.

As I have mentioned, Lancaster preferred to work with the model defined over characteristics. However, for many purposes it is useful, having started with the "primitive" preferences over characteristics, to work in terms of induced preferences over goods. For example, finance theory deals with individual and aggregate demands for securities, of which non-interest-bearing money is an example. Typically, such securities are imagined as generating characteristics, which are interpreted as vectors of dated or contingent commodities. It is these, not securities themselves, that form the primitive objects of preference. An implication of the present analysis, which is discussed more rigorously and at a more general level by Milne (1981), is that demand functions for securities may be defined that have the properties of the demand functions discussed in Chapters 2 and 3. The continuing controversies in the theory of the demand for money concern the precise nature of the services or characteristics that money generates. Another example is the supply of labor. For most of us, labor is supplied not merely for its own sake, but because it generates a characteristic called purchasing power. The labor/leisure choice is made more complex by the fact that other, perhaps less desirable, characteristics are associated with work.

The linear characteristics model has some interesting properties. Let there be two marketed goods, q_1 and q_2, and two characteristics, z_1 and z_2. The purchase of each unit of q_1 generates 2 units of z_1 and 1 of z_2. Each unit of q_2 generates 1 unit of z_1 and 2 of z_2. The prices of the marketed goods are both unity, so that an income of, say, 12 units implies the budget constraint BC in Figure 6.1. The rays $0R_1$ and $0R_2$ show the

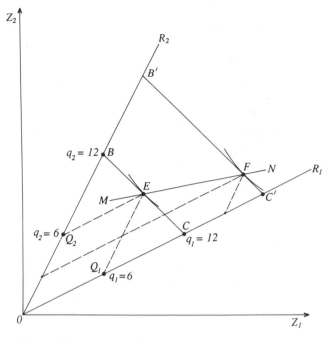

Figure 6.1

proportions of z_1 and z_2 generated by q_1 and q_2, respectively, and distances along those rays can be used to measure purchases of the marketed goods. For example, if preferences are such that the consumer's optimum is at E, where (z_1, z_2) is $(18, 18)$, completion of the parallelogram as shown leads to the observation that 6 units of q_1 are being purchased, generating 12 units of z_1 and 6 units of z_2. This is the vector $0Q_1$. The vector $0Q_2$ represents the characteristics generated through the purchase of q_2.

Now suppose preferences do, indeed, place the optimum at E. Now let income double. Suppose the slope of the income expansion path through E is positive but less than that of $0R_1$. Both characteristics are therefore normal characteristics, by assumption. The relevant segment of the new budget constraint, $B'C'$, is parallel to BC, and the new consumer optimum is at F. Consumption of both characteristics has risen, but completion of the relevant parallelogram immediately shows that purchases of q_2 have fallen. For example, if at $F(z_1, z_2) = (44, 28)$, it is easy to work out that $(q_1, q_2) = (20, 4)$. Thus, although both characteristics are normal, one of the marketed goods turns out to be inferior.

Preferences over prices again

Antonelli's use of the indirect utility function, which we analyzed more systematically in Chapter 2, represents another example of induced preferences. The primitive preferences are over the quantities **q**. The consumer is confronted with a vector of objects, the money prices **P**, and income M. The budget constraint defines the set of quantities made available by any vector $(\mathbf{P}, M)$. Because $(\mathbf{P}, M)$ determines the most preferred bundle and the associated utility level, we can define the induced preferences over $(\mathbf{P}, M)$. In this case, we know the indirect utility function to be decreasing and quasi-convex in **P**. Suitable modification of Milne's general argument runs as follows: Any given $(\mathbf{P}', M')$ defines a set of attainable quantities, defined by the inequalities $\mathbf{P}' \cdot \mathbf{q} \leq M'$, $\mathbf{q}' \geq 0$. If an individual price, P_i, is increased, this defines a new set, which is itself a subset of the original budget set. Let income be fixed at the value M throughout. Because the constraint set has shrunk, the associated maximum attainable utility, $V(\mathbf{P}, M)$, must fall. $V(\cdot)$ is therefore decreasing in **P**. To establish quasi-convexity, consider two price vectors: Faced with $\mathbf{P}'$, the consumer attains the utility level $v' = V(\mathbf{P}', M)$, whereas the vector $\mathbf{P}''$ leads to $v'' = V(\mathbf{P}'', M)$. Suppose that $v' \geq v''$. Now consider the maximum attainable utility when the price vector is $\theta\mathbf{P}' + (1-\theta)\mathbf{P}''$, $0 \leq \theta \leq 1$. The implied budget constraint is $[\theta\mathbf{P}' + (1-\theta)\mathbf{P}''] \cdot \mathbf{q} \leq M$. This defines a set that lies within the union of the two initial budget sets. This implies that there is no point attainable with this budget constraint that cannot be attained with one or the other of the original constraints. In Figure 6.2, the hatched set $0EF$ lies wholly within the set $0AIB$. Therefore the maximum attainable utility implied by $\theta\mathbf{P}' + (1-\theta)\mathbf{P}''$ is no more than that implied by $\mathbf{P}'$. Put more briefly,

$$V(\theta\mathbf{P}' + (1-\theta)\mathbf{P}'', M) \leq V(\mathbf{P}', M) \quad \text{for } 0 \leq \theta \leq 1.$$

But this is precisely the definition of quasi-convexity. The mapping from prices and income to quantities enables us to induce preferences over $(\mathbf{P}, M)$, the implied utility function being the indirect utility function. This is something we already know. The present treatment simply emphasizes that this result is a special case of preference induction.

Preferences over net trades

A further example of induced preferences is well known to and widely exploited by trade theorists. Consider first a single consumer with an initial

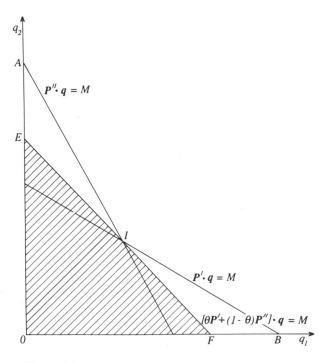

Figure 6.2

endowment of goods. This is the single-consumer exchange economy of Caves and Jones (1977, ch. 2). Denote endowments by $\bar{q}$ and consumption by q. Figure 6.3 is a conventional representation of this very conventional model. A moment's reflection suggests that we can, if we wish, simply shift the origin of this diagram to the endowment point, $0'$. If we do this, we have a figure in which the horizontal axis measures the excess demand for commodity 1, $z_1 = q_1 - \bar{q}_1$, and the vertical axis measures the excess demand for commodity 2, $z_2 = q_2 - \bar{q}_2$. The indifference map has the same qualitative features – higher quantities are associated with higher values of utility, and preferences over (z_1, z_2) remain convex. All that has happened is that the origin has shifted. The indifference map in the new figure and the corresponding utility function $\hat{U}(z_1, z_2)$ are defined over excess demands, or net trades. Negative values for such trades make perfectly good economic sense and represent net excess supplies. Offer, or trading, curves can be generated, and by superimposing the trading curve of a second country we can analyze the equilibrium terms of trade, the effects of tariffs on trade flows, and so on.

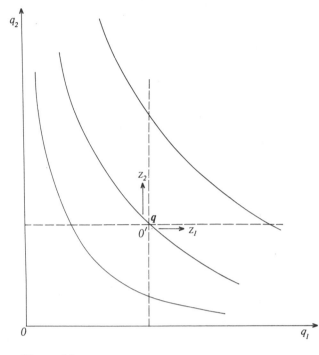

Figure 6.3

All this is straightforward. More interesting, and certainly less obvious, is the fact that the same trick can be employed even when there is production of commodities, and even though the supply of individual commodities is sensitive to price changes. The idea of trade indifference curves was effectively exploited by Meade (1952, ch. 2) and was treated more formally by Dixit and Norman (1980, pp. 67–9). Krauss (1979, pp. 29–32) and Ethier (1983, pp. 79–82) have provided simple geometric expositions.

Suppose the consumer, or single-consumer economy, has an endowment of inputs ℓ from which a vector of consumable goods $\mathbf{y}$ may be produced. The production possibilities set is assumed to be convex and is expressed by the constraint $T(\mathbf{y}, \ell) \leq 0$. Follow Dixit and Norman in supposing that the country receives an exogenous gift of a vector $\mathbf{z}$ of consumable commodities. Some components of $\mathbf{z}$ may be negative, indicating a gift by the country to the rest of the world. For any gift $\mathbf{z}$, the country can consume the vector $\mathbf{q} = \mathbf{z} + \mathbf{y}$, the sum of what is received from the rest of the world and the level of production from its own resources. The country, we suppose, chooses its output mix so as to maximize its utility,

$U(\mathbf{q}) = U(\mathbf{z}+\mathbf{y})$, subject to its input endowment, the technology, and the value of $\mathbf{z}$. This defines a function $\hat{U}(\cdot)$:

$$\hat{U}(\mathbf{z}, \ell) \equiv \max_{\mathbf{y}}\{U(\mathbf{z}+\mathbf{y}) \mid T(\mathbf{y}, \ell) \le 0\}.$$

In many applications, ℓ is held fixed and can therefore be suppressed. We are then left with the Meade utility function $\hat{U}(\mathbf{z})$ defined over the gifts, or net trades, $\mathbf{z} = \mathbf{q}-\mathbf{y}$. $\hat{U}(\cdot)$ is clearly increasing in its arguments. It is also quasi-concave in $\mathbf{z}$. In short, $\hat{U}(\mathbf{z})$ has all the properties of a direct utility function. An advantage of working with $\hat{U}(\mathbf{z})$ is that it allows us to amalgamate production and consumption, so that the details of the production sector do not need to be modeled explicitly.

An associated indirect utility function can also be defined. Consider a single-consumer open economy. Given an endowment of primary resources ℓ, and facing a world price vector $\mathbf{P}$ for tradable commodities, the value of output generated by a competitive production sector consisting of profit-maximizing plants is given by the revenue function, $R(\mathbf{P}, \ell)$. Total income is then $R(\cdot)+B$, where B is the value of any transfers from the rest of the world. B will be positive for an aid recipient, and negative for a donor. The budget constraint then requires that the value of domestic consumption, $\mathbf{P}\cdot\mathbf{q}$, should not exceed $R(\cdot)+B$. A conventional indirect utility function, $V(\mathbf{P}, R(\mathbf{P}, \ell)+B)$, can be defined. Now define the function

$$\hat{V}(\mathbf{P}, \ell, B) \equiv V(\mathbf{P}, R(\mathbf{P}, \ell)+B).$$

Because this is an identity, partial differentiation with respect to P_i yields

$$\hat{V}_i = V_i + V_M R_i,$$

where $M \equiv R(\mathbf{P}, \ell)+B$, total income. Partial differentiation with respect to B yields

$$\hat{V}_B = V_M.$$

Combining these gives

$$\hat{V}_i/\hat{V}_B = V_i/V_M + R_i.$$

Application of Roy's identity to the right-hand side of this expression tells us that $V_i/V_M = x_i(\cdot)$, and Shephard's lemma implies that $R_i = y_i(\cdot)$. The consequence of this is that there is a variant of Roy's identity associated with $\hat{V}(\cdot)$:

$$\hat{V}_i/\hat{V}_B = -x_i(\cdot) + y_i(\cdot) = -z_i(\cdot)$$

$\hat{V}(\mathbf{P}, \ell, B)$ has a natural interpretation as an indirect utility function defined over net trades, or excess demands, and may be related to $\hat{U}$ by noting that

$$\hat{V}(\mathbf{P}, \ell, B) \equiv \max_{\mathbf{z}} \{\hat{U}(\mathbf{z}, \ell) \mid \mathbf{P} \cdot \mathbf{z} \leq B\}.$$

If trade in commodities is required to balance, the analysis can capture this requirement by evaluating $\hat{V}(\cdot)$ and its partial derivatives at a point where $B = 0$. The function $\hat{V}(\cdot)$ has been applied in several recent papers on international trade theory, as cited at the end of this chapter.

6.2 Hedonic prices

Having seen how preferences over characteristics induce preferences over marketed goods, I want to reverse the procedure and show how it is possible, and sometimes useful, to translate or induce the constraint set, initially defined over goods, into a production possibilities set in characteristics space. This allows us to define shadow, or "hedonic," prices associated with characteristics.

First consider the close analogy between the characteristics model of consumer behavior and the standard model of producer behavior presented in Chapter 5. A plant uses factor inputs ℓ to produce outputs $\mathbf{y}$ so as to maximize profits Π. The consumer uses marketed goods $\mathbf{q}$ to produce characteristics $\mathbf{z}$ to maximize utility $U(\mathbf{z})$. As we did in Chapter 5, we can break the optimizing exercise up into two parts. Whatever vector $\mathbf{z}$ is being produced, it must be produced at minimum cost. This is necessary, though not sufficient, for utility maximization. Given that $\mathbf{z}$ is so produced, we can then determine its utility-maximizing level. The cost-minimizing part of this exercise defines the cost function:

$$C(\mathbf{P}, \mathbf{z}) \equiv \min_{\mathbf{q}} \{\mathbf{P} \cdot \mathbf{q} \mid D_1(\mathbf{q}, \mathbf{z}) \geq 1\}. \tag{1}$$

Assume that the production possibilities set is convex and that its frontier is everywhere differentiable. $C(\cdot)$, being a minimum value function, has standard properties. In particular, its derivative with respect to P_i is the demand function for the ith marketed good, and its derivative with respect to z_j is a shadow price associated with characteristic j. It is the marginal cost of characteristic j.

Now turn to the second part of the optimization exercise. From among all those $\mathbf{z}$ vectors that can be produced within the budget constraint, and given that the chosen bundle will be producd at minimum cost, we wish to maximize utility:

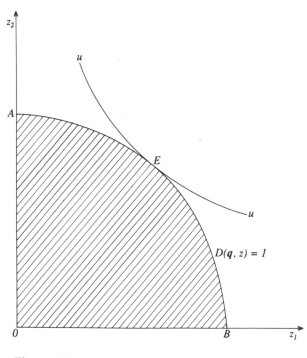

Figure 6.4

$$V(\mathbf{P}, M) \equiv \max_{\mathbf{z}}\{U(\mathbf{z}) \mid C(\mathbf{P}, \mathbf{z}) = M\}. \tag{2}$$

First-order conditions require

$$(\partial U(\cdot)/\partial z_j)/\lambda = \partial C(\cdot)/\partial z_j, \tag{3}$$

where λ is the Lagrangian multiplier associated with (2) and can readily be shown, using the envelope theorem, to equal the marginal utility of money, $\partial V(\mathbf{P}, M)/\partial M$. The right-hand side of (3) is the supply price of characteristic j, and the left-hand side is the demand price. The equality between the two can be seen in Figure 6.4, which shows the production possibilities set in characteristics space, $0AB$, an indifference curve, and the utility-maximizing bundle of characteristics at E. Denote $\partial C(\cdot)/\partial z_j$ by ϕ_j; ϕ_j is simply a virtual price, and in the context of the characteristics model it is called a hedonic price. The vector ϕ is a vector of characteristics prices that if confronted by the consumer would support the allocation E. Their absolute level is indeterminate, because of the homogeneity of the system. However, if there are constant returns to scale in the technology that converts marketed goods into characteristics, so that a doubling of the target $\mathbf{z}$ requires a doubling of the cost, then Euler's theorem tells us that

$$\sum_j \phi_j z_j = C(\mathbf{P}, \mathbf{z}) = M = \sum_i P_i q_i.$$

This pins down the absolute values of the ϕ variables. We can then model the consumer's equilibrium as if the consumer were facing a single linear constraint, $\sum_j \phi_j z_j = M$, and maximizing utility in the usual way. This has advantages that are pointed out by Deaton and Muellbauer (1980a, pp. 247-50). However, an important problem has to be faced. The virtual prices are themselves endogenous. Consider two consumers, each with 10 units of income. Suppose there are three marketed commodities, each having a price of unity. Let there be two characteristics. The following table indicates the level of each characteristic generated by a unit of each market good:

Marketed good	Characteristic	
	1	2
1	$\frac{4}{5}$	0
2	$\frac{1}{2}$	$\frac{1}{2}$
3	$\frac{1}{5}$	$\frac{3}{5}$

Each consumer faces the same feasible consumption set over characteristics. This is the hatched area in Figure 6.5. If their preferences differ, so that their utility-maximizing bundles differ, so too may the associated virtual or hedonic prices. Such a situation is shown in the figure, because the consumers' equilibria lie on different facets of the frontier. Individual a chooses the bundle A, and individual b chooses B. In general, unless restrictions are placed on preference differences or the technology for transforming goods into characteristics, hedonic prices will vary across individuals. They are not directly observable.

Because this observation clearly implies difficulties in estimating hedonic prices, it is sensible to pause and ask why we should be interested in them. The hedonic approach has been used to analyze the demand for new commodities. An automobile, for example, can be thought of as simply a bundle of characteristics – speed, comfort, passenger and baggage capacity, reliability, appeal to one's machismo, and so on. If it were possible to estimate the hedonic prices attached by an individual to each of these characteristics, it would then be possible to estimate the valuation

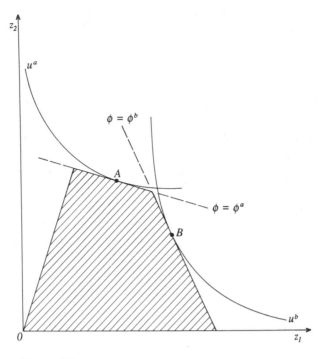

Figure 6.5

placed on a given alternative package of characteristics. A new automobile is just such a package. Housing is another example of a marketed good that often is analyzed in terms of the characteristics generated – such as distance from shops, schools, and office, number of rooms, size of garden – and individuals' valuations of those characteristics.

An important class of nonmarketed characteristics is the subject of a large and growing literature on externalities, public goods and public bads such as pollution and congestion. Usually, the evaluation of any project involving significant externalities requires that they be valued. Many studies have explored the use of econometric techniques to estimate hedonic prices for such environmental characteristics. Sources are cited in the comments that conclude this chapter.

6.3   Separability

For certain purposes, generality is a virtue. For example, the sign and symmetry properties of compensated demand responses are all the more interesting because they require only a fairly general set of axioms. However, for many purposes it is helpful, even necessary, to impose additional structure on preferences. Econometricians particularly often rely on rather meager data sets to estimate parameters. The number of degrees of freedom, hence the power of their estimation procedures, often is disappointingly low. Additional degrees of freedom can be achieved if we are prepared to impose more a priori structure on a model. Purely theoretical work also can achieve richer insights if we can treat certain problems in isolation without having to worry about countless complex interactions between innumerable endogenous variables. In this context, Gorman's general comments on the usefulness of the notion of separability are worth quoting:

> Separability has to do with the structure of a problem. Perfect competition and the absence of external economies, which allow us to examine the behaviour of individual firms, in isolation; constant returns, permitting us to discuss the structure of a firm's production plan without knowing its scale; Samuelson's weak independence axiom which says that, in an uncertain world, what we do if it shines is quite independent of what we would have done had it rained; and Bergson's social welfare function based on the sovereignty of self-regarding consumers: all embody separability assumptions, whose function is to allow us to examine one aspect of a problem in at least relative isolation from others. [Gorman 1976, p. 212].

There is not universal agreement on the terminology of separability. I shall stick to that of Gorman, whose work has inspired many developments in this area. In the spirit of Gorman's quotation, let us start with the following simple problem. Suppose a consumer spends income on many commodities. Under what circumstances can we determine the allocation of a given amount of income between, say, commodities 1 and 2 independently of the allocation among the remaining commodities? In other words, when is information about P_1, P_2, and $P_1 q_1 + P_2 q_2$ sufficient to determine $x_1(\cdot)$ and $x_2(\cdot)$?

In geometric terms, we are envisaging an indifference map in (q_1, q_2) space that is unaffected by whatever the quantities of remaining commodities may be. This implies that the marginal rate of substitution between q_1 and q_2 depends only on q_1 and q_2, and not at all on $q_3, q_4, \ldots, q_n$. This structure is captured by writing the utility function in the form

$$U(\mathbf{q}) = F(g(q_1, q_2), q_3, \ldots, q_n).$$

The function $g(\cdot)$ is often called a subutility function. It defines a kind of intermediate good, produced by combining q_1 and q_2, and itself then being combined with $q_3, \ldots, q_n$ to produce $U(\cdot)$. If the allocation of resources between q_1 and q_2 can be separated from the rest of the system in the manner here described, the vector (q_1, q_2) is said to be separable.

Now go further, and suppose that it is possible to partition the vector of commodities into a set of subvectors, so that $\mathbf{q} = (\mathbf{q}_1, \mathbf{q}_2, \ldots, \mathbf{q}_T)$, and to represent preferences by the function

$$U(\mathbf{q}) = F(g_1(\mathbf{q}_1), g_2(\mathbf{q}_2), \ldots, g_T(\mathbf{q}_T)). \tag{4}$$

We now have a set of subutility functions, $g_1(\cdot), \ldots, g_T(\cdot)$. If we take any pair of commodities both lying in the same group – that is, their quantities are arguments of the same subutility function – then again their marginal rate of substitution is independent of quantities of commodities not included in that group. Preferences that can be represented by a function of the form (4) are said to be weakly separable, as is the utility function $U(\cdot)$. Denote expenditure on group t by $M_t = \mathbf{P}_t \cdot \mathbf{q}_t$, $t = 1, \ldots, T$. Then demand functions for commodities in group t can be defined that are of the form $q_i = x_i(\mathbf{P}_t, M_t)$.

The consumer can be thought of as maximizing in two stages. Given $M_1, \ldots, M_T$, optimization is undertaken within each group subject to that group's expenditure level and the relevant price subvector. An indirect utility function can be defined of the form

$$I(\mathbf{P}, M_1, \ldots, M_T) \equiv \max_{\mathbf{q}_1, \ldots, \mathbf{q}_T} \{ F(g_1(\mathbf{q}_1), \ldots, g_T(\mathbf{q}_T)) \mid \mathbf{P}_t \cdot \mathbf{q}_t = M_t, t = 1, \ldots, T \} \tag{5}$$

In addition, there is the problem of distributing total expenditure amongst the various groups in an optimal way. This defines the conventional indirect utility function:

$$V(\mathbf{P}, M) \equiv \max_{M_1, \ldots, M_T} \left\{ I(\mathbf{P}, M_1, \ldots, M_T) \mid \sum_{t=1}^{T} M_t = M \right\}. \tag{6}$$

What this means is that if (and only if) the utility function is separable, then once the M_i's have been correctly chosen, the allocation of each between the commodities in that group can be determined without reference to any other group. Given appropriate separability, once total expenditure on food is known, its allocation between bagels and bacon depends only on food prices, not on those of Scotch whisky or socks. If indeed individuals do budget in this two-stage manner, it makes sense in empirical work to assume separable utility at the outset so as to reduce the number of independent parameters to be estimated.

To assume separability is to impose significant extra restrictions on behavior. To emphasize this important observation, consider its implications for the cross-responses $\partial c_i(\cdot)/\partial P_j$ when goods i and j belong to different groups. Suppose commodities can be partitioned into $\mathbf{q} = (\mathbf{q}_I, \mathbf{q}_J)$ and the utility function written as

$$U(\mathbf{q}) = U(U_I(\mathbf{q}_I), U_J(\mathbf{q}_J)),$$

where $U_I(\cdot)$ and $U_J(\cdot)$ are subutility functions. Uncompensated demand functions $x_i(\mathbf{P}, M)$ can alternatively be expressed in a conditional form:

$$q_i = x_i^\dagger(\mathbf{P}_I, M_I), \quad i \in I,$$

where $M_I = \mathbf{P}_I \cdot \mathbf{q}_I$, the level of income spent on goods in group I. M_I is itself endogenous and may be written as either $m_I(\mathbf{P}, M)$ or $\mu_I(\mathbf{P}, u)$. In equilibrium, therefore, we can write

$$q_i = c_i(\mathbf{P}, u) = x_i^\dagger(\mathbf{P}_I, \mu_I(\mathbf{P}, u)).$$

The cross-response can therefore be expressed as

$$c_{ij} = x_{iM}^\dagger \mu_{Ij},$$

where $\mu_{Ij} \equiv \partial \mu_I(\cdot)/\partial P_j$. But $c_{ij} = c_{ji}$, so that

$$x_{iM}^\dagger \mu_{Ij} = x_{jM}^\dagger \mu_{Ji} \quad \text{for all } i \in I, j \in J.$$

Therefore, $\mu_{Ji}/x_{iM}^\dagger = \mu_{Ij}/x_{jM}^\dagger = \Lambda_{IJ}$. But the first of these two expressions is independent of the choice of j, and the second is independent of i. Their common value, denoted by Λ_{IJ}, is therefore independent of both i and j. Therefore, compensated responses can be expressed as

$$c_{ij} = \Lambda_{IJ} x_{iM}^\dagger x_{jM}^\dagger.$$

The parameters of the conditional functions, $x_i^\dagger(\cdot)$ and $x_j^\dagger(\cdot)$, can be replaced by those of the conventional uncompensated demand functions, because

$$x_i(\mathbf{P}, M) = x_i^\dagger(\mathbf{P}_I, m_I(\mathbf{P}, M))$$

so that $x_{iM} = x_{iM}^\dagger m_{IM}$. The response c_{ij} is therefore

$$c_{ij} = \left(\frac{\Lambda_{IJ}}{m_{IM} m_{JM}}\right) x_{iM} x_{jM} \quad \text{for all } i \in I, j \in J.$$

The expression in parentheses does not depend on the particular choices of i and j. Given a value for this expression, there is therefore a very simple set of relationships between the compensated price responses and the conventional income responses.

Econometricians often make an assumption that is even stronger than separability, as I defined it earlier, and assume that $U(\cdot)$ is additively separable: That is, it takes the form

$$U(\cdot) = g_1(\mathbf{q}_1) + g_2(\mathbf{q}_2) + \cdots + g_T(\mathbf{q}_T). \tag{7}$$

Additive separability of the direct utility function can be linked with separable preferences in an interesting way. Consider a three-commodity example. Suppose an individual's preferences are such that the vectors $(\mathbf{q}_1, \mathbf{q}_2)$ and $(\mathbf{q}_2, \mathbf{q}_3)$ are both separable, where $\mathbf{q} = (\mathbf{q}_1, \mathbf{q}_2, \mathbf{q}_3)$. The direct utility function can then be written as

$$U(\mathbf{q}_1, \mathbf{q}_2, \mathbf{q}_3) = F(f(\mathbf{q}_1, \mathbf{q}_2), \mathbf{q}_3) = G(\mathbf{q}_1, g(\mathbf{q}_2, \mathbf{q}_3)).$$

When separable vectors overlap in this way, it can be shown that the utility function can be written in the form

$$U(\cdot) = g_1(\mathbf{q}_1) + g_2(\mathbf{q}_2) + g_3(\mathbf{q}_3),$$

which is precisely the additively separable form shown in (7). Such a structure is commonly assumed in analysis of intertemporal choice, in which $\mathbf{q}_t$ is interpreted as the vector of consumption at time t. Once total expenditure in any period is determined, the matter of its allocation between commodities can be divorced from events in other periods. Similarly, extension of the model to situations involving uncertainty, in which $\mathbf{q}_s$ is interpreted as the consumption vector given that the state of the world s occurs, typically uses the same assumption. It implies that what I shall do tomorrow if it is cold, wet, and miserable will be independent of what would happen in alternative states.

Additive separability has further implications that make it an attractive assumption to work with if this can be done without too much violence to the facts. Consider, for example, the implications for producer theory of an additively separable production function. The profit function associated with a single-output plant is

$$\Pi(P, \mathbf{W}) \equiv \max_{\boldsymbol{\ell}} \{ PF(\boldsymbol{\ell}) - \mathbf{W} \cdot \boldsymbol{\ell} \}.$$

If the production function has the form $F(\boldsymbol{\ell}) = \sum_i f_i(\ell_i)$, then the profit function is

$$\Pi(\cdot) = \max_{\boldsymbol{\ell}} \left\{ P \sum_{i=1}^{n} f_i(\ell_i) - W_i \ell_i \right\}$$

$$= \max_{\boldsymbol{\ell}} \left\{ \sum_{i=1}^{n} [Pf_i(\ell_i) - W_i \ell_i] \right\}$$

$$= \sum_{i=1}^{n} \Pi_i(P, W_i),$$

where $\Pi_i(\cdot) \equiv \max_{\ell_i}\{Pf_i(\ell_i) - W_i\ell_i\}$. The profit function, then, conveniently factorizes into n subprofit functions. This observation is given a very clear statement by Koopmans (1957, pp. 10–14).

There are many slightly different separability concepts, and their implications are far-reaching. The reader will find further references to the large, and sometimes quite sophisticated, literature on these matters at the end of this chapter.

6.4   Joint and nonjoint production

Recall the analysis in Chapter 5 of the multiproduct plant. Under common assumptions, various alternative representations of the technology are available. In quantity space, we can use the distance function. In the example that I gave, $D(\cdot)$ was given by

$$D(\cdot) = \sqrt{\ell_1\ell_2}/(y_1^2 + y_2^2)^\rho. \tag{8}$$

I showed that this technology could be represented by a cost function $C(\mathbf{W}, \mathbf{y})$, a revenue function $R(\ell, \mathbf{P})$, or, if $\rho > \frac{1}{2}$, a profit function $\Pi(\mathbf{P}, \mathbf{W})$. Nowhere was a production function mentioned. There was a simple reason for that. Without imposing special structure on the technology, it is not always possible to define explicit production functions, and the technology described by (8) is an example in which production functions are, indeed, not defined. To understand what is at issue, suppose that we can define such functions for some technology, and consider the implications. If the maximum attainable output of commodity j is given by

$$y_j = F^j(\ell_{1j}, \dots, \ell_{mj}),$$

then the minimum cost of producing y_j is, as we know from Chapter 5,

$$C_j(\mathbf{W}, y_j) = \min_{\ell_j}\{\mathbf{W}\cdot\ell_j \mid y_j = F^j(\ell_j)\}.$$

where $\ell_j \equiv (\ell_{1j}, \dots, \ell_{mj})$. The cost of output j depends on the vector of input prices and the level of y_j. It does not depend on any other output levels. The cost of producing the given vector of outputs, $\mathbf{y}$, is therefore

$$C(\mathbf{W}, \mathbf{y}) = \sum_{j=1}^{n} C_j(\mathbf{W}, y_j).$$

In short, if the technology can be described by individual production functions, then a very particular structure is implied for the cost function. This structure is not possessed by the cost function associated with (8).

Kohli (1983) provides a useful discussion of these issues. A technology is called nonjoint in input quantities if it is possible to split up the total quantity of each input and assign each component to the production of a single output. Following Kohli, suppose there are constant returns to scale. A technology involving m inputs and n outputs is defined as nonjoint in input quantities if it is possible to define individual quasi-concave, nonnegative, nondecreasing functions $F^j(\cdot)$ – that is, production functions – and also to define nonnegative quantities ℓ_{ij} such that

$$y_j \leq F^j(\ell_{1j}, \ldots, \ell_{mj}), \quad j = 1, \ldots, n,$$

and

$$\sum_{j=1}^{n} \ell_{ij} \leq \ell_i, \quad i = 1, \ldots, m.$$

The quantity ℓ_{ij} is that part of the endowment of input i that is assigned to production of output j. The following result may be shown:

Nonjointness in input quantities.   *The technology is nonjoint in input quantities if and only if the cost function $C(\mathbf{y}, \mathbf{W})$ can be written as*

$$C(\mathbf{y}, \mathbf{W}) = \sum_{j=1}^{n} y_j g^j(\mathbf{W}), \tag{9}$$

where the $g^j(\cdot)$ functions are nonnegative, nondecreasing, homogeneous of degree 1, and concave.

It is nonjointness that implies the factorization of $C(\cdot)$ into functions of output quantities and input prices, and constant returns to scale that allows us to interpret $g^j(\cdot)$ as the unit cost of producing y_j, the total cost being $C^j(\cdot) = y_j g^j(\mathbf{W})$.

Nonjointness and constant returns to scale imply that the marginal cost of producing, say, y_j is independent of all output levels, because marginal cost is given by

$$m_j^*(\cdot) = \partial C(\cdot)/\partial y_j = g^j(\mathbf{W}),$$

so that $\partial m_j^*(\cdot)/\partial y_k = 0$, for all $j, k = 1, \ldots, n$. Geometrically, it is the nonjointness assumption that permits us to draw an isoquant diagram relating the arguments of the production function to the output level. The constant-returns-to-scale assumption enables a single unit isoquant to contain all information about the technology. These two assumptions are also necessary if we are to draw an iso-cost curve, depicting the pairs of values of W_1 and W_2 in a two-input economy to a given unit cost level. If there is joint production, the unit cost of producing y_j cannot be defined independently of the level of, say, y_k.

Kohli also defines a second concept of nonjointness. Nonjointness in output quantities holds if the total quantity of each output can be split up and each part assigned to a particular input. A constant-returns-to-scale technology is nonjoint in output quantities if it is possible to define individual quasi-convex, nonnegative, nondecreasing functions $G^i(\cdot)$ – factor requirements functions – and also to define nonnegative quantities y_{ij} such that

$$\ell_i \geq G^i(y_{i1}, \ldots, y_{in}), \quad i = 1, \ldots, m,$$

and

$$\sum_{i=1}^{m} y_{ij} \geq y_j, \quad j = 1, \ldots, n,$$

where y_{ij} is that part of the total output of good j that can be ascribed to input i. The following result can be shown:

Nonjointness in output quantities. *The technology is nonjoint in output quantities if and only if the revenue function $R(\ell, \mathbf{P})$ can be written as*

$$R(\ell, \mathbf{P}) = \sum \ell_i \gamma^i(\mathbf{P}),$$

where the $\gamma^i(\cdot)$ functions are nonnegative, nondecreasing, homogeneous of degree 1, and convex.

Again, nonjointness implies the ability to factorize $R(\cdot)$, and constant returns to scale allows an interesting interpretation of $\gamma^i(\mathbf{P})$. It is the contribution to total revenue made by a unit of input i. It is also the marginal revenue attributable to input i and is independent of any input level, being a function of output prices alone. Denote the marginal revenue function by $r_i(\ell, \mathbf{P})$. Then

$$r_i(\cdot) = \partial R(\cdot)/\partial \ell_i = \gamma^i(\mathbf{P}),$$

so that $\partial r_i(\cdot)/\partial \ell_k = 0$ for all $k = 1, \ldots, m$.

There is no particular a priori reason to suppose that technology is nonjoint in either input or output quantities. Whether indeed these are good assumptions is an empirical matter. Nevertheless, though little empirical work has been done to investigate these matters, economic theory has generally proceeded by making assumptions that necessarily imply nonjointness. There are, for example, some famous propositions in international trade theory that require technology to be nonjoint in input quantities. Let us examine two of these propositions.

Consider the production sector of the two-input, two-output Heckscher–Ohlin model of international trade. This is presented by Caves and Jones (1977, ch. 7) and Ethier (1983). The assumptions of constant returns to scale and nonjointness in input quantities imply that unit cost functions can be defined for each output, and unit costs depend only on the input prices. In a competitive equilibrium, profits are zero, and output prices equal unit costs:

$$P_j = C_j(\mathbf{W}, y_j)/y_j = g_j(\mathbf{W})$$
$$= a_{1j}(\mathbf{W})W_1 + a_{2j}(\mathbf{W})W_2, \quad j = 1, 2. \tag{10}$$

The $a_{ij}(\cdot)$ functions are input demand functions per unit output, obtained by using Shephard's lemma. Treat output prices as exogenous. Within a given economy, to any pair of values (P_1, P_2) there corresponds a unique pair of input prices that satisfy (10). Consider how input prices are affected by changes in output prices. Both before and after any change, (10) must hold in a zero-profit equilibrium. Consequently,

$$dP_j = a_{1j}(\mathbf{W})dW_1 + a_{2j}(\mathbf{W})dW_2, \quad j = 1, 2. \tag{11}$$

In writing this, I have exploited the fact that although the unit input demands change in response to input price changes, the weighted sum $W_1 da_{1j}(\cdot) + W_2 da_{2j}(\cdot)$ is zero. This is a consequence of the envelope theorem. Consequently, the a_{ij} quantities may be treated as fixed coefficients in the present exercise. Expressed in proportional terms,

$$dP_j/P_j = (a_{1j}W_1/P_j)(dW_1/W_1) + (a_{2j}W_2/P_j)(dW_2/W_2), \quad j = 1, 2.$$

Jones (1965), who popularized the use of unit cost functions by trade theorists, writes this pair of equations using a somewhat more efficient notation:

$$\hat{P}_1 = \theta_{11}\hat{W}_1 + \theta_{21}\hat{W}_2,$$
$$\hat{P}_2 = \theta_{12}\hat{W}_1 + \theta_{22}\hat{W}_2.$$

where a "hat" over a variable denotes a proportional change, and $\theta_{ij} = a_{ij}W_i/P_j$, the share of input i in the unit cost of producing output j. Clearly, $\theta_{1j} + \theta_{2j} = 1$, because under constant returns to scale the unit cost is precisely exhausted by payments to inputs. Cramer's rule may now be used to solve for the factor price changes brought about by small changes in output prices. To keep matters simple, suppose $\hat{P}_2 = 0$. Then $\hat{W}_1$ and $\hat{W}_2$ are given by

$$\hat{W}_1 = \theta_{22}\hat{P}_1/|\Theta|, \qquad \hat{W}_2 = -\theta_{12}\hat{P}_1/|\Theta|$$

where $|\Theta|$ is the determinant of factor shares. It is easily shown that

$$|\Theta| = \frac{W_1 W_2}{P_1 P_2}|A|$$

where $|A|$ is the determinant of unit input requirements. An immediate implication of all this is that if the ratio of inputs a_{11}/a_{21} exceeds the ratio a_{12}/a_{22} – that is, if commodity 1 makes relatively intensive use of factor input 1 – then $|A|$ is positive, so that $|\Theta|$ is positive, $\hat{W}_1/\hat{P}_1$ is positive, and $\hat{W}_2/\hat{P}_1$ negative. Moreover, because $\theta_{1j} + \theta_{2j} = 1$,

$$\hat{W}_1/\hat{P}_1 = \theta_{22}/[\theta_{11}\theta_{22} - \theta_{12}\theta_{21}]$$
$$= \theta_{22}/[\theta_{11}\theta_{22} - (1 - \theta_{22})(1 - \theta_{11})]$$
$$= \theta_{22}/(\theta_{22} + \theta_{11} - 1)$$
$$> 1.$$

The general result is called the Stolper–Samuelson theorem. It asserts that proportional input price changes are magnified reflections of output price changes. An increase in the price of the commodity that is relatively intensive in the use of, say, factor i will lead to a greater proportional increase in W_i, while the price of the other input will decline relative to both output prices. Using the hat notation, if commodity 1 uses input 1 relatively intensively, and if $\hat{P}_1 > \hat{P}_2$, the theorem states that

$$\hat{W}_1 > \hat{P}_1 > \hat{P}_2 > \hat{W}_2.$$

If technology were intrinsically joint in input quantities, it would not be possible to write (11) without reference to output quantities. Subsequent algebra would include extra terms and would not lead to the Stolper–Samuelson theorem. A general treatment is not particularly enlightening, but recall that earlier we generated inverse input demand functions for a joint production technology in Section 5.7. In that model, the responses of input demand prices to output price changes were all positive.

Nonjointness in input quantities is also required for another celebrated theorem in international trade theory, the Rybczynski theorem. Let commodity prices be fixed in the two-input, two-output model, and consider the response of competitive output levels to exogenous changes in factor endowments. Both before and after any such change, the total employment of each factor must equal the total quantity available, ℓ_j. But Shephard's lemma tells us that the employment level is the derivative of the cost function. The requirement that input markets clear therefore implies that

$$\ell_i = \partial C(\mathbf{W}, \mathbf{y})/\partial W_i, \quad i = 1, 2. \tag{12}$$

In the present model, these two conditions allow us to solve for the two unknowns y_1 and y_2. If production is nonjoint and subject to constant returns to scale, the cost function takes the form given by (9), so that the full-employment requirements become

$$\ell_i = y_1(\partial g_1(\cdot)/\partial W_i) + y_2(\partial g_2(\cdot)/\partial W_i)$$
$$= a_{i1}(\mathbf{W})y_1 + a_{i2}(\mathbf{W})y_2.$$

In the present exercise, output and input prices are constant, so that the a_{ij}'s are constant. Consequently, the full-employment conditions can be written as linear relations between ℓ and $\mathbf{y}$:

$$\ell_1 = a_{11}y_1 + a_{12}y_2 \quad \text{and} \quad \ell_2 = a_{21}y_1 + a_{22}y_2.$$

Reasoning similar to that involved in the Stolper–Samuelson theorem leads to the Rybczynski theorem, which asserts that proportional output responses are magnified reflections of endowment changes. An increase in the endowment of that factor that is relatively intensively used in the production of, say, output j will lead to a greater proportional increase in y_j, while the level of the other output will decline. Using the hat notation, if commodity 1 uses input 1 relatively intensively, and if $\hat{\ell}_1 > \hat{\ell}_2$, the theorem states that

$$\hat{y}_1 > \hat{\ell}_1 > \hat{\ell}_2 > \hat{y}_2.$$

Changes in input quantities generate magnified proportional adjustments in output levels. If production were joint, the initial statement of the full-employment equations could not be formulated in terms of constant a_{ij} coefficients. Again, the example of Chapter 5 provides an instructive contrast, because in that model the supply responses $\partial s_j^*(\ell, \mathbf{P})/\partial \ell_i$ are all positive.

6.5   Economies of scope and scale

Consider a technology that exhibits constant returns to scale and is nonjoint in input quantities, so that the cost function takes the form

$$C(\mathbf{W}, \mathbf{y}) = \sum_{j=1}^{n} y_j g^j(\mathbf{W}).$$

Now imagine two production plants, each with access to this technology, one of which produces the vector $\mathbf{y}'$, and the other $\mathbf{y}''$. The total cost of operating the two plants is then

$$C(\mathbf{W}, y') + C(\mathbf{W}, y'') = \sum_j y_j' g^j(\mathbf{W}) + \sum_j y_j'' g^j(\mathbf{W})$$

$$= \sum_j (y_j' + y_j'') g^j(\mathbf{W})$$

$$= C(\mathbf{W}, y' + y'').$$

The implication of this is that precisely the same cost would be incurred by a single plant producing the vector $y' + y''$. There is neither advantage to be gained nor disadvantage to be incurred by concentrating production in a single plant.

However, there are circumstances in which the number of plants, and the distribution of a given output target among them, will affect total costs. Consider first the production of a single homogeneous output. Let each plant have access to the same technology, represented by the cost function $C(\mathbf{W}, y)$. I want to consider whether or not a given output target is more efficiently produced at a single plant than by splitting the output up between, say, two plants. Let the output of one plant be y', and that of the other y''. The cost function is said to be subadditive at the point $C(\mathbf{W}, y' + y'') \leq C(\mathbf{W}, y') + C(\mathbf{W}, y'')$. It is strictly subadditive if the inequality is a strong one. The expression on the left is the cost of producing $y' + y''$ at a single plant. Consequently, if $C(\cdot)$ is strictly subadditive at $(\mathbf{W}, y' + y'')$, the target is more efficiently produced at one plant.

This result is very transparent and seems to say little more than that a single plant is more efficient if it produces at a lower cost. It is useful, therefore, to try to relate it to familiar ideas concerning falling average cost and marginal cost curves. Economies of scale often are defined as synonymous with a falling average cost as output rises. Adopting this definition, it is interesting to note that scale economies are not necessary for subadditivity of the cost function and therefore are not necessary for the superiority of concentrating production in a single plant. What is true is that $C(\cdot)$ is subadditive if either there are economies of scale at all output levels or $C(\cdot)$ is strictly concave in output at all output levels and $C(\mathbf{W}, 0) \geq 0$. The first of these conditions involves declining average costs, and the latter involves declining marginal costs. The misleading tendency to identify economies of scale with the superiority of single-plant production probably arises from the habit of confining attention to production functions that are homogeneous of a constant degree. Suppose, for example, that for any positive scalar θ, $F(\theta\ell) = \theta^r F(\ell)$, where $r > 1$. Then it may be shown that both average and marginal costs are declining functions of output. Not only are there universal economies of scale, but also $C(\cdot)$ is everywhere a strictly concave function of y. If $r < 1$, there are universal diseconomies of scale, and $C(\cdot)$ is everywhere strictly convex in y. However, once we move away from homogeneous production functions, the two alternative sufficient conditions for subadditivity of $C(\cdot)$ cease to go hand in hand. It is easy to concoct examples in which one condition holds while the other fails to hold.

Turning to multiproduct technologies, there is a natural extension of the subadditivity assumption introduced earlier. The cost function $C(\mathbf{W}, \mathbf{y})$ is strictly ray-subadditive if, for any two output targets $\mathbf{y}'$ and $\theta\mathbf{y}'$, where θ is a positive scalar,

$$C(\mathbf{W}, \mathbf{y}') + C(\mathbf{W}, \theta\mathbf{y}') > C[\mathbf{W}, (1+\theta)\mathbf{y}'].$$

As its name suggests, this concept confines attention to the properties of $C(\cdot)$ along a ray through the origin in output space. In multiproduct technologies, ray subadditivity is neither necessary nor sufficient to render single-plant production more efficient than multiplant production.

To see this, consider the technology described by the cost function

$$C(\cdot) = 2\sqrt{W_1 W_2 (y_1^2 + y_2^2)}. \tag{13}$$

This is weakly ray-subadditive. In fact, because it is homogeneous of degree 1 in outputs, there are globally constant returns to scale. If two plants produce $\mathbf{y}'$ and $\theta\mathbf{y}'$, respectively, their amalgamation into a single plant producing $(1+\theta)\mathbf{y}'$ will have no effect on total cost. Now consider the following definition of orthogonal subadditivity. $C(\mathbf{W}, \mathbf{y})$ is orthogonally subadditive if

$$C(\mathbf{W}, \mathbf{y}') + C(\mathbf{W}, \mathbf{y}'') \geq C(\mathbf{W}, \mathbf{y}' + \mathbf{y}'')$$

for any pair of vectors $\mathbf{y}'$ and $\mathbf{y}''$ such that $\sum_{j=1} y_j' y_j'' = 0$. This definition then restricts attention to vectors such that whenever either of y_j' and y_j'' is positive, the other must be zero. Let us look at this in the light of (13). For simplicity, let $W_1 = W_2 = 1$ throughout. Consider the target output vectors $\mathbf{y}' = (0, 7)$ and $\mathbf{y}'' = (7, 0)$. Putting these values into the cost function, we find that the total cost of having one plant produce $\mathbf{y}'$ and the other $\mathbf{y}''$ is

$$C(\mathbf{W}, 0, 7) + C(\mathbf{W}, 7, 0) = 14 + 14 = 28.$$

Suppose the same total output is now produced by assigning the output target $(3, 4)$ to one plant and $(4, 3)$ to the other. The total cost then becomes

$$C(\mathbf{W}, 3, 4) + C(\mathbf{W}, 4, 3) = 10 + 10 = 20.$$

Finally, consider the assignment $\mathbf{y}' = (3 \cdot 5, 3 \cdot 5)$, $\mathbf{y}'' = (3 \cdot 5, 3 \cdot 5)$. This implies a total cost

$$C(\mathbf{W}, 3 \cdot 5, 3 \cdot 5) + C(\mathbf{W}, 3 \cdot 5, 3 \cdot 5) = 19 \cdot 8.$$

Costs, then, are reduced by having each plant jointly produce the two outputs in equal quantities. In the present example, if a single plant were to produce the total target output, $\mathbf{y}' + \mathbf{y}'' = (7, 7)$, the total cost would again be $19 \cdot 8$. The cost function is strongly orthogonally subadditive. This implies not that a single plant is more efficient but that multiproduct production within each plant is more efficient than specialist single-product plants. Orthogonal subadditivity of $C(\cdot)$ is synonymous with economies of scope.

6.6   Frisch demand functions

Consider a consumer whose preferences are representable by an additive utility function:

$$U(\mathbf{q}) = U_1(q_1) + \cdots + U_n(q_n),$$

where each function $U_i(\cdot)$ is everywhere an increasing, strictly concave, and twice differentiable function of q_i. Maximization of utility subject to the budget constraint $\mathbf{P} \cdot \mathbf{q} \le M$ yields the first-order conditions

$$U_i'(q_i) = \lambda P_i = P_i / r,$$

where λ is the familiar Lagrangian multiplier and r is its reciprocal. The variable r has the interpretation of the marginal cost of utility, or the price of utility. Monotonicity and strict concavity of $U_i(\cdot)$ allow us to invert the first-order conditions to obtain

$$q_i = \chi_i(P_i/r), \quad i = 1, \ldots, n. \tag{14}$$

$\chi_i(\cdot)$ is a demand function, expressing the demand for commodity i as a function of that commodity's price and the price of utility. Browning, Deaton, and Irish (1985) call $\chi_i(\cdot)$ a Frisch demand function, after the pioneering work of Ragnar Frisch (1932).

The analysis is easily extended to deal with situations in which each subutility function is defined over a group of commodities. Partition the vector $\mathbf{q}$ into $\mathbf{q}_1, \mathbf{q}_2, \ldots, \mathbf{q}_T$, where $\mathbf{q}_t$ is interpreted as a vector of consumption at time t. The utility function is

$$U(\mathbf{q}) = U_1(\mathbf{q}_1) + \cdots + U_t(\mathbf{q}_t) + \cdots U_T(\mathbf{q}_T).$$

Let the vector $\mathbf{P}_t$ denote the vector of money prices of goods at time t. P_{it} and q_{it} are the price and quantity of commodity i at time t. First-order conditions associated with maximization of $U(\cdot)$ subject to a single budget constraint imply a set of demand functions:

$$q_{it} = \chi_{it}((1/r)\mathbf{P}_t). \tag{15}$$

Notice that the commodity prices appearing in (15) all relate to period t. The link between q_{it} and other time periods is entirely captured by the "price-of-utility" term r.

Having introduced the idea of utility having a price, and having also derived demand functions that display close analogies with the input demand functions of a profit-maximizing firm, it is natural to explore the analogy further. Utility can be thought of as output, and if r is given, the consumer can be modeled as choosing $\mathbf{q}_t$ so as to maximize the value of output in time t net of the cost of generating it, $\mathbf{P}_t \cdot \mathbf{q}_t$. This defines a profit function:

$$\Pi_t(\mathbf{P}_t, r) \equiv \max_{\mathbf{q}_t} \{ru_t - \mathbf{P}_t \cdot \mathbf{q}_t \mid u_t = U_t(\mathbf{q}_t)\}.$$

Following the discussion in Chapter 5, we know that the consumer will minimize the cost of attaining whatever utility level is achieved in period t, so that

$$\Pi_t(\mathbf{P}_t, r) = ru_t - E(\mathbf{P}_t, u_t). \tag{16}$$

The demand functions defined in (15) can be obtained by applying Hotelling's lemma to the profit function:

$$\chi_{it}(\mathbf{P}_t, r) = c_{it}(\mathbf{P}_t, u_t) = c_{it}(\mathbf{P}_t, \partial\Pi(\cdot)/\partial r); \tag{17}$$

$$\therefore \ \partial\chi_{it}(\cdot)/\partial P_{jt} = \partial c_{it}(\cdot)/\partial P_{jt} + (\partial c_{it}(\cdot)/\partial u_t)(\partial^2\Pi(\cdot)/\partial P_{jt}\partial r).$$

Young's theorem implies that

$$\partial^2\Pi(\cdot)/\partial P_{jt}\partial r = \partial^2\Pi(\cdot)/\partial r\,\partial P_{jt} = -\partial\chi_{jt}(\cdot)/\partial r.$$

Returning to (17) for commodity j, differentiation with respect to r yields the result that

$$\partial\chi_{jt}(\cdot)/\partial r = (\partial c_{jt}(\cdot)/\partial u_t)(\partial^2\Pi(\cdot)/\partial r^2).$$

Consequently,

$$\partial\chi_{it}(\cdot)/\partial P_{jt} = \partial c_{it}(\cdot)/\partial P_{jt} - (\partial c_{it}(\cdot)/\partial u_t)(\partial c_{jt}/\partial u_t)(\partial^2\Pi(\cdot)/\partial r^2).$$

This not only demonstrates the symmetry of the price responses $\partial \chi_{it}(\cdot)/ \partial P_{jt}$, something that we already know, but also provides a link between these responses and the more conventional compensated price responses $\partial c_{it}(\cdot)/\partial P_{jt}$. Notice that the trick used in establishing the link is no more than a judicious substitution for u_t in (17), in the spirit of the strategy suggested by Cook (1972) in the more familiar context of the Slutsky decomposition.

6.7   Concluding comments and suggestions for further study

Since the original contributions of Gorman and Lancaster, the characteristics model of consumer behavior has been extensively used. Lancaster (1971) provides a book-length treatment, and Deaton and Muellbauer (1980a, pp. 243–54) exploit duality in their exposition of its logical structure. Some econometric aspects are discussed by Boyle, Gorman, and Pudney (1977), and Lipsey and Rosenbluth (1971) use it to take a look at the notorious case of the Giffen good. My discussion of the possibility of an inferior marketed good is based on their analysis. A promised sequel, looking at the empirical literature on Giffen goods, has not, as far as I am aware, been published.

Prior to the work of Milne (1981), which stresses the general idea of induced preferences, of which the characteristics model, the indirect utility function, and preferences defined over net trades are special cases, earlier work had been done by Rader (1964, 1978). More recently, Machina (1984) exploits the same basic idea in modeling risky choice. The trick of defining preferences over net trades is given a rigorous treatment by Chipman (1979). The indirect utility function over net trades was defined, and its properties set out, by Woodland (1980). Subsequently it was further discussed by Woodland (1982) and has been applied to a number of problems in international trade theory by Neary and Schweinberger (1986).

As we have seen, hedonic prices emerge naturally from the idea of characteristics. However, the importance of estimating them and the difficulties in obtaining such estimates have produced a large body of literature with a life of its own. Again, Deaton and Muellbauer (1980a, pp. 254–67) can be recommended for a good overview. There are classic papers by Rosen (1974), Muellbauer (1974), and Pollak and Wachter (1975). For more recent discussions of estimation and interpretation problems, see Follain and Jimenez (1985), Epple (1987), and Bartik (1987).

The literature on separability is not always easy. Gorman (1959, 1968) is one of the pioneers. His papers require considerable effort to absorb, and the best course probably is to start with the broadly sketched survey (Gorman 1976). Much space is devoted to separability and its implications for multistage budgeting and intertemporal models by Blackorby et al. (1978b).

Dual formulations of multiproduct technologies are discussed by Lau (1972) and Hall (1973). Both of these authors, together with Hasenkamp (1976) and Kohli (1983), make effective use of cost and profit functions in providing amenable characterizations of joint and nonjoint technologies. Recent work by students of industrial organization or natural monopoly and the idea of contestability has led to renewed interest in joint production technologies and in the roles played by economies of scope and scale in determining industrial structure – see, for example, Baumol, Panzar, and Willig (1982) and Sharkey (1982, ch. 3 and 4). Chambers (1988) devotes a whole chapter to a useful exposition of the literature on multiproduct technologies. The use of flexible functional forms in estimating technologies enables one to admit the possibility of intrinsic jointness, a fact that has not been lost on Evans and Heckman (1983), among others. At a more aggregate level, Burgess (1976) and Kohli (1978, 1981) have estimated revenue and cost functions at the economy level and have tested the hypothesis of nonjointness. Finally, Teece (1980) sounds a cautionary note about the dangers of drawing hasty inferences about the size and structure of firms from assumptions concerning scope and scale economies at a purely technological level.

Frisch demand functions (Frisch 1932) have recently become popular in empirical studies of labor supply and of life-cycle consumption patterns: Browning et al. (1985), Heckman and MaCurdy (1980), MaCurdy (1981). The roles of separability and of Frisch demand functions in facilitating econometric analysis of life-cycle labor supply are surveyed by Blundell (1986).

CHAPTER 7

Consumer theory with many constraints

Much of the power of the simple model of individual consumer behavior can be traced to the simple environment within which choices are made. It is summarized by a single linear constraint that is readily described by reference to the set of prices and the money income that the individual takes as given. One can interpret the model as one in which there are additional relevant constraints or variables, such as the state of the weather, that are assumed constant for the problem at hand and may therefore be suppressed as explicit variables.

There are, however, many interesting and important problems that involve multiple constraints in such a way as to require their explicit modeling. The wartime rationing experience in many countries during the 1940s, when consumers required ration coupons in addition to money, and even then often found that desired goods were unavailable, stimulated a brief flurry of interest among economists. The consequent literature was comprehensively surveyed by Tobin (1952), but then rather petered out as economists turned their attention to other matters. The waning of interest undoubtedly was attributable in part to the gradual phasing out of formal rationing devices. But in addition to feeling that models of quantity-constrained behavior were less relevant to economic conditions of the 1950s and 1960s, economists also must have felt discouraged by the difficulties encountered in applying the traditional formulation of consumer behavior to situations involving multiple constraints. Since the latter half of the 1970s it has become clear that this class of models is both of much wider applicability and also, with the aid of dual techniques of analysis, susceptible to much simpler analysis than had formerly been recognized.

In Section 7.1 we survey the various possible applications of multiple-constraint models of consumer behavior. Section 7.2 provides an analysis of a simple model in which, in addition to the budget constraint, the consumer faces a single quantity constraint for one of the commodities. We derive various comparative static responses, and in Section 7.3 we derive

167

relationships between these "restricted" responses and their conventional counterparts in the absence of a quantity constraint. Section 7.4 argues that some of the qualitative results of this analysis are quite robust and suggests an interpretation of multiple-constraint models as depicting short-run behavior. An alternative interpretation is offered in Section 7.5, where the additional constraint reflects not just a temporary short-run friction, but rather the idea that many consumption activities inherently involve time as well as money. Finally, Section 7.6 shows in greater detail how multiple constraints arise in situations in which the set of markets is, in some sense, incomplete.

7.1   Applications of the model with quantity constraints

Consider first the range of possible applications of the multiple-constraint model. In the wake of a change in prices or income, the consumer's short-run response may well differ from his long-run response. Certain commitments may have been made, and certain adjustments may be difficult to make quickly, so that in the short run there are other constraints in addition to his budget that must be respected. Turning to macroeconomics, events since the mid-1970s have given us good cause to worry about the chronic failure of markets – particularly that for labor – to clear. The quantity constraints to which some individuals find themselves subjected in the labor market appear to be rather more than an ephemeral attribute of short-run adjustment, and their consequences for behavior are likely to be important in determining the behavior of the macroeconomy. In addition, the very concept of an externality implies constraints on behavior in addition to the budget. The beekeeper in Meade's famous example can consume pollen services generated by the orchardist without paying a price. But at that price of zero, he generally will wish to consume more of those services than are currently supplied – therein lies the source of inefficiency. In short, his consumption of the pollen-generating services of the orchard encounters a quantity constraint. The same is true of detrimental externalities. The recipient may prefer, and would therefore be prepared to pay a price, in order to consume zero quantity of smoke, but is constrained to consume a positive quantity, there being no established market in this particular "bad." The simple model of a public good is a special case. The noncooperative solution envisages each individual as taking the current contribution by the rest of the community as given. This contribution may be thought of as a commodity. Subject to the implied quantity constraint and his budget constraint, the individual optimizes with respect to his own contribution and his consumption of private goods.

The list of applications of the multiple-constraint model is far from exhausted. Two more are worth mentioning. First, there has been a gradual realization that consumption activities require time as well as money and that the constraint imposed by the strictly finite life-span that each of us enjoys on this planet has significant implications for our behavior. This suggests a model in which two budget constraints play roles, one incorporating money prices, the other time prices. The final application concerns the modeling of situations involving incomplete systems of markets. Suppose that there are several time periods or, alternatively, states of nature – the reader may choose whichever interpretation is easier, because the formal argument is the same for both. Within each state the consumer may allocate his income for that state among the currently available goods and services. As regards allocation between states, there are two extreme possibilities. At one extreme there may be such a rich set of assets, or securities, that he can trade freely between states, in which case his consumption set is defined, in the usual way, by a single budget constraint. At the other extreme there may be no such opportunities, so that even if he wishes to give up one unit of a commodity in state 1 in exchange for one unit in state 2, there is no opportunity to do so. In such a world, he will have as many separate budget constraints as there are states. In between these two extremes are situations in which securities exist, but are fewer in number than the states of nature. Again, such a world implies multiple constraints for the consumer.

There are, then, good reasons for wanting to investigate the properties of multiple-constraint models of consumer behavior. The tools of duality now provide an elegant and relatively painless means of conducting such an investigation. I shall confine attention to models in which the constraints are linear in the quantities. Honesty compels me to draw attention to another feature of the exposition that follows. I assume that each of the exogenously imposed constraints holds with strict equality both before and after a comparative static change. This is less easy to justify in a multiple-constraint model than in a single-constraint model, and the analysis itself should really be used to determine endogenously which potential constraints are actually binding. The use of Kuhn–Tucker theory can deal with inequalities, but it introduces complications that are perhaps best avoided in an elementary treatment.

7.2 Consumer behavior with a single quantity constraint: Restricted behavioral functions

Consider a consumer whose utility depends on the quantities consumed of three commodities. Of these, q_1 and q_2 may be chosen subject only to his budget constraint, but q_3 is exogenously imposed. Assume that he pays a positive price for q_3, but P_3 can be put equal to zero if desired. The consumer's problem is

$$\max_{q_1, q_2}\{U(q_1, q_2, q_3) \mid P_1 q_1 + P_2 q_2 + P_3 q_3 = M, q_3 = Q_3\}. \qquad (1)$$

Our task is to generate, and explore the properties of, the "restricted" demand functions that characterize the consumer's behavior. The uncompensated and compensated demand functions will be denoted by $x_i^*(\cdot)$ and $c_i^*(\cdot)$, respectively, to distinguish them from the unrestricted demand functions $x_i(\cdot)$ and $c_i(\cdot)$ that describe the price-taker's behavior. The particular questions to which answers are sought are these: How do exogenous changes in the quantity constraint affect demands for unconstrained goods? How are responses to price and income changes affected by the presence of a constraint that prevents adjustment in the market for commodity 3? This second question touches on the distinction drawn in macroeconomics between notional and effective, or recalculated, demands.

Figure 7.1 illustrates the problem. In the absence of the quantity constraint, the consumer will choose the preferred bundle from those lying on the budget plane, depicted by the plane ABC, at which one of the indifference surfaces in (q_1, q_2, q_3) space just touches the plane. Such a point of tangency is shown as the point W. Each of the closed loops around W represents the intersection of the plane ABC with an indifference surface corresponding to a bundle less preferred than the one associated with price-taking equilibrium at W. Convexity of preferences implies that the set enclosed by any given loop is a convex set. The imposition of the quantity constraint restricts the consumer to points on the segment RS, those points on the budget plane for which $q_3 = Q_3$. When subjected to this additional constraint, the consumer's most preferred bundle is at the tangency of RS with an indifference loop – this is the point E in Figure 7.1. The composition of this restricted optimal bundle, and the implied utility level, will depend on the exogenous variables P_1, P_2, P_3, M, and Q_3, because they determine the constraint set. Before defining the appropriate indirect utility and demand functions, consider in more detail the role played by P_3. Suppose P_3 is increased by ΔP_3, and at the same

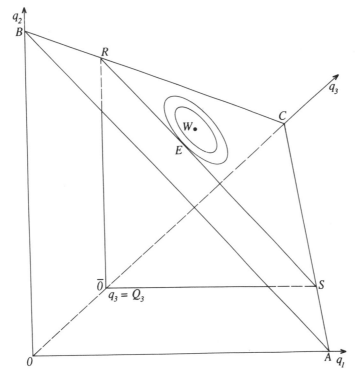

Figure 7.1

time total income is increased by $\Delta M = Q_3 \Delta P_3$. The value of income available for expenditure on commodities 1 and 2 is unchanged, as is their relative price P_1/P_2. Geometrically, the line RS, to which the consumer is constrained, remains unaffected by the change, which simply rotates the budget plane around RS, so that it becomes the plane $A'B'C'$ in Figure 7.2. Consequently, the consumer's choice and maximum attainable utility are unchanged. This means that the restricted demands for q_1 and q_2, and the implied utility level, can be regarded as functions of P_1, P_2, Q_3, and $\tilde{M}$, where $\tilde{M} = M - P_3 Q_3$, the value of discretionary income. More formally, the maximizing problem posed in (1) leads to the definition of a maximum value function, the *restricted indirect utility function:*

$$V^*(P_1, P_2, Q_3, \tilde{M}) \equiv \max_{q_1, q_2}\{U(q_1, q_2, q_3) \mid P_1 q_1 + P_2 q_2 = \tilde{M}, q_3 = Q_3\}. \quad (2)$$

One may think of the quantity constraint as confining the individual to the plane defined by the axes $\bar{0}R$ and $\bar{0}S$. Within this plane, preferences

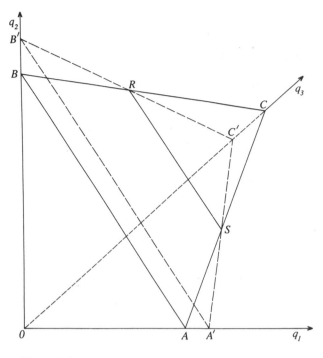

Figure 7.2

over goods 1 and 2 may be represented by standard indifference curves, representing the intersection of the plane with the indifference surfaces in (q_1, q_2, q_3) space, and the budget constraint is simply RS. The consumer is, in effect, confronted with the standard problem of allocating a given value of discretionary income, at fixed prices, among a set of competitively traded commodities. Seen in this way, the duality between direct and indirect utility functions that we analyzed in Chapter 2 extends naturally to the present context. In particular, equation (5) of that chapter becomes, in the present context,

$$U(q_1, q_2, q_3) = \min_{P_1, P_2} \{V^*(P_1, P_2, Q_3, \tilde{M}) \mid P_1 q_1 + P_2 q_2 = \tilde{M}\}. \quad (3)$$

The associated Lagrangian function is

$$L^*(P_1, P_2, Q_3, \tilde{M}) = V^*(P_1, P_2, Q_3, \tilde{M}) - \lambda[P_1 q_1 + P_2 q_2 - \tilde{M}].$$

From this, first-order conditions can be obtained that, upon elimination of the multiplier λ, yield Roy's identity for *restricted uncompensated demand functions*

$$x_i = -\frac{\partial V^*(P_1, P_2, Q_3, \tilde{M})/\partial P_i}{\partial V^*(P_1, P_2, Q_3, \tilde{M})/\partial \tilde{M}} = x_i^*(P_1, P_2, Q_3, \tilde{M}), \quad i = 1, 2. \tag{4}$$

Inspection of (3) and (4) reveals that for a given value of Q_3, $V^*(\cdot)$ and $x_i^*(\cdot)$ have the same properties with respect to P_1, P_2, and $\tilde{M}$ as do their unrestricted counterparts with respect to all prices and money income. In particular they are both homogeneous of degree 0 with respect to $(P_1, P_2, \tilde{M})$. Further, $V^*(\cdot)$ is decreasing with respect to P_1 and P_2, and increasing with respect to $\tilde{M}$. In addition, it is quasi-convex in (P_1, P_2).

Further results are obtained by defining the inverse of $V^*(P_1, P_2, Q_3, \tilde{M})$, the *restricted minimum expenditure function:*

$$E^*(P_1, P_2, Q_3, u)$$
$$\equiv \min_{q_1, q_2}\{P_1 q_1 + P_2 q_2 + P_3 q_3 \,|\, U(q_1, q_2, q_3) = u, \, q_3 = Q_3\}$$
$$= P_3 Q_3 + \min_{q_1, q_2}\{P_1 q_1 + P_2 q_2 \,|\, U(q_1, q_2, q_3) = u, \, q_3 = Q_3\}. \tag{5}$$

Because both P_3 and Q_3 are exogenous, the presence of the term $P_3 Q_3$ makes no difference to the nature of the optimizing problem, and it is possible to work in terms of the discretionary expenditure function, from which the compulsory component $P_3 Q_3$ has been netted out:

$$\tilde{E}^*(P_1, P_2, Q_3, u) \equiv E^*(\cdot) - P_3 Q_3. \tag{6}$$

Both (5) and (6) define minimum value functions and allow one to exploit the envelope property. We shall adopt (5) as our starting point, because this is the more commonly used function, although (6) makes clearer the fact that the ration $q_3 = Q_3$ simply reduces the problem to a standard expenditure-minimizing problem in two dimensions, involving the two unrationed goods and discretionary expenditure.

$E^*(\cdot)$ is clearly increasing in P_i for $i = 1, 2, 3$. Equally clearly, it is increasing in u. It is also homogeneous of degree 1 in (P_1, P_2, P_3), because equal proportional increases in all prices leave the real situation unchanged, so that nominal expenditure must rise by the same proportion. The argument used earlier to establish the concavity of the conventional expenditure function also establishes the concavity of the restricted expenditure function with respect to the prices of freely chosen goods, (P_1, P_2). Finally, the envelope property again implies that "restricted" compensated demand functions may be derived by partial differentiation of $E^*(\cdot)$:

$$\partial E^*(P_1, P_2, P_3, Q_3, u)/\partial P_i = c_i^*(P_1, P_2, P_3, Q_3, u), \quad i = 1, 2.$$

The responses of $E^*(\cdot)$ and $\tilde{E}^*(\cdot)$ to changes in the ration Q_3 merit further attention. $\partial E^*(\cdot)/\partial Q_3$ indicates the change in the level of total

expenditure required to provide exact compensation for a change in the
tion when all prices are held constant, and $\partial \tilde{E}^*(\cdot)/\partial Q_3$ is the required
change in discretionary expenditure. Suppose Q_3 varies exogenously, while
all prices and money income remain fixed. Then, both before and after
the change,

$$E^*(P_1, P_2, P_3, Q_3, u) = M.$$

Substituting the restricted indirect utility function for u,

$$E^*(P_1, P_2, P_3, Q_3, V^*(P_1, P_2, P_3, Q_3, M)) = M,$$

from which partial differentiation with respect to Q yields,

$$E_Q^* + E_u^* V_Q^* = 0$$

or

$$V_Q^* = -E_Q^*/E_u^*.$$

Alternatively, we can use the discretionary expenditure function:

$$\tilde{E}^*(P_1, P_2, Q_3, V^*(\cdot)) = M - P_3 Q_3,$$

from which

$$\tilde{E}_Q^* + E_u^* V_Q^* = -P_3$$

or

$$V_Q^* = -(\tilde{E}_Q^* + P_3)/\tilde{E}_u^*.$$

Figure 7.3, which measures the rationed commodity along the horizontal
axis, and the Hicksian composite commodity consisting of an aggregate
of all the freely chosen commodities along the vertical axis, shows that if
Q_3 is initially chosen to equal the quantity that would be freely chosen
anyway – that is, if $Q_3 = x_3(P_1, P_2, P_3, M)$ – then small changes in Q_3
produce only a second-order effect on utility. This is so at the initial point
I, where an infinitesimal change, dQ_3, would move the consumer along
the indifference curve. At I, $E_Q^* = \tilde{E}_Q^* + P_3 = 0$. However, at J, an increase
in Q_3 by itself raises utility, because $E_Q^* = \tilde{E}_Q^* + P_3 < 0$. The increase in
$P_3 Q_3$ reduces discretionary expenditure by less than would be required
to effect precise compensation. Finally, at K, the reduction in discretionary expenditure required by the additional expenditure on Q_3 is so great
that the consumer will be made worse off by increases in Q_3 is so great
that the consumer will be made worse off by increases in Q_3 unless he receives
additional compensating income. In short, we have established that

$$dU/dQ_3 \gtreqless 0 \quad \text{according to whether} \quad Q_3 \lesseqgtr x_3(\mathbf{P}, M).$$

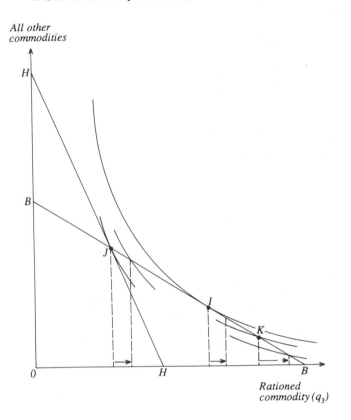

All other commodities

Rationed commodity (q_3)

Figure 7.3

There is another helpful way of characterizing $\partial \tilde{E}^*(\cdot)/\partial Q_3$. Suppose, as in Figure 7.3, that the quantity constraint leads the consumer who faces the budget constraint BB to consume at the point J. There exists a set of prices and a money income that would support consumption at J. This is the hypothetical budget line HH, which touches an indifference curve at J. This budget line is consistent with the actual market prices P_1 and P_2 faced in the quantity-constrained situation, together with a hypothetical, or "virtual," price for commodity 3, which we shall denote by ϕ_3. In other words, there exists a price ϕ_3 such that if the individual were to face the prices (P_1, P_2, ϕ_3), J would represent the least-cost way of achieving the utility level associated with the quantity-constrained equilibrium at J. This implies that

$$\tilde{E}^*(P_1, P_2, Q_3, u) + \phi_3 Q_3 = E(P_1, P_2, \phi_3, u).$$

Let Q_3 change. Then differentiation yields the result that

$$\partial \tilde{E}^*(\cdot)/\partial Q_3 \equiv \tilde{E}_Q^* = -\phi_3.$$

The definition of ϕ_3 makes it clear that it reflects the slope of the indifference curve at J. Indeed, ϕ_3/P_i for $i = 1, 2$, evaluated at the quantity-constrained allocation, is the marginal rate of substitution between commodities 3 and i at that point. Hence, $\partial \tilde{E}^*(\cdot)/\partial Q_3$ is simply the demand, or virtual, price of the rational commodity, which can therefore be defined as a function $\phi_3(P_1, P_2, Q_3, u)$.

This completes the groundwork necessary for analysis of the restricted uncompensated demand functions, $x_i^*(P_1, P_2, P_3, Q_3, M)$, and their compensated counterparts $c_i^*(P_1, P_2, P_3, Q_3, u)$. Recall that for a given value of Q_3, $x_i^*(\cdot)$ and $c_i^*(\cdot)$ are perfectly well behaved demand functions in (q_1, q_2) space. Their qualitative properties have already been analyzed in Chapters 3 and 4, and Figures 7.2 and 7.3 clearly show that the effect of introducing the constraint $q_3 = Q_3$ is simply to reduce the consumer's problem into an orthodox one in as many dimensions as there are freely chosen goods. Equation (6) further clarifies the one new element, which is the pure income effect generated by changes in P_3.

What can be said about $\partial x_i^*(\cdot)/\partial Q_3$ and $\partial c_i^*(\cdot)/\partial Q_3$? The uncompensated response may be decomposed into a pure compensated substitution term and a pure income response by using Cook's substitution trick, replacing M with $E^*(\cdot)$:

$$x_i^*(P_1, P_2, P_3, Q_3, E^*(\cdot)) = c_i^*(P_1, P_2, P_3, Q_3, u).$$

Partial differentiation with respect to Q_3 yields

$$x_{iQ}^* + x_{im}^* E_Q^* = c_{iQ}^*.$$

Rearranging, and exploiting the fact that $E_Q^* = P_3 + \tilde{E}_Q^* = P_3 - \phi_3$,

$$x_{iQ}^* = c_{iQ}^* + (\phi_3 - P_3) x_{im}^*$$

$$= \text{pure substitution} + \text{real income}$$
$$\quad\;\; \text{response} \qquad\qquad \text{response}.$$

The form of the real income component is intuitively reasonable. The implications for utility of a change in the ration must clearly depend on the difference between the price actually paid for units of the rational good, P_3, and the demand price, ϕ_3.

What can be said about the compensated responses, $\partial c_i^*(\cdot)/\partial Q_3 \equiv c_{iQ}^*$? Briefly, not very much. Their price-weighted sum will be negative, because

$$P_1 c_1^*(\cdot) + P_2 c_2^*(\cdot) + P_3 Q_3 = E^*(\cdot);$$

$$\therefore \; P_1 c_{1Q}^* + P_2 c_{2Q}^* = E_Q^* - P_3.$$

So long as the rationed commodity is, indeed, a good, ϕ_3 is positive, so that at least one out of c_{1Q}^* and c_{2Q}^* must be negative. However, the individual responses c_{iQ}^* may be of either sign. An increase in the ration of bread may, at constant real income, stimulate the demand for jam while curtailing that for cake – this certainly seems plausible if we share Marie Antoinette's judgment that bread and cakes are close substitutes.

7.3   Relationships between restricted and unrestricted behavior

The last comment, whimsical as it sounds, raises an issue that has interested students of quantity-constrained behavior since the 1940s. Is it possible to relate the value of the restricted responses – $\partial x_i^*/\partial P_j$, $\partial x_i^*/\partial Q_3$, $\partial c_i^*/\partial P_j$, $\partial c_i^*/\partial Q_3$, and so on – to the values of the conventional responses? One advantage of this would be that the signs and magnitudes of restricted responses could, with luck, be related to whether pairs of goods are substitutes or complements according to the various conventional measures used. We might be able to say that $\partial c_i^*/\partial Q_3$ will be negative if, according to some familiar criterion, goods i and 3 are close substitutes.

    Consider an initial price-taking equilibrium. The consumer's compensated demand for commodity i ($i = 1, 2$) may be described as usual by $c_i(P_1, P_2, P_3, u)$. But an equally valid description is provided by the restricted demand function, on the assumption that the "ration," Q_3, is in fact the consumer's optimal price-taking quantity:

$$c_i^*(P_1, P_2, P_3, Q_3, u) = c_i^*(P_1, P_2, P_3, c_3(P_1, P_2, P_3, u), u). \qquad (7)$$

Yet again, this is simply Cook's substitution trick. The allocation process is in effect split into two stages: $c_3(\cdot)$ is chosen optimally, and in the light of that choice $c_1^*(\cdot)$ and $c_2^*(\cdot)$ are determined. Now consider the effect of a small change in P_3 on the demand for commodity i, with other prices and utility held constant. Both before and after the change, the price-taker's behavior is equally well represented by $c_i(\cdot)$ or $c_i^*(\cdot)$, bearing in mind that commodity 3 is always optimally chosen:

$$c_i^*(P_1, P_2, P_3, c_3(P_1, P_2, P_3, u), u) = c_i(P_1, P_2, P_3, u); \qquad (8)$$

$$\therefore \; \frac{\partial c_i^*}{\partial P_3} + \frac{\partial c_i^*}{\partial Q_3} \frac{\partial c_3}{\partial P_3} = \frac{\partial c_i}{\partial P_3}. \qquad (9)$$

But $\partial c_i^*/\partial P_3 = 0$, because if dP_3 is accompanied by an offsetting change in income, while consumption of commodity 3 is held constant, the choice between commodities 1 and 2 is quite unaffected. Therefore,

$$\frac{\partial c_i^*}{\partial Q_3} = \frac{\partial c_i/\partial P_3}{\partial c_3/\partial P_3}. \tag{10}$$

Because we know that $\partial c_3/\partial P_3$ is negative, (10) states that the restricted quantity response $\partial c_i^*/\partial Q_3$ is of opposite sign from the unrestricted price response, $\partial c_i/\partial P_3$. If beer and wine are net substitutes in the sense that the unrestricted compensated cross-price response is positive, then a compensated reduction in the beer ration will stimulate consumption of wine, and vice versa. On the other hand, if bread and butter are net complements, a compensated reduction in the bread ration will reduce butter consumption.

Other responses can be related in a similar way. Of particular interest are the responses $\partial c_i^*/\partial P_j$, where j is an unrationed commodity. Consider (8) again:

$$\frac{\partial c_i^*}{\partial P_j} + \frac{\partial c_i^*}{\partial Q_3}\frac{\partial c_3}{\partial P_j} = \frac{\partial c_i}{\partial P_j}, \quad i, j = 1, 2.$$

Using (10), and rearranging,

$$\frac{\partial c_i^*}{\partial P_j} = \frac{\partial c_i}{\partial P_j} - \frac{\partial c_i/\partial P_3}{\partial c_3/\partial P_3}\frac{\partial c_3}{\partial P_j}. \tag{11}$$

A special case of (11) arises when $i = j$. Because $\partial c_3/\partial P_3 < 0$ and $\partial c_i/\partial P_3 = \partial c_3/\partial P_i$, (11) implies that

$$\left|\frac{\partial c_i^*}{\partial P_i}\right| < \left|\frac{\partial c_i}{\partial P_i}\right|. \tag{12}$$

The restricted compensated own-price response is numerically smaller than its unrestricted counterpart.

This result can be seen in a geometric way. Suppose we graph minimum expenditure against P_i, as we did in Chapter 4. Initially the price is P_i^0, and the level of expenditure of a price-taking consumer is E^0. Now let P_i increase. If Q_3 is held constant, then the consumer will require at least as much additional expenditure to maintain his original utility level, and generally more, than if he is allowed to adjust his consumption of commodity 3. In Figure 7.4, the graph of $E^*(\cdot)$ lies everywhere on or above that of $E(\cdot)$. Translated into statements about changes in slopes, the slope of $E^*(\cdot)$ declines more slowly as P_i increases than does that of

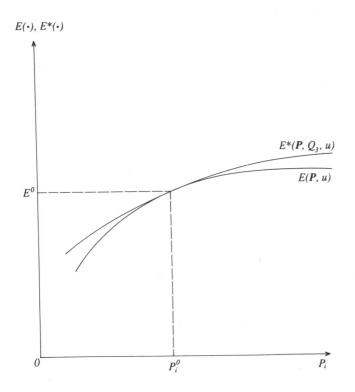

Figure 7.4

$E(\cdot)$. The slope is itself the quantity demanded, so that the inequality (12) follows from the geometric argument.

7.4   Short- and long-run responses

One of the most striking of the results obtained in the preceding section is (12), which tells us that the restricted compensated own-price response, $\partial c_i^*/\partial P_i$, is numerically smaller than its unrestricted counterpart. Obtained under the assumption of a single quantity constraint, this result is in fact extremely robust, in the sense that it holds in the presence of much more general constraints. It is an example of Le Chatelier's principle, as expounded by Samuelson (1947). Suppose that the single quantity constraint is replaced by any arbitrary function of the q_i's. The important point is that it should not contain P_i as an argument. Denote the constraint by $K(\mathbf{q}) = 0$. Then we can define the restricted expenditure function as

$$E^*(\cdot) = \min_{\mathbf{q}} \{ \mathbf{P} \cdot \mathbf{q} \mid U(\mathbf{q}) = u, K(\mathbf{q}) = 0 \}.$$

$K(\mathbf{q})$ may be a single quantity constraint, a vector of such constraints, a linear relationship of the form $q_1 = 2q_2$, or indeed almost anything. Suppose that initially the consumer is at a price-taking equilibrium at which the constraint happens to be precisely satisfied. Now P_i changes. In the presence of the additional constraint the consumer cannot be better off and will generally be worse off than in its absence. This implies that the expenditure required to maintain his original utility level generally will be greater when the constraint $K(\mathbf{q}) = 0$ is imposed:

$$E^*(\cdot) \geq E(\cdot),$$

with the equality holding at the initial price-taking equilibrium. The argument proceeds exactly as in the preceding section. Shephard's lemma is still valid, restricted compensated demand functions can be defined as partial derivatives of $E^*(\cdot)$, and the inequality presented in (12) remains true.

The importance of this is that $K(\mathbf{q}) = 0$ can represent any set of additional constraints that can impede the individual's adjustment to price-taking equilibrium in the short run. In response to a large increase in the price of gasoline, the individual may find it difficult or inconvenient to adjust immediately by exchanging one automobile for another, or moving to a different neighborhood, or sending his children to a school closer to home. In time, he may acquire a smaller car. Eventually his adjustments may involve relocating himself, after his children have gone to college. Clearly, there are all sorts of constraints that are felt in the short run. The purpose of this section is to show that the logic behind the restricted behavioral functions continues to hold even in the face of more complex systems of constraints than the simple single-quantity ration.

7.5   Time and money: Behavior subject to two budget constraints

In addition to emphasizing the money cost of consumption, economists have drawn attention to the limitations imposed by the fact that consumption uses up the scarce resource of time. No amount of technical progress, however fiendishly ingenious, will allow one to enjoy a Mahler symphony without setting aside an hour or two for that purpose. This suggests that the consumer faces two constraints. Suppose that a unit of activity j, which is synonymous with the consumption of one unit of good j, costs P_j units of money and t_j hours. Activities cannot be undertaken simultaneously; so an hour spent jogging cannot also be made available for eating a dinner. The consumer's problem is then

$$\max_{\mathbf{q}} U(\mathbf{q}) \quad \text{subject to } \mathbf{P} \cdot \mathbf{q} \le M \text{ and } \mathbf{t} \cdot \mathbf{q} \le T, \tag{13}$$

where T is the total endowment of available hours. With two budget constraints, there is not a single minimum expenditure function. However, we can use the fact that given one of the constraints, the consumer will minimize his expenditure of the other resource. We assume that, at the consumer's equilibrium, both constraints are binding. Then we can define the minimum money expenditure function as

$$E^*(\mathbf{P}, \mathbf{t}, T, u) = \min_{\mathbf{q}} \{\mathbf{P} \cdot \mathbf{q} \mid \mathbf{t} \cdot \mathbf{q} = T, U(\mathbf{q}) = u\}.$$

The time constraint simply restricts the choice of $\mathbf{q}$ to a convex subset in quantity space. The definition of $E^*(\cdot)$ guarantees that it retains its familiar properties. It is increasing and concave in $\mathbf{P}$ and increasing in u, and its derivative with respect to P_i yields a demand function for q_i:

$$\partial E^*(\cdot)/\partial P_i = c_i^*(\mathbf{P}, \mathbf{t}, T, u).$$

The reasoning is precisely the same as that used in Chapter 4. The simple quantity ration is a special case in which $\mathbf{t}$ is a unit vector, $(0, 0, \dots, 1, \dots, 0)$, and T is interpreted as the fixed ration. The convex subset thereby defined is then a (hyper)plane orthogonal to one of the quantity axes.

An indirect utility function can also be defined:

$$V^*(\mathbf{P}, \mathbf{t}, M, T) \equiv \max_{\mathbf{q}} \{U(\mathbf{q}) \mid \mathbf{P} \cdot \mathbf{q} = M, \mathbf{t} \cdot \mathbf{q} = T\}$$

$$= U(\mathbf{x}^*(\mathbf{P}, \mathbf{t}, M, T)).$$

Again, a form of Roy's identity can be generated and used to assist comparative static analysis. One has to be careful, because the extra constraint reduces the degrees of freedom available to the consumer. This was obvious in the example with straight rationing, because q_3 could not be freely chosen. In the present, more general, setting it is less obvious, but equally true, that a degree of freedom has disappeared. To make this clear, let us look at a special case that has attracted attention. Suppose that one of three commodities, say q_3, is leisure. Further, suppose that leisure as such does not enter into the individual's utility function. He cares only about the quantities consumed of goods 1 and 2, expenditure on which is determined by the hours of work – or sacrificed leisure – and the wage received for that work, w. Consumption of goods also takes time. The consumer's problem is

$$\max U(q_1, q_2) \quad \text{subject to} \quad P_1 q_1 + P_2 q_2 = M + w\ell \quad \text{and} \quad t_1 q_1 + t_2 q_2 = T - \ell,$$

where T is the total time endowment, and ℓ is the number of hours worked. In terms of the more general notation, $\ell = q_3$, $w = -P_3$, and $t_3 = 1$. In this example it is possible to eliminate the commodity ℓ – or q_3 – and simultaneously eliminate one of the two constraints, by simple substitution, so as to yield the problem

$$\max U(q_1, q_2) \quad \text{subject to} \quad (P_1 + wt_1)q_1 + (P_2 + wt_2)q_2 = M + wT.$$

This is a conventional single-constraint problem in which the terms $P_i + wt_i$ may be interpreted as "total" prices, incorporating both the money and time costs of consumption. Such a problem is easily analyzed with the help of unrestricted expenditure and indirect utility functions, $E(\phi_1, \phi_2, u)$ and $V(\phi_1, \phi_2, M + wT)$, where ϕ_i is the total price of commodity i.

As an exercise, consider the compensated response in the demand for commodity i to a change in the wage. We know that

$$c_i(\cdot) = c_i(P_1 + wt_1, P_2 + wt_2, u) = c_i(\phi_1, \phi_2, u) = E_i(\phi_1, \phi_2, u);$$
$$\therefore \ \partial c_i / \partial w = E_{i1}(\partial \phi_1 / \partial w) + E_{i2}(\partial \phi_2 / \partial w).$$

But $\phi_i = P_i + t_i w$, so that $\partial \phi_i / \partial w = t_i$. Therefore,

$$\partial c_i / \partial w = t_1 E_{i1} + t_2 E_{i2}. \tag{14}$$

Now $c_i(\cdot)$, being a compensated demand function, is homogeneous of degree 0 in (ϕ_1, ϕ_2). Therefore,

$$0 = (P_1 + t_1 w)E_{i1} + (P_2 + t_2 w)E_{i2}. \tag{15}$$

Put $i = 1$, and use (14) and (15) to solve for $\partial c_1 / \partial w$, eliminating E_{12}:

$$\frac{\partial c_1}{\partial w} = \frac{P_2 t_1 - P_1 t_2}{P_2 + wt_2} E_{11}$$

$$= \frac{P_1 P_2}{P_2 + wt_2}\left[\frac{t_1}{P_1} - \frac{t_2}{P_2}\right] E_{11}.$$

Because we know that E_{11}, the compensated own-price response, is negative, the sign of $\partial c_1 / \partial w$ depends on the comparison between t_1/P_1 and t_2/P_2. If good 1 is relatively time-intensive, so that $t_1/P_1 > t_2/P_2$, an increase in w will reduce its compensated demand. My derivation closely follows that of Atkinson and Stern (1979), who, besides showing the power of the expenditure function in this context, warn that this particular result does not hold if there are more than two commodities in addition to leisure.

7.6   Specific applications of the multiple-constraint model

Much of the early work on rationing – see, for example, Tobin (1952) – was concerned with points rationing. Individuals in wartime economies received ration books and faced given coupon prices – so many coupons for a dozen eggs, so many for a quart of milk, and so on. Denoting the coupon prices by R_i, and the total endowment of coupons as N, the individual faced a constraint $\sum R_i q_i = N$, in addition to the money income constraint. This is formally identical with the problem formulated in (13). The relevance of points rationing may not be immediately apparent, but similar systems of constraints arise in other contexts that economists take seriously. In particular, the analysis of intertemporal resource allocation, especially under uncertainty, raises the possibility of the set of available markets being, in some sense, incomplete, so that individuals face multiple constraints. I raised this possibility at the beginning of this chapter. I now spell out in more detail how multiple constraints can arise.

Suppose there are two time periods: today and tomorrow. It is not currently known which of two states of the world will obtain tomorrow – for instance, it may be wet or dry. Let q_{ij} and P_{ij} denote the quantity and price of a commodity of type i given state j. Today's values are denoted by putting $j = 0$, and the two possible states tomorrow are denoted by $j = 1, 2$. Thus, q_{12} is the quantity of commodity 1 in the event of tomorrow being dry. We suppose there are two physically distinct commodities. Also, we denote by M_j the individual's exogenous money income in state j. Consider the consumer's utility maximization problem in a world in which there are no assets or securities that allow him to exchange purchasing power between states. If the commodities are perishable, and cannot be stored, the problem is

$$\max_q U(q_{10}, q_{20}, q_{11}, q_{21}, q_{12}, q_{22}) \quad \text{subject to } P_{10}q_{10} + P_{20}q_{20} = M_0,$$
$$P_{11}q_{11} + P_{21}q_{21} = M_1, \quad (16)$$
$$P_{12}q_{12} + P_{22}q_{22} = M_2.$$

This is a straightforward multiple-constraint problem with a special structure – each commodity appears in only one constraint, there being as many constraints as there are states.

Now suppose, instead, that there is one asset. The individual can buy a unit of this asset at time 0 at the given price w. In return, if state 1 occurs, he receives the commodity bundle (z_{11}, z_{21}) tomorrow, where z_{ij} is the quantity of commodity i in the state j. If state 2 occurs, he receives (z_{12}, z_{22}) tomorrow. If he purchases s units of the asset today, his constraints become

$$P_{10}q_{10} + P_{20}q_{20} + ws = M_0,$$

$$P_{11}q_{11} + P_{21}q_{21} = M_1 + (P_{11}z_{11} + P_{21}z_{21})s, \tag{17}$$

$$P_{12}q_{12} + P_{22}q_{22} = M_2 + (P_{12}z_{12} + P_{22}z_{22})s.$$

The quantity s, though endogenous, does not appear in his direct utility function. This reflects the assumption that assets are important to the individual only insofar as they help to generate preferred commodity bundles. It is natural to eliminate s from the constraints, so that they and the objective function will contain precisely the same endogenous variables. Because there is the one variable, s, this procedure eliminates one constraint. For example, eliminating the current budget constraint from (17) yields two equations of the form

$$\frac{P_{11}z_{11} + P_{21}z_{21}}{w}(P_{10}q_{10} + P_{20}q_{20}) + P_{1j}q_{1j} + P_{2j}q_{2j}$$

$$= \frac{P_{11}z_{11} + P_{21}z_{21}}{w}M_0 + M_j, \quad j = 1, 2,$$

which are of the form

$$\rho_{10}q_{10} + \rho_{20}q_{20} + \rho_{1j}q_{1j} + \rho_{2j}q_{2j} = \mu_j, \quad j = 1, 2, \tag{18}$$

where the ρ_{ij}'s and μ_j's may be interpreted as exogenous price and income variables. It is a straightforward utility maximization problem with two linear constraints. Its comparative static analysis has to be done with care. If P_{11} changes, this implies a change in ρ_{11}, which appears in the first constraint, and also in ρ_{10} and ρ_{20}, which appear in both constraints. For this reason, the reduced-form price and income variables that appear in (18) may not always be the most helpful formulation. However, (18) makes the most important point, which is that the incompleteness of the set of markets can lead to situations in which the individual's constraint set is defined by a system of linear constraints precisely identical with the points-rationing model discussed by Tobin and others. It would be a useful exercise for the reader to introduce a second security into the example and confirm that, in general, the system can then be collapsed into an orthodox one of utility maximization subject to a single linear constraint.

7.7   Concluding comments and suggestions for further study

The survey article by Tobin (1952) represents the culmination of a period of intense interest by economists in nonprice rationing problems. Two earlier pieces are particularly notable. Rothbarth (1941) was responsible for introducing the concept of virtual prices, which was later used by Malmquist (1953). The analysis by Tobin and Houthakker (1951) is particularly instructive, because it shows how hard one must work to obtain comparative static properties of rationed behavior if the direct utility function is used as the starting point.

More recently, Muellbauer and Portes (1978) have drawn on the work of Malinvaud (1977) to indicate the relevance of the microeconomic model of constrained behavior to the analysis of macroeconomic models. Its relevance to models involving externalities and public goods has been argued by Cornes (1980), and restricted indirect utility and expenditure functions, together with virtual prices, will be encountered again in Chapter 10.

The systematic application of dual techniques to quantity-constrained choice began in a flurry of papers in the late 1970s. The theory was set out by Cornes (1979), Latham (1980), Mackay and Whitney (1980), and Neary and Roberts (1980) and has been expounded by Deaton and Muellbauer (1980a, pp. 109–15). Deaton and Muellbauer (1981) use the theory to examine plausible functional forms for restricted commodity demand functions in the presence of labor supply constraints and explore the implications for consumer preferences of the commonly estimated linear labor supply function. Both theoretical and empirical considerations have been surveyed by Deaton (1981). See also Blundell and Walker (1982) for an analysis of labor constraints from an empirical viewpoint. Following Samuelson (1965), Chavas (1984) has explored the properties of "mixed" demand functions, which have as their arguments a mixed set of prices and quantities.

The important role of time as an input to the consumption process has been stressed by Becker (1965). It naturally suggests a household production model, similar in spirit to Lancaster's characteristics model, in which time and traded commodities are combined to produce desired characteristics. The possible implications of the scarcity of time were further explored by Burenstam Linder (1970), whose work provoked a symposium in the *Quarterly Journal of Economics,* edited by Schelling (1973), in which the most relevant contribution from the point of view of the present chapter is by Baumol (1973). Baumol's analysis prompted the comment by Atkinson and Stern (1979) on which this treatment draws. Atkinson and Stern (1981) used the time-and-money model as the basis for serious empirical analysis of consumer behavior. The combination of a household production model with recent developments in functional forms can produce a particularly rich and versatile structure.

Cornes and Milne (1989) have analyzed a model with incomplete securities markets in a way that emphasizes its formal parallels with the models of points rationing surveyed by Tobin (1952) – see also Diamond and Yaari (1972). Shefrin and Heineke (1979) have discussed how the set of constraints may be reduced to a set of the kind appearing as (18) in this chapter, and they warn against the mechanical and illegitimate application of Roy's identity to systems in which such substitutions have been made.

The addition of linear rationing constraints to the standard budget constraint represents the simplest way of introducing nonlinearity into the consumer's problem. Blomquist (1985, 1989) and Epstein (1981a) have considered nonlinear constraints more generally, and Hausman (1985) has discussed the implications of such nonlinearity for econometric work. Recently, Bronsard and Salvas-Bronsard (1986) have suggested that consumption data that, at first glance, may not appear to be reconcilable with rational behavior can be so reconciled if one takes account of possible quantity constraints. Finally, Goodspeed and Schwab (1988) have suggested a number of problems in public economics that lend themselves to simple analysis using some of the tricks introduced in this chapter.

PART III

Applying the model of individual behavior

CHAPTER 8

Aggregation analysis

For certain purposes, the economist can enjoy the luxury of working at a very disaggregated level. For example, analyses of the conditions under which a competitive equilibrium is guaranteed to exist follow similar lines whether there are two commodities or 2 million. This being so, it makes good sense to accommodate the possibility of a large number of commodities. As with commodities, so with agents. Indeed, it can be a positive advantage to assume a large number of agents with different preferences. Local nonconvexities in the preferences of some particular group may then get washed out at the aggregate level.

Nevertheless, when it comes to qualitative comparative statics and empirical analysis of data sets, aggregation over things and people often is extremely helpful. It is therefore important to know whether, and under what assumptions, such aggregation is legitimate and also to know what useful properties, if any, of the disaggregated system survive the aggregation process.

Those who like neat, simple answers, and who would like to be able to believe that aggregated systems possess simple properties, will derive little comfort from aggregation analysis. The assumptions required to justify aggregation are quite stringent and are almost never satisfied in the world that generates the data. In a recent study of the subject, van Daal and Merkies (1984, p. 14) express the leitmotiv of aggregation analysis thus: "aggregation is nearly always impossible; nevertheless one nearly always has to aggregate, hence let us, therefore, investigate how serious are the inconsistencies due to aggregation we have committed and make the best of it."

Despite its disappointingly weak results, indeed because of them, aggregation analysis is important. When one is on thin ice, it is important to know that fact.

8.1 Aggregation over commodities: Hicksian composite commodities

Consider a consumer who faces a vector of money prices $P_1, \ldots, P_n$. Suppose that we are interested in analyzing his behavior in situations in which

P_1 and money income, M, may vary in arbitrary ways, but in which the relative prices of commodities $2, 3, \ldots, n$ remain constant. Hicks (1946, pp. 312–13) suggested that in this circumstance, commodites 2 through n may be aggregated into a single composite commodity, so that the consumer can be modeled as choosing between two commodities, with preferences being represented by a direct utility function $U^c(q_1, q_c)$ or, alternatively, an indirect utility function $V^c(P_1, P_c, M)$, where q_c and P_c are the quantity and price of the composite commodity.

Hicks's composite commodity theorem is easy to demonstrate using duality. Let the consumer's preferences over the n commodities be represented by the indirect utility function $V(P_1, P_2, \ldots, P_n, M)$. Let initial prices be $P_1^0, \ldots, P_n^0$. By assumption, we restrict our attention to situations in which there exists some scalar θ such that

$$P_j = \theta P_j^0, \quad j = 2, \ldots, n.$$

Define the function $V^c(P_1, \theta, M)$:

$$V^c(P_1, \theta, M) = \{V(P_1, P_2, \ldots, P_n, M) \mid P_j = \theta P_j^0 \text{ for } j = 2, \ldots, n\} \tag{1}$$

$$= V(P_1, \theta P_2^0, \ldots, \theta P_n^0, M). \tag{2}$$

I wish to show that $V^c(\cdot)$ is an indirect utility function and that the scalar θ can be interpreted as the price of the composite commodity, P_c, the quantity of which in any situation can be defined as $x_c \equiv \sum_{j=2}^{n} P_j^0 x_j$.

It is a straightforward matter to show that $V^c(\cdot)$ satisfies the conditions required of an indirect utility function. Using (2), it is clearly a nonincreasing function of P_1 and of $P_c \ (= \theta)$ and a nondecreasing function of M. It is also homogeneous of degree 0 in P_1, θ, and M. Finally, quasi-convexity of $V^c(\cdot)$ in P_1 and P_c is equally clearly inherited from quasi-convexity of $V(\cdot)$ in $P_1, \ldots, P_n$. The present thought experiment simply confines attention to a particular subset of those price vector comparisons that are considered in the definition of quasi-convexity.

Having established that $V^c(P_1, \theta, M)$ is an indirect utility function, it remains only to exploit Roy's identity to generate the appropriate definition of quantity of the composite commodity, and then show that the scalar θ is the composite commodity's price.

First, observe that partial differentiation of (2) yields the results that

$$\partial V^c(\cdot)/\partial P_1 = \partial V(\cdot)/\partial P_1,$$

$$\partial V^c(\cdot)/\partial M = \partial V(\cdot)\partial M,$$

and

$$\partial V^c(\cdot)/\partial\theta = \sum_{j=2}^{n} P_j^0 \partial V(\cdot)/\partial P_j.$$

Consequently, Roy's identity may be exploited to yield the results that

$$-\frac{\partial V^c(\cdot)/\partial P_1}{\partial V^c(\cdot)/\partial M} = -\frac{\partial V(\cdot)/\partial P_1}{\partial V(\cdot)/\partial M} = x_1(P_1, \theta, M),$$

and

$$-\frac{\partial V^c(\cdot)/\partial\theta}{\partial V^c(\cdot)/\partial M} = -\frac{\sum_{j=2}^{n} P_j^0 \partial V(\cdot)/\partial P_j}{\partial V(\cdot)/\partial M} = \sum_{j=2}^{n} P_j^0 x_j(\cdot) = x_c(\cdot).$$

The price of the composite commodity should certainly have the property of being consistent with the budget constraint. We require, therefore, that $P_1 x_1 + P_c x_c = M$. From the definition of θ we know that

$$\sum_{j=2}^{n} P_j^0 x_j = \sum_{j=2}^{n} (P_j/\theta) x_j,$$

$$\sum_{j=2}^{n} P_j x_j = \sum_{j=2}^{n} \theta P_j^0 x_j = \theta \sum_{j=2}^{n} P_j^0 x_j = \theta x_c.$$

Therefore,

$$P_1 x_1 + \sum_{j=2}^{n} P_j x_j = P_1 x_1 + \theta x_c.$$

As with consumers, so with producers. Consider a competitive firm that produces a given output at minimum cost with n inputs, and suppose that the relative prices of the inputs $\ell_2, \ldots, \ell_n$ remain constant throughout the analysis. Then we can define the function

$$C^c(y, W_1, \theta) \equiv C(y, W_1, W_2, \ldots, W_n)$$
$$= C(y, W_1, \theta W_2^0, \ldots, \theta W_n^0),$$

where $W_2^0, \ldots, W_n^0$ is a given vector of factor returns. The argument parallels our treatment of the consumer. Partial differentiation yields

$$\partial C^c(\cdot)/\partial W_1 = \partial C(\cdot)/\partial W_1 = \ell_1(y, W_1, \theta),$$

$$\partial C^c(\cdot)/\partial\theta = \sum_{j=2}^{n} W_j^0 \partial C(\cdot)/\partial W_j = \sum_{j=2}^{n} W_j^0 \ell_j(y, W_1, \theta).$$

The weighted sum of individual factor demands, $\sum_{j=2}^{n} W_j^0 \ell_j$, provides a measure of the quantity of the composite input, and θ is its price. The cost function defined over the composite inputs, $C^c(\cdot)$, is again easily shown to possess the properties that characterize a cost function. In circumstances that permit definition of a profit function, the composite commodity theorem can be established in exactly the same way using $\Pi(\cdot)$.

Hicks's composite commodity theorem has proved extremely useful. It implies that if the relative prices of commodities 2 through n are fixed, then we can treat the resulting model as a two-commodity model. The analysis of the consumer's problem, for example, can then proceed with the help of indifference curves in two-dimensional space, with the quantity of commodity 1, say, measured along one axis, and the quantity of the composite good measured along the other. International trade theory exploits the theorem to advantage in modeling the small, open economy. This is an economy that, for whatever reason, faces exogenously given world prices for its importables and exportables. If the terms of trade are assumed to be fixed, then these two categories of commodities can be aggregated into the single category of tradable goods. The analyses of Swan (1955), Salter (1959), and, more recently, Jones (1974) demonstrate the convenience of being able to deal with a single composite tradable commodity.

8.2   Aggregation over agents: Exact aggregation

The theory of consumer behavior developed in Chapters 2–4 imagines a single individual maximizing utility subject to a single budget constraint. In reality, the data with which our models are estimated and tested relate to groups of individuals. Even the individual household typically is a group of three or more. It would be extremely convenient if we could treat a group as if it were a single consumer, with its aggregate demand behavior in competitive situations precisely obeying the restrictions that characterize the behavior of a rational individual. Total demand for commodity i, $\sum_h x_i^h$, could then be modeled by a single aggregate demand function, such as $X_i(\mathbf{P}, \sum_h M^h)$. Aggregate compensated demand functions, together with aggregate expenditure and indirect utility functions, could also be defined. Because this is precisely what is usually done in empirical work, it is important that we know exactly what has to be assumed in order to justify the application of such macroeconomic analogues to microeconomic demand systems. It turns out that the conditions under which aggregation is possible are very stringent.

Intuition suggests, and analysis confirms, that there are two alternative types of restrictions that give rise to aggregate uncompensated demand functions. We can place restrictions on admissible income distributions, in the hope that there exists a subset of distributions for which the associated aggregate demands will behave as if they were generated by a single individual. Alternatively, if we want to allow arbitrary redistributions of income, we must impose some restriction on the form of individual preferences. Let us explore this second route first, because it is the more commonly encountered.

Restrictions on preferences

Let there be two consumers whose demands for commodity i are $x_i^1(\mathbf{P}, M^1)$ and $x_i^2(\mathbf{P}, M^2)$. If there is to be an aggregate demand function of the form $X_i(\mathbf{P}, M^1 + M^2)$, it must be the case that a redistribution of a given total income between the two individuals will leave the aggregate demand unchanged. Let an amount dM^1 be taken from individual 1 and transferred to individual 2. This keeps aggregate income unchanged, because $d(M^1 + M^2) = dM^1 + dM^2 = 0$. Under what conditions does this leave X_i unchanged? Clearly, a sufficient condition is that

$$\partial x_i^1(\cdot)/\partial M^1 = \partial x_i^2(\cdot)/\partial M^2 = 0.$$

If individual income responses are zero, so too must be the aggregate response $dX_i = dx_i^1 + dx_i^2$. However, this condition is very stringent and is not consistent with the empirical observation that commodities generally have positive income responses. Fortunately, the condition is not necessary. Equality of the two individuals' income responses, whether they are zero or not, is sufficient. If taking the amount dM^1 away from individual 1 changes that individual's demand for commodity i by dx_i^1, and if giving it to individual 2 changes x_i^2 by $dx_i^2 = -dx_i^1$, then X_i will be unchanged. This clearly will be the case if demand functions are of the form

$$x_i^h = aM^h + b^h, \quad h = 1, 2, \tag{3}$$

where a, b^1, and b^2 are exogenous parameters. Observe that the parameter a is common to both individuals. These are rather odd demand functions, because prices do not appear. However, because both individuals are assumed to face a common set of prices, the coefficients a and b^h can themselves be made functions of prices. The demand functions then become

$$x_i^h = a(\mathbf{P})M^h + b^h(\mathbf{P}), \quad h = 1, 2. \tag{4}$$

Again, the function $a(\mathbf{P})$ is common to both individuals. The function $b^h(\cdot)$, by contrast, need not be. Let us check that income responses do indeed have the desired property:

$$\partial x_i^h(\cdot)/\partial M^h = a(\mathbf{P}), \quad h = 1, 2.$$

Therefore, if prices remain constant and income is redistributed so that $dM^1 + dM^2 = 0$, we have

$$dX_i = (\partial x_i^1(\cdot)/\partial M^1)dM^1 + (\partial x_i^2(\cdot)/\partial M^2)dM^2$$
$$= a(\mathbf{P})dM^1 + a(\mathbf{P})dM^2$$
$$= a(\mathbf{P})[dM^1 + dM^2]$$
$$= 0.$$

If individual demand functions, then, are of the form given by (4), then aggregate demand is independent of income distribution.

The next question is, What, if anything, does (4) imply for the structure of preferences as reflected in the utility function? The answer to this question comes in two parts. First, it can be shown that if preferences of individual h can be represented by an indirect utility function of the form

$$V^h(\mathbf{P}, M^h) = A(\mathbf{P})M^h + B^h(\mathbf{P}), \tag{5}$$

then demand functions take the form shown in (4). This is easily shown by exploiting Roy's identity. Differentiating (5), we obtain

$$x_i^h(\cdot) = -\frac{\partial V^h(\cdot)/\partial P_i}{\partial V^h(\cdot)/\partial M^h} = -\frac{(\partial A(\cdot)/\partial P_i)M^h + \partial B^h(\cdot)/\partial P_i}{A(\cdot)}$$
$$= a_i(\mathbf{P})M^h + b_i^h(\mathbf{P}),$$

where $a_i(\cdot) \equiv (\partial A(\cdot)/\partial P_i)/A(\cdot)$ and $b_i^h(\cdot) \equiv (\partial B^h(\cdot)/\partial P_i)/A(\cdot)$. If $V^h(\cdot)$ is to be decreasing and quasi-convex in prices and increasing in income, certain restrictions must be imposed on $A(\cdot)$ and $B^h(\cdot)$. However, such restrictions are easier to analyze by considering the implied expenditure function. Equation (5) can be inverted to show the implied form of the expenditure function, which is

$$E^h(\cdot) = [u^h - B^h(\mathbf{P})]/A(\mathbf{P}) \tag{6}$$
$$= \alpha(\mathbf{P})u^h + \beta^h(\mathbf{P}),$$

where $\alpha(\cdot) \equiv 1/A(\cdot)$ and $\beta^h(\cdot) \equiv -B^h(\cdot)/A(\cdot)$. The functions that appear in (6) have an intuitive interpretation; $\beta^h(\cdot)$ is the cost of attaining the standard of living corresponding to $u = 0$, and $\alpha(\cdot)$ is the marginal, or incremental, cost of utility. In order that the expenditure function be concave in prices, it is necessary and sufficient that the functions $\alpha(\cdot)$ and $\beta(\cdot)$ be concave in prices.

It should be stressed that the analysis is, in an important sense, local. Figure 8.1 shows that I mean by this. The length of the horizontal axis

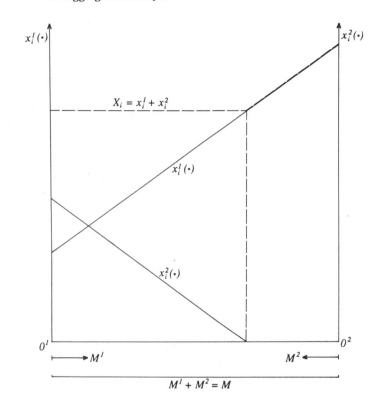

Figure 8.1

measures the total income in a two-person economy. Individual 1's demand for commodity i is measured on the vertical axis and plotted against that individual's income using 0^1 as the origin. Individual 2's demand is plotted using the origin 0^2. Because both have preferences represented by (5) with identical $A(\cdot)$ functions, both have the same income responses. Over the range of income distributions along the segment 0^1B, both individuals demand a positive level of commodity i. Over this range, income redistribution leaves aggregate demand unchanged. However, at B, individual 2's demand has fallen to zero. It cannot fall further, so that additional transfers from 2 to 1 must raise aggregate demand by an amount dependent on individual 1's income response. A full set of sufficient conditions for aggregate demand to be independent of distribution must therefore not only specify the form of the individual's preferences but also restrict attention to price and income configurations that imply strictly positive demands for every commodity by every consumer. Outside this range, the property breaks down.

Subject to this additional condition, I have argued that a sufficient condition for aggregate demand to be independent of income distribution is that preferences be representable by $V^h(\cdot) = A(\mathbf{P})M^h + B^h(\mathbf{P})$. It can be shown that this condition is also necessary. This is harder, and it requires us to start with the demand functions and integrate them in order to recover the indirect utility function that generated them. The interested reader is invited to explore the sources cited at the end of this chapter for rigorous treatments of this matter.

The form of the indirect utility function $V(\cdot) = A(\mathbf{P})M + B(\mathbf{P})$ is called the Gorman polar form, because it was Gorman (1953) who first suggested it and provided a rigorous treatment of its properties. Gorman himself called such a utility function quasi-homothetic. It allows us to define not merely a representative consumer but, more specifically, an arithmetic mean consumer. A community of n such consumers, each with a different income, behaves exactly as if there were n consumers each with the arithmetic mean income $(1/n)\sum_h M^h$. The cost of being able to work with a representative "arithmetic mean man" is that income expansion paths must be linear. Recently, Muellbauer (1976a) has generalized the analysis to accommodate nonlinear income expansion paths. Observe that the expenditure function (6) can be written in a slightly modified form:

$$
\begin{aligned}
E^h(\cdot) &= \alpha(\mathbf{P})u + \beta(\mathbf{P})u - \beta(\mathbf{P})u + \beta(\mathbf{P}) \\
&= [\alpha(\mathbf{P}) + \beta(\mathbf{P})]u + (1-u)\beta(\mathbf{P}) \\
&= u\gamma(\mathbf{P}) + (1-u)\beta(\mathbf{P}),
\end{aligned} \tag{7}
$$

where $\gamma(\cdot) \equiv \alpha(\cdot) + \beta(\cdot)$. The function $\gamma(\mathbf{P})$ is the sum of two concave functions. It is therefore itself concave. Equation (7) has an interesting interpretation. $\beta(\mathbf{P})$ defines a "poor" consumer's indifference curve, because the equation $M = \beta(\mathbf{P})$ defines the budget lines that touch the indifference curve corresponding to $U(\cdot) = 0$. Similarly, the function $\gamma(\mathbf{P})$ defines the indifference curve of a "rich" consumer, for whom $U(\cdot) = 1$. Equation (7) therefore expresses the expenditure level of an individual facing $\mathbf{P}$ and attaining the utility target u as a linear combination of the rich and the poor individuals' expenditures, the weights being u and $(1-u)$. It therefore defines an indifference curve that is a weighted average of rich and poor curves. Muellbauer suggests a generalization of (7) in which the expenditure level is a constant elasticity of substitution (CES) function of $\gamma(\cdot)$ and $\beta(\cdot)$:

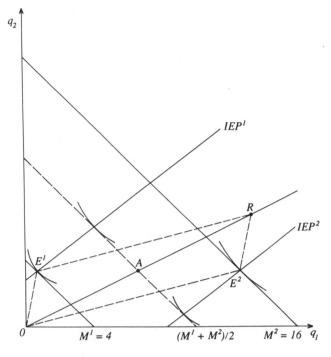

Figure 8.2

$$E(\mathbf{P}, u) = \{u[\gamma(\mathbf{P})]^{\rho} + (1-u)[\beta(\mathbf{P})]^{\rho}\}^{1/\rho}, \tag{8}$$

where $[\gamma(\mathbf{P})]^{\rho} \equiv [\alpha(\mathbf{P})]^{\rho} + [\beta(\mathbf{P})]^{\rho}$.

Equation (8) defines a class of preferences exhibiting "price-independent generalized linearity" (PIGL). The reason for this label and a good intuitive discussion of how such a generalization of Gorman's polar form works are given by Muellbauer (1976*b*, pp. 37–9). The right-hand side of (8) can be thought of as a "generalized mean," of which equation (7) represents the special case, the arithmetic mean, for which $\rho = 1$. Another interesting special case arises when $\rho \to 0$. it may be shown that this implies the following form of expenditure function:

$$E(\mathbf{P}, u) = [\gamma(\mathbf{P})]^{u}[\beta(\mathbf{P})]^{1-u}. \tag{9}$$

This defines $E(\cdot)$ as a geometric mean of β and γ. Figures 8.2 and 8.3 illustrate the linear and nonlinear examples. In Figure 8.2, the two individuals have preferences of the Gorman polar form, with identical $A(\cdot)$ functions. One has an income of 4 and consumes the bundle E^1; the other

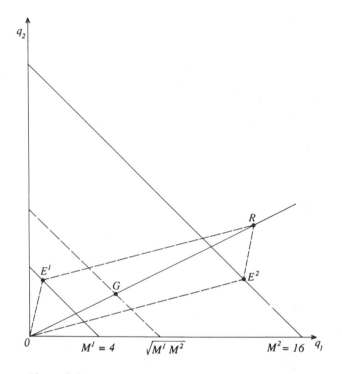

Figure 8.3

receives 16 and consumes the bundle E^2. By adding the consumption vectors chosen by each, the aggregate consumption bundle at R can be generated. The proportions of aggregate consumption of the two commodities are given by the ray $0R$.

The same outcome would result if each consumer received the arithmetic mean income of 10 units. Indeed, because the individuals' income expansion paths – denoted by IEP^1 and IEP^2 in the figure – are linear and parallel to one another, any distribution of income that leaves the arithmetic mean unaffected and that results in both individuals consuming quantities in the strictly positive orthant will produce the same aggregate outcome, just as if there were two identical representative consumers, each with the arithmetic mean income and each consuming the bundle A.

Figure 8.3 depicts the nonlinear geometric case. Again, initial incomes are 4 and 16, and the chosen bundles are E^1 and E^2. In this case, which corresponds to the expenditure function shown in (9), the shapes of the nonlinear income expansion paths – not shown – are such that distributions of income having the same geometric mean as $(M^1, M^2) = (4, 16)$

will result in the same observed aggregate budget shares, so long as each individual continues to consume a bundle in the positive orthant. For example, if $M^1 = M^2 = 8$, the per capita consumption bundle is the point G, where $0R$ intersects the budget constraint corresponding to $M = 8$. In general, G will not be the actual consumption bundle of either, because preferences are not identical. However, it is the midpoint between the actual bundles chosen by the two consumers when they each receive 8 units of income. In this sense, G is the consumption bundle of the representative geometric mean consumer. In such a community of n consumers, the aggregate budget shares associated with a given distribution of income $(M^1, M^2, ..., M^n)$ are identical with those resulting from a situation in which each consumer receives the geometric mean, $M^g = (M^1 M^2 \cdots M^n)^{1/n}$. In general, of course, the number of "geometric mean" consumers whose aggregate behavior is exactly like that of the community with tastes given by (9) may not be an integer. In the numerical example, 2.5 geometric mean consumers are required. In this respect, the situation seems a little odd. However, the peculiarity has no particularly sinister implications. By extending the analysis of aggregation to situations captured by (8), in which aggregate budget shares can be expressed as functions of $\mathbf{P}$ and of a function of incomes $f(M^1, ..., M^n)$, not necessarily the arithmetic mean, we can go beyond the class of preferences for which Engel curves are linear. How important it is that we should be able to do this is an empirical matter.

Restrictions on income distribution

Samuelson (1956) has drawn attention to another circumstance in which the aggregate commodity demands in a competitive economy behave as though they were individual demands. Suppose that in such an economy of H households, income is always distributed in such a way as to maximize a social welfare function. For example, suppose the income distribution is such that of all the points on the utility possibilities frontier implied by the current technology and world prices, the realized allocation is the one that maximizes the Benthamite sum of utilities. Then the aggregate demands can be rationalized as though they were generated by a single consumer.

   Interestingly enough, this aggregation theorem over agents can be demonstrated very simply by applying the aggregation theorem over commodities – in short, Hicks's composite commodity theorem. This is indeed Samuelson's approach. In a competitive economy, each consumer faces the same set of prices. Consequently, the various quantities of commodity i

consumed by each can be aggregated: $q_i = \Sigma_{h=1}^{H} q_i^h$. By assumption, there exists a function $F(\cdot)$ such that any realized allocation solves the problem

$$\max_{q^1, \ldots, q^H} \left\{ F(U^1(q^1), \ldots, U^H(q^H)) \,|\, \mathbf{P} \cdot \sum_{h=1}^{H} \mathbf{q}^h = \sum_{h=1}^{H} M^h \right\}. \tag{10}$$

But the composite commodity theorem enables us to work with the aggregate vector of commodities $\mathbf{q} \equiv \Sigma_{h=1}^{H} \mathbf{q}^h$. The problem defined by (10) then becomes

$$\max_{\mathbf{q}} \left\{ G(\mathbf{q}) \,|\, \mathbf{P} \cdot \mathbf{q} = \sum_{h=1}^{H} M^h \right\}. \tag{11}$$

The aggregate demand functions implied by (11) have standard properties, because the problem is itself a standard maximization subject to a single linear budget constraint.

The practical relevance of this result is perhaps not great. Its interest in the present context derives largely from the lateral thinking involved in applying the composite commodity theorem to a problem involving aggregation over optimizing agents. It should also be stressed that the social welfare function $F(\cdot)$ or $G(\cdot)$ has no normative significance. The theorem simply states that if allocations are consistent with optimization of such a function, then the individual agents can be aggregated.

8.3   The almost ideal demand system

In Chapters 2 and 3 I referred to a number of attempts to estimate demand systems by applying utility or expenditure functions to aggregate data. Much of that work did not address the aggregation issue explicitly, relying instead on the assumption, often little more than an article of faith, that aggregate relationships could be formulated directly from the theory of individual consumer behavior. Phlips (1983, p. 101) was representative of that approach. Others have worried more about the problem and have tried, at least, to be more explicit about the assumptions required if we are to be able to treat aggregate systems in this manner. The "almost ideal demand system" (AIDS) of Deaton and Muellbauer is a good example of a more explicit treatment of aggregation issues in empirical work.

The AIDS model, as it is often, somewhat unfortunately, referred to, is a flexible functional form that builds on Muellbauer's extension of Gorman's polar form. Let the expenditure function take the form given by (9), which in logarithmic form is

$$\ln E(\mathbf{P}, u) = u \ln \gamma(\mathbf{P}) + (1 - u) \ln \beta(\mathbf{P}). \tag{12}$$

This implies an indirect utility function of the form

$$u = V(\mathbf{P}, M) = (\ln M - \ln \beta(\mathbf{P})) / (\ln \gamma(\mathbf{P}) - \ln \beta(\mathbf{P}))$$
$$= \ln(M/\beta(\mathbf{P}))/\alpha(\mathbf{P}),$$

where $\alpha(\mathbf{P}) \equiv \ln \gamma(P) - \ln \beta(\mathbf{P})$. To use this as the basis for estimation, particular functional forms must be assumed for $\gamma(\cdot)$ and $\beta(\cdot)$ or $\alpha(\mathbf{P})$. These forms should be flexible enough to allow the derivatives of $E(\cdot)$ at any point to equal those of any admissible expenditure function, while being consistent with those properties generally possessed by expenditure or indirect utility functions. Deaton and Muellbauer chose the following:

$$\ln \beta(\mathbf{P}) = a_0 + \sum_k a_k \ln P_k + \frac{1}{2} \sum_k \sum_j a_{kj}^\dagger \ln P_k \ln P_j,$$

and

$$\ln \gamma(\mathbf{P}) = \ln \beta(\mathbf{P}) + b_0 P_1^{b_1} P_2^{b_2} \cdots P_n^{b_n}.$$

Substituting these expressions into (12) gives the expenditure function

$$\ln E(\cdot) = a_0 + \sum_k a_k \ln P_k + \frac{1}{2} \sum_k \sum_j a_{kj}^\dagger \ln P_k \ln P_j$$
$$+ \beta_0 u P_1^{b_1} P_2^{b_2} \cdots P_n^{b_n}. \tag{13}$$

Several properties of this function are worth noting. First, $E(\cdot)$ is homogeneous of degree 1 in all prices, as an expenditure function must be, if $\sum_{k=1}^n a_k = 1$ and $\sum_{k=1}^n a_{kj}^\dagger = \sum_{j=1}^n a_{kj}^\dagger = \sum_{j=1}^n b_j = 0$. Second, $\partial^2 E(\cdot)/\partial u^2 = 0$. This is not such a special restriction as might initially be thought, once we realize that an ordinal utility function can be subjected to any monotonic increasing transformation. It simply reflects a particular normalization that makes a linear relationship between M and u at a given set of prices. Third, consider the demand functions obtained by Shephard's lemma. Expressed in terms of budget shares, they are

$$P_i x_i(\cdot)/M = (P_i/E(\cdot))(\partial E(\cdot)/\partial P_i) = \partial \ln E(\cdot)/\partial \ln P_i$$
$$= a_i + \sum_j a_{ij} \ln P_j + b_i u \beta_0 (P_1^{b_1} P_2^{b_2} \cdots P_n^{b_n}), \tag{14}$$

where

$$a_{ij} = (a_{ij}^\dagger + a_{ji}^\dagger)/2.$$

The variable u can be replaced by the indirect utility function to obtain uncompensated budget-share equations:

$$P_i x_i(\cdot)/M = a_i + \sum_j a_{ij} \ln P_j + b_i \ln(M/\text{PI}).$$ (15)

The variable PI is a price index, defined as

$$\text{PI} = a_0 + \sum_{k=1}^{n} a_k \ln P_k + \frac{1}{2} \sum_j \sum_k a_{kj} \ln P_k \ln P_j.$$ (16)

At this point, it is worth following Deaton and Muellbauer (1980b) in reminding the reader of the following restrictions imposed on the parameters:

$$\sum_{i=1}^{n} a_i = 1, \quad \sum_{i=1}^{n} a_{ij} = \sum_{j=1}^{n} a_{ij} = 0, \quad \sum_{i=1}^{n} b_i = 0, \quad a_{ij} = a_{ji}.$$

The restrictions on the a_{ij}'s follow from their definitions in terms of the $a_{ij}^{\dagger}$'s. Given these restrictions, equation (15) represents a demand system consistent with utility maximization.

At this point it is certainly possible to use the expression for the price index provided by (16) in the budget-share equation (15). Doing so produces an equation that is nonlinear in the parameters. Although this does not present insurmountable problems, Deaton and Muellbauer (1980b, p. 316) suggest that simpler linear estimation procedures can be adopted if the price index PI is approximated by some other simple form.

8.4   Concluding comments and suggestions for further study

Hicks's composite commodity theorem has been stated by Hicks (1946, pp. 312–13), Samuelson (1947, pp. 141–3), Gorman (1953, pp. 77–8), and Green (1971, pp. 111–13, 308–10). Liviatan (1968) discussed the theorem in the context of production theory and did so with the help of cost and profit functions. Diewert (1978a) also exploited duality theory, and his discussion embraced both consumer and producer behavior. I should remind the reader of the discussion of induced preferences in Chapter 6, because Hicks's theorem is a special case of preference induction. A more general discussion of "aggregation over miscellaneous objects," with particular reference to the confused and often unenlightening controversies concerning the aggregation of capital, has been presented by Bliss (1975, pt. III).

Aggregation over agents has a large literature that shows no sign of abating. Discussion of the forms of demand functions required to ensure that aggregate demand will be invariant with respect to changes in income distribution goes back to Antonelli, but it was Gorman (1953) who first traced the analysis back to the required form of indirect utility function, now generally known as the Gorman polar form. Gorman's insights have influenced much recent empirical work – see, for example, Blackorby et al. (1978*a*), Blundell and Walker (1982), and Blundell and Meghir (1986). Gorman (1961) discussed the associated expenditure function. It is surprisingly difficult to find proofs of Gorman's results. A theorem proved by Bergstrom and Cornes (1981) can be adapted to deal with Gorman's problem. The extension to nonlinear aggregation is largely due to Muellbauer (1975, 1976*a*), of which Muellbauer (1976*b*) is a useful nontechnical summary. Exact aggregation over individuals is the subject of an interesting paper by Heineke and Shefrin (1988), who stress the importance of looking beyond the formal manipulations at the informational motivation for the whole exercise. Diewert (1977) followed a number of earlier papers in exploring the role of the number of consumers relative to the number of commodities in determining the extent to which aggregate behavior fails to mimic that of a single utility-maximizing consumer.

Following the original paper by Deaton and Muellbauer (1980*b*) on the almost ideal demand system, there have been several attempts to modify and extend it, particularly to produce more dynamic specifications. See, for example, papers by Simmons (1980), Ray (1982), Kooreman and Kapteyn (1986), Weissenberger (1986), and Coondoo and Majumder (1987).

CHAPTER 9

Consumer theory and welfare evaluation

Dual formulations of consumer behavior, in particular the expenditure function, have played a significant role in simplifying welfare evaluation. The source of this simplicity is the fact that elementary revealed preference arguments are naturally built into the dual approach. For this reason, I begin this chapter with a discussion of the revealed preference approach. Although this provides the conceptual core of normative analysis, the exploitation of duality allows us to go further than the simple welfare ranking of alternative allocations. The concepts of equivalent and compensating variations provide unambiguous answers to easily understood questions that one might want to pose concerning the ranking of alternative price-taking situations, and it has been argued that the equivalent variation can provide us with a money metric – that is, a money measure that has all the properties of a utility function and consequently can be thought of as a utility function. Situations involving quantity constraints may be handled by slight modifications of these measures. Furthermore, the use of duality considerably simplifies the definition and analysis of a variety of index numbers. These topics form the subject matter of this chapter.

9.1   Revealed preference arguments

Let us begin in simple and familiar territory. A consumer faces a linear budget constraint, $\mathbf{P}^0 \cdot \mathbf{q} \leq M^0$. Call this the situation $(\mathbf{P}^0, M^0)$, and denote the chosen bundle by $\mathbf{q}^0$ and the attained utility level by u^0. I shall retain the assumption that preferences are strictly convex, so that there is a unique most preferred bundle associated with any given situation. It would be a useful exercise for the reader to relax this assumption and trace through the minor modifications needed in the following argument. Assuming that choice reflects preference, we can immediately infer that $\mathbf{q}^0$ must be strongly preferred to any other bundle that could have been, but was not, purchased in the situation $(\mathbf{P}^0, M^0)$. Put more succinctly,

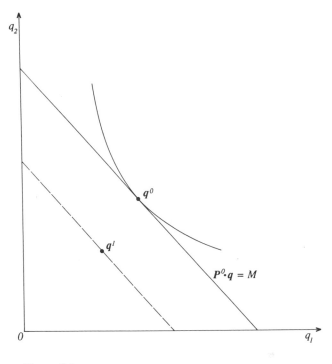

Figure 9.1

if a comparison with some alternative bundle $\mathbf{q}^1$ is made, it can be stated that

$$\mathbf{P}^0 \cdot \mathbf{q}^1 \leq \mathbf{P}^0 \cdot \mathbf{q}^0 \to \mathbf{q}^0 > \mathbf{q}^1 \quad \text{for} \quad \mathbf{q}^1 \neq \mathbf{q}^0. \tag{1}$$

This simple inference, illustrated in Figure 9.1, has far-reaching implications. In Chapter 4 we used it to establish a positive proposition, the law of overcompensated demand. It also plays an important role in normative economics. Suppose that the consumer has an endowment not of final commodities but of inputs that can be combined to produce goods. What is produced can then be consumed or exchanged at exogenous prices. This is the standard single-consumer economy of international trade theory. I want to show that the opportunity to trade is gainful to the individual. Let the autarkic, or pretrade, levels of output, consumption, and utility be $\mathbf{y}^a$, $\mathbf{q}^a$, and u^a, respectively. Values attained in the trading equilibrium are distinguished by the superscript t. The exogenous trading prices are given by $\mathbf{P}^t$. The argument proceeds through a small number of simple steps and is easy to follow in Figure 9.2.

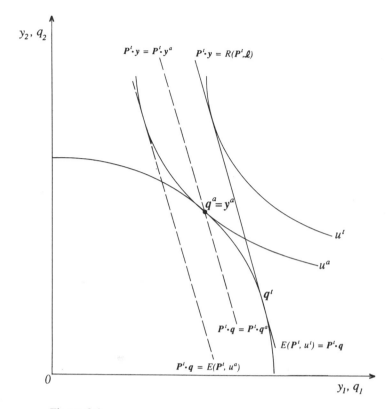

Figure 9.2

To begin with, the autarkic bundle $\mathbf{q}^a$, which attains u^a, cannot cost less at prices $\mathbf{P}^t$ than the least-cost method of attaining u^a when confronted with $\mathbf{P}^t$:

$$E(\mathbf{P}^t, u^a) \leq \mathbf{P}^t \cdot \mathbf{q}^a. \tag{2}$$

This observation follows from the very definition of $E(\cdot)$. Again by definition, the autarkic consumption and production bundles are identical, so that

$$E(\mathbf{P}^t, u^a) \leq \mathbf{P}^t \cdot \mathbf{y}^a.$$

Now recall the revenue function. At the trading equilibrium the consumer – or, in the case of a single-consumer economy, the competitive production sector – will choose output so as to maximize its value at the prevailing prices. The resulting value is given by the revenue function, $R(\mathbf{P}, \ell)$. Again by definition, it must be the case that

$$R(\mathbf{P}^t, \ell) \geq \mathbf{P}^t \cdot \mathbf{y}^a. \tag{3}$$

Finally, the value of income must equal that of expenditure, so that in the trading equilibrium

$$R(\mathbf{P}^t, \ell) = E(\mathbf{P}^t, u^t).$$

Following through the chain of inequalities, we can conclude that

$$E(\mathbf{P}^t, u^a) \leq E(\mathbf{P}^t, u^t).$$

But at a given price vector the level of expenditure is an increasing function of utility. Hence, the final conclusion can be drawn that $u^a \leq u^t$.

An understandable reaction to all of this is that I have made very heavy weather of establishing a very simple and obvious result. In defense, two points should be made. First, the algebra can accommodate as many inputs and outputs as required. Second, the revealed preference inequalities (2) and (3) appear in many contexts, often helping to establish less intuitively obvious results than the present one. Ohyama (1972) used precisely this type of reasoning to establish a host of welfare propositions for trading economies.

More recently, Dixit and Norman (1980) have extended the classic gains from trade results to the many-consumer economy when lump-sum transfers are not possible. The problem is the following: If there are many consumers with different tastes and endowments, an opening up of trade will benefit some, but hurt others. If lump-sum redistribution is not permitted, it is not obvious that recourse to distortionary taxes and subsidies can help to attain a trading equilibrium in which all consumers are at least as well off, and at least one better off, than in autarky. Dixit and Norman show that one can, indeed, attain such an outcome. Let $\mathbf{q}^{ha}$ and ℓ^{ha} denote consumption demands and input supplies of household h in autarky. Total input supplies are $\ell^a = \sum_h \ell^{ha}$, and so on. In the absence of lump-sum transfers, each household obeys the autarkic budget constraint

$$\mathbf{P}^a \cdot \mathbf{q}^{ha} = \mathbf{W}^a \cdot \ell^{ha}. \tag{4}$$

Consider a set of commodity taxes that are set at such levels that the consumers continue to face the autarky price vector, $(\mathbf{P}^a, \mathbf{W}^a)$. Under such a regime, because all consumers' budget constraints are unchanged, so are their commodity demands and factor supplies. In particular, this means that producers face the same factor supplies. However, producers face world prices $\mathbf{P}^t$ for all traded goods. Let $\mathbf{y}^t$ be the output chosen in the trading equilibrium. Because $(\mathbf{y}^t, \ell^a)$ and $(\mathbf{y}^a, \ell^a)$ are both feasible, it must be true that at the trading equilibrium, the chosen output $\mathbf{y}^t$ is at least as profitable as the autarkic output $\mathbf{y}^a$:

$$\mathbf{P}^t \cdot \mathbf{y}^t - \mathbf{W}^t \cdot \boldsymbol{\ell}^a \geq \mathbf{P}^t \cdot \mathbf{y}^a - \mathbf{W}^t \cdot \boldsymbol{\ell}^a. \tag{5}$$

Two further steps are required. First, it must be shown that such an equilibrium results in the government's net tax revenue being positive. The revenue is simply

$$T = (\mathbf{P}^a - \mathbf{P}^t) \cdot \sum_h \mathbf{q}^{ha} + (\mathbf{W}^t - \mathbf{W}^a) \cdot \sum_h \boldsymbol{\ell}^{ha}.$$

Using the budget equality (4), this can be written as

$$T = -\mathbf{P}^t \cdot \sum_h \mathbf{q}^{ha} + \mathbf{W}^t \cdot \sum_h \boldsymbol{\ell}^{ha}$$

$$= -\mathbf{P}^t \cdot \mathbf{q}^a + \mathbf{W}^t \cdot \boldsymbol{\ell}^a.$$

At this point, we use the revealed preference inequality (5) to infer that

$$T \geq -\mathbf{P}^t \cdot \mathbf{q}^t + \mathbf{W}^t \cdot \boldsymbol{\ell}^a = 0.$$

The government, therefore, runs a budget surplus. It finally remains to be shown that the tax structure can be slightly perturbed so as to return some of this surplus to consumers without making anyone worse off. Suppose there is a commodity of which no domestic consumer is a net supplier and some are net demanders. Then a reduction in the tax on this commodity (or an increase in the subsidy) will benefit net demanders, while having a second-order effect on those with zero net demands. Such a tax change therefore results in a Pareto improvement upon the autarkic equilibrium.

This section has done enough, I hope, to show the potential power of simple revealed preference arguments in determining the welfare ranking of alternative situations. Much of the normative literature, however, addresses itself to the more ambitious problem of securing cardinal measures of welfare change and of uncovering a utility function from observed behavior and from estimated systems of demand functions. To investigate these questions, we must look at the notions, due to Hicks (1946), of the equivalent and compensating variations.

9.2   Equivalent and compensating variations

Consider a consumer with an initial budget $(\mathbf{P}^0, M^0)$. We wish to obtain a measure of the welfare change implied by the move from this situation to some alternative, say $(\mathbf{P}^1, M^1)$. Because utility functions generally are assumed to be ordinal, there is not a unique real number that represents the change in utility $V(\mathbf{P}^1, M^1) - V(\mathbf{P}^0, M^0)$. However, this does not necessarily prevent us from defining a natural monetary measure, or money metric, of welfare change. Hicks's notion of an equivalent variation is a useful starting point from which to develop such a measure.

The equivalent variation

The equivalent variation associated with the move from $(\mathbf{P}^0, M^0)$ to $(\mathbf{P}^1, M^1)$ is defined as that amount of income that if given to the consumer would have exactly the same effect on his welfare as the move from $(\mathbf{P}^0, M^0)$ to $(\mathbf{P}^1, M^1)$. It is most conveniently defined by using the indirect utility function. Denote the equivalent variation associated with the move from $(\mathbf{P}^0, M^0)$ to $(\mathbf{P}^1, M^1)$ by EV^{01}. Suppose the individual is paid an income equal to $M^0 + \mathrm{EV}^{01}$, while prices are maintained at their initial values, $\mathbf{P}^0$. By definition, we require the utility attainable with this price-income pair to equal that attained with $(\mathbf{P}^1, M^1)$. That is, we require

$$V(\mathbf{P}^0, M^0 + \mathrm{EV}^{01}) = V(\mathbf{P}^1, M^1) = u^1. \tag{6}$$

Whereas equation (6) is the most natural way of defining EV^{01}, its development into an operational concept exploits the expenditure function. The quantity $(M^0 + \mathrm{EV}^{01})$ is the minimum expenditure required to attain the utility level u^1 when prices are $\mathbf{P}^0$:

$$M^0 + \mathrm{EV}^{01} = E(\mathbf{P}^0, u^1),$$

from which the equivalent variation is

$$\begin{aligned} \mathrm{EV}^{01} &= E(\mathbf{P}^0, u^1) - M^0 \\ &= E(\mathbf{P}^0, u^1) - E(\mathbf{P}^0, u^0). \end{aligned} \tag{7}$$

Figure 9.3 shows the EV associated with the move from $(\mathbf{P}^0, M^0)$ to $(\mathbf{P}^1, M^1)$. It involves calculating the expenditure level associated with the dashed budget line that reflects the initial prices and just allows attainment of the final utility level. From this expenditure, the EV is obtained by subtracting the initial expenditure level. Measured in terms of commodity 1, EV^{01} is measured by the distance AB. As depicted in Figure 9.3, the EV is positive. If situation 1 were less attractive to the individual than situation 0, the EV would be negative.

It is important to notice a crucial feature of the EV as expressed in equation (7) and depicted in Figure 9.3. It is defined with respect to a fixed reference price vector, $\mathbf{P}^0$. Given this vector, there is a one-to-one

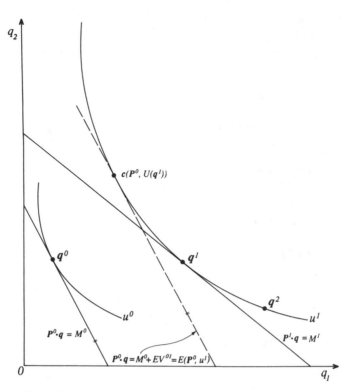

Figure 9.3

mapping between indifference curves and points on the income expansion path passing through $(\mathbf{P}^0, M^0)$, and hence between indifference curves and income levels, given $\mathbf{P}^0$. For example, any bundle on the indifference curve corresponding to $V(\cdot) = u^1$ can just be matched with the income $M^0 + \mathrm{EV}^{01}$, so long as the prices are $\mathbf{P}^0$. Algebraically, this is a consequence of the fact that for any given $\mathbf{P}$, $V(\mathbf{P}, M)$ is a strictly increasing function of M. Given any budget or commodity bundle that produces the utility level $\bar{u}$ for a given utility representation, there exists a unique value of income $\bar{M}$ such that $V(\mathbf{P}^0, \bar{M}) = \bar{u}$.

An alternative representation of EV^{01} uses compensated demand functions. Suppose, to make things simple, $M^0 = M^1$. Then, in equation (7), M^0 may be replaced by M^1, which in turn equals $E(\mathbf{P}^1, u^1)$:

$$\mathrm{EV}^{01} = E(\mathbf{P}^0, u^1) - E(\mathbf{P}^1, u^1). \tag{8}$$

Recall that compensated demand curves are the derivatives of the expenditure function with respect to prices. The converse of this proposition tells us that equation (8) is the definite integral, from $\mathbf{P}^1$ to $\mathbf{P}^0$, of the compensated demand curves with respect to prices. Suppose only P_j changes. Then we know that

$$\mathrm{EV}^{01} = \int_{P_j^1}^{P_j^0} c_j(\mathbf{P}, u^1)\, dP_j. \tag{9}$$

Because integrals can be thought of as areas under curves, (9) enables us to identify EV^{01} with an appropriate area associated with the compensated demand curve for commodity j in a way that I shall clarify shortly, after I have introduced the compensating variation.

The compensating variation

The equivalent variation provides an answer to the following question: What amount of income would have to be given to a consumer initially facing a price vector $\mathbf{P}^0$ and receiving an income M^0 in order to make him precisely as well off as in the alternative situation $(\mathbf{P}^1, M^1)$? Let us now ask a slightly different question: How much income would have to be taken away from the consumer in order precisely to negate the effect of moving from $(\mathbf{P}^0, M^0)$ to $(\mathbf{P}^1, M^1)$, in the sense that it takes the consumer back to his original utility level? This is Hicks's compensating variation, and is again best defined with the help of the indirect utility function. Denoting the compensating variation by CV^{01}, its definition implies the following relationship:

$$u^0 = V(\mathbf{P}^0, M^0) = V(\mathbf{P}^1, M^1 - \mathrm{CV}^{01}). \tag{10}$$

The CV associated with the move from $(\mathbf{P}^0, M^0)$ to $(\mathbf{P}^1, M^1)$ is shown in Figure 9.4.

Inverting the indirect utility function allows us to express the CV explicitly as

$$M^1 - \mathrm{CV}^{01} = E(\mathbf{P}^1, u^0),$$
$$\mathrm{CV}^{01} = M^1 - E(\mathbf{P}^1, u^0)$$
$$= E(\mathbf{P}^1, u^1) - E(\mathbf{P}^1, u^0). \tag{11}$$

In Figure 9.4 we construct the dashed budget line that reflects the final prices and just allows attainment of the initial utility level u^0. The CV is obtained by subtracting this expenditure level from the final expenditure level M^1. In terms of commodity 1, CV^{01} is measured by the distance CD. Comparison of (11) with (7) reveals the difference between EV^{01} and CV^{01}. The former uses the base prices, $\mathbf{P}^0$, when identifying the required income

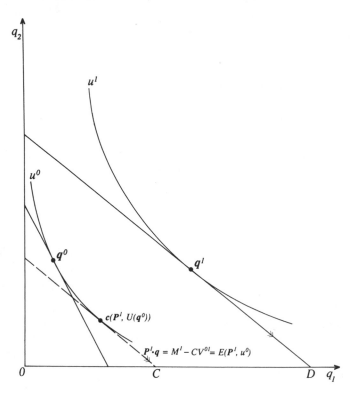

Figure 9.4

transfer, and the latter uses the final prices, $\mathbf{P}^1$. Again, if the further assumption is made that $M^0 = M^1$, then (11) may be rewritten in a form that explicitly involves both $\mathbf{P}^0$ and $\mathbf{P}^1$:

$$\mathrm{CV}^{01} = E(\mathbf{P}^0, u^0) - E(\mathbf{P}^1, u^0). \tag{12}$$

This has the attraction of being interpretable as an integral of compensated demand functions. For example, if P_j alone changes,

$$\mathrm{CV}^{01} = \int_{P_j^1}^{P_j^0} c_j(\mathbf{P}, u^0)\, dP_j. \tag{13}$$

The integral representations of the EV and CV suggest that they may be depicted as areas associated with demand curves. Suppose P_j alone falls, while all other prices and money income remain constant. In Figure 9.5, we suppose this takes the utility-maximizing consumer from an initial equilibrium I to the final equilibrium F. The points I and F are both on the uncompensated demand curve $x_j(P_j)$, which I have deliberately

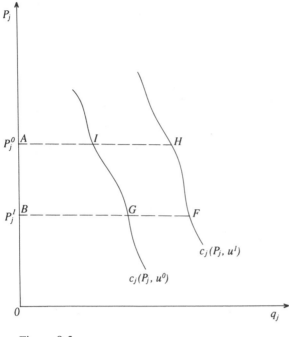

Figure 9.5

not drawn. Equation (13) suggests that in order to represent CV^{01}, we first draw the compensated demand curve corresponding to the utility level attained at the initial equilibrium. If commodity j is a normal good, the compensated demand curve will be steeper than the uncompensated curve, because the beneficial income effect of the price fall will further increase the uncompensated demand for a normal good. The magnitude of CV^{01} as it is expressed in (13) is represented by the area bounded by the compensated demand curve $C_j(\mathbf{P}, u^0)$ and the price axis, and also by the initial and final prices, P_j^0 and P_j^1. It is the area $BAIG$.

The equivalent variation, by contrast, takes the final utility level as its reference value. To depict EV^{01}, therefore, we must draw the compensated demand curve corresponding to $U(\cdot) = u^1$. Because a price fall raises utility, we know that the relevant demand curve for a normal good will be everywhere to the right of $c_j(\mathbf{P}, u^0)$. In Figure 9.5 it is the curve through the points H and F. Again, inspection of the integral definition of EV^{01} given by equation (9) shows that it is measured by an area to the left of the demand curve, in this case the area $BAHF$. The geometric representation provided by Figure 9.3 is often used to show that if the price of a single normal good changes, the EV and CV provide the upper and lower bounds, respectively, of the traditional Marshallian consumer surplus.

In an important sense, the EV and the CV are very similar. Indeed, it is clear from their definitions and from their geometric representations that a certain symmetry is present, so that $EV^{01} = -CV^{10}$ and $CV^{01} = -EV^{10}$. However, the asymmetric treatment of situation 0 as the base, or status quo, situation and of situation 1 as some hypothetical, or final, alternative makes it important to note differences. The CV features prominently in contemporary discussions of the time-hallowed concept of willingness to pay. It is, after all, the maximum amount that the individual will be prepared to pay in order to bribe fellow citizens to carry out the move from $(\mathbf{P}^0, M^0)$ to $(\mathbf{P}^1, M^1)$. This provides a very natural definition of the willingness to pay for a project and yields a well-defined answer in terms of a given number of dollars. The EV is more often encountered in discussions of money metrics. In order to elucidate the distinctions that some writers are careful to draw between the EV and the CV, let us first note that they are both special cases of a more general function. Observe that there is nothing that requires us to use either $\mathbf{P}^0$ or $\mathbf{P}^1$ as the reference price vector at which to evaluate income changes. Let us define a slight variant of the expenditure function called the indirect compensation function. This may be written as

$$\mu(\mathbf{P}^r; \mathbf{P}, M) \equiv E(\mathbf{P}^r, V(\mathbf{P}, M)), \tag{14}$$

where $\mu(\cdot)$ defines the minimum expenditure required, when faced with some arbitrarily chosen reference price vector $\mathbf{P}^r$, to attain that level of utility that is just attainable when prices are $\mathbf{P}$ and money income is M. In the binary comparison of situations 0 and 1, the EV is derived by letting the reference price vector be $\mathbf{P}^0$, thereby generating (7), and the CV is obtained by using $\mathbf{P}^1$ as the reference price vector. However, as long as the same vector is used throughout the comparison, it matters little what it is. Given any particular reference price vector, the quantity defined by $\mu(\mathbf{P}^r; \mathbf{P}, M)$ is a perfectly acceptable welfare indicator. This follows from the simple fact that it is a monotonic increasing transformation of $V(\mathbf{P}, M)$.

What, then, are we to make of the claim, strongly advanced by McKenzie (1983, p. 37), that the EV is a money metric, whereas the CV is not? The explanation is simple. Suppose that the issue is not just a binary choice, but requires us to rank a number of alternatives to the status quo in terms of welfare. Let the ith alternative be $(\mathbf{P}^i, M^i)$. Then, for a given reference price vector, the most preferred alternative is that for which

$\mu(\mathbf{P}^r; \bar{\mathbf{P}}^i, M^i)$ is maximized. If $(\mathbf{P}^0, M^0)$ is singled out as the status quo, then the EV is defined as

$$E^{0j} = \mu(\mathbf{P}^0; \mathbf{P}^j, M^j) - \mu(\mathbf{P}^0; \mathbf{P}^0, M^0).$$

The most preferred project is that for which this is a maximum. This may, of course, be the status quo, for which $j = 0$. The CV associated with the comparison between situations 0 and j is

$$\mathrm{CV}^{0j} = \mu(\mathbf{P}^j; \mathbf{P}^j, M^j) - \mu(\mathbf{P}^j; \mathbf{P}^0, M^0).$$

Notice that with this definition, each binary comparison uses a different reference price vector. What prevents the CV from being a welfare measure is not its failure to use the base prices as its reference set, but rather its use of a different reference set for each comparison. If we chose to use, say, $\mathbf{P}^3$ as our reference vector for all calculations of $\mu(\cdot)$, we would obtain a perfectly acceptable welfare indicator. McKenzie's advocacy of the EV rests on the natural feeling that the status quo vector is in some sense the obvious candidate.

9.3   Equivalent and compensating surpluses

Consider now a consumer who is quantity-constrained in some subset of commodity markets. Accordingly, the quantity vector is partitioned: $\mathbf{q} = (\mathbf{q}_f, \mathbf{q}_r)$, where $\mathbf{q}_f$ and $\mathbf{q}_r$ are, respectively, the freely traded and rationed commodities. The money price vector is similarly partitioned. The vector of rationed quantities is assumed to be exogenously imposed: $\mathbf{q}_r = \mathbf{Q}_r$. We wish now to obtain a welfare measure of the move from $(\mathbf{P}_f^0, \mathbf{P}_r^0, \mathbf{Q}_r^0, M^0)$ to $(\mathbf{P}_f^1, \mathbf{P}_r^1, \mathbf{Q}_r^1, M^1)$. One obvious possibility is to calculate the virtual prices associated with each situation and use them in the definition of the equivalent variation. In Chapter 7 we discussed the notion of a virtual price – it is the money price at which, acting as a price-taker, the consumer will choose to consume a specified bundle. Situations 0 and 1 can be re-placed by the situations $(\mathbf{P}_f^0, \mathbf{\Pi}_r^0, \tilde{M}^0 + \mathbf{\Pi}_r^0 \cdot \mathbf{Q}_r^0)$ and $(\mathbf{P}_f^1, \mathbf{\Pi}_r^1, \tilde{M}^1 + \mathbf{\Pi}_r^1 \cdot \mathbf{Q}_r^1)$, where $\mathbf{\Pi}_r^0$ and $\mathbf{\Pi}_r^1$ are the virtual price vectors at which the consumer will choose the bundles observed in situations 0 and 1, and $\tilde{M}$ is the income available for expenditure on freely traded commodities, $M - \mathbf{P}_r \cdot \mathbf{Q}_r$. Having now effectively defined two price-taking situations, the analysis proceeds as in the preceding section.

An alternative approach is to define measures corresponding to what Hicks called the equivalent and compensating surpluses. The equivalent surplus is that amount of money that if paid to a consumer who continues to face prices $\mathbf{P}_f^0$ and quantity constraints $\mathbf{Q}_r^0$, makes him precisely as well off as at $(\mathbf{P}_f^1, \mathbf{P}_r^1, \mathbf{Q}_r^1, M^1)$. The restricted indirect utility function offers a precise and clear definition of the equivalent surplus, denoted by ES:

$$V^*(\mathbf{P}_f^0, \mathbf{Q}_r^0, \tilde{M}^0 + \mathrm{ES}^{01}) = V^*(\mathbf{P}_f^1, \mathbf{Q}_r^1, \tilde{M}^1) = u^1. \tag{15}$$

The ES can, like its counterpart the EV, be expressed explicitly by inverting $V^*(\cdot)$ and using the restricted expenditure function:

$$\tilde{M}^0 + \mathrm{ES}^{01} = E^*(\mathbf{P}_f^0, \mathbf{Q}_r^0, u^1),$$
$$\mathrm{ES}^{01} = E^*(\mathbf{P}_f^0, \mathbf{Q}_r^0, u^1) - \tilde{M}^0. \tag{16}$$

The ES provides a determinate answer to a question that is perfectly well defined and has a straightforward intuitive meaning. It and the EV based on virtual prices give different numerical answers when applied to any given comparison, but each is an acceptable money metric. The choice between them will depend partly on one's preferences between the intuitive appeal of the thought experiments that lie behind them, and more importantly on the ease with which they can be computed. Of this I shall have more to say in the next section.

By now it should be possible for the reader to make a good guess at the meaning of the compensating surplus. I shall simply define it formally, for the sake of completeness. Denoted by CS, it is implicitly defined by the following condition:

$$u^0 = V^*(\mathbf{P}_f^0, \mathbf{Q}_r^0, \tilde{M}^0) = V^*(\mathbf{P}_f^1, \mathbf{Q}_r^1, \tilde{M}^1 - \mathrm{CS}^{01}). \tag{17}$$

Its explicit statement in terms of the restricted expenditure function is

$$\mathrm{CS}^{01} = M^1 - E^*(\mathbf{P}_f^1, \mathbf{Q}_r^1, u^0). \tag{18}$$

Figure 9.6 provides a simple illustration of the ES and CS when the freely traded and the constrained quantities are scalars. Observe that there is a one-to-one relationship between the level of the final indifference curve and the magnitude of the equivalent surplus, which is a reflection of its nature as a money metric. On the other hand, different points on the indifference curve corresponding to $u = u^1$ produce different magnitudes for the compensating surplus, indicating its unsuitability as a welfare indicator.

9.4   Computation of a welfare measure

I argued in the preceding section that the EV and the ES are, at least in principle, attractive candidates as money metrics. In practice, even the EV

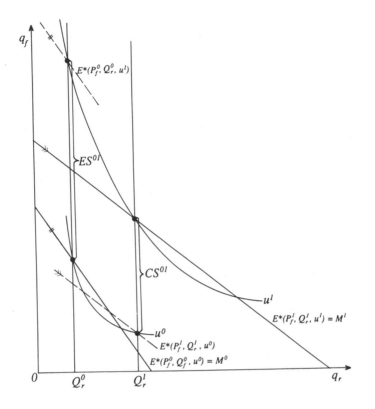

Figure 9.6

is not commonly encountered. Advocates of the widely used Marshallian consumer surplus measure argue that the EV demands more information than is generally available and that even if information problems are overcome, the EV is computationally demanding.

This is not an appropriate place to explore the intricacies of the confused debate on the pros and cons of various welfare measures – for that, consult McKenzie (1983) or Morey (1984). My objective in this section is simply to show that the information contained in an estimated system of uncompensated demand functions is sufficient to allow calculation of the EV. As a preliminary step, observe that if we take any direct utility function consistent with a given set of demand observations, Taylor's expansion can provide as good an approximation as desired of the change in utility associated with any given discrete move. Let $\Delta V \equiv V(\mathbf{P}^1, M^1) - V(\mathbf{P}^0, M^0)$. Then

$$\Delta V = \sum_i V_i \Delta P_i + V_M \Delta M + \frac{1}{2} \sum_i \sum_j V_{ij} \Delta P_i \Delta P_j$$

$$+ \sum_i V_{iM} \Delta P_i \Delta M + \frac{1}{2} V_{MM} (\Delta M)^2 + \cdots, \tag{19}$$

where

$$\Delta P_i \equiv P_i^1 - P_i^0, \quad \Delta M \equiv M^1 - M^0, \quad V_i \equiv \partial V(\cdot)/\partial P_i, \quad \text{and} \quad V_M \equiv \partial V(\cdot)/\partial M.$$

I want to show that adoption of the particular money metric $\mu(\mathbf{P}^0; \mathbf{P}, M)$ defined in (14) as our utility function implies a set of relationships that enable us to express the various partial derivatives of the utility function in (19) in terms of partial derivatives of the observable demand functions, $x_i(\mathbf{P}, M)$. Consider again the definition of $\mu(\cdot)$: $\mu(\mathbf{P}^0; \mathbf{P}, M)$ is the minimum expenditure, when facing $\mathbf{P}^0$, required to attain the utility level $V(\mathbf{P}, M)$. Therefore, by its very definition, $\mu(\mathbf{P}^0; \mathbf{P}^0, M) = M$. Consequently, in the neighborhood of any situation in which the individual faces $\mathbf{P}^0$, it must be true that

$$\partial\mu(\mathbf{P}^0; \mathbf{P}^0, M)/\partial M = 1, \quad \text{or} \quad \mu_M = 1,$$

and

$$\partial^n\mu(\mathbf{P}^0; \mathbf{P}^0, M)/\partial M^n = 0, \quad \text{or} \quad \mu_{MM} = \mu_{MMM} = \cdots = 0.$$

The basic idea is very simple. Return to Figure 9.3 and imagine the income expansion path through $\mathbf{q}^0$ generated by varying M while prices remain at $\mathbf{P}^0$. Along this path, because higher values of M are associated with preferred bundles, we are justified in taking M itself as a utility indicator. If the level of expenditure associated with the bundle labeled $\mathbf{c}(\mathbf{P}^0, U(q^1))$ is twice that associated with $\mathbf{q}^0$, our chosen measure will record its utility as twice that of $\mathbf{q}^0$. Along this path, then, utility is defined to equal expenditure, so that the partial derivatives have the values just given. The function $\mu(\mathbf{P}^0; \mathbf{P}, M)$ associates all other bundles in quantity space with the equivalent bundle on the income expansion path, and hence with its associated expenditure level. Because $\mathbf{q}^1$ and $\mathbf{q}^2$ are on the same indifference curve, they are both mapped into $\mathbf{c}(\mathbf{P}^0, u^1)$ and therefore into the utility level $\mathbf{P}^0 \cdot \mathbf{c}(\mathbf{P}^0, u^1) = E(\mathbf{P}^0, u^1)$. In general, it is not true that $\partial\mu(\mathbf{P}^0; \mathbf{P}^1, M^1)/\partial M = 1$ when $\mathbf{P}^1 \neq \mathbf{P}^0$. The normalization is specifically along one income expansion path, so that second derivatives with respect to prices must be computed. However, this, too, turns out to be straightforward. Roy's identity tells us that because $\mu(\cdot)$ is a utility function,

$$\partial\mu(\mathbf{P}^0; \mathbf{P}^0, M^0)/\partial P_i = -x_i \, \partial\mu(\mathbf{P}^0; \mathbf{P}^0, M^0)/\partial M.$$

I should emphasize that in interpreting these derivatives, the reference price vector is held fixed throughout. It is the prices and income faced by the consumer in a given allocation that are being varied. Using more economical notation,

$$\mu_i = -x_i(\mathbf{P}^0, M^0)\mu_M. \tag{20}$$

Bearing in mind that μ_M is itself a function of the prices and income faced by the consumer, a partial differentiation of (20) yields

$$\mu_{iM} = -x_i\mu_{MM} - \mu_M x_{iM} = \mu_{Mi} \quad \text{for all } i, j,$$

and

$$\mu_{ij} = -x_i\mu_{Mj} - \mu_M x_{ij}.$$

Now exploit the normalization that sets $\mu_M = 1$ and $\mu_{MM} = 0$. Substituting these values, we get

$$\mu_i = -x_i,$$

$$\mu_{iM} = -x_{iM} = \mu_{Mi},$$

and

$$\mu_{ij} = x_i x_{jM} - x_{ij} \quad \text{for all } i, j.$$

If desired, the third and further derivatives of $\mu(\cdot)$ in the neighborhood of $(\mathbf{P}^0; \mathbf{P}^0, M^0)$ may be replaced by observable parameters in the same way. Plugging these into (19) yields an expression for the change in utility measured in monetary units:

$$\Delta\mu = -\sum_i x_i\Delta P_i + \Delta M + \frac{1}{2}\sum_i\sum_j(x_i x_{jM} - x_{ij})\Delta P_i\Delta P_j$$

$$- \sum_i x_{iM}\Delta P_i\Delta M + \cdots, \tag{21}$$

where it is understood that x_i and the partial derivatives of x_i are evaluated at $(\mathbf{P}^0, M^0)$. Notice that the expression for the change in utility contains only exogenous price and income changes and parameters of the demand system.

The use of Taylor's expansion to generate a welfare measure from observed behavior has the merit of involving no more than familiar first principles. It has the drawback, however, of involving an intrinsic approximation, because the series has to be truncated, leaving a remainder of unknown magnitude. There is an attractive alternative procedure that both provides an exact measure and is based on an intuitively simple idea. Recall that the equivalent variation associated with the move from $(\mathbf{P}^0, M^0)$ to $(\mathbf{P}^1, M^1)$ is

$$\begin{aligned}
EV^{01} &= E(\mathbf{P}^0, u^1) - E(\mathbf{P}^0, u^0) \\
&= E(\mathbf{P}^0, u^1) - E(\mathbf{P}^1, u^1) + E(\mathbf{P}^1, u^1) - E(\mathbf{P}^0, u^0) \\
&= E(\mathbf{P}^0, u^1) - E(\mathbf{P}^1, u^1) + (M^1 - M^0).
\end{aligned}$$

In order to calculate the troublesome term $E(\mathbf{P}^0, u^1) - E(\mathbf{P}^1, u^1)$, observe that it can be split up into a sequence of stages, each representing the equivalent variation associated with a single price change:

$$\begin{aligned}
&E(\mathbf{P}^0, u^1) - E(\mathbf{P}^1, u^1) \\
&= E(P_1^0, P_2^1, \ldots, u^1) - E(P_1^1, P_2^1, \ldots, u^1) \\
&\quad + E(P_1^0, P_2^0, P_3^1, \ldots, u^1) - E(P_1^0, P_2^1, P_3^1, \ldots, u^1) \\
&\quad \vdots \\
&\quad + E(P_1^0, \ldots, P_j^0, P_{j+1}^1, \ldots, u^1) - E(P_1^0, \ldots, P_{j-1}^0, P_j^1, \ldots, u^1) \\
&\quad \vdots \\
&\quad + E(P_1^0, \ldots, P_{n-1}^0, P_n^0, u^1) - E(P_1^0, \ldots, P_{n-1}^0, P_n^1, u^1).
\end{aligned}$$

Line j of this expression is simply the equivalent variation associated with the change in the jth price when $P_1, \ldots, P_{j-1}$ are held at their original level and $P_{j+1}, \ldots, P_n, u$ are held at their final level. It turns out that we can solve for each stage of the sequence in turn. Begin with the first, in which P_1 changes from P_1^0 to P_1^1. For convenience, define the function

$$g_1(P_1) \equiv E(P_1, P_2^1, \ldots, P_n^1, u^1) - E(P_1^1, P_2^1, \ldots, P_n^1, u^1).$$

By definition of $E(\mathbf{P}^1, u^1)$,

$$g_1(P_1) = E(P_1, P_2^1, \ldots, P_n^1, u^1) - M^1.$$

Now, using Shephard's lemma,

$$\frac{dg_1(P_1)}{dP_1} = c_1(P_1, P_2^1, \ldots, P_n^1, u^1).$$

The demand for commodity 1 can be expressed alternatively in terms of the uncompensated demand function:

$$\frac{dg_1(P_1)}{dP_1} = x_1(P_1, P_2^1, \ldots, P_n^1, E(P_1, P_2^1, \ldots, P_n^1, u^1)).$$

The expenditure function can itself be replaced using the expression that defines $g_1(P_1)$:

$$\frac{dg_1(P_1)}{dP_1} = x_1(P_1, P_2^1, \ldots, P_n^1, M^1 + g_1(P_1)).$$

The attraction of this is that if we know the uncompensated demand function $x_1(\cdot)$, we can solve this first-order differential equation for the function $g_1(P_1)$. Then, by evaluating $g_1(P_1)$ at the value P_1^0, we compute the equivalent variation associated with the change from $(P_1^0, P_1^1, ..., P_n^1)$ to $(P_1^1, P_2^1, ..., P_n^1)$.

Having done this, the second stage can be calculated in the same way. At the jth stage,

$$\frac{dg_j(P_j)}{dP_j} = x_j\left(P_1^0, ..., P_{j-1}^0, P_j, P_{j+1}^1, ..., M^1 + \sum_{i=1}^{j-1} g_i(P_i^0) + g_j(P_j)\right).$$

Because $g_i(P_i^0)$ is already known for $i = 1, ..., j-1$, this is also an ordinary first-order differential equation. Numerical methods have to be used to iterate toward the solution, but the procedure itself is based on an exact measure of welfare change.

Whatever specific procedure is used, the basic thrust of this section remains, which is that there is a natural choice of money metric, the calculation of which requires no more than is usually assumed anyway, namely, a system of estimated uncompensated demand functions. Finally, the ever increasing power of computer – indeed, supercomputer – technology makes the computational burden of calculating $\mu(\cdot)$ seem relatively light.

9.5   Economic index numbers

Price indices

Consider now a consumer who initially faces the price vector $\mathbf{P}^0$ and is observed to choose the bundle $\mathbf{q}^0$. The prices of various commodities now change, so that the price vector becomes $\mathbf{P}^1$ in the new situation. Many economists and national income statisticians have been interested in answering this question: By how much would money income have to be adjusted in order to enable the consumer facing the new prices to be precisely as well off as in the initial situation? That was the question to which the compensating variation provided an answer in Section 9.2. Cost-of-living indices attempt to answer this question in terms of the ratio of the final required income level to the initial actual income level. The expenditure function provides a natural way of writing a cost-of-living index.

The initial income level can be expressed in various ways. It is $M^0 = \mathbf{P}^0 \cdot \mathbf{q}^0 = E(\mathbf{P}^0, U(\mathbf{q}^0))$. This is, by assumption, known. If the individual now faces $\mathbf{P}^1$, then in order to attain the initial utility level the required income level is given by $E(\mathbf{P}^1, U(\mathbf{q}^0))$. If $\mathbf{P}^1$ is not a scalar multiple of $\mathbf{P}^0$, then if he received the required income he would no longer consume $\mathbf{q}^0$, but would instead choose the point $\mathbf{c}(\mathbf{P}^1, u^0)$ in Figure 9.4. This creates a problem. If we knew the individual's indifference map, $\mathbf{c}(\mathbf{P}^1, u^0)$ could be located, and the "true" cost-of-living, or price, index could be calculated. This is defined as

$$PI_{K0}^{01} = \frac{E(\mathbf{P}^1, U(\mathbf{q}^0))}{E(\mathbf{P}^0, U(\mathbf{q}^0))} = \frac{\mathbf{P}^1 \cdot \mathbf{c}(\mathbf{P}^1, u^0)}{\mathbf{P}^0 \cdot \mathbf{q}^0}. \tag{22}$$

PI_{K0}^{01} simply expresses the minimum expenditure required to attain the initial utility level when facing the new prices $\mathbf{P}^1$ relative to the actual initial cost of reaching that standard of living. The K subscript refers to the Russian statistician Konüs (1939), who suggested the adoption of a reference utility, or real income, level. The 0 subscript refers to the adoption of the specific value u^0 as that reference level. If all prices had risen by, say, $b\%$, then PI_{K0}^{01} would be $(100+b)/100$. More generally it is an indicator of the change in the level of prices. The difficulty that arises is simply that we may not know the individual's preferences, in which case the hypothetical bundle $\mathbf{c}(\mathbf{P}^1, u^0)$ cannot be located. Suppose we can observe simply the prices faced and the quantities chosen in both situations 0 and 1, but no more than this. One possible way to obtain a measure of the change in the price level is to use the base quantity $\mathbf{q}^0$ in both the numerator and denominator of the index. Define the Laspeyres price index:

$$PI_L^{01} = \frac{\mathbf{P}^1 \cdot \mathbf{q}^0}{\mathbf{P}^0 \cdot \mathbf{q}^0}. \tag{23}$$

Because the hypothetical vector $\mathbf{c}(\mathbf{P}^1, u^0)$ is, by definition, the least-cost way of attaining u^0 when prices are $\mathbf{P}^1$, it follows that

$$\mathbf{P}^1 \cdot \mathbf{q}^0 \geq \mathbf{P}^1 \cdot \mathbf{c}(\mathbf{P}^1, u^0) = E(\mathbf{P}^1, u^0).$$

Consequently, the Laspeyres index generally overstates the true price index as defined in (22).

If, instead, we use the final quantities as weights, the result is the Paasche cost-of-living index:

$$PI_P^{01} = \frac{\mathbf{P}^1 \cdot \mathbf{q}^1}{\mathbf{P}^0 \cdot \mathbf{q}^1}.$$

There is, in general, no particular relationship between PI_P^{01} and PI_{K0}^{01}, the true cost-of-living index associated with the base utility level. However, there is nothing to stop us from defining a true cost-of-living index associated with the final utility level $U(\mathbf{q}^1)$:

$$PI_{K1}^{01} \equiv \frac{E(\mathbf{P}^1, U(\mathbf{q}^1))}{E(\mathbf{P}^0, U(\mathbf{q}^1))} = \frac{\mathbf{P}^1 \cdot \mathbf{q}^1}{\mathbf{P}^0 \cdot \mathbf{c}(\mathbf{P}^0, u^1)}. \tag{24}$$

It may then be shown that the true index, PI_{K1}^{01}, generally exceeds the Paasche index. If preferences are homothetic, stronger results can be obtained. Homotheticity implies that

$$\frac{\mathbf{P}^1 \cdot \mathbf{c}(\mathbf{P}^1, u^0)}{\mathbf{P}^1 \cdot \mathbf{q}^1} = \frac{\mathbf{P}^0 \cdot \mathbf{q}^0}{\mathbf{P}^0 \cdot \mathbf{c}(\mathbf{P}^0, u^1)},$$

or, slightly rearranging,

$$PI_{K0}^{01} = \frac{\mathbf{P}^1 \cdot \mathbf{c}(\mathbf{P}^1, u^0)}{\mathbf{P}^0 \cdot \mathbf{q}^0} = \frac{\mathbf{P}^1 \cdot \mathbf{q}^1}{\mathbf{P}^0 \cdot \mathbf{c}(\mathbf{P}^0, u^1)} = PI_{K1}^{01}.$$

Thus, if preferences are homothetic, it does not matter whether the reference utility level is u^0 or u^1. It follows, then, that the true index lies between the Laspeyres and Paasche indices:

$$PI_L^{01} \geq PI_{K0}^{01} = PI_{K1}^{01} \geq PI_P^{01}.$$

A slightly more general result may, if desired, be obtained. In defining the "true" cost-of-living index, we may choose any arbitrary reference quantity $\mathbf{q}^r$, so that the general index is defined as

$$PI_{Kr}^{01} \equiv \frac{E(\mathbf{P}^1, U(\mathbf{q}^r))}{E(\mathbf{P}^0, U(\mathbf{q}^r))}. \tag{25}$$

This shows the expenditure required to reach the utility level associated with $\mathbf{q}^r$ when faced with the price vector $\mathbf{P}^1$ relative to the expenditure required at prices $\mathbf{P}^0$. Figure 9.7 shows as dashed lines the budget constraints corresponding to the numerator and denominator of (25). It may be shown that if preferences are homothetic and $\mathbf{q}^r$ is strictly positive,

$$PI_L^{01} \geq PI_{Kr}^{01} \geq PI_P^{01}. \tag{26}$$

The result obtained earlier is simply a special case of (26), obtained by choosing the initial or final bundles as the reference quantity vector.

The literature on index numbers seems to be particularly bedeviled by confusing controversies that often rest, ultimately, on semantic issues. For example, McKenzie (1983) goes out of his way to distinguish between a price index suggested by himself and Pearce – see McKenzie and Pearce (1976) – and the Konüs index. In fact, the McKenzie–Pearce price index is simply PI_{K1}^{01}, which I defined in (24). Other writers would recognize this as a Konüs index that uses the final utility as the reference level. This

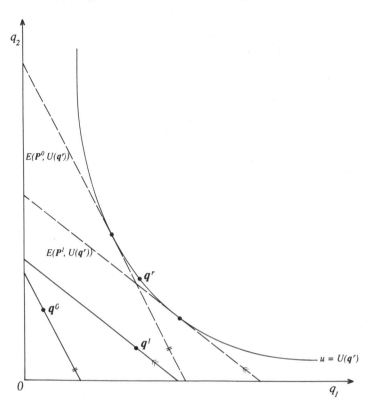

Figure 9.7

index is of particular interest for a reason that will emerge from our discussion of quantity indices.

Quantity indices

As with prices, so too with quantities. The desire to make such comparative statements as "real consumption rose by 3% last year" or "in 1963 the gross domestic product per capita was $2,790 in the United States, compared with U.S.$40 in Ethiopia" requires us to confront index number problems similar to those encountered in the construction of cost-of-living or price inflation statistics. Some, such as Moroney (1956, pp. 48–54), argue that such desires are unwholesome and should be suppressed. A more moderate stance was adopted in the excellent treatment by Usher (1968), who was concerned to show simply what could and what could not be read into index numbers. The present treatment can be brief, because

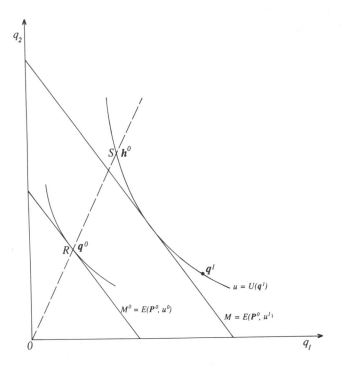

Figure 9.8

we shall see shortly that development of quantity indices leads us back into familar territory.

Forget all about prices for the moment, and consider a consumer who initially consumes the bundle q^0, and who in a later time period consumes the bundle q^1. If every element of q has risen by the same proportion, so that $q_i^1 = (1+\theta)q_i^0$ for all i, it would be natural to say that consumption had risen by the proportion θ, or that final consumption was $(1+\theta)$ times initial consumption. However, we wish to deal with situations in which there is no simple proportional relationship between the elements of q^0 and q^1. It may even be the case that while some consumption levels are higher in the final situation than initially, others are lower. Figure 9.8 suggests one way of defining a quantity index. Starting from q^0, there is a scalar multiple bundle, h^0, that just permits the same utility level as is achieved with q^1. The move from q^0 to q^1 is, in an obvious sense, equivalent to the radial move from q^0 to h^0. But the relationship between h^0 and q^0 is easy to express, because h^0 is a scalar multiple of q^0. In Figure 9.8, we can see that $\mathbf{h}^0 = (0S/0R)\mathbf{q}^0$. But $0S/0R$ is nothing more than the reciprocal of the distance function $D(\mathbf{q}^0, u^1)$.

The quantity index number that I have just defined is a special case of what is commonly known as the Malmquist quantity index. In defining the value of the index associated with the move from $\mathbf{q}^0$ to $\mathbf{q}^1$, there is no logical necessity to use either $u^0 = U(\mathbf{q}^0)$ or $u^1 = U(\mathbf{q}^1)$ as a reference utility level. More generally, if an arbitrary utility level u^r is chosen, the index is defined as

$$\mathrm{QI}_{Mr}^{01} \equiv D(\mathbf{q}^1, u^r)/D(\mathbf{q}^0, u^r). \tag{27}$$

When u^r is chosen to equal u^1, the numerator in (27) becomes unity, so that

$$\mathrm{QI}_{M1}^{01} = 1/D(\mathbf{q}^0, u^1). \tag{28}$$

If, on the other hand, $u^r = u^0$, it is the denominator that becomes unity, and the index becomes

$$\mathrm{QI}_{M0}^{01} = D(\mathbf{q}^1, u^0). \tag{29}$$

Equation (29) provides an answer to the following question: By how much should the final bundle be scaled up or down in order to provide the consumer with the initial utility level? The Malmquist index has some attractive properties. If $\mathbf{q}^1$ generates the same level of utility as does $\mathbf{q}^0$, then $\mathrm{QI}_{M0}^{01} = \mathrm{QI}_{M1}^{01} = 1$. Also, if the change in the bundle is proportional, so that $\mathbf{q}^1 = (1+\theta)\mathbf{q}^0$, then $\mathrm{QI}_{Mr}^{01} = (1+\theta)$, whatever reference utility is used. This follows directly from the fact that the distance function is homogeneous of degree 1 in all quantities. Finally, if preferences are homothetic, the value of the index associated with the move from $\mathbf{q}^1$ to $\mathbf{q}^2$ is independent of the choice of the reference utility level.

The Malmquist index considers proportional changes in a given bundle that would produce a particular target level. For this reason, it is often encountered in analyses of technical efficiency of production. The Farrell measure of technical efficiency, which was discussed in Chapter 5, is a Malmquist index. An alternative index, suggested by Allen (1949), asks what proportional income change, at some set of reference prices, would have the same effect on utility as an observed change in the quantity vector. Such an index clearly uses prices as an integral component. If the individual is a price-taker, and if the reference prices are taken to be the base or initial price vector, Allen's quantity index may be written as

$$\mathrm{QI}_{A0}^{01} \equiv \frac{E(\mathbf{P}^0, U(\mathbf{q}^1))}{E(\mathbf{P}^0, U(\mathbf{q}^0))} = \frac{\mu(\mathbf{P}^0; \mathbf{P}^1, M^1)}{\mu(\mathbf{P}^0; \mathbf{P}^0, M^0)}. \tag{30}$$

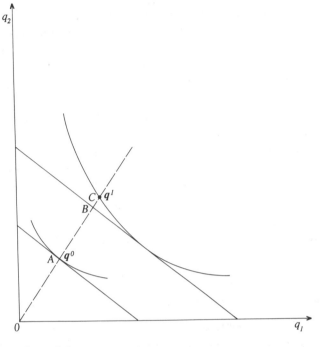

Figure 9.9

In Figure 9.8, the move from $\mathbf{q}^0$ to $\mathbf{q}^1$ is equivalent, in terms of welfare, to the move from the initial expenditure level, $M^0 = E(\mathbf{P}^0, u^0)$, to the level defined by $E(\mathbf{P}^0, u^1)$.

Allen's quantity index does not generally equal the Malmquist index. This is hardly surprising, because the two answer different questions. Figure 9.9, which considers the special case in which $\mathbf{q}^1$ is proportional to $\mathbf{q}^0$, shows the difference and suggests under what circumstances the two indices coincide. As drawn, $\mathbf{q}^1 = 2\mathbf{q}^0$. The Malmquist index QI_{M0}^{01} will take on the value $0C/0A = 2$. The Allen index QI_{A0}^{01} will take on the value $0B/0A < 2$. If, indeed, income were doubled, the individual would be able to improve on $\mathbf{q}^1$ and therefore on u^1, by substituting into commodity 1. The one situation in which the two indices coincide arises when preferences are homothetic.

Comparison of (30) with (7) reveals that Allen's quantity index uses precisely the same information as does the money metric associated with the move from $\mathbf{q}^0$ to $\mathbf{q}^1$. it simply presents it in a slightly different form. For this reason, Deaton and Muellbauer (1980a, p. 180) and McKenzie (1983, p. 130) refer to Allen's index as a welfare, or money metric, index.

One last comment may be helpful in linking together price and quantity index numbers. By this stage, the reader will have realized that there is a plethora of definable index numbers. To help in weeding out less interesting candidates, researchers have suggested properties that ought to be obeyed by economically sensible price and quantity index numbers. One such property is the weak factor reversal criterion. This requires that whatever our choice of price index and quantity index, their product should equal the ratio of actual expenditures in the two periods considered: $(\mathrm{PI}^{01} \times \mathrm{QI}^{01}) = M^1/M^0$. Suppose we adopt Allen's suggested quantity index, QI_{A0}^{01}, having been persuaded by its virtues as a money metric. It forms a natural pairing with the Konüs price index, PI_{K1}^{01}, in the sense that, as (24) and (30) show, they satisfy this criterion. At the same time, the duality between cost and distance functions suggests a strong formal link between the Konüs cost-of-living index and the Malmquist quantity index. The formal symmetry between the two is neatly brought out by Russell (1983).

9.6   Measurement of deadweight loss

Application of the welfare measures that we have developed here to particular contexts often encounters difficulties and ambiguities that can provoke controversy and confuse the reader. As an example, consider the problem of measuring deadweight loss. The problem is as follows: Governments wish to tax individuals in order to acquire real resources. From the point of view of economic efficiency, the least painful way of effecting such a transfer is through lump-sum taxation. Suppose an individual can supply labor hours to produce a final commodity according to the production frontier 0F in Figure 9.10. One can think in terms of either the two goods, leisure and commodities, measured from the point N, or work and commodities, measured from 0. N0 is the initial endowment of hours available as leisure or labor time. In the absence of government intervention, 0F is also the consumption frontier. Now suppose the government wishes to acquire a fixed number of man-hours for its own use. Lump-sum confiscation of, say, z man-hours, in effect through conscription, would shift the consumption possibilities frontier for the consumer to the left by z units, so that it would become 0'F'. The utility-maximizing consumer would then choose the point B, which would put him on the indifference curve marked u^0. Suppose, however, that lump-sum confiscation is not permissible. Instead, the government has to rely on taxing one of the commodities. A tax on labor income has the effect of reducing the amount of final commodity q that is made available for consumption by

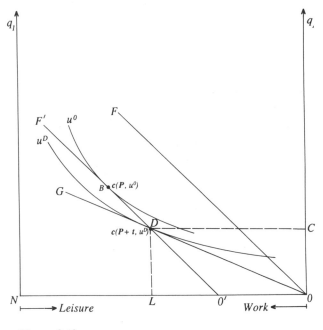

Figure 9.10

virtue of any given input of labor. There is a tax rate, for example, that confronts the individual with the consumption frontier $0G$. As drawn, the utility-maximizer will consume at the point D. At D, the individual's labor supply is $0L$, and his final goods consumption is $0C$. It is as if the individual is working $00'$ ($= z$ man-hours) for the government, and $0'L$ hours in order to generate consumption for himself. The deadweight loss associated with the tax-distorted equilibrium D is reflected in the fact that at D the same tax revenue is collected as by the lump-sum tax described earlier, but the allocation at D makes the consumer worse off than at the allocation B. The price-distorting nature of the tax, while generating tax revenue, creates an additional source of welfare loss. It is this that is termed the deadweight loss.

Suppose that in the absence of any tax the price vector faced by the consumer is $\mathbf{P}$. The distortionary tax system is represented by the vector $\mathbf{t}$, so that in the tax-distorted equilibrium the consumer faces the price vector $\mathbf{P}+\mathbf{t}$. Notice that the formal statement of the problem can accommodate as many commodities as we wish. My notation also emphasizes that we can allow all commodities to be goods of which the consumer, given an exogenous income, is a net demander. I shall denote the utility level attained at the distorted equilibrium by u^D.

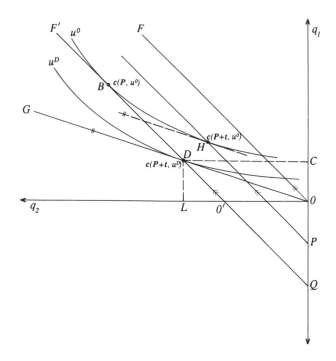

Figure 9.11

Diamond and McFadden (1974) suggest the following deadweight loss measure. Suppose that the consumer is compensated so that while still facing the distorted prices $\mathbf{P}+\mathbf{t}$, he is now able to attain the utility level that would result from the lump-sum tax, u^0. This will take him to the point H in Figure 9.11. Now take the values of the allocations at D and H at the undistorted prices. The difference between these two values is a measure of deadweight loss. In Figure 9.11, if commodity 1 is used as the numeraire, the loss is represented by the distance PQ. Algebraically, the bundle chosen at H is, in terms of compensated demand functions, the bundle $\mathbf{c}(\mathbf{P}+\mathbf{t}, u^0)$. At D, the bundle is $\mathbf{c}(\mathbf{P}+\mathbf{t}, u^D)$. Consequently, the deadweight loss (DWL) is

$$\text{DWL}^1 = \mathbf{P}\cdot\mathbf{c}(\mathbf{P}+\mathbf{t}, u^0) - \mathbf{P}\cdot\mathbf{c}(\mathbf{P}+\mathbf{t}, u^D).$$

But the bundle at D has the same value as that at B, valued at undistorted prices: $\mathbf{P}\cdot\mathbf{c}(\mathbf{P}+\mathbf{t}, u^D) = \mathbf{P}\cdot\mathbf{c}(\mathbf{P}, u^0)$. Therefore,

$$\text{DWL}^1 = \mathbf{P}\cdot\mathbf{c}(\mathbf{P}+\mathbf{t}, u^0) - \mathbf{P}\cdot\mathbf{c}(\mathbf{P}, u^0). \tag{31}$$

To obtain Diamond and McFadden's expression, observe that the first term on the right-hand side of (31) can be written as

$$(\mathbf{P}+\mathbf{t})\cdot\mathbf{c}(\mathbf{P}+\mathbf{t}, u^0) - \mathbf{t}\cdot\mathbf{c}(\mathbf{P}+\mathbf{t}, u^0) = E(\mathbf{P}+\mathbf{t}, u^0) - \mathbf{t}\cdot\mathbf{c}(\mathbf{P}+\mathbf{t}, u^0).$$

Using this fact, (31) can be written

$$\text{DWL}^1 = E(\mathbf{P}+\mathbf{t}, u^0) - E(\mathbf{P}, u^0) - \mathbf{t}\cdot\mathbf{c}(\mathbf{P}+\mathbf{t}, u^0). \tag{32}$$

Two things are worth noting about this expression. First, it uses the undistorted utility level as its reference point. Second, the tax revenue term is not the actual tax revenue. It is the hypothetical revenue that would result if, while facing the distorted price vector, the consumer were compensated so as to return him to the utility level u^0.

While Diamond and McFadden's measure provides a correct answer to a perfectly coherent question, its use of the hypothetical tax revenue has been criticized by Kay (1980). He points out that it gives the suggested measure some undesirable characteristics. We would like our measure of deadweight loss to have the property that in the comparison between two tax vectors that raise the same actual revenue, its value is smaller for the vector associated with the higher distorted utility level. This would imply that among all such tax vectors, the one that allows the consumer the highest utility level is also the one that minimizes the value of the deadweight loss. The Diamond–McFadden measure does not possess these properties.

Kay suggests an alternative measure. Moving from the lump-sum equilibrium at B to the tax-distorted equilibrium at D is equivalent, he notes, to having income taken away in a lump-sum manner so as to take the consumer to the point J in Figure 9.12. This equivalent variation, measured in terms of commodity 1, is represented by the distance QR. Clearly, this measure uses the undistorted price vector in valuing the situations B and J. Algebraically, it is given by

$$\text{DWL}^2 = \mathbf{P}\cdot\mathbf{c}(\mathbf{P}, u^0) - \mathbf{P}\cdot\mathbf{c}(\mathbf{P}, u^D).$$

Reasoning similar to that applied to the earlier measure enables us to write

$$\begin{aligned}
\text{DWL}^2 &= \mathbf{P}\cdot\mathbf{c}(\mathbf{P}+\mathbf{t}, u^D) - \mathbf{P}\cdot\mathbf{c}(\mathbf{P}, u^D) \\
&= (\mathbf{P}+\mathbf{t})\cdot\mathbf{c}(\mathbf{P}+\mathbf{t}, u^D) - \mathbf{P}\cdot\mathbf{c}(\mathbf{P}, u^D) - \mathbf{t}\cdot\mathbf{c}(\mathbf{P}+\mathbf{t}, u^D) \\
&= E(\mathbf{P}+\mathbf{t}, u^D) - E(\mathbf{P}, u^D) - \mathbf{t}\cdot\mathbf{c}(\mathbf{P}+\mathbf{t}, u^D). \tag{33}
\end{aligned}$$

This measure uses the tax-distorted equilibrium utility level as its reference point. Notice, too, that the last term is the actual tax revenue collected at the distorted equilibrium.

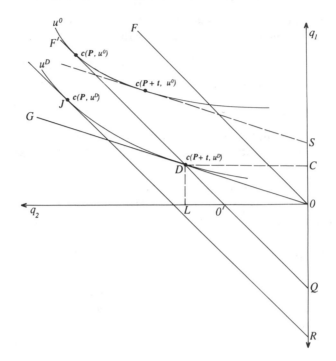

Figure 9.12

It is tempting to characterize these two measures by calling DWL^1 the compensating variation and DWL^2 the equivalent variation associated with the comparison between the base situation B and the distorted situation D. However, Zabalza (1982) has pointed out that DWL^1 is not the only, and perhaps not the most natural, measure of the compensating variation. He suggests asking how much income would have to be paid to the consumer at the tax-distorted equilibrium D in order to bring him back to his original utility level u^0, evaluated at the distorted prices. Like Diamond and McFadden's analysis, this generates the hypothetical situation H. The comparison is now between H and D. Geometrically, this compensating variation is the distance $0S$. Algebraically, it can be expressed as

$$\text{DWL}^3 = (\mathbf{P}+\mathbf{t})\cdot\mathbf{c}(\mathbf{P}+\mathbf{t}, u^0) - (\mathbf{P}+\mathbf{t})\cdot\mathbf{c}(\mathbf{P}+\mathbf{t}, u^D)$$
$$= E(\mathbf{P}+\mathbf{t}, u^0) - \mathbf{P}\cdot\mathbf{c}(\mathbf{P}+\mathbf{t}, u^D) - \mathbf{t}\cdot\mathbf{c}(\mathbf{P}+\mathbf{t}, u^D)$$
$$= E(\mathbf{P}+\mathbf{t}, u^0) - \mathbf{P}\cdot\mathbf{c}(\mathbf{P}, u^0) - \mathbf{t}\cdot\mathbf{c}(\mathbf{P}+\mathbf{t}, u^D)$$
$$= E(\mathbf{P}+\mathbf{t}, u^0) - E(\mathbf{P}, u^0) - \mathbf{t}\cdot\mathbf{c}(\mathbf{P}+\mathbf{t}, u^D). \qquad (34)$$

This expression is certainly in the spirit of the compensating variation, because the expenditure levels are associated with the base utility level u^0. It differs from the Diamond–McFadden measure by virtue of the last term. In (34), the tax revenue $t \cdot c(P+t, u^D)$ is, as in Kay's measure, the revenue actually collected.

There is little to be gained from arguments concerning the superiority of one measure over the other. Kay's equivalent variation has the attractive property of being a money metric, because the magnitude of his measure correctly ranks alternative equal-revenue tax structures according to their implied utility levels. All three measures, however, provide precise and correct answers to unambiguous and readily understood questions. All three, too, are easy to define with the help of the expenditure function.

9.7   Concluding comments and suggestions for further study

Samuelson (1938, 1950) was a pioneer in the development of simple re-vealed preference arguments. A good discussion of precisely how far one can go in drawing welfare conclusions from observed behavior was pro-vided by Pearce (1970, ch. 13). He was skeptical about the value of becom-ing too preoccupied with devices such as utility possibility frontiers and compensation tests, notions that loom large in the literature. The treat-ment by Ohyama (1972) has greatly influenced international trade theo-rists. Dixit and Norman (1986) have recently attempted to clarify their analysis of gainful trade in the absence of lump-sum transfers. Their meth-od of argument has been exploited by other writers such as Smith (1982).

Since their introduction by Hicks (1943), the equivalent and compen-sating variations have become standard tools in welfare economics. Boad-way and Bruce (1984) provide a helpful discussion of these and related matters. Dixit and Weller (1979) provide a useful comparison of alterna-tive measures. McKenzie (1983) is certainly worth consulting. His desire to differentiate his own product sometimes leads him to fail to do justice to earlier literature, but his argument that the EV provides a natural money metric and is computable from the information sets normally assumed to be available is compelling and should be more widely heeded. Equivalent and compensating surpluses are less commonly encountered. Again, Hicks (1943, 1956) was a pioneer. Recently there has been renewed interest, with papers by Hammond (1983) on the CS and by Lankford (1986) on the ES.

McKenzie's book (1983) on welfare measures follows earlier work by McKenzie and Pearce (1976) and Hausman (1981). Another contribution is by Vartia (1983). The idea of breaking the EV up into a sequence of exact first-order differential equations, each amenable to numerical solution, was expounded by McKenzie and Ulph (1986), following Vartia's earlier application of the same idea to generate the CV. The application of such procedures to quantity-constrained allocations, for which the equivalent surplus is used by Lankford (1986), encounters difficult data problems in estimating values for unobserved virtual prices. These, rather than conceptual difficulties or computational burden, represent the major obstacle here. Johansson (1987) provides a good discussion, both of the conceptual and theoretical concerns of this chapter and also of attempts to deal with the problem of obtaining the necessary data, in the context of environmental economics.

The literature on index numbers is large, complicated, and not always enlightening. Deaton and Muellbauer (1980*a*, pp. 170–82) are helpful and commendably brief; Deaton (1979) emphasizes the usefulness of the distance function in defining certain indices. Malmquist (1953), to whom I referred in earlier chapters, exposes very clearly the parallels between the representation of a price index using price indifference curves and the representation of a quantity index using quantity indifference curves. Debreu's analysis of the coefficient of resource utilization, referred to in Chapter 5, is a discussion of a quantity index. The reader desiring a comprehensive technical survey should consult Diewert (1980). Pollak (1989) provides an excellent discussion, sophisticated but not cluttered by intricate mathematics, of both conceptual and practical aspects of constructing and interpreting the cost-of-living index; it is a collection of papers, most of which have appeared elsewhere – for example, it includes Pollak (1971, 1981) – but it also has some previously unpublished pieces. I recommend it highly. Blackorby and Russell (1978) and Pollak (1989) also discuss the problems of constructing and interpreting subindices – that is, indices involving subsets of commodities, such as food or clothing.

In addition to the papers cited in Section 9.6, there are several recent papers by Diewert (1983, 1984, 1985) discussing alternative measures of deadweight loss and welfare change. Expenditure and distance functions are prominent, as one would expect of this author and the topic. Pauwels (1986) has recently provided a critical review of some of the issues raised in the debate on alternative measures of deadweight loss – see also Stutzer (1982). Interesting applications of the ideas in this chapter to bodies of data are now beginning to be generated – see, for example, King (1983), Schwab (1985), and De Borger (1989). It is an area ripe for cultivation by graduate students.

With some misgivings, I have decided to stop short of a discussion of the problems that arise when the focus switches from the individual to the idea of social welfare. The literature on social welfare functions is vast, and recent analyses have increasingly exploited the simplicity that results from dual formulations. A number of recent contributions may be of particular interest to readers of this book. McKenzie (1983, ch. 8) discusses how to go from individual welfare, as measured by money metrics, to social welfare evaluation. King (1983, 1987) has made extensive use of the equivalent income concept in analyzing tax reform, and Blackorby and Donaldson (1988) have noted a problem with using money metric utility measures in evaluating social states. Pollak (1981, 1989, ch. 7) defines and uses the idea of a social expenditure function. This is the minimum level of aggregate expenditure, at a given set of prices, required to attain a target level of social welfare in a many-consumer economy. Ahlheim (1988) and Kay and Keen (1988) discuss the use of distance functions in the analysis of social welfare and the welfare loss due to taxation. Roberts (1980) notes that the indirect social welfare function, $W(\mathbf{P}, m_1, \ldots, m_H) = W(V^1(\mathbf{P}, m_1), \ldots, V^H(\mathbf{P}, m_H))$, is often written as a function of individual incomes alone, without any prices among its arguments. He contends that this can be justified only on the basis of very special assumptions about individual preferences. There are, of course, many more papers on welfare economics, in addition to the small sample cited here, that use dual arguments along the way in order to simplify analysis. In particular, I should finish by mentioning a simple and useful expository paper by Greenberg and Denzau (1988) that looks at applications of duality to various public finance problems.

CHAPTER 10

Externalities and public goods

I asserted in Chapter 7 that externalities and public goods can usefully be modeled as quantity constraints. The restricted indirect utility and expenditure functions can then be used, together with the implied demand and inverse demand functions, to analyze the comparative static and optimality properties of equilibrium. Much of the literature on externalities has been concerned with the idea that in their presence, a decentralized market equilibrium may fail to attain a Pareto optimum. The Pigouvian tradition has gone on to explore the possibility of finding a set of taxes and subsidies that will sustain a Pareto-optimal equilibrium. In general, there is no presumption that an arbitrary Pareto optimum will be Pareto-superior to a given equilibrium established in the absence of taxes. It is of interest to explore the possibility of Pareto-improving moves from an equilibrium – that is, moves that make no individual worse off and that make at least one individual better off than at an initial equilibrium. It turns out that in many situations Pigouvian taxes and subsidies are not enough to secure a Pareto improvement. They must be supplemented by some means, whether lump-sum or distortionary, of redistributing real income. A further concern of students of externalities has been the possibility that in the move from an equilibrium to an optimal allocation, the level of activities associated with detrimental externalities, such as air pollution, may rise. Conversely, the level of those activities that generate beneficial externalities may fall. Such possibilities have been regarded as anomalous by some writers, and deserving of explanation. Section 10.1 uses dual formulations to analyze the various normative and positive aspects of externalities mentioned earlier in the context of a simple two-person model of a one-way externality – that is, a model in which there is a single externality, produced by one individual, the "generator," and imposed on the other, the "recipient." Section 10.2 briefly analyzes a model of reciprocal externalities, in which each individual is both a generator and a recipient.

Models of reciprocal externalities can quickly become very complex, and often it is helpful to simplify them by making additional assumptions.

One class of models, in which the recipient views the externality as a perfect substitute for one of the marketed commodities, has particularly attractive properties. It also provides the formal framework for analyzing situations involving so-called pure public goods. Section 10.3 is devoted to this topic. The issues are the same as those raised in the context of general externalities, although the special structure allows us to explore some themes rather more deeply.

10.1   A simple externality model

Consider an individual who cares about the quantities of two types of commodities. The first, denoted by $\mathbf{q}$, may be bought or sold in competitive markets, but the quantities of the second, denoted by $\mathbf{e}$, are beyond the control of the consumer, there being no associated markets. Examples might include the quality of downstream water available for drinking and other domestic purposes, the level and duration of noise from neighbors' lawnmowers and power drills, or the fragrance and attractive scenery resulting from a nearby orchard in bloom. By contrast with the marketed commodities, such goods – or bads – may be called environmental commodities. Our present interest is in those environmental commodities the quantities of which are determined by the activities of other members of the community. The recipient is a quantity-taker with respect to environmental commodities. They represent flows of services or disservices that are not channeled through, or "internalized" by, the market system. Rather, they have a direct effect on the well-being and/or choices of the involuntary recipient. Such commodities, endogenous to the economy but exogenous to the individual, are commonly called externalities or external effects.

Formally, the recipient's problem is simply a special case of quantity-constrained behavior. The direct utility function is maximized subject to a budget constraint and a set of quantity constraints:

$$\max_{\mathbf{q}}\{U(\mathbf{q},\mathbf{e})\,|\,\mathbf{P}\cdot\mathbf{q} \leq M,\ \mathbf{e}\ \text{given}\}. \tag{1}$$

Environmental commodities have zero prices, but their quantities $\mathbf{e}$ are exogenously imposed on the recipient. As indicated by our examples, they may be goods or bads. The latter will be reflected in a negative marginal utility, $\partial U/\partial e_k$.

Alternative representations of the individual's preferences are provided by the restricted indirect utility function $V^*(\mathbf{P},\mathbf{e},M)$ and the restricted expenditure function $E^*(\mathbf{P},\mathbf{e},u)$. There is no need to run systematically through the derivation and properties of the various demand and inverse demand functions that can be generated, because that was done in Chapter 7. Recall simply that uncompensated and compensated demand functions for the marketed goods can be generated, respectively, through Roy's identity,

$$x_i^*(\mathbf{P}, \mathbf{e}, M) = -\frac{\partial V^*(\mathbf{P}, \mathbf{e}, M)/\partial P_i}{\partial V^*(\mathbf{P}, \mathbf{e}, M)/\partial M},$$

and Shephard's lemma,

$$c_i^*(\mathbf{P}, \mathbf{e}, u) = \partial E^*(\mathbf{P}, \mathbf{e}, u)/\partial P_i.$$

A change in, say, e_k produces a response in the demand for the marketed commoditity i that can be split up into compensated and real income components, using the substitution trick of Cook (1972):

$$x_i^*(\mathbf{P}, \mathbf{e}, E^*(\mathbf{P}, \mathbf{e}, u)) = c_i^*(\mathbf{P}, \mathbf{e}, u).$$

Therefore, differentiating with respect to e_k while holding $\mathbf{P}$, u, and other environmental quantities fixed yields, after a little rearrangement,

$$\partial x_i^*(\cdot)/\partial e_k = \partial c_i^*(\cdot)/\partial e_k - (\partial E^*(\cdot)\partial e_k)(\partial x_i^*(\cdot)/\partial M), \tag{2}$$

which is reminiscent of the standard Slutsky or Hicks decomposition of the price response.

Uncompensated and compensated virtual price functions, indicating the recipient's willingness to pay for environmental commodities, may be generated from $V^*(\cdot)$ and $E^*(\cdot)$ in a similar fashion. Figure 10.1 depicts a situation in which all marketed commodities have been aggregated into a single Hicksian composite commodity. Suppose that money prices are all fixed, so that the composite marketed good can be thought of as money income, M, measured along the horizontal axis. The vertical axis measures the quantity of a single environmental commodity, e_k. As drawn, e_k is a beneficial externality. Suppose e_k rises by de_k. The monetary value placed by the recipient on de_k is represented by the amount of income that can be given up so as to leave the individual precisely as well off as at the initial point, I. This is the quantity dM. The changes in M and e_k that maintain an unchanged utility level can be derived by differentiating the indirect utility function and putting $dV = 0$:

$$dV = 0 = (\partial V^*(\cdot)/\partial e_k)de_k + (\partial V^*(\cdot)/\partial M)dM.$$

Therefore, rearranging,

$$-\frac{dM}{de_k}\bigg|_{dV=0} = \frac{\partial V^*(\mathbf{P}, \mathbf{e}, M)/\partial e_k}{\partial V^*(\mathbf{P}, \mathbf{e}, M)/\partial M}. \tag{3}$$

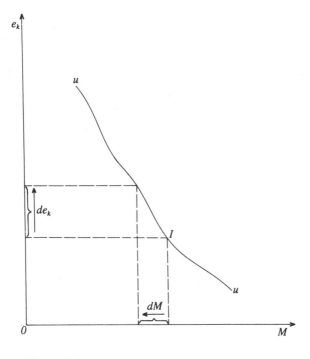

Figure 10.1

As the figure clearly suggests, this is simply the marginal rate of substitution between the externality and the composite marketed good, which reflects the willingness to pay for the externality. We can, in the manner suggested in Chapter 7, write this as an uncompensated inverse demand, or virtual price, function:

$$\phi_k^*(\mathbf{P}, \mathbf{e}, M) \equiv \frac{\partial V^*(\cdot)/\partial e_k}{\partial V^*(\cdot)/\partial M}. \tag{4}$$

Alternatively, the restricted expenditure function can be used to generate the compensated inverse demand function:

$$\psi_k^*(\mathbf{P}, \mathbf{e}, u) \equiv -\partial E^*(\mathbf{P}, \mathbf{e}, u)/\partial e_k. \tag{5}$$

A detrimental externality will be reflected in a negative value for the virtual price and in an upward-sloping indifference curve in Figure 10.1. Whether beneficial or detrimental, there is no necessary presumption that the set of preferred bundles in Figure 10.1 is convex, and indeed there are many instances of externalities that strongly suggest nonconvexity. For definitions of $\phi_k^*(\cdot)$ and $\psi_k^*(\cdot)$ this does not matter. Nonconvexities become important in the usual way when we consider the possibility of sustaining a given allocation with the help of some decentralized price-based mechanism. In the present thought experiment, in which the recipient is a quantity-taker, such nonconvexities pose no problem.

Certain comparative static properties of externality-ridden economies have attracted attention in recent years and will be examined later in this chapter. Their analysis is simplified, and properties that have struck others as anomalous can be readily understood, if we bear in mind the recipient's response to changes in e_k presented in (2). Using the virtual price function (4) and (5), the response $dx_i^*(\cdot)/de_k$ can be written alternatively as

$$x_{ik}^* = c_{ik}^* + \psi_k^* x_{iM}^* \tag{6}$$

or

$$x_{ik}^* = c_{ik}^* + \phi_k^* x_{iM}^*, \tag{7}$$

where $x_{ik}^* \equiv \partial x_i^*(\cdot)/\partial e_k$, and so on. The parallels with the Slutsky decomposition, and the way in which the quantity and price of the independent variable are swapped around, come across very clearly in this formulation.

Equilibrium and optimality

The general importance of externalities in the economic literature stems from the suboptimality of equilibrium in their presence. If all interdependence is channeled through competitive prices, a fundamental theorem of welfare economics tells us that a competitive equilibrium is efficient and, indeed, Pareto-optimal. In an exchange economy, individual h equates the marginal private cost of a commodity – its market price P_i – with his own virtual price ϕ_i^h.

Consider a two-person economy. Each individual receives a fixed money income and faces a given set of prices $\mathbf{P}$ for the marketed commodities. The generator of the externality, individual b, chooses the consumption vector $\mathbf{q}^b$ to maximize utility $U^b(\mathbf{q}^b)$ in the usual way. The recipient, individual a, chooses $\mathbf{q}^a$ to maximize the utility function $U^a(\mathbf{q}^a, \mathbf{e}^a)$. Let us suppose that there is a single environmental commodity e_2^a that is equal to individual b's chosen consumption of q_2^b. With prices given, we can exploit Hicks's composite commodity theorem. In Figure 10.2, individual b's equilibrium is depicted on the left, where I have distinguished between q_2^b on the one hand and "all other marketed goods" on the other. Think of this as the commodity q_1, with price $P_1 = 1$. On the right in Figure 10.2 an indifference map for the recipient is drawn in which one of the objects of preference is the single environmental commodity e_2^a, and the other is

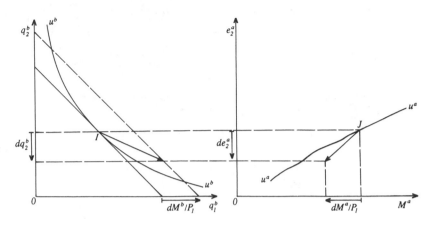

Figure 10.2

the composite of all marketed goods consumed by individual a, which can be equated with money income. I have depicted a situation in which e_2^a is detrimental to the recipient. Lying behind the indifference map is the assumption that for any given value of e_2^a the recipient is allocating income optimally. In short, the individuals are solving the following problems:

individual a: $\max_{\mathbf{q}^a}\{U^a(\mathbf{q}^a, e_2^a) \mid \mathbf{P}\cdot\mathbf{q}^a = M^a, e_2^a = q_2^b\};$ \hfill (8)

individual b: $\max_{\mathbf{q}^b}\{U^b(\mathbf{q}^b) \mid \mathbf{P}\cdot\mathbf{q}^b = M^b\}.$ \hfill (9)

At the initial equilibrium, individual b is at I. Given the implied value of e_2^a and the exogenous value of individual a's income, we can read off the utility level of the recipient, who is at J. What I wish to show now is that there exist alternative allocations that are feasible – that is, consistent with the aggregate budget constraint – and Pareto-superior to the equilibrium. This establishes the Pareto suboptimality of equilibrium.

First, note that if the generator were to curb consumption of q_2 by a small amount, while incomes remained unchanged, the recipient would be made better off. The generator would move down and to the right, away from I, along the budget line on the left in Figure 10.2. This implies a utility loss for the generator, but of "second order." An infinitesimal reduction in q_2^b would, as explained in Chapter 7, have no adverse welfare effect. Because the adverse effect on the generator of a small finite change is of second order, whereas the beneficial effect on the recipient is of first order, it follows that a small reduction in q_2^b can be accompanied by a redistribution of income away from a to b in such a way as to make both better off than at equilibrium. The short arrows originating at I and J in Figure 10.2 show a possible combination of income changes, ΔM^b and ΔM^a ($= -\Delta M^b$), and adjustment in q_2^b, $\Delta q_2^b = \Delta e_2^a$, that makes both better off.

A comparison between the first-order conditions necessary for Pareto optimality and the conditions fulfilled at equilibrium confirms the suboptimality of equilibrium. Equilibrium is characterized by the first-order conditions associated with the individual's problems (8) and (9). Among these conditions are the following equalities between the relative price P_2/P_1 and the marginal rate of substitution for each individual between q_2 and q_1:

$$P_2/P_1 \ [=P_2] = \frac{\partial U^a(\cdot)/\partial q_2^a}{\partial U^a(\cdot)/\partial q_1^a} = \frac{\partial U^b(\cdot)/\partial q_2^b}{\partial U^b(\cdot)/\partial q_1^b}.$$

In writing the relative price as P_2, I am regarding commodity 1 as the numeraire and putting P_1 equal to unity. Using virtual price functions, this can be written as

$$P_2 = \phi_2^a = \phi_2^b, \tag{10}$$

where ϕ_j^h is individual h's virtual price for the marketed commodity. Equation (10) simply expresses the fact that each will allocate resources to the point at which the marginal cost to that individual of consuming an extra unit of commodity 2, which is P_2, will equal its marginal benefit to that individual, ϕ_2^h.

Now consider a Pareto optimum. Necessary conditions can be generated by exploiting the fact that there is a weighted sum of utilities, $\alpha U^a(\cdot) + \beta U^b(\cdot)$, such that a Pareto optimum satisfies the first-order necessary conditions associated with maximization of this weighted sum. For this exercise, I wish to allow income to be redistributed. Consequently, there is a single budget constraint. The maximization problem is

$$\max_{\mathbf{q}^a, \mathbf{q}^b}\{\alpha U^a(\mathbf{q}^a, e_2^a) + \beta U^b(\mathbf{q}^b) \,|\, q_1^a + q_1^b + P_2(q_2^a + q_2^b) \le M^a + M^b\}. \tag{11}$$

Observe that because first-order conditions characteristically involve equalities between market and virtual prices, the latter being thought of as directly dependent on the consumption bundle, the direct utility function is a natural formulation in the present context. A little manipulation of the first-order conditions associated with (11), required to eliminate α, β, and the Lagrange multiplier, yields among the conditions the requirement that

$$P_2 = U_2^a/U_1^a = U_2^b/U_1^b + U_e^a/U_1^a,$$

or, using virtual price functions,

$$P_2 = \phi_2^a(\cdot) = \phi_2^b(\cdot) + \phi_e^a(\cdot), \tag{12}$$

where $\phi_e^a(\cdot)$ is the virtual price of the externality e from the recipient's point of view. Equation (12) presents the important first-order necessary condition for a Pareto optimum on which Pigou's tax/subsidy remedy is based. P_2 is the exogenous market price that rules in the absence of any distortionary policies. Suppose we were to consider imposing a tax, t_2^b, on b's consumption of commodity 2, so that the price faced by b would become $P_2^b = P_2 + t_2^b$. We know that utility-maximizing behavior on the part of b implies the equating of the virtual price ϕ_2^b with the price facing b, P_2^b. In any tax-distorted equilibrium,

$$P_2 + t_2^b = \phi_2^b(\cdot). \tag{13}$$

However, (12) tells us that for an allocation to be an optimum, we must have

$$P_2 - \phi_e^a(\cdot) = \phi_2^b(\cdot). \tag{14}$$

Consequently, Pareto optimality requires that

$$t_2^b = -\phi_e^a(\cdot). \tag{15}$$

Recall that a negative or detrimental externality implies a negative value for the recipient's marginal valuation. The specific tax t_2^b imposed on the generator must equal the level of the marginal cost imposed on the recipient. This makes intuitive sense, because the tax is in effect internalizing the external costs. The generator is being forced to take into account the costs imposed on the recipient, albeit in the form of a tax. A beneficial externality implies a positive value for $\phi_e^a(\cdot)$, so that the tax implied by (15) is negative. In other words, it is a subsidy.

Before moving on to the analysis of two-way, or reciprocal, externalities, notice the following points about the optimal allocation. First, (12) is simply a necessary condition for optimality. By itself, it does not enable us to solve for the optimum. Indeed, generally there will be an infinite number of points on the contract curve in the standard Edgeworth box diagram. Further, because ϕ_e^a is a function of P_2, e_2^g, and M^a, we need to know the value of the function ϕ_e^a in the neighborhood of an optimal allocation in order for (12) to be of any value to us. Finally, notice that even if we have enough information to identify an optimum, (12) gives no presumption concerning the comparison between equilibrium and optimal quantities consumed. Consider the generator of the detrimental externality. Individual b's demand for commodity 2 is given by the demand function

$x_2^b(P_1, P_2^b, M^b)$. Starting from an initial tax-free equilibrium, the Pigouvian policy involves a tax that increases P_2^b. By itself, this generally will reduce x_2^b and certainly will do so if commodity 2 is a normal good. However, the tax may be accompanied – indeed, for a Pareto improvement it must be accompanied – by an increase in M^b. The net result is indeterminate, and it is certainly possible that x_2^b may be higher at a given Pareto optimum than at the initial equilibrium. The recipient's demand for commodity 2 may similarly either rise or fall. Suppose that the optimal value of the q_2^b is lower than its initial equilibrium level. Equation (2) tells us that the change in the externality level influences the recipient's demand for commodity 2 through both a substitution term and also a real income term. Suppose we ignore the real income term. Even the pure compensated substitution response can be of either sign. We know from our analysis in Chapter 7 that this response is related in a straightforward way to compensated price responses:

$$\partial c_2^{*a}/\partial e_2^a = \frac{\partial c_2^a(\cdot)/\partial \phi_e^a}{\partial c_2^a(\cdot)/\partial P_2}. \tag{16}$$

If e_2^a and q_2^a are close substitutes, in the sense that a change that increases ϕ_e^a while holding P_1, P_2, and u^a constant leads to an increase in q_2^a – that is, if they are close p-substitutes – then the response in (16) is negative. In the move from equilibrium to optimum, therefore, even though b's consumption of commodity 2 may generate a negative externality, it is possible that q_2^b or q_2^a, or both, may rise, so that aggregate consumption of commodity 2 may rise. This possibility carries over to situations involving reciprocal externalities. Although it has been regarded by some as a puzzling anomaly, it is relatively simple to identify the forces at work if we use restricted demand functions and explicitly decompose responses to quantity and price changes in the way associated with Slutsky and Hicks. Similar comments, with signs appropriately reversed, apply to situations involving a unilateral beneficial externality.

10.2   Reciprocal externalities

Let us modify the model of Section 10.1 by allowing each individual to impose an externality on the other. Suppose that their restricted indirect utility and expenditure functions take the form

$$V^{*h}(\cdot) = V^{*h}(P_1, P_2, e_2^h, M^h), \quad E^{*h}(\cdot) = E^{*h}(P_1, P_2, e_2^h, u^h), \quad h = a, b,$$

where $e_2^a = q_2^b$ and $e_2^b = q_2^a$. Let us suppose, for the sake of argument, that the externalities are detrimental, so that $\partial V^{*h}(\cdot)/\partial e_2^h < 0$, $h = a, b$. As an exercise in using the dual formulation, I want to establish two propositions about this model. First, suppose that taxes may be imposed on each individual's consumption of q_2, but that tax revenues must be returned in lump-sum manner to the individual from whom they are raised. In other words, there can be no redistribution of money income. I want to show that in contrast to the model involving a unilateral externality, it is possible to make both individuals better off than in the initial tax-free equilibrium. Consider the individual's indirect utility function under such a scheme. With tax revenue returned, $V^{*h}(\cdot)$ takes the form

$$V^{*h}(\cdot) = V^{*h}(P_1, P_2 + t_2^h, e_2^h, \bar{M}^h + t_2^h x_2^h), \quad h = a, b,$$

where $\bar{M}^h$ is the exogenous component of income. In what follows, I shall denote actual income in the usual way by $M^h = \bar{M}^h + t_2^h x_2^h$. The introduction of taxes on q_2^a and q_2^b affects $V^{*h}(\cdot)$ through three channels: They distort the price $P_2^h = P_2 + t_2^h$; the revenues get returned as lump-sum income $t_2^h x_2^h$; and they influence the level of the externality experienced by each. The net effect of infinitesimal tax changes is given by

$$dV^{*h}(\cdot) = V_2^{*h} dt_2^h + V_e^{*h} de_2^h + V_M^{*h} dM^h.$$

Roy's identity enables us to substitute $V_2^{*h} = -V_M^{*h} x_2^h$, and (4) similarly enables us to substitute for $V_e^{*h} = V_M^{*h} \phi_e^{*h}$. Finally, $dM^h = t_2^h dx_2^h + x_2^h dt_2^h$. Using these facts, the welfare change for individual h can be written as

$$dV^{*h}(\cdot) = V_M^{*h}[-x_2^h dt_2^h + \phi_e^{*h} de_2^h + t_2^h dx_2^h + x_2^h dt_2^h].$$

Therefore, if taxes are initially zero, the change in utility is

$$dV^{*h}(\cdot) = \phi_2^{*h} V_M^{*h} de_2^h.$$

In words, the net effect on the individual's welfare level of introducing a system of small taxes is dominated by their effect on the externality experienced by each. In the case of reciprocal detrimental externalities, a Pareto improvement will be achieved by any system of taxes and subsidies that leads to reductions in e_2^a and e_2^b.

By itself, this statement is of limited interest, because $x_2^a(\cdot)$ and $x_2^b(\cdot)$ are both endogenous. It would be more helpful to obtain expressions for the tax changes dt_2^a and dt_2^b that would promote Pareto improvement. Consider the uncompensated demand functions

$$x_2^{*a}(P_1, P_2 + t_2^a, e_2^a, \bar{M}^a + t_2^a q_2^a) \quad \text{and} \quad x_2^{*b}(P_1, P_2 + t_2^b, e_2^b, \bar{M}^b + t_2^b q_2^b).$$

Recall that in any equilibrium, $e_2^a = q_2^b = x_2^{*b}(\cdot)$, and $e_2^b = q_2^a = x_2^{*a}(\cdot)$. We wish to find values of t_2^a and t_1^b that will make de_2^b and de_2^a negative. Differentiation yields the following conditions:

$$de_2^a = dx_2^{*b}(\cdot) = x_{22}^{*b}dt_2^b + x_{2e}^{*b}dx_2^{*a}(\cdot) + x_{2M}^{*b}(x_2^{*b}dt_2^b + t_2^b dx_2^{*b}(\cdot))$$
$$= c_{22}^{*b}dt_2^b + x_{2e}^{*b}dx_2^{*a}(\cdot) < 0, \tag{17}$$

and

$$dx_2^{*a}(\cdot) = c_{22}^{*a}dt_2^a + x_{2e}^{*a}dx_2^{*b}(\cdot) < 0. \tag{18}$$

In deriving these conditions I have decomposed the uncompensated price responses into compensated and real income terms. The latter cancel out, so that the only real income terms that remain are those associated with the externality changes.

Using Cramer's rule, let us solve for $dx_2^{*a}(\cdot)$. This is given by

$$dx_2^{*a}(\cdot) = \frac{c_{22}^{*a}dt_2^a + c_{22}^{*b}x_{2e}^{*a}dt_2^b}{1 - x_{2e}^{*a}x_{2e}^{*b}}. \tag{19}$$

It has been shown by Cornes (1980) that local stability considerations require the sign of the denominator in (19) to be positive. The required tax changes must then be such as to make the numerator of (19), and of the corresponding expression for $dx_2^{*b}(\cdot)$, negative. A slight rearrangement leads to the following conditions:

$$(c_{22}^{*a}/c_{22}^{*b})dt_2^a + x_{2e}^{*a}dt_2^b > 0,$$

$$(c_{22}^{*a}/c_{22}^{*b})x_{2e}^{*b}dt_2^a + dt_2^b > 0.$$

The expression c_{22}^{*a}/c_{22}^{*b}, being the ratio of compensated own-price responses, must be positive. It is easy to confirm that at least one of the taxes must be positive. This may be done by assuming that both represent subsidies and showing that this implies a violation of the stability condition. However, it is certainly possible for one of dt_2^a or dt_2^b to be negative. Panels (i) and (ii) of Figure 10.3 summarize some possibilities. Panel (i) corresponds to a situation in which x_{2e}^{*a} and x_{2e}^{*b} are both negative. The crosshatched area represents those values for dt_2^a and dt_2^b that generate Pareto improvement. As shown, a tax on q_2^a alone will make individual b better off, through its effect on q_2^a and e_2^b. However, faced with a reduction in e_2^b, individual b is encouraged to expand consumption of q_2^b. Hence e_2^a increases, and individual a's welfare is consequently reduced. Panel (ii) corresponds to the assumption that the uncompensated responses x_{2e}^{*a} and x_{2e}^{*b} are positive. Here it is possible for one or other of the taxes to be negative, that is, a subsidy. But our analysis indicates that no part of the crosshatched region of Pareto improvements can lie in the quadrant below and to the left of the origin. The stability condition also implies that in the case of two detrimental externalities, some part of the region of Pareto-improving tax changes must lie in the positive quadrant.

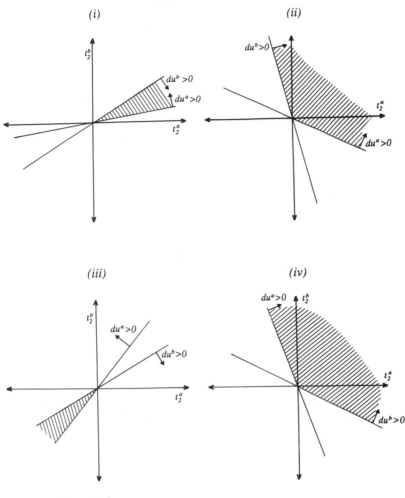

Figure 10.3

Panel (*iii*) of Figure 10.3 is therefore inconsistent with stability, as is panel (*iv*). In this last panel the hatched area indicating directions of Pareto improvement is identical with that in panel (*ii*). However, the relative slopes of the two half-lines that bound that area are inconsistent with stability.

The second proposition that I want to establish in the context of this model is simply that even though both consumption activities are taxed, it is still possible for one of the consumption levels, and indeed for the sum $x_2^a + x_2^b$, to be higher at a Pareto optimum than at the initial equilibrium. This is a slight generalization of the analysis of the unilateral externality. I shall do this by simply showing that if both consumption levels are taxed at the same rate, so that the individuals face a common relative price vector, $q_2^a + q_2^b$ may still rise. This implies that the relevant demand curves slope upward.

Our interest is in $X_2 = x_2^{*a}(\cdot) + x_2^{*b}(\cdot)$, and particularly in how X_2 responds when infinitesimal taxes $dt_2^a = dt_2^b = dt_2$ are imposed on a's and b's consumptions of commodity 2. As before, I assume that tax revenues are returned to their source in a lump-sum manner, so that income effects arising from redistribution do not arise. The response can be written down using (19):

$$dX_2 = dx_2^{*a}(\cdot) + dx_2^{*b}(\cdot);$$

$$\therefore \ dX_2/dt_2 = (c_{22}^{*a} + c_{22}^{*b} + c_{22}^{*a} x_{2e}^{*b} + c_{22}^{*b} x_{2e}^{*a})/(1 - x_{2e}^{*a} x_{2e}^{*b}).$$

We know that stability requires the denominator to be positive. However, the bounds that this places on x_{2e}^{*a} and x_{2e}^{*b} do not ensure that the numerator is negative. It is certainly possible for either x_{2e}^{*a} or x_{2e}^{*b} to be sufficiently large and negative for its associated product with the compensated price response in the numerator to be positive and to dominate the whole expression. Cornes (1980) analyzes this possibility. The mechanism, once exposed, is straightforward. Suppose that in the move to the optimum, q_2^a falls. The effect of this on q_2^b is captured by the parameter x_{2e}^b, the response of individual b's demand for commodity 2 to a fall in the level of externality e_2^b. If q_2^b and e_2^b are very close substitutes, then b's demand for commodity 2 may, through this mechanism, rise. Moreover, this may dominate the direct effect of the tax distortion in discouraging q_2^b. The algebra merely confirms that such an outcome is consistent with local stability. It also shows how simply the comparative statics can be analyzed if externalities are thought of as additional quantity constraints and modeled with the help of dual techniques.

10.3   Pure public goods

From a purely formal point of view, the next model to be considered appears to be a very simple special case of reciprocal externalities. However, the wide variety of possible interpretations of the model, together with its relative simplicity, has given it particular prominence. Suppose that again there are two individuals, a and b, each of whom likes both food and open-air fireworks displays. From an economic point of view, fireworks have two significant characteristics. First, their enjoyment by either consumer does not reduce the amount available for consumption by the other.

This property is sometimes inelegantly called "nonrivalness." Second, it is expensive, if not impossible, to exclude nonpayers from their enjoyment. Individual a, having paid nothing, can sit on top of the nearest hill and enjoy b's fireworks. This is the "nonexcludability" property. These two characteristics sharply distinguish pure nonexcludable public goods from pure private goods such as bread. The reason for the appearance of public goods in this book is that they may naturally be modeled as yet another example of quantity-constrained behavior. Each individual takes as given not only his income and the prices of marketed commodities but also the levels of others' contributions, or subscriptions, to the public good. Formally, the public-good model is a special case of an externality in which the subscriptions of different individuals appear as perfect substitutes in the utility function of each, their sum appearing as an argument:

$$U^i(\cdot) = U^i(q_1^i, q_2^i, q_2^j) = U^i(q_1^i, q_2^i + q_2^j), \quad i, j = a, b, \ i \neq j.$$

It helps to vary the notation somewhat. In order to dispense with subscripts, I shall henceforth denote the private commodity by y and set its price at unity. The subscript that identifies public-good contributions may also be dropped, it being understood that they are represented simply by q. The individual's problem is now

$$\max_{y^i, q^i}\{U^i(y^i, q^i + q^j) \mid y^i + P_Q q^i \le M^i, \ q^j \text{ given}\}.$$

Indeed, we can drop superscripts in our analysis of the individual by the simple expedient of defining Q as the community's total contribution to the public good – $Q = q^a + q^b$ in the present two-person example, and $Q = \sum_{i=1}^{n} q^i$ in a community of n individuals – and by defining $\tilde{Q}$ as the rest of the community's contribution. For individual i, $\tilde{Q}^i \equiv Q - q^i$. Our undistinguished typical individual now has the problem

$$\max_{y, q}\{U(y, q - \tilde{Q}) \mid y + P_Q q \le M, \ \tilde{Q} \text{ given}\}. \tag{20}$$

The remainder of this section will use expenditure and indirect utility functions to analyze the nature and properties of equilibrium and of optimal allocations in a community of individuals facing the problem described in (20).

Figure 10.4 shows the individual's most preferred allocation, E, in response to given values of P_Q, $\tilde{Q}$, and M. The contributions of others are, in effect, a component of income that the individual happens to receive in kind. The initial endowment point is I, and the slope of the budget line that passes through I is determined by the price P_Q. Preferences are

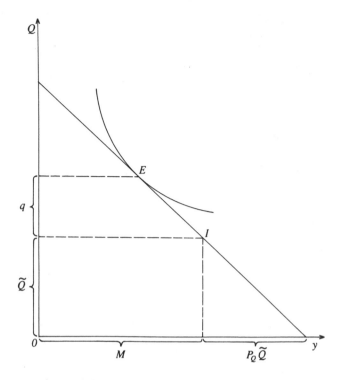

Figure 10.4

represented by an orthodox utility function defined over y and Q, and consequently by a standard indifference map in (y, Q) space. At E, the individual is minimizing the cost of attaining the realized utility level by choice of y and q:

$$E^*(P_Q, \tilde{Q}, u) \equiv \min\{y + P_Q q \mid U(y, q + \tilde{Q}) \geq u, \; \tilde{Q} \text{ given}\}.$$

I should at this point be explicit about my assumption that the equilibrium implies a strictly positive value of q. This need not be true, but is an important assumption for some comparative static properties of the model. The first-order conditions of this optimizing problem imply that

$$P_Q = U_Q/U_y, \tag{21}$$

which is evident from the figure. This result will shortly be useful when we compare the equilibrium with optimal allocations. First, however, let us consider some comparative statics. In particular, consider the response of q to a change in $\tilde{Q}$. It is possible to perform the analysis by applying

Roy's identity to the restricted indirect utility function, $V^*(P_Q, \tilde{Q}, M)$. An aggregate restricted subscription function can be defined, which I shall write as $S^*(P_Q, \tilde{Q}, M)$. $S^*(\cdot)$ is the most preferred level of total community provision of the public good from the representative individual's point of view. The individual restricted subscription function is defined as

$$s^*(P_Q, \tilde{Q}, M) \equiv S^*(P_Q, \tilde{Q}, M) - \tilde{Q} \qquad (22)$$

and denotes the individual's most preferred level of his own subscription. Rather than work with these functions alone, things can be simplified by defining the subscription functions in a slightly modified form. Inspection of Figure 10.4 suggests that we can think of the individual as choosing y and Q as a price-taker, given "total" income $T = M + P_Q \tilde{Q}$. The indirect utility function can be written as an unrestricted function:

$$V^*(P_Q, \tilde{Q}, M) = V(P_Q, M + P_Q \tilde{Q}) = V(P_Q, T), \qquad (23)$$

from which an aggregate unrestricted subscription function can be generated using Roy's identity:

$$S(P_Q, T) = -\frac{\partial V(\cdot)/\partial P_Q}{\partial V(\cdot)/\partial T}.$$

$S(\cdot)$ simply expresses the most preferred level of total community provision as a function of price and total income.

Using (22) as the starting point, consider the effect of varying $\tilde{Q}$ on $s^*(\cdot)$ and $S^*(\cdot)$:

$$\partial s^*(\cdot)/\partial \tilde{Q} = \partial S^*(\cdot)/\partial \tilde{Q} - 1. \qquad (24)$$

But by definition,

$$S^*(P_Q, \tilde{Q}, M) = S(P_Q, T) = S(P_Q, M + P_Q \tilde{Q}). \qquad (25)$$

Consequently,

$$\partial S^*(\cdot)/\partial \tilde{Q} = (\partial S(\cdot)/\partial T) \cdot P_Q.$$

Using (25), consider a change in income, M:

$$\partial S^*(\cdot)/\partial M = \partial S(\cdot)/\partial T.$$

Finally, inspection of (22) shows that $\partial s^*(\cdot)/\partial M = \partial S^*(\cdot)/\partial M$. Exploiting these various simple substitutions in (24), we can conclude that

$$\partial s^*(\cdot)/\partial \tilde{Q} = P_Q \partial s^*(\cdot)/\partial M - 1. \qquad (26)$$

The uncompensated response of the subscription level to a change in the rest of the community's contribution is equal to the marginal propensity

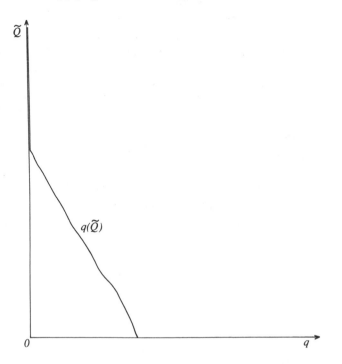

Figure 10.5

to subscribe less 1. If P_Q and M are held constant, the equilibrium value of q can be graphed against $\tilde{Q}$, the resulting curve being the "reaction" curve in Figure 10.5. Equation (26) implies that if both y and Q are normal goods, so that $0 < P_Q \partial s^*(\cdot)/\partial M < 1$, then the reaction curve is downward-sloping, and the absolute value of the slope cannot be less than 45°. The relationship expressed in equation (26) has an interesting further implication for the equilibrium of an economy with a pure public good.

The equilibrium concept used is variously called a Nash, or independent adjustment, or subscription, equilibrium. Hold the price P_Q and all incomes constant. Each individual's optimal subscription is, as we have seen, a function of the rest of the community's contribution. At a Nash equilibrium, each individual is choosing his most preferred subscription given the current contribution of the rest of the community. In other words, for all i,

$$q^i = s^i(P_Q, M^i + P_Q \tilde{Q}^i), \quad \text{where } \tilde{Q}^i = \sum_{\substack{j=1,\ldots,n \\ j \neq i}} s^j(\cdot).$$

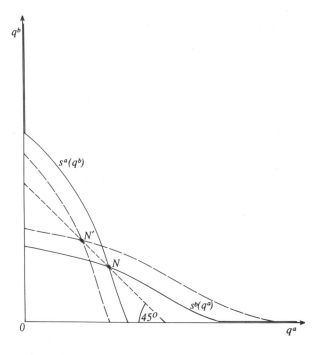

Figure 10.6

The two-person economy offers a simple representation. The reaction curve
of each individual is graphed in Figure 10.6, and their intersection N is a
Nash equilibrium. Equation (26) implies that if both private and public
goods are normal goods in each individual's preferences, then there will
be a unique Nash equilibrium. Moreover, if at that equilibrium both individuals are making strictly positive contributions to the public good, then
redistribution of a given income between the individuals will leave unchanged the equilibrium value of total public-good provision, as well as
each individual's consumption of the private good, and hence each individual's utility level. This result, rather surprising at first, can be confirmed by examining the indirect utility functions. Suppose, for example,
we start at a Nash equilibrium at which both $s^a(\cdot)$ and $s^b(\cdot)$ are positive.
We know that

$$V^a(\cdot) = V^a(P_Q, M^a + P_Q q^b),$$

and

$$V^b(\cdot) = V^b(P_Q, M^b + P_Q q^a).$$

Let M^a fall by one unit, while $P_Q q^b$ rises by one unit. Then a's maximum attainable utility is unchanged, because P_Q and T^a $(=M^a+P_Q q^b)$ are unchanged. In addition, because his budget constraint is unchanged, his most preferred y^a and Q are unchanged. Thus, $ds^a = -dq^b$, so that $P_Q s^a$ falls by one unit. Now if b receives the unit of income taken from a and also experiences the reduction of one unit in $P_Q q^a$, b's real situation is similarly unaffected. The fall in a's contribution is precisely offset by the rise in b's, the equal level of Q is unchanged, and each consumes an unchanged quantity of the private good in the new equilibrium. Figure 10.6 shows the new position of the reaction curves as the dashed lines, and the new equilibrium N'. The points N and N' both correspond to the same value of the sum q^a+q^b.

Let us now characterize an optimum in the presence of public goods in an n-person economy. The direct utility function provides a very convenient way of doing this, because the optimum is characterized by a relationship between marginal cost and the individuals' demand prices, and the latter are obtained by simple differentiation of $U(y, Q)$. A Pareto optimum satisfies the first-order conditions for maximization of a weighted sum of utilities subject to the economy's resource constraint:

$$\max_{y^1, \ldots, y^n, Q} \left\{ \sum_{i=1}^{n} \alpha^i U^i(y^i, Q) \mid \sum_i y^i + P_Q Q = \sum_i M^i \right\}.$$

The first-order conditions imply that

$$\alpha^i \partial U^i(\cdot)/\partial y^i - \lambda = 0, \quad i = 1, \ldots, n,$$

and also $\sum_i \alpha^i \partial U^i(\cdot)/\partial Q - \lambda P_Q = 0$, where λ is the Lagrangian multiplier. The weights $\alpha^1, \ldots, \alpha^n$ may be eliminated, and thereby the multiplier also conveniently disappears, leaving the following first-order necessary condition for the Pareto-optimal provision of the public good:

$$P_Q = \sum_{i=1}^{n} \left(\frac{\partial U^i(\cdot)/\partial Q}{\partial U^i(\cdot)/\partial y^i} \right) = \sum_{i=1}^{n} \phi_Q^i(y^i, Q). \tag{27}$$

This is the well-known Samuelson condition, requiring the cost of an extra unit of the public good, P_Q, to be equal to the sum over individuals of marginal benefits, measured by the marginal valuations or virtual prices $\phi_Q^i(\cdot)$.

There is an equally straightforward alternative derivation that uses the indirect utility function. Suppose the government takes upon itself the task of providing the public good, financing it by means of lump-sum taxation. Denote by R^i the amount of tax revenue raised from individual i.

Exogenous pretax income is $\bar{M}^i$, and income after tax is $M^i = \bar{M}^i - R^i$. Subject to the government's taxation and public-good provision activities, individuals allocate their remaining income among a vector of private goods, $\mathbf{y}$, the market prices of which are denoted by the vector $\mathbf{P}$. In any equilibrium, i's utility level is given by the value of the restricted indirect utility function $V^{*i}(\mathbf{P}, Q, \bar{M}^i - R^i)$. Notice that it is the total provision Q that appears as an argument here, not $\tilde{Q}$. If government provision is optimal, no individual will have an incentive to supplement it with any private contribution. Consequently, government provision and total provision are synonymous. A Pareto-optimal allocation satisfies the necessary first-order conditions associated with the following problem:

$$\max_{Q, R^1, \ldots, R^n} \left\{ \sum_i \alpha^i V^{*i}(\mathbf{P}, Q, \bar{M}^i - R^i) \,|\, P_Q Q = \sum_i R^i \right\}. \tag{28}$$

Again, the α's are positive weights. The constraint simply requires lumpsum tax revenue to cover the cost of providing the public good. The first-order conditions are

$$\sum_{i=1}^n \alpha^i \partial V^{*i}(\cdot)/\partial Q - \lambda P_Q = 0,$$

and

$$\alpha^i \partial V^{*i}(\cdot)/\partial M^i + \lambda = 0, \quad i = 1, \ldots, n.$$

Again, the α's and λ can be removed, leaving the condition

$$P_Q = \sum_i \left(\frac{\partial V^{*i}(\cdot)/\partial Q}{\partial V^{*i}(\cdot)/\partial M^i} \right) = \sum_i \phi_Q^{*i}(\mathbf{P}, Q, \bar{M}^i - R^i).$$

The only difference between this condition and (27) is that here the virtual price is defined as a function of the variables that appear as arguments of the restricted indirect utility function. It still equates marginal cost with the sum of marginal benefits.

The Lagrangian multiplier, λ, has a straightforward interpretation. Observe that because $M^i = \bar{M}^i - R^i$, the maximization problem can be posed in a way that treats the government as choosing $M^1, \ldots, M^n$ given the initial exogenous incomes, $\bar{M}^1, \ldots, \bar{M}^n$, the tax variables having been eliminated. The Lagrangian associated with (28) can then be written as

$$L(\cdot) = \sum_i \alpha^i V^{*i}(\mathbf{P}, Q, M^i) - \lambda \left[P_Q Q + \sum_i (M^i - \bar{M}^i) \right].$$

Denote the maximized value of social welfare by $W^{\max}(\mathbf{P}, \bar{M}^1, \ldots, \bar{M}^n)$. Then the envelope theorem implies that $\partial W^{\max}(\cdot)/\partial \bar{M}^i = \partial L(\cdot)/\partial \bar{M}^i = \lambda$.

The variable λ, then, measures the extra increment of "social welfare" accruing from an extra unit of exogenous income; λ is the same, regardless of the identity of the recipient, by virtue of the fact that income is optimally distributed according to the social welfare function.

The necessary condition for optimal allocation in the presence of a public good does not determine a unique optimal level of public-good provision Q^{opt}. As one moves around the utility possibilities frontier of the public-good economy by redistributing the private good, the optimal level of the public good will generally change. Discussions of "the" optimal level of public-good provision therefore either presuppose a particular distribution or rely on special assumptions about the structure of preferences that make Q^{opt} independent of private-goods distribution. Consider now what these special assumptions might be. Let us start with an allocation in the two-person economy that we know to be Pareto-optimal. Denote the quantities at this allocation by $(\hat{y}^a, \hat{y}^b, \hat{Q})$. Pareto optimality implies that

$$P_Q = \phi_Q^a(\hat{y}^a, \hat{Q}) + \phi_Q^b(\hat{y}^b, \hat{Q}). \tag{29}$$

Suppose that $\hat{Q}$ remains unchanged, while a redistribution of the private good is effected. Specifically, one unit is taken from individual a and given to b. The question now is, Under what circumstances is $(\hat{y}^a - 1, \hat{y}^b + 1, \hat{Q})$ a Pareto optimum? Clearly, if $\phi_Q^a(\cdot)$ and $\phi_Q^b(\cdot)$ are independent of y^a and y^b, respectively, then the optimality condition (29) will continue to hold, because P_Q, $\phi_Q^a(\cdot)$, and $\phi_Q^b(\cdot)$ will all be unchanged. However, this may be assuming too much. It implies that each individual's preferences over y and Q have income expansion paths parallel to the private-good axis, or a zero income elasticity of demand for the public good. For this property to hold, it is both necessary and sufficient that preferences be representable by the "quasi-linear" form:

$$U^i(y^i, Q) = y^i + G^i(Q).$$

Differentiation yields the marginal valuation function

$$\phi_Q^i(\cdot) = \frac{\partial U^i(\cdot)/\partial Q}{\partial U^i(\cdot)/\partial y^i} = \frac{g^i(Q)}{1} = \phi_Q^i(Q).$$

This confirms the sufficiency of quasi-linear preferences for $\phi_Q^i(\cdot)$ to be independent of y^i. Necessity is slightly trickier, because it involves integrating back from $\phi_Q^i(\cdot)$ to $U^i(\cdot)$.

A little reflection, however, reveals that we do not require $\phi_Q^i(\cdot)$ to be independent of y^i. Suppose the loss of one unit of private good reduces a's valuation of Q by an amount ϵ. If b's valuation increases by ϵ on receipt of that extra unit, then the aggregate valuation $\phi_Q^a(\cdot) + \phi_Q^b(\cdot)$ will be unchanged. Consequently, the optimality condition (29) will continue to hold. This will be the case if $\phi_Q^i(\cdot)$ takes the form

$$\phi_Q^i(\cdot) = f(Q)y^i + g^i(Q), \quad i = a, b. \tag{30}$$

Notice that the function $f(Q)$ is the same for both individuals. This ensures that $\partial \phi_Q^a(\cdot)/\partial y^a = \partial \phi_Q^b(\cdot)/\partial y^b = f(Q)$. In order that marginal valuation functions take the required form (30), it is necessary and sufficient that preferences be representable by the following functional form:

$$U^i(y^i, Q) = F(Q)y^i + G^i(Q). \tag{31}$$

Differentiation shows that

$$f(Q) = F'(Q)/F(Q) \quad \text{and} \quad g^i(Q) = G^{i'}(Q)/F(Q).$$

Again, sufficiency is easy to show, necessity less so. For details, consult Bergstrom and Cornes (1981). This form of direct utility function is particularly interesting because it has precisely the same structure as the indirect utility function discussed by Gorman (1953) in his analysis of private-good aggregation. Gorman shows that if individual i's indirect utility function takes the form $V^i(\mathbf{P}, M^i) = A(\mathbf{P})M^i + B^i(\mathbf{P})$, then redistributing income at given prices in a private-good economy will not affect the sum of individual demands. Bergstrom and Cornes (1981) show that if individual i's direct utility function takes the form $U^i(y^i, Q) = F(Q)y^i + G^i(Q)$, then redistributing the private good at a given level of provision of Q in a public-good economy will not affect the sum of individual demand prices. In a private-good economy, individuals face a common price vector, and Gorman is interested in the sum of quantities demanded. In our public-good economy, individuals face a common quantity Q, and, following Samuelson, we are interested in the sum of individual inverse demands. Seen in this light, it is not surprising that the analysis has such strong parallels with Gorman's. Bergstrom and Cornes (1983) have investigated further implications of such preferences and provided a more rigorous discussion of the precise sense in which preferences of this form are necessary and sufficient for the Pareto-optimal level of public goods to be independent of income distribution.

10.4 Taxation and provision of public goods

I showed in the preceding section that over a certain range, redistribution of initial income endowments has no effect on the Nash equilibrium values of total public-good provision, individual private-good consumptions, or individual utilities. This neutrality property has interesting implications. Suppose a planning agency is concerned to augment the private provision of Q. This it does by levying lump-sum taxes and using the revenue to finance public production of the public good. An individual who loses a dollar in taxes and finds that public production of Q has risen by a dollar's worth will simply reduce his private contribution by a dollar's worth. There is full crowding out, and no real change has been effected. This result breaks down only when the tax drives the individual to the point at which his own voluntary contribution is zero. Thereafter the individual's ability to undo the planner's intervention ceases, and there is a real effect.

Bernheim (1986) has recently established an even stronger neutrality property. He has shown that even if supposedly distortionary consumption taxes are used to finance the public-sector production of the public good, there may still be complete crowding out. The "distortionary" taxes may distort nothing, leaving the real resource allocation unaffected at the Nash equilibrium. This counterintuitive result may be understood by forgetting about public goods for a moment and instead considering a somewhat different and commonly undertaken thought experiment. Suppose there is a private-goods economy with n identical consumers. A planner imposes consumption taxes on a vector of commodities. The revenue is then returned in a lump-sum manner so that each consumer receives a transfer equal to that consumer's tax payment. In the new equilibrium, the value of consumption at pretax prices is unchanged, but if the tax is imposed on just one commodity, then consumption of that commodity is reduced. Indeed, this is precisely the thought experiment associated with the "law of undercompensated demand" encountered in Chapter 4. For this result to follow it is important that the representative individual regard his lump-sum receipt as independent of his own actions. This seems an innocuous assumption. Suppose he considers increasing his consumption of the taxed commodity by one unit, and suppose that this increases tax revenue by \$10. This revenue is handed back to a population of n consumers. If we suppose an equal share is given to each consumer, and if n is a large number, the extra revenue of \$10/n that is returned to the representative individual is not going to affect his private cost/benefit calculus. The representative consumer's uncompensated demand function for commodity j may be written as

$$x_j(\cdot) = x_j(\mathbf{P}+\mathbf{t}, T) = x_j(\mathbf{P}+\mathbf{t}, M+t_j\bar{x}_j),$$

where T is total income and $\bar{x}_j$ is the average level of consumption of commodity j: $\bar{x}_j \equiv (1/n)\sum_{h=1}^{n} x_j^h$. Each individual regards the consumption decisions of others as exogenous and ignores the negligible effect of adjustments in his own consumption on that average, so that a change in the tax t_j has an effect given by

$$dx_j = x_{jj}dt_j + x_{jT}\bar{x}_j dt_j.$$

In this economy of identical individuals, the representative consumer's consumption x_j equals the average consumption $\bar{x}_j$. Consequently,

$$\begin{aligned} dx_j &= x_{jj}dt_j + x_{jT}\bar{x}_j dt_j \\ &= (c_{jj} - x_j x_{jT})dt_j + x_{jT}\bar{x}_j dt_j \\ &= c_{jj}dt_j. \end{aligned}$$

Now suppose that the representative individual assumes instead that any change in tax revenue from his own consumption activity will be reflected in the level of the lump-sum receipt. It is as if tax revenue is paid in bills that have his name on them, and these are returned in lump-sum fashion. The individual no longer treats the lump-sum receipt as exogenous, and the indirect utility function, if required, is defined as

$$V(\mathbf{P}, \mathbf{t}, M) \equiv \max_{\mathbf{y}}\{U(\mathbf{y}) \mid (\mathbf{P}+\mathbf{t})\cdot\mathbf{y} = M + \mathbf{t}\cdot\mathbf{y}\}.$$

Inspection of the budget constraint suggests that the tax gets washed out of the system. If this argument is not persuasive, simple application of the envelope property will confirm that $V(\cdot)$ is, in fact, independent of the value of $\mathbf{t}$. Because $V(\cdot)$ is unaffected, Roy's identity tells us that the uncompensated demands, $x_j(\cdot)$, must also be unchanged. The simple truth is that the tax is no tax at all, because whatever the individual does, the tax revenue must come back to him.

In the context of the private-good economy, the assumption that each individual views his lump-sum receipts as identically equal to his tax payment is highly implausible. However, it is the most natural assumption to make if tax revenue is spent providing a public good that the individual values and to which he continues to contribute. I have already argued that in this situation an extra increment of the public good is, in effect, income. It happens to be income in kind, but if the individual is a positive contributor, this creates no additional constraint or complication.

Application of the envelope theorem confirms the point. The individual's problem is

$$\max_{\mathbf{y},q}\{U(\mathbf{y}, q+\tilde{Q}) \mid (\mathbf{P}+\mathbf{t})\cdot\mathbf{y} + P_Q q = M, P_Q \tilde{Q} = \mathbf{t}\cdot\mathbf{y}\}.$$

To emphasize the fact that $\tilde{Q}$ is not exogenous, but is determined by the tax revenue, let us substitute this constraint into the direct utility function. An indirect utility function can be defined:

$$V(\mathbf{P}, \mathbf{t}, M) = \max_{\mathbf{y}, q} \{U(\mathbf{y}, q + (\mathbf{t} \cdot \mathbf{y})/P_Q) \mid (\mathbf{P} + \mathbf{t}) \cdot \mathbf{y} + P_Q q = M\}.$$

Denote the multiplier associated with this optimizing problem by λ in the usual way; λ has its usual interpretation as the marginal utility of income. Application of the envelope theorem tells us that

$$\partial V / \partial t_j = U_Q y_j / P_Q - \lambda y_j.$$

Consider the first-order condition associated with the individual's choice of q. It requires that if the equilibrium level of q is positive, $\partial U / \partial Q = \lambda P_Q$. Consequently, $\partial V / \partial t_j = 0$. The intuition is straightforward. An adjustment in the individual's consumption plan generally changes the tax revenue by an amount $\mathbf{t} \cdot d\mathbf{y}$, but this comes straight back to the individual in a form that is equivalent to income. There is therefore no genuine distortion of choice.

10.5   Concluding comments and suggestions for further study

The emphasis of this chapter has been on fairly narrow technical aspects of modeling externalities and public goods. A more wide-ranging treatment can be found in Cornes and Sandler (1986). The treatment of unilateral externalities draws on that and on Cornes (1980). Mäler (1974) makes effective use of the restricted expenditure function in modeling externalities – see also Mäler and Wyzga (1976, pp. 29–44, 124–9). Concern with "anomalies" uncovered in the comparison between equilibrium and optimum dates from Buchanan and Kafoglis (1963). More recent contributions to this literature include Diamond and Mirrlees (1973), Sandmo (1980), Cornes (1980), and Cornes and Homma (1979). An understanding of real income and compensated responses to quantity changes should dispel any feeling of paradox about such matters. Johansson (1987), already referred to in Chapter 9, provides an excellent discussion of many aspects of measuring environmental benefits and costs and of evaluating social states in the presence of externalities.

The original discussion by Samuelson (1954, 1955) of the optimality condition for public-good provision hinted at the duality property, but thoughtfully left its formal development for others to exploit. The Bergstrom–Cornes utility function, if I may call it that, has been further studied by Bergstrom, Simon, and Titus (1983) in the context of the Groves–

Ledyard demand-revealing mechanism. It is also used by Bergstrom (1989) to simplify the analysis of the "rotten kid" theorem suggested by Becker (1974).

The neutrality property of Nash equilibrium in the presence of a pure public good is suggested by the work of Becker (1974), and a special case has been developed by Jeremias and Zardkoohi (1976). Warr (1983) has provided a formal demonstration, and Cornes and Sandler (1984, 1985) have suggested a more direct and transparent method of proof. This was adopted by Bergstrom, Blume, and Varian (1986) in their extension of earlier analyses. In addition to his analysis of the impotence of consumption taxes in the presence of a pure public good, Bernheim (1986) joins Bergstrom and associates in emphasizing the importance of the assumption that individuals' voluntary contributions are strictly positive. Bernheim and Bagwell (1988) have an interesting discussion of intertemporal manifestations of the neutrality property, in which they draw attention to neutrality propositions of a similar flavor familiar to macroeconomists through the work of Barro (1974).

Epilogue

This book has, I hope, provided a digestible introduction to the formal structure of dual relationships and their role in economic analysis, together with some appreciation of the tremendous variety of applications in both qualitative and quantitative work. A few final comments may be helpful.

First, let me emphasize again that the possibility of alternative formulations of economic problems presents the researcher with a choice, and this choice should be made in the light not only of the model under analysis but also of the precise questions that the analyst wishes to address. The literature on optimal indirect taxation, which I have not treated, provides a good example of this. Atkinson and Stiglitz (1980, ch. 12) discuss the problem of picking a set of commodity taxes that raise a given revenue target while imposing the minimum welfare cost on the taxed individuals, each of whom continues to behave as a price-taking optimizer in the face of the tax-distorted prices. The behavior of the taxed individuals can be modeled using their indirect utility functions. If this is done, the natural variables to be determined in the resulting optimization problem are the prices, or taxes. Individuals' utility responses to price changes appear in the first-order conditions, and Roy's identity eliminates them and replaces them with quantities. The result is a set of first-order conditions that tell us how quantities must adjust to the imposition of the optimal tax structure, whatever that may be – see Atkinson and Stiglitz (1980, p. 373).

This, though interesting, may be less so than statements about the magnitude of the taxes themselves. Suppose that instead of indirect utility functions, we use the individuals' direct utility functions. We might then think of the government as choosing quantities, rather than prices. Derivatives of the form $\partial U(\mathbf{q})/\partial q_j$ appear in the first-order conditions, and these tell us something about individuals' demand prices, which are equal to tax-distorted market prices. This route leads to a statement of necessary conditions that tells us something about the structure of prices, or taxes, that may be of more interest than information about quantities.

It transpires that compensated price responses play a key role in determining the structure of optimal indirect taxes; so with the benefit of hindsight it seems worthwhile to investigate the expenditure function. If we minimize Kay's measure of the deadweight loss associated with taxation, this leads very quickly to the characterization in terms of quantities provided by the indirect utility function. Finally, as Deaton (1979) indicates, the distance function provides a direct derivation of the conditions obtained more circuitously with the help of the direct utility function. These conditions concern the structure of the taxes themselves and allow us to consider such matters as whether, and under what conditions, uniform taxes may be optimal. In short, the adopted formulation should depend on the questions to be asked.

I am conscious of omitted topics. There is little explicit treatment in this book of intertemporal, or dynamic, issues. If time is modeled discretely, the device of defining dated commodities allows the standard framework of microeconomic analysis to be applied, together with the apparatus of duality as developed here. If time is thought of as continuous, fresh problems arise. Epstein (1981*b*) provides some discussion of the usefulness of dual analysis in intertemporal models. Risk is another topic that makes little explicit appearance in these pages. Again, the state preference approach provides a formal framework for analysis of risky choice that is identical with the standard atemporal model. The references in Chapter 7 to Diamond and Yaari (1972) and to Cornes and Milne (1989) are relevant here, as is the discussion by Machina (1984) on induced preferences and risk, to which I referred in Chapter 6. For analyses of various aspects of decision making in the face of risk that make use of duality, see also Epstein (1975), Pope (1980), and Dalal (1983). A final omission is monopoly. Certainly, duality comes into its own as a simplifier of the analysis of price-taking behavior. However, its insights can also simplify models with market power. This is suggested by the analysis of nonlinear constraints in Chapter 7, and an explicit discussion of the application of dual and envelope arguments to monopoly appears in Diewert (1982). See also Guesnerie and Laffont (1978) for a discussion of the monopolist's profit function and for an analysis of taxation in the presence of monopoly.

It should be clear that the dual and envelope arguments expounded in this book rest on properties of convex sets and on the structure of optimizing problems. These topics have a large literature, with which the serious student and user of duality should, in time, become acquainted. The books by Eggleston (1963) and Valentine (1964) are useful, as is Rockafellar (1970). This last reference is quite challenging, and a more leisurely

treatment, which I have found helpful, is provided by Roberts and Varberg (1973). See also Ponstein (1980). Among treatments with an emphasis
on the mathematics of duality in an economic context, I have already referred to Shephard's seminal contributions and to Blackorby et al. (1978b).
In addition, useful discussions are given by Weddepohl (1970), Ruys and
Weddepohl (1979), and Richter (1979). Familiarity with such sources will
give one a feel for methods of proving, in more general contexts, the various results for which I have merely given heuristic arguments under rather
restrictive simplifying assumptions. Even if the desire to prove new theorems is weak, a deeper understanding of the nature and scope of dual
arguments is helpful in making judgments about their limitations and
scope. For example, I have generally restricted attention to strictly convex preferences and technologies and to strictly positive price and quantity vectors, as well as relying on differentiability. For certain arguments,
none of these simplifying assumptions is crucial. For others, extra work
has to be done to come to grips with greater generality. It is useful to be
familiar with these matters, and dangerous to apply the arguments in an
unthinking cookbook approach. An intelligent understanding of duality
can certainly simplify and clarify the structure of economic arguments
and make economic analysis a truly enjoyable experience.

Bibliography

Afriat, S. N. (1967), "The Construction of a Utility Function from Expenditure Data," *International Economic Review* 8: 67–77.

(1972), "Efficiency Estimates of Production Functions," *International Economic Review* 13: 569–98.

Ahlheim, M. (1988), "A Reconsideration of Debreu's Coefficient of Resource Utilization," in *Welfare and Efficiency in Public Economics,* edited by D. Bös, M. Rose, and C. Seidl. Heidelberg: Springer-Verlag, pp. 21–48.

Allen, R. G. D. (1933), "On the Marginal Utility of Money," *Economica* 12: 186–209.

(1938), *Mathematical Analysis for Economists.* London: Macmillan.

(1949), "The Economic Theory of Index Numbers," *Economica* 16: 197–203.

Anderson, R. W. (1980), "Some Theory of Inverse Demand for Applied Demand Analysis," *European Economic Review* 14: 281–90.

Antonelli, G. B. (1886), "Sulla Teoria Matematica della Economia Politica." Translated (1971) as "On the Mathematical Theory of Political Economy," in *Preferences, Utility and Demand,* edited by J. S. Chipman, L. Hurwicz, M. K. Richter, and H. F. Sonnenschein. New York: Harcourt Brace Jovanovich, pp. 333–64.

Arrow, K. J., and Enthoven, A. C. (1961), "Quasi-concave Programming," *Econometrica* 29: 779–800.

Atkinson, A. B., and Stern, N. (1979), "A Note on the Allocation of Time," *Economics Letters* 3: 119–23.

(1981), "On Labour Supply and Commodity Demands," in *Essays in the Theory and Measurement of Consumer Behaviour,* edited by A. S. Deaton. Cambridge University Press, pp. 265–96.

Atkinson, A. B., and Stiglitz, J. E. (1980), *Lectures on Public Economics.* New York: McGraw-Hill.

Avriel, M. (1976), *Nonlinear Programming: Analysis and Methods.* Englewood Cliffs, NJ: Prentice-Hall.

Avriel, M., Diewert, W. E., Schaible, S., and Zang, I. (1988), *Generalized Concavity.* New York: Plenum Press.

Barro, R. (1974), "Are Government Bonds Net Wealth?" *Journal of Political Economy* 84: 1095–17.

Barten, A. P., and Bettendorf, L. J. (1989), "Price Formation of Fish: An Application of an Inverse Demand System," *European Economic Review* 33: 1509–25.

Bartik, T. (1987), "The Estimation of Demand Parameters in Hedonic Price Models," *Journal of Political Economy* 95: 81-8.

Baumol, W. J. (1973), "Income and Substitution Effects in the Linder Theorem," *Quarterly Journal of Economics* 87: 629-33.

Baumol, W. J., Panzar, J. C., and Willig, R. D. (1982), *Contestable Markets and the Theory of Industry Structure*. New York: Harcourt Brace Jovanovich.

Bazaraa, M. D., and Shetty, C. M. (1979), *Nonlinear Programming: Theory and Algorithms*. New York: Wiley.

Bear, D. V. T. (1965), "Inferior Inputs and the Theory of the Firm," *Journal of Political Economy* 73: 287-9.

Becker, G. S. (1965), "A Theory of the Allocation of Time," *Economic Journal* 75: 493-517.

(1974), "A Theory of Social Interactions," *Journal of Political Economy* 82: 1063-94.

Bergstrom, T. C. (1989), "A Fresh Look at the Rotten Kid Theorem – and Other Household Mysteries," *Journal of Political Economy* 97: 1138-59.

Bergstrom, T. C., Blume, L., and Varian, H. (1986), "On the Private Provision of Public Goods," *Journal of Public Economics* 29: 25-49.

Bergstrom, T. C., and Cornes, R. C. (1981), "Gorman and Musgrave are Dual – An Antipodean Theorem on Public Goods," *Economics Letters* 7: 371-8.

(1983), "Independence of Allocative Efficiency from Distribution in the Theory of Public Goods," *Econometrica* 51: 1753-65.

Bergstrom, T. C., Simon, C. P., and Titus, C. J. (1983), "Counting Groves-Ledyard Equilibria via Degree Theory," *Journal of Mathematical Economics* 12: 167-84.

Berndt, E. R., Darrough, M. N., and Diewert, W. E. (1977) "Flexible Functional Forms and Expenditure Distributions: An Application to Canadian Consumer Demand Functions," *International Economic Review* 18: 651-76.

Bernheim, B. D. (1986), "On the Voluntary and Involuntary Provision of Public Goods," *American Economic Review* 76: 789-93.

Bernheim, B. D., and Bagwell, K. (1988), "Is Everything Neutral?" *Journal of Political Economy* 96: 308-39.

Blackorby, C., Boyce, R., and Russell, R. R. (1978a), "Estimation of Demand Systems Generated by the Gorman Polar Form: A Generalization of the S-Branch Utility Tree," *Econometrica* 46: 345-63.

Blackorby, C., and Donaldson, D. (1988), "Money Metric Utility: A Harmless Normalization?" *Journal of Economic Theory* 46: 120-9.

Blackorby, C., Primont, D., and Russell, R. R. (1978b), *Duality, Separability and Functional Structure: Theory and Economic Applications*. New York: American Elsevier.

Blackorby, C., and Russell, R. R. (1978), "Indices and Subindices of the Cost of Living and the Standard of Living," *International Economic Review* 19: 229-40.

Blaug, M. (1980), *The Methodology of Economics*. Cambridge University Press.

Bliss, C. J. (1975), *Capital Theory and the Distribution of Income*. Amsterdam: North Holland.

Blomquist, N. S. (1985), "Labour Supply in a Two-Period Model: The Effect of a Nonlinear Progressive Income Tax," *Review of Economic Studies* 52: 515–24.

(1989), "Comparative Statics for Utility Maximization with Nonlinear Budget Constraints," *International Economic Review* 30: 275–96.

Blundell, R. (1986), "Econometric Approaches to the Specification of Life-cycle Labour Supply and Commodity Demand Behaviour," *Econometric Reviews* 5: 89–146.

(1988), "Consumer Behaviour: Theory and Empirical Evidence – A Survey," *Economic Journal* 98: 16–65.

Blundell, R., and Meghir, C. (1986), "Selection Criteria for a Microeconometric Model of Labour Supply," *Journal of Applied Econometrics* 1: 55–80.

Blundell, R., and Walker, I. (1982), "Modelling the Joint Distribution of Household Labour Supplies and Commodity Demands," *Economic Journal* 92: 351–64.

Boadway, R. W., and Bruce, N. (1984), *Welfare Economics*. Oxford: Blackwell.

Boyle, J. R., Gorman, W. M., and Pudney, S. E. (1977), "Demand for Related Goods," in *Frontiers of Quantitative Economics, Vol. IIIA*, edited by M. Intriligator. Amsterdam: North Holland, pp. 87–101.

Bronsard, C., and Salvas-Bronsard, L. (1984), "On Price Exogeneity in Complete Demand Systems," *Journal of Econometrics* 24: 235–47.

(1986), "Commodity and Asset Demands with and without Quantity Constraints in the Labour Market," *Journal of Applied Econometrics* 1: 185–206.

Bronsard, C., Salvas-Bronsard, L., and Delisle, D. (1978), "Computing Optimal Tolls in a Money Economy," in *Econometric Contributions to Public Policy*, edited by R. Stone and W. Peterson. London: Macmillan, pp. 206–25.

Browning, M., Deaton, A., and Irish, M. (1985), "A Profitable Approach to Labor Supply and Commodity Demands over the Life-Cycle," *Econometrica* 53: 503–43.

Buchanan, J. M., and Kafoglis, M. Z. (1963), "A Note on Public Goods Supply," *American Economic Review* 53: 403–14.

Burenstam Linder, S. (1970), *The Harried Leisure Class*. New York: Columbia University Press.

Burgess, D. F. (1976), "Tariffs and Income Distribution: Some Empirical Evidence for the United States," *Journal of Political Economy* 84: 17–45.

Caves, R. E., and Jones, R. W. (1977), *World Trade and Payments: An Introduction*, 2nd ed. Boston: Little, Brown.

Chambers, R. (1988), *Applied Production Analysis: A Dual Approach*. Cambridge University Press.

Chavas, J.-P. (1984), "The Theory of Mixed Demand Functions," *European Economic Review* 24: 321–44.

Chiang, A. C. (1984), *Fundamental Methods of Mathematical Economics*, 3rd ed. New York: McGraw-Hill.

Chipman, J. S. (1972), "The Theory of Exploitative Trade and Investment Policies," in *International Economics and Development*, edited by L. E. Di Marco. New York: Academic Press, pp. 209–44.

(1979), "The Theory and Application of Trade Utility Functions," in *General Equilibrium, Growth, and Trade,* edited by J. R. Green and J. A. Scheinkman. New York: Academic Press, pp. 277-96.

Chipman, J. S., Hurwicz, L., Richter, M. K., and Sonnenschein, H. F. (1971), *Preferences, Utility and Demand.* New York: Harcourt Brace Jovanovich.

Chipman, J. S., and Moore, J. C. (1980), "Compensating Variation, Consumer's Surplus, and Welfare," *American Economic Review* 70: 933-49.

Christensen, L. R., Jorgenson, D. W., and Lau, L. J. (1975), "Transcendental Logarithmic Utility Functions," *American Economic Review* 65: 367-83.

Cook, P. J. (1972), "A One-Line Proof of the Slutsky Equation," *American Economic Review* 62: 139.

Coondoo, D., and Majumder, A. (1987), "A System of Demand Equations Based on Price Independent Generalized Linearity," *International Economic Review* 28: 213-28.

Cornes, R. C. (1979), "Duality, Quantity Constraints, and Consumer Behaviour." Warwick economic research paper No. 149, Warwick University, Coventry, U.K.

(1980), "External Effects: An Alternative Formulation," *European Economic Review* 14: 307-21.

Cornes, R. C., and Homma, M. (1979), "Consumption Externalities and Stability," *Economics Letters* 4: 301-6.

Cornes, R. C., and Milne, F. (1989), "A Simple Analysis of Mutually Disadvantageous Trading Opportunities," *Economic Studies Quarterly* 40: 122-34.

Cornes, R. C., and Sandler, T. (1984), "Easy Riders, Joint Production, and Public Goods," *Economic Journal* 94: 580-98.

(1985), "The Simple Analytics of Public Good Provision," *Economica* 52: 103-16.

(1986), *The Theory of Externalities, Public Goods, and Club Goods.* Cambridge University Press.

Dalal, A. J. (1983), "Comparative Statics and Asset Substitutability/Complementarity in a Portfolio Model: A Dual Approach," *Review of Economic Studies* 50: 355-67.

Darrough, M. N., and Southey, C. (1977), "Duality in Consumer Theory Made Simple: The Revealing of Roy's Identity," *Canadian Journal of Economics* 10: 307-17.

Deaton, A. S. (1979), "The Distance Function and Consumer Behaviour with Applications to Index Numbers and Optimal Taxation," *Review of Economic Studies* 46: 391-405.

(1981), "Theoretical and Empirical Approaches to Consumer Demand under Rationing," in *Essays in the Theory and Measurement of Consumer Behaviour,* edited by A. S. Deaton. Cambridge University Press, pp. 55-72.

(1986), "Demand Analysis," in *Handbook of Econometrics, Vol. III,* edited by Z. Griliches and M. D. Intriligator. Amsterdam: North Holland, pp. 1767-839.

Deaton, A. S., and Muellbauer, J. (1980a), *Economics and Consumer Behavior.* Cambridge University Press.

(1980*b*), "An Almost Ideal Demand System," *American Economic Review* 70: 312–26.

(1981), "Functional Forms for Labor Supply and Commodity Demands with and without Quantity Restrictions," *Econometrica* 49: 1521–32.

De Borger, B. (1989), "Estimating the Welfare Implications of In-Kind Government Programs: A General Numerical Procedure," *Journal of Public Economics* 38: 215–26.

Debreu, G. (1951), "The Coefficient of Resource Utilization," *Econometrica* 19: 273–92.

(1954*a*), "A Classical Tax-Subsidy Problem," *Econometrica* 22: 14–22.

(1954*b*), "Representation of a Preference Ordering by a Numerical Function," in *Decision Processes,* edited by R. M. Thrall, C. H. Coombs, and R. L. Davis. New York: Wiley, pp. 159–65.

Diamond, P. A., and McFadden, D. L. (1974), "Some Uses of the Expenditure Function in Public Finance," *Journal of Public Economics* 3: 3–21.

Diamond, P. A., and Mirrlees, J. (1973), "Aggregate Consumption with Production Externalities," *Quarterly Journal of Economics* 87: 1–24.

Diamond, P. A., and Yaari, M. E. (1972), "Implications of the Theory of Rationing for Consumer Choice under Uncertainty," *American Economic Review* 62: 333–43.

Diewert, W. E. (1971), "An Application of the Shephard Duality Theorem: A Generalized Leontief Production Function," *Journal of Political Economy* 79: 481–507.

(1973*a*), "Functional Forms for Profit and Transformation Functions," *Journal of Economic Theory* 6: 284–316.

(1973*b*), "Separability and a Generalization of the Cobb-Douglas Cost, Production and Indirect Utility Functions." Technical report No. 86, Institute for Mathematical Studies in the Social Sciences, Stanford University.

(1974*a*), "Functional Forms for Revenue and Factor Requirements Functions," *International Economic Review* 15: 119–30.

(1974*b*), "Applications of Duality Theory," in *Frontiers of Quantitative Economics, Vol. II,* edited by M. D. Intriligator and D. A. Kendrick. Amsterdam: North Holland, pp. 106–71.

(1976), "Exact and Superlative Index Numbers," *Journal of Econometrics* 4: 115–45.

(1977), "Generalized Slutsky Condition for Aggregate Demand Functions," *Journal of Economic Theory* 15: 353–62.

(1978*a*), "Hicks' Aggregation Theorem and the Existence of a Real Value-Added Function," in *Production Economics: A Dual Approach to Theory and Applications, Vol. 2,* edited by M. Fuss and D. McFadden. Amsterdam: North Holland, pp. 17–51.

(1978*b*), "Superlative Index Numbers and Consistency in Aggregation," *Econometrica* 46: 883–900.

(1980), "The Economic Theory of Index Numbers: A Survey," in *Essays in the Theory and Measurement of Consumer Behaviour,* edited by A. S. Deaton. Cambridge University Press, pp. 163–208.

272   **Bibliography**

(1982), "Duality Approaches to Microeconomic Theory," in *Handbook of Mathematical Economics, Vol. II,* edited by K. J. Arrow and M. D. Intriligator. Amsterdam: North Holland, pp. 535-99.

(1983), "The Measurement of Waste within the Production Sector of an Open Economy," *Scandinavian Journal of Economics* 85: 159-79.

(1984), "The Measurement of Deadweight Loss in an Open Economy," *Economica* 51: 23-42.

(1985), "The Measurement of Waste and Welfare in Applied General Equilibrium Models," in *New Developments in Applied General Equilibrium Analysis,* edited by J. R. Piggott and J. Whalley. Cambridge University Press, pp. 42-103.

Diewert, W. E., and Edlefsen, L. E. (1984), "Consumption Theorems in Terms of Over and Under Compensation Revisited," *International Economic Review* 25: 379-84.

Diewert, W. E., and Parkan, C. (1983), "Linear Programming Tests of Regularity Conditions for Production Frontiers," in *Quantitative Studies on Production and Prices,* edited by W. Eichhorn, R. Henn, K. Neumann, and R. W. Shephard. Würzburg: Physica-Verlag, pp. 131-58.

Diewert, W. E., and Wales, T. J. (1987), "Flexible Functional Forms and Global Curvature Conditions," *Econometrica* 55: 43-68.

Dixit, A. K. (1976), *Optimization in Economic Theory.* Oxford University Press.

Dixit, A. K., and Norman, V. (1980), *Theory of International Trade.* Cambridge University Press.

(1986), "Gains from Trade without Lump-Sum Compensation," *Journal of International Economics* 21: 111-22.

Dixit, A. K., and Weller, P. A. (1979), "The Three Consumer's Surpluses," *Economica* 46: 125-35.

Eggleston, H. G. (1963), *Convexity.* Cambridge University Press.

Epple, D. (1987), "Hedonic Prices and Implicit Markets: Estimating Demand and Supply Functions for Differentiated Products," *Journal of Political Economy* 95: 59-80.

Epstein, L. G. (1975), "A Disaggregate Analysis of Consumer Choice Under Uncertainty," *Econometrica* 43: 877-92.

(1981a), "Generalized Duality and Integrability," *Econometrica* 49: 655-78.

(1981b), "Duality Theory and Functional Forms for Dynamic Factor Demands," *Review of Economic Studies* 48: 81-95.

Ethier, W. (1983), *Modern International Economics.* New York: Norton.

Evans, D. S., and Heckman, J. J. (1983), "Multiproduct Cost Function Estimates and Natural Monopoly Tests for the Bell System," in *Breaking up Bell,* edited by D. S. Evans. Amsterdam: North Holland, pp. 253-82.

Färe, R. (1988), *Fundamentals of Production Theory.* Heidelberg: Springer-Verlag.

Färe, R., Grosskopf, S., and Lovell, C. A. K. (1985), *The Measurement of Efficiency of Production.* Boston: Kluwer-Nijhoff.

(1988), "An Indirect Approach to the Evaluation of Producer Performance." *Journal of Public Economics* 37: 71-89.

Färe, R., and Lovell, C. A. K. (1978), "Measuring the Technical Efficiency of Production," *Journal of Economic Theory* 19: 150–62.

Farrell, M. J. (1957), "The Measurement of Productive Efficiency," *Journal of the Royal Statistical Society, Series A* 120: 253–81.

Follain, J. R., and Jimenez, E. (1985), "Estimating the Demand for Housing Characteristics," *Regional Science and Urban Economies* 15: 77–107.

Frisch, R. (1932), *New Methods of Measuring Marginal Utility*. Tübingen: J. C. B. Mohr.

Fuss, M., and McFadden, D. (1978), *Production Economics: A Dual Approach to Theory and Applications*, 2 vols. Amsterdam: North Holland.

Gallant, R. A. (1981), "On the Bias in Flexible Functional Forms and an Essentially Unbiased Form: The Fourier Flexible Form," *Journal of Econometrics* 15: 211–45.

Glaister, S. (1984), *Mathematical Methods for Economists*, 3rd ed. Oxford: Blackwell.

Goodspeed, T., and Schwab, R. (1988), "Some Applications of the Theory of Rationing to Problems in Public Economics." Working paper No. 88-31, Department of Economics, University of Maryland.

Gorman, W. M. (1953), "Community Preference Fields," *Econometrica* 21: 63–80.

(1956), "A Possible Procedure for Analysing Quality Differentials in the Egg Market." Mimeograph, Department of Economics, Iowa State College, Ames; reprinted in 1980: *Review of Economic Studies* 47: 843–56.

(1959), "Separable Utility and Aggregation," *Econometrica* 27: 469–81.

(1961), "On a Class of Preference Fields," *Metroeconomica* 13: 53–6.

(1968), "The Structure of Utility Functions," *Review of Economic Studies* 35: 369–90.

(1976), "Tricks with Utility Functions," in *Essays in Economic Analysis*, edited by M. Artis and R. Nobay. Cambridge University Press, pp. 211–43.

(1984), "Le Chatelier and General Equilibrium," in *Demand, Equilibrium and Trade: Essays in Honour of Ivor F. Pearce*, edited by A. Ingham and A. M. Ulph. London: Macmillan, pp. 1–18.

Green, H. A. J. (1971), *Consumer Theory*. London: Penguin.

Greenberg, E., and Denzau, A. (1988), "Profit and Expenditure Functions in Basic Public Finance: An Expository Note," *Economic Inquiry* 26: 145–58.

Guesnerie, R., and Laffont, J.-J. (1978), "Taxing Price Makers," *Journal of Economic Theory* 19: 423–55.

Hall, R. E. (1973), "The Specification of Technology with Several Kinds of Output," *Journal of Political Economy* 81: 878–92.

Hammond, P. J. (1983), "Approximate Measures of the Social Welfare Benefits of Large Projects." Technical report No. 410, Institute for Mathematical Studies in the Social Sciences, Stanford University.

Hanoch, G. (1978), "Symmetric Duality and Polar Production Functions," in *Production Economics: A Dual Approach to Theory and Applications, Vol. I*, edited by M. Fuss and D. McFadden. Amsterdam: North Holland, pp. 111–31.

Hanoch, G., and Rothschild, M. (1972), "Testing the Assumptions of Production Theory: A Nonparametric Approach," *Journal of Political Economy* 80: 256-75.

Hasenkamp, G. (1976), *Specification and Estimation of Multiple-Output Production Functions.* Berlin: Springer-Verlag.

Hatta, T. (1980), "Structure of the Correspondence Principle at an Extremum Point," *Review of Economic Studies* 47: 987-97.

Hatta, T., and Willke, R. J. (1982), "Mosak's Equality and the Theory of Duality," *International Economic Review* 23: 361-4.

Hausman, J. A. (1981), "Exact Consumer's Surplus and Deadweight Loss," *American Economic Review* 71: 662-76.

  (1985), "The Econometrics of Nonlinear Budget Sets," *Econometrica* 53: 1255-82.

Heckman, J., and MaCurdy, T. (1980), "A Life Cycle Model of Female Labour Supply," *Review of Economic Studies* 47: 47-74.

Heineke, J. M., and Shefrin, H. M. (1988), "Exact Aggregation and the Finite Basis Property," *International Economic Review* 29: 525-38.

Hicks, J. R. (1943), "The Four Consumers' Surpluses," *Review of Economic Studies* 11: 31-41.

  (1946), *Value and Capital,* 2nd ed. Oxford University Press.

  (1956), *A Revision of Demand Theory.* Oxford University Press.

Hirshleifer, J. (1988), *Price Theory and Applications,* 4th ed. Englewood Cliffs, NJ: Prentice-Hall.

Hotelling, H. (1932), "Edgeworth's Taxation Paradox and the Nature of Demand and Supply Functions," *Journal of Political Economy* 40: 577-616.

Houthakker, H. S. (1951-2), "Compensated Changes in Quantities and Qualities Consumed," *Review of Economic Studies* 19: 155-64.

  (1960), "Additive Preferences," *Econometrica* 28: 224-56.

Hurwicz, L. (1971), "On the Problem of Integrability of Demand Functions," in *Preferences, Utility and Demand,* edited by J. S. Chipman, L. Hurwicz, M. K. Richter, and H. F. Sonnenschein. New York: Harcourt Brace Jovanovich, pp. 174-214.

Hurwicz, L., and Uzawa, H. (1971), "On the Integrability of Demand Functions," in *Preferences, Utility and Demand,* edited by J. S. Chipman, L. Hurwicz, M. K. Richter, and H. F. Sonnenschein. New York: Harcourt Brace Jovanovich, pp. 114-48.

Intriligator, M. D. (1971), *Mathematical Optimization and Economic Theory.* Englewood Cliffs, NJ: Prentice-Hall.

Jacobsen, S. E. (1972), "On Shephard's Duality Theorem," *Journal of Economic Theory* 4: 458-64.

Jeremias, R., and Zardkoohi, A. (1976), "Distributional Implications of Independent Adjustments in an Economy with Public Goods," *Economic Inquiry* 14: 305-8.

Johansson, P. -O. (1987), *The Economic Theory and Measurement of Environmental Benefits.* Cambridge University Press.

Jones, R. W. (1965), "The Structure of Simple General Equilibrium Models," *Journal of Political Economy* 73: 557-72.

(1974), "Trade with Non-Traded Goods: The Anatomy of Interconnected Markets," *Economica* 41: 111–38.

Karlin, S. (1959), *Mathematical Methods and Theory in Games, Programming, and Economics, Vol. I.* London: Pergamon.

Kay, J. A. (1980), "The Deadweight Loss from a Tax System," *Journal of Public Economics* 13: 111–19.

Kay, J. A., and Keen, M. (1988), "Measuring the Inefficiencies of Tax Systems," *Journal of Public Economics* 35: 265–87.

Kim, H. Y. (1988), "Analyzing the Indirect Production Function for U.S. Manufacturing," *Southern Economic Journal* 54: 494–504.

King, M. A. (1983), "Welfare Analysis of Tax Reforms Using Household Data," *Journal of Public Economics* 21: 183–214.

(1987), "The Empirical Analysis of Tax Reforms," in *Advances in Econometrics – Fifth World Congress, Vol. II,* edited by T. F. Bewley. Cambridge University Press, pp. 61–90.

Kohli, U. J. R. (1978), "A Gross National Product Function and the Derived Demand for Imports and Supply of Exports," *Canadian Journal of Economics* 11: 167–82.

(1981), "Nonjointness and Factor Intensity in U.S. Production," *International Economic Review* 22: 3–18.

(1983), "Non-joint Technologies," *Review of Economic Studies* 50: 209–19.

Konüs, A. A. (1939), "The Problem of the True Index of the Cost of Living," *Econometrica* 7: 10–29. (Originally published in Russian, 1924.)

Koopmans, T. C. (1957), *Three Essays on the State of Economic Science.* New York: McGraw-Hill.

(1970), "Uses of Prices," in *Scientific Papers of Tjalling C. Koopmans,* edited by M. Beckmann, C. F. Christ, and M. Nerlove. Heidelberg: Springer-Verlag, pp. 243–57.

Kooreman, P., and Kapteyn, A. (1986), "Estimation of Rationed and Unrationed Household Labour Supply Functions using Flexible Functional Forms," *Economic Journal* 96: 398–412.

Kopp, R. J. (1981), "The Measurement of Productive Efficiency," *Quarterly Journal of Economics* 96: 477–503.

Kopp, R. J., and Diewert, W. E. (1982), "The Decomposition of Frontier Cost Function Deviations into Measures of Technical and Allocative Efficiency," *Journal of Econometrics* 19: 319–31.

Krauss, M. (1979), *A Geometric Approach to International Trade.* Oxford: Blackwell.

Lancaster, K. (1966), "A New Approach to Consumer Theory," *Journal of Political Economy* 74: 132–57.

(1971), *Consumer Demand: A New Approach.* New York: Columbia University Press.

Lankford, R. H. (1988), "Measuring Welfare Changes in Settings with Imposed Quantities," *Journal of Environmental Economics and Management* 15: 45–63.

Latham, R. (1980), "Quantity Constrained Demand Functions," *Econometrica* 48: 307–13.

Lau, L. J. (1972), "Profit Functions of Technologies with Multiple Inputs and Outputs," *Review of Economics and Statistics* 59: 281-9.
  (1974), "Applications of Duality Theory: Comments," in *Frontiers of Quantitative Economics, Vol. II,* edited by M. D. Intriligator and D. A. Kendrick. Amsterdam: North Holland, pp. 176-99.
  (1976), "A Characterization of the Normalized Restricted Profit Function," *Journal of Economic Theory* 12: 131-63.
  (1977), "Complete Systems of Consumer Demand Functions through Duality," in *Frontiers of Quantitative Economics, Vol. IIIA,* edited by M. D. Intriligator. Amsterdam: North Holland, pp. 59-86.
  (1978), "Applications of Profit Functions," in *Production Economics: A Dual Approach to Theory and Applications, Vol. I,* edited by M. Fuss and D. McFadden. Amsterdam: North Holland, pp. 133-216.
  (1986), "Functional Forms in Econometric Model Building," in *Handbook of Econometrics, Vol. III,* edited by Z. Griliches and M. D. Intriligator. Amsterdam: North Holland, pp. 1515-66.
Lipsey, R. G., and Rosenbluth, G. (1971), "A Contribution to the New Theory of Demand: A Rehabilitation of the Giffen Good," *Canadian Journal of Economics* 4: 131-63.
Liviatan, N. (1968), "The Principle of Two-Stage Maximization in Price Theory," in *Value, Capital and Growth. Papers in Honour of Sir John Hicks,* edited by J. N. Wolfe. Edinburgh University Press, pp. 291-303.
McCloskey, D. N. (1982), *The Applied Theory of Price.* New York: Macmillan.
MaCurdy, T. E. (1981), "An Empirical Model of Labor Supply in a Life Cycle Setting," *Journal of Political Economy* 89: 1059-85.
McFadden, D. (1978), "Cost, Revenue and Profit Functions," *Production Economics: A Dual Approach to Theory and Applications, Vol. I,* edited by M. Fuss and D. McFadden. Amsterdam: North Holland, pp. 3-109.
Machina, M. J. (1984), "Temporal Risk and the Nature of Induced Preferences," *Journal of Economic Theory* 33: 199-231.
Mackay, R. J., and Whitney, G. A. (1980), "The Comparative Statics of Quantity Constraints and Conditional Demands: Theory and Applications," *Econometrica* 48: 1727-44.
McKenzie, G. W. (1983), *Measuring Economic Welfare: New Methods.* Cambridge University Press.
McKenzie, G. W., and Pearce, I. F. (1976), "Exact Measures of Welfare and the Cost of Living," *Review of Economic Studies* 43: 465-8.
McKenzie, G. W., and Ulph, D. (1986), "An Exact Welfare Measure," in *Economic Perspectives: An Annual Survey of Economics, Vol. 4,* edited by D. W. Pearce and N. J. Rau. Chur: Harwood, pp. 1-43.
McKenzie, L. W. (1957), "Demand Theory Without a Utility Index," *Review of Economic Studies* 24: 185-9.
Mäler, K.-G. (1974), *Environmental Economics: A Theoretical Inquiry.* Baltimore: Johns Hopkins University Press.
Mäler, K.-G., and Wyzga, R. E. (1976), *Economic Measurement of Environmental Damage.* Paris: Organization for Economic Co-operation and Development.

Malinvaud, E. (1977), *The Theory of Unemployment Reconsidered.* Oxford: Blackwell.

Malmquist, S. (1953), "Index Numbers and Indifference Surfaces," *Estatistica* 4: 209–42.

Mangasarian, O. (1969), *Nonlinear Programming.* New York: McGraw-Hill.

Meade, J. (1952), *A Geometry of International Trade.* London: Allen & Unwin.

Milne, F. (1981), "Induced Preferences and the Theory of the Consumer," *Journal of Economic Theory* 24: 205–17.

Morey, E. F. (1984), "Confuser Surplus," *American Economic Review* 74: 163–73.

Moroney, M. J. (1956), *Facts from Figures.* Harmondsworth: Penguin.

Mosak, J. (1942), "On the Interpretation of the Fundamental Equation of Value Theory," in *Studies in Mathematical Economics and Econometrics,* edited by O. Lange, T. O. Yntema, and F. McIntyre. University of Chicago Press, pp. 69–74.

Muellbauer, J. (1974), "Household Production Theory, Quality, and the 'Hedonic Technique'," *American Economic Review* 64: 977–94.

  (1975), "Aggregation, Income Distribution and Consumer Demand," *Review of Economic Studies* 62: 525–43.

  (1976a), "Community Preferences and the Representative Consumer," *Econometrica* 44: 979–99.

  (1976b), "Economics and the Representative Consumer," in *Private and Enlarged Consumption,* edited by L. Solari and J.-N. Du Pasquier. Amsterdam: North Holland, pp. 29–53.

Muellbauer, J., and Portes, R. (1978), "Macroeconomic Models with Quantity Rationing," *Economic Journal* 88: 788–821.

Neary, J. P., and Roberts, K. W. S. (1980), "The Theory of Household Behaviour under Rationing," *European Economic Review* 13: 25–42.

Neary, J. P., and Schweinberger, A. G. (1986), "Factor Content Functions and the Theory of International Trade," *Review of Economic Studies* 53: 421–32.

Ohyama, M. (1972), "Trade and Welfare in General Equilibrium," *Keio Economic Studies* 9: 37–73.

Pauwels, W. (1979), "On Some Results in Comparative Statics Analysis," *Journal of Economic Theory* 21: 483–90.

  (1986), "Correct and Incorrect Measures of the Deadweight Loss of Taxation," *Public Finance* 41: 267–76.

Pearce, I. F. (1964), *A Contribution to Demand Analysis.* Oxford University Press.

  (1970), *International Trade.* New York: Macmillan.

Phlips, L. (1983), *Applied Consumption Analysis,* rev. ed. Amsterdam: North Holland.

Pollak, R. (1971), "The Theory of the Cost-of-Living Index." Research discussion paper No. 11, Research Division, Office of Prices and Living Conditions, U.S. Bureau of Labor Statistics; reprinted in Diewert, W. E. and Montmarquette, C. (1983), *Price Level Measurement* (Ottawa: Ministry of Supply and Services), and in Pollak, R. A. (1989).

  (1981), "The Social Cost of Living Index," *Journal of Public Economics* 15: 311–36; reprinted in Pollak, R. A. (1989).

  (1989), *The Theory of the Cost-of-Living Index.* Oxford University Press.

Pollak, R. A., and Wachter, M. L. (1975), "The Relevance of the Household Production Function and Its Implications for the Allocation of Time," *Journal of Political Economy* 83: 255–77.

Ponstein, J. (1980), *Approaches to the Theory of Optimization.* Cambridge University Press.

Pope, R. D. (1980), "The Generalized Envelope Theorem and Price Uncertainty." *International Economic Review* 21: 75–86.

Rader, T. (1964), "Edgeworth Exchange and General Economic Equilibrium," *Yale Economic Essays* 4: 133–80.

(1978), "Induced Preferences on Trades when Preferences may be Intransitive and Incomplete," *Econometrica* 46: 137–46.

Ray, R. (1982), "The Testing and Estimation of Complete Demand Systems on Household Budget Surveys: An Application of AIDS," *European Economic Review* 17: 348–69.

Richter, M. K. (1979), "Duality and Rationality," *Journal of Economic Theory* 20: 131–81.

Roberts, A. W., and Varberg, D. E. (1973), *Convex Functions.* New York: Academic Press.

Roberts, K. W. S. (1980), "Price-independent Welfare Prescriptions," *Journal of Public Economics* 13: 277–97.

Rockafellar, R. T. (1970), *Convex Analysis.* Princeton University Press.

Rosen, S. (1974), "Hedonic Prices and Implicit Markets: Product Differentiation in Pure Competition," *Journal of Political Economy* 82: 34–55.

Rothbarth, E. (1941), "The Measurement of Change in Real Income under Conditions of Rationing," *Review of Economic Studies* 8: 100–7.

Roy, R. (1942), *De l'Utilité.* Paris: Hermann.

(1947), "La Distribution du Revenu Entre Les Divers Biens," *Econometrica* 15: 205–25.

Russell, R. R. (1983), "Comments on the Theory of the Cost-of-Living Index and the Measurement of Welfare Change, by Diewert," in *Price-Level Measurement,* edited by W. E. Diewert and C. Montmarquette. Ottawa: Ministry of Supply and Services, pp. 234–9.

Ruys, P. H. M., and Weddepohl, H. N. (1979), "Economic Theory and Duality," in *Convex Analysis and Mathematical Economics,* edited by J. Kriens. Berlin: Springer-Verlag, pp. 1–71.

Salter, W. E. G. (1959), "Internal and External Balance: The Role of Price and Expenditure Effects," *Economic Record* 35: 226–38.

Salvas-Bronsard, L., Leblanc, D., and Bronsard, C. (1977), "Estimating Demand Functions: The Converse Approach," *European Economic Review* 9: 301–21.

Samuelson, P. A. (1938), "A Note on the Pure Theory of Consumer Behaviour," *Economica* 5: 61–71.

(1947), *Foundations of Economic Analysis.* Harvard University Press.

(1950), "Evaluation of Real National Income," *Oxford Economic Papers* 2: 1–29.

(1953a), "Prices of Factors and Goods in General Equilibrium," *Review of Economic Studies* 21: 1–20.

(1953*b*), "Consumption Theorems in Terms of Overcompensation Rather than Indifference Comparison," *Economica* 20: 1-9.

(1954), "The Pure Theory of Public Expenditure," *Review of Economics and Statistics* 36: 387-9.

(1955), "A Diagrammatic Exposition of a Theory of Public Expenditure," *Review of Economics and Statistics* 37: 350-6.

(1956), "Social Indifference Curves," *Quarterly Journal of Economics* 70: 1-22.

(1965), "Using Full Duality to Show that Simultaneously Additive Direct and Indirect Utilities Implies Unitary Price Elasticity of Demand," *Econometrica* 33: 781-96.

(1966), "The Fundamental Singularity Theorem for Non-Joint Production," *International Economic Review* 7: 34-41.

Sandmo, A. (1980), "Anomaly and Stability in the Theory of Externalities," *Quarterly Journal of Economics* 94: 799-807.

Schelling, T. C. (1960), *The Strategy of Conflict*. Oxford University Press.

(ed.) (1973), "Symposium: Time in Economic Life," *Quarterly Journal of Economics* 87: 629-75.

(1978), *Micromotives and Macrobehavior*. New York: Norton.

Schmidt, P. (1985-6), "Frontier Production Functions," *Econometric Reviews* 4: 289-328.

Schwab, R. M. (1985), "The Benefits of In-Kind Government Programs," *Journal of Public Economics* 27: 195-210.

Sharkey, W. W. (1982), *The Theory of Natural Monopoly*. Cambridge University Press.

Shefrin, H. M., and Heineke, J. (1979), "On Duality Theory in Intertemporal Choice with Uncertainty," *Economics Letters* 3: 19-23.

Shephard, R. W. (1953), *Cost and Production Functions*. Princeton University Press.

(1970), *Theory of Cost and Production Functions*. Princeton University Press.

(1974), *Indirect Production Functions*. Meisenheim am Glan: Verlag Anton Hain.

Silberberg, E. (1971), "The Le Chatelier Principle as a Corollary to a Generalized Envelope Theorem," *Journal of Economic Theory* 3: 146-55.

(1974), "A Revision of Comparative Statics Methodology in Economics, or, How to Do Economics on the Back of an Envelope," *Journal of Economic Theory* 7: 159-72.

(1978), *The Structure of Economics*. New York: McGraw-Hill.

Simmons, P. J. (1974), *Choice and Demand*. New York: Macmillan.

(1980), "Evidence on the Impact of Income Distribution on Consumer Demand in the U.S. 1955-68," *Review of Economic Studies* 47: 893-906.

Simmons, P. J., and Weiserbs, D. (1979), "Translog Flexible Functional Forms and Associated Demand Systems," *American Economic Review* 69: 892-901.

Smith, A. (1982), "Some Simple Results on the Gains from Trade, from Growth and from Public Production," *Journal of International Economics* 13: 215-30.

Stern, N. (1986), "A Note on Commodity Taxation, the Choice of Variable and the Slutsky, Hessian and Antonelli Matrices (SHAM)," *Review of Economic Studies* 53: 293-9.

Stoneman, P. (1983), *The Economic Analysis of Technological Change.* Oxford University Press.

Stutzer, M. J. (1982), "Another Note on Deadweight Loss," *Journal of Public Economics* 18: 277-84.

Swamy, G., and Binswanger, H. P. (1983), "Flexible Consumer Demand Systems and Linear Estimation: Food in India," *American Journal of Agricultural Economics* 65: 675-84.

Swan, T. W. (1955), "Longer-Run Problems of the Balance of Payments," in *The Australian Economy: A Volume of Readings,* edited by H. W. Arndt and W. M. Corden. Melbourne: Cheshire, pp. 384-95.

Takayama, A. (1972), *International Trade.* New York: Holt, Rinehart & Winston.

Teece, D. J. (1980), "Economies of Scope and the Scope of the Enterprise," *Journal of Economic Behavior and Organization* 1: 223-47.

Tobin, J. (1952), "A Survey of the Theory of Rationing," *Econometrica* 20: 512-53.

Tobin, J., and Houthakker, H. S. (1951), "The Effects of Rationing on Demand Elasticities," *Review of Economic Studies* 18: 140-53.

Usher, D. (1968), *The Price Mechanism and the Meaning of National Income Statistics.* Oxford University Press.

Valentine, F. A. (1964), *Convex Sets.* New York: McGraw-Hill.

van Daal, J., and Merkies, A. H. Q. M. (1984), *Aggregation in Economic Analysis: From Individual to Macro Relations.* Dordrecht: Reidel.

Varian, H. R. (1982), "The Non-parametric Approach to Demand Analysis," *Econometrica* 50: 945-73.

  (1983), "Non-parametric Tests of Consumer Behaviour," *Review of Economic Studies* 50: 99-110.

  (1984*a*), "The Non-parametric Approach to Production Analysis," *Econometrica* 52: 579-98.

  (1984*b*), *Microeconomic Analysis,* 2nd ed. New York: Norton.

  (1985), "Non-parametric Analysis of Optimizing Behavior with Measurement Error," *Journal of Econometrics* 30: 445-58.

Vartia, Y. O. (1983), "Efficient Methods of Measuring Welfare Change and Compensated Income in Terms of Ordinary Demand Functions," *Econometrica* 51: 79-98.

Ville, J. (1951-2), "The Existence Conditions of a Total Utility Function," *Review of Economic Studies* 19: 123-8.

Wales, T. J., and Woodland, A. D. (1976), "Estimation of Household Utility Functions and Labor Supply Functions," *International Economic Review* 17: 397-410.

  (1977), "Estimation of the Allocation of Time for Work, Leisure and Housework," *Econometrica* 45: 115-32.

Warr, P. (1983), "The Private Provision of a Public Good Is Independent of the Distribution of Income," *Economics Letters* 13: 207-11.

Weddepohl, H. N. (1970), *Axiomatic Choice Models and Duality.* Groningen: Rotterdam University Press.

Wegge, L. (1974), "Notes on the Regional Product Function," *Tijdschrift voor Economie* 19: 165–85.

Weintraub, E. R. (1982), *Mathematics for Economists: An Integrated Approach.* Cambridge University Press.

Weissenberger, E. (1986), "An Intertemporal System of Dynamic Consumer Demand Functions," *European Economic Review* 30: 859–91.

Weymark, J. A. (1980), "Duality Results in Demand Theory," *European Economic Review* 14: 377–95.

Woodland, A. D. (1977), "A Dual Approach to Equilibrium in the Production Sector in International Trade Theory," *Canadian Journal of Economics* 10: 50–68.

(1980), "Direct and Indirect Trade Utility Functions," *Review of Economic Studies* 47: 907–26.

(1982), *International Trade and Resource Allocation.* Amsterdam: North Holland.

Zabalza, A. (1982), "Compensating and Equivalent Variations, and the Deadweight Loss of Taxation," *Economica* 49: 355–9.

Zieschang, K. D. (1983), "A Note on the Decomposition of Cost Efficiency into Technical and Allocative Components," *Journal of Econometrics* 23: 401–5.

Author index

283

Subject index